When Opponents Cooperate

# When Opponents Cooperate
## Great Power Conflict and Collaboration in World Politics

Benjamin Miller

Ann Arbor
THE UNIVERSITY OF MICHIGAN PRESS

Copyright © by the University of Michigan 1995
All rights reserved
Published in the United States of America by
The University of Michigan Press
Manufactured in the United States of America
∞ Printed on acid-free paper

1998  1997  1996  1995    4  3  2  1

*A CIP catalogue record for this book is available from the British Library.*

Library of Congress Cataloging-in-Publication Data

Miller, Benjamin, 1953–
    When opponents cooperate : great power conflict and collaboration in world politics / Benjamin Miller.
      p. cm.
    Includes bibliographical references and index.
    ISBN 0-472-10458-6 (hardcover : alk. paper)
    1. International relations. 2. Great powers. 3. International cooperation. I. Title.
JX1391.M52   1995
327.1′7′09045—dc20                                                94-36794
                                                               CIP

*To Liora and Adi
and to the memory of
my mother and father*

# Contents

Introduction: Recent International Changes and International Relations Theory — 1

1. Intended and Unintended Conflict and Cooperation under International Anarchy — 9
2. Explaining Great Power Cooperation in Conflict Management — 33
3. Polarity, Nuclear Weapons, and Major War — 57
4. Explaining the Emergence and the Form of Great Power Concerts — 89
5. The Superpowers and Middle East Crises during the Cold War: Tacit Cooperation — 125
6. Explaining Superpower Diplomacy: Attempts at U.S.-Soviet Collaboration in Resolving the Arab-Israeli Conflict — 173

Conclusions: Intended and Unintended Consequences—Past and Future — 223

Notes — 253

Bibliography — 303

Index — 335

# Preface and Acknowledgments

I was born and grew up in Israel. Thus, I naturally became interested at a relatively young age in questions of war and peace and international conflict and cooperation. My participation in the intense Yom Kippur battles on the Golan Heights[1] did much to sharpen my concern about these issues, as did my service in the Israeli Foreign Ministry, which included a mission to the United Nations (UN). Yet both the 1973 war and the UN mission have also made me aware of the great importance of the role of the great powers in international politics. Indeed, great power cooperation faces many difficulties but is critical for world peace and prosperity. Accordingly, this book suggests some of the conditions not only for the occurrence of great power conflict but also for the emergence of cooperation—both intended and unintended.

While writing this book I have also learned the importance of cooperation on the personal level. Indeed, what made possible completing this project was that I have been fortunate to meet many helpful people who were willing to cooperate; thus, I have accumulated a great number of debts. It is a great pleasure to acknowledge them here. All responsibility for what follows rests, of course, with me.

I started the project at the University of California, Berkeley. I owe a particular debt of gratitude to Professors Kenneth N. Waltz, George W. Breslauer, Aaron Wildavsky, Ernst Haas, Nelson Polsby, and William Brinner as well as to Professors Alexander George of Stanford University and Steven Spiegel of the University of California, Los Angeles. I am especially grateful to Kenneth Waltz for both his support and his stimulating criticism. My friends and colleagues Clay Moltz, Ronnie Lipschutz, Jeff Kopstein, and Jim Goldgeier deserve special thanks for sharing ideas and providing detailed comments on different chapters. Hugh and Sunny Dewitt provided a feeling of home to my family despite the long distance away from our home country.

I also appreciate the stimulating ideas kindly provided by the following scholars and decision makers: Jack Citrin, Neil MacFarlane, Dennis Ross, William Quandt, Harold Saunders, Alfred Atherton, Raymond Garthoff, Reuven Gal, Aaron Yariv, Abba Eban, Haim Bar-Lev, Yossi Sarid, Hagai Eshed, Shimcha Dinitz, Shlomo Avineri, Shai Feldman, and Shimon Shamir. The University of California Institute on Global Conflict and Cooperation

(IGCC) and the Berkeley MacArthur Foundation Fellowship in International Peace and Security provided much needed financial help. I would like to thank Herbert York and everyone associated with the IGCC.

I was fortunate to carry out the next stage of the project in the stimulating atmosphere of Cambridge, Massachussets: first at Harvard University and later at the Massachusetts Institute of Technology (MIT). At Cambridge I benefited from the help of Samuel Huntington, Barry Posen, Stephen Van Evera, Bob Art, Roger Smith, Michael Desch, Ed Rhodes, Jonathan Shimshoni, Steve Weber, Bob Powell, Saadia Touval, Herbert Kelman, Peter Katzenstein, Stanley Hoffmann, Richard Betts, and Catherine Gjerdingen. Financial assistance was provided by the Olin Fellowship in National Security of the Center for International Affairs at Harvard University and by the Defense and Arms Control Program of the MIT Center for International Studies.

I have completed the project at the Hebrew University of Jerusalem, where the manuscript was revised in some major ways. Among many other changes, I have tried to address some of the conceptual and policy implications of the end of the cold war for international politics, particularly for great power conflict and cooperation. Some of those who have provided valuable advice and assistance in Israel include Emanuel Adler, Uri Bar-Joseph, Arie Kacowicz, Uri Bialer, Zeev Maoz, Alan Dowty, Joel Peters, Nissan Oren, the late Dan Horowitz, Amnon Sella, Galia Golan, Sasson Sofer, Yaacov Bar Siman-Tov, Yair Evron, Michael Brecher, and Avi Ben-Zvi. I would also like to thank Robert Jervis, Jacob Berkovitz, Michael Doyle, George Downs, Steven David, Jack Levy, Jack Snyder, Richard Herrmann, Aaron Miller, and the helpful team of the University of Michigan Press: the reviewers, director Colin Day, editor Malcolm Litchfield, and assistant Robin Moir. The index was prepared by Matthew Spence.

Two dear friends and colleagues deserve special gratitude: Raymond Cohen and Korina Kagan. Both provided an enormous amount of intellectual stimulus. Korina has also provided extremely helpful editorial assistance. I doubt whether this project would ever have come to completion in its present form without her wise advice and useful assistance.

The research and writing during the last stage were made possible by financial support from the following sources: the Israel Foundations Trustees; the United States Institute of Peace; the Davis Institute for International Relations, the Hebrew University; and the Truman Institute for the Advancement of Peace, the Hebrew University.

Somewhat different versions of portions of this book have been published previously in "Explaining the Emergence of Great Power Concerts," *Review of International Studies* (October 1994); "Polarity, Nuclear Weapons, and Major War," *Security Studies* 3, no. 4 (Summer 1994); and "Explaining Great Power Cooperation in Conflict Management," *World Politics* 45, no. 1 (October

1992): 1–46. I appreciate the cooperation of these journals in permitting me to use material that first appeared in their pages.

Finally, there are five people without whom I would never have arrived at this point: my wife Liora, my daughter Adi, my sister Eti, and my late father and mother. My love and gratitude to them cannot be expressed in words.

# Introduction: Recent International Changes and International Relations Theory

After more than four decades of continuity, recent years have seen far-reaching changes in international politics. The changes have appeared at both the unit level and the international system level. In the former instance, they occurred within the political and socioeconomic systems of states, taking the form of democratization and transition to market economies, notably in Latin America, Eastern Europe, and, so far to a more limited extent, the former Soviet Union. Changes at the international system level include the decline of bipolarity due to the disintegration of Soviet power and its disengagement from Eastern Europe and other parts of the globe and the potential for an integrated Europe or a united Germany and for China and Japan to become major world powers. In many ways, these changes have been the most dramatic since the end of World War II and the onset of the Cold War in the late 1940s.

What does international relations theory lead us to expect concerning the effects of these changes on stability and conflict management in the post–Cold War world? On the one hand, it raises concerns about the expected changes at the systems level: the classic debate on the relative merits of bipolarity and multipolarity notwithstanding, many analysts have recently come to accept the Waltzian argument about the greater basic stability of bipolar systems.[1] Indeed, pessimists in the realist camp anticipate greater instability in post–Cold War Europe because of the structural transition from bipolarity to multipolarity.[2] On the other hand, optimists in the liberal camp would find the unit-level changes reassuring,[3] because of the anticipated pacifying effects of the democratization process (the Kantian argument that democracies never fight each other having been recently confirmed empirically) and of economic liberalism (expressed by the rise of the trading state, the transition to free-market economies, and the related growing economic interdependence).[4] These contradictory predictions have not so far been reconciled in a coherent theoretical argument.

Indeed, contemporary international relations theory fails to provide an adequate and parsimonious (i.e., elegant) model that can both explain patterns of great power cooperation and conflict in earlier eras and predict these patterns for the post–Cold War era, though it is so important for issues of war and peace. More specifically, no theoretical model has attempted to explain the conditions for the occurrence of both intended and unintended cooperation and conflict in international politics.[5] In the present book, I attempt to provide such a model. Indeed, for the post–Cold War era, the proposed model differs from both the pessimists and the optimists by predicting that the likelihood of failure in crisis management, and thus of inadvertent wars, will increase but that at the same time, intended cooperation in conflict resolution will be more likely than during the Cold War.

The proposed model explains two types of outcomes or dependent variables: great power conflict and cooperation. Each of these outcomes is divided into two ideal types,[6] the two conflictual outcomes being intended war and inadvertent war, while the cooperative ones are cooperation in crisis management and in conflict resolution. These four ideal types of outcomes are distinguished according to a basic criterion: whether they are intended or unintended by the great powers. Indeed, the recurrence and frequency of unintended outcomes, that is, outcomes that cannot be deduced from actors' intentions and attributes, is one of the most puzzling phenomena in international relations. Such outcomes can be more cooperative or more conflictual than what the actors initially wanted. Namely, the actors may unintentionally achieve a higher level of cooperation or conflict than they desired. This distinction between intended and unintended outcomes is one of the major themes of the book. A second major theme is the distinction between crises and normal times.[7] The proposed model combines these two themes by arguing that *intended outcomes occur in normal times, while unintended ones take place in crises.*

The third major theme of the book is that different levels of analysis account for different types of international outcomes.[8] Broadly speaking, international relations theory can be divided into two main families according to the distinction between the system and the unit levels of analysis: inside-out or unit-level theories (which focus on state attributes and on cognitive factors)[9] and structural-systemic theories.[10] Assuming that both these major theoretical approaches have some explanatory power with respect to international outcomes,[11] in this book I introduce one way of reconciling their competing claims, at least in the areas of conflict and cooperation. Thus, based on a combination of the three themes into a single coherent theoretical argument, I develop the proposed model (see tables 1 and 2) and argue that *whereas*

**TABLE 1. The Outcomes (dependent variables)**

|  | Conflict | Cooperation |
| --- | --- | --- |
| Intended | Premeditated wars | Conflict resolution |
| Unintended | Inadvertent wars | Crisis management |

**TABLE 2. The Main Causal Relations**

|  | The Setting | Explanation |
|---|---|---|
| Intended outcomes | Normal times | Unit-level |
| Unintended outcomes | Crises | Structural |

*structural factors account for the unintended crisis outcomes* (namely, inadvertent wars and unexpected success in crisis management), *unit-level factors explain the intended outcomes in normal times* (that is, the results of decisions to resort to premeditated wars and conflict resolution).

## Overview of the Book

The conflictual and the cooperative outcomes studied in this book are considerably affected by the central attribute of international politics—anarchy, namely, the absence of an international authority. In chapter 1, I introduce two different conceptions of international order that are both compatible with the condition of anarchy: the structural balance-of-power and the international society schools. I then discuss two major implications of anarchy for conflict and cooperation in international politics. The first is the special role of the great powers as the managers of the international system, thus justifying the focus of this book on great power conflict and cooperation. The second major implication of anarchy is its permissiveness for conflict—most notably, wars (Waltz 1959), and the constraints it places on cooperation (Grieco 1990; Jervis 1978; Waltz 1979).

However, the linkages between anarchy, war, and cooperation, although important, are too general and unspecified to provide a theoretical explanation of either conflict or cooperation. One crucial step in developing an explanatory model of both the outbreak of war and the emergence of cooperation is to distinguish between intended and unintended outcomes. In chapter 1, I provide such a distinction by presenting the four ideal types of outcomes. I also relate them to the two schools referred to above, by demonstrating that the international society school is mainly concerned with intended outcomes, while the structural school provides theoretical background for unintended ones. With regard to great power wars, I draw on the important distinction between premeditated and inadvertent wars.[12] Such a distinction is more difficult for great power cooperation, however.

Indeed, although the literature on cooperation under anarchy has demonstrated that international cooperation is possible even in the absence of a world authority,[13] one of the problems with this literature is its insufficient differentiation among kinds, degrees, and objectives of collaboration.[14] I address this problem in chapter 1 by differentiating between two modes of cooperation and between two substantive categories of joint great power action in conflict management. The two ideal modes of cooperation are the spontaneous-tacit avoidance type (associated with the structural approach) and the consciously explicit and affirmative type (related to the international society approach; see table 3).[15] The two major substantive categories of cooperation in conflict management are closely related to these two modes: tacit rules for regulating the use of force during crises are a manifestation of unintended spontaneous cooperation, whereas joint diplomacy for the purpose of conflict resolution is a reflection of the consciously affirmative type of collaboration. Thus, chapter 1 concentrates on the dependent variables and provides a broader theoretical background for them. In the subsequent chapters, I discuss the conditions for the occurrence of these outcomes.

Another major shortcoming of the literature on cooperation is the failure to advance parsimonious (that is, elegant) explanations of different types of collaboration by linking different sets of causal factors with different cooperative categories. Similarly, the literature on wars has not introduced a parsimonious model that can explain the occurrence of intended and unintended wars.[16] In chapters 2, 3, and 4, I address these shortcomings by developing and specifying the general argument introduced above that structural factors (namely, polarity) best explain unintended outcomes (which take place in times of crisis), whereas unit-level elements account for intended outcomes (which are not related to crisis situations). At the same time, unit-level theories fail to explain unintended outcomes, while structural theory is unable to account for intended ones. Chapter 2 is mainly concerned with the two cooperative outcomes. In that chapter, I introduce the general model of the book, which links causal factors at different levels of analysis with the two major kinds of collaboration in crisis and noncrisis settings (that is, structural factors are linked with crisis management and state-cognitive elements with conflict resolution). More specifically, bipolarity is conducive to successful crisis management, while the combination of the unit-level attributes of similarity and moderation bring about cooperation in conflict resolution.

In chapter 3, I apply the above argument to explaining the two conflictual outcomes: inadvertent and intended wars. In explaining the outbreak of major wars, it is inevitable that we consider the effects of another systemic variable—military technology.[17] Inadvertent wars are accounted for by the international structure. More specifically, multipolarity is prone to such wars, whereas bipolarity is conducive to their avoidance. Indeed, in bipolar systems tacit rules for regulating the use of force in crises tend to emerge. Although the substance and the implications of these rules are unintended, their emergence considerably reduces the likelihood of failure in crisis management and thus of inadvertent wars.

**TABLE 3. Two Modes of Order, Cooperation, and Conflict in International Politics**

| General Perspective on the International Order (see chap. 1) | Structural Balance-of-Power Theory | International Society |
|---|---|---|
| General type of outcomes | Unintended | Intended |
| Setting | Crises | Normal times |
| Mode of cooperation (see chap. 1) | Spontaneous, self-generating | Deliberate |
| Means of cooperation | Tacit rules | Explicit agreements and joint actions; concerted diplomacy, security regimes, concerts |
| Objectives of cooperation | Negative—avoid an unwanted outcome | Affirmative—achieve a set of goals |
| Application to conflict management | Crisis management; regulation of use of force; war termination | Conflict resolution; crisis prevention |
| Explanation of origins (see chap. 2) | Situational factors; distribution of capabilities (under bipolarity) | A shared cognitive-normative framework |
| Manifestations of cooperative relations among the great powers (see chaps. 3–4) | Tacit recognition of spheres of influence, the status quo, and the coequal status of the great powers | Explicit legitimation of the status quo or of peaceful change; explicit acceptance of the coequal status of the great powers |
| Historical application (see chaps. 3–6) | Postwar superpower crisis management | Nineteenth century Concert of Europe |
| Sources of war | Counterhegemonic; inadvertent | Intentions and attributes of the actors; ideological differences |
| Main danger (see chap. 3) | Inadvertent escalation due to unclarity of structural factors under multipolarity | Eruption of intended wars because of political-ideological differences and calculated decisions by aggressive leaders and states |
| Application to post–Cold War (see Conclusions) | Inadvertent wars due to the likely transition to multipolarity | Concerted diplomacy at conflict resolution because of growing democratization and liberalization |

Intended wars are caused by unit-level factors, yet their outbreak is conditioned by the type of military technology: conventional or nuclear. Indeed, because of the critical effects on warfare of the revolution in military technology after World War II, the chapter focuses on these conditioning effects rather than going into detail regarding the specific relations between unit-level factors and intended wars. Thus, the presence of nuclear weapons in the postwar era contributed to the Long Peace by making premeditated wars obsolete.[18] But the structural change—the transition from multipolarity to bipolarity—was the major factor that precluded unintended wars.

Since anarchy constrains cooperation, especially intended affirmative cooperation, only restrictive unit-level factors can make possible the emergence of such cooperation. In chapter 4 I am concerned with a very high level of intended cooperation, namely, a great power concert in conflict resolution, and further elaborate the unit-level conditions necessary for its emergence and durability. The emergence of great power concerts requires a shared vision of the international order, or at least a convergence of leaders' perceptions and a related process of cognitive learning by elites. These are achieved by a compatibility of state attributes and an explicit legitimation of the status quo (or of acceptable means for revising it), which help to resolve conflicts and thereby minimize the probability of crises and wars. The absence of these conditions, which prevents the emergence of a concert, may also constrain lower forms of intended cooperation.

Both chapters 3 and 4 include some historical examples, especially from the Concert era and from the Cold War. In chapters 5 and 6, I provide more detailed empirical case studies of the superpower involvement in the Middle East. In chapter 5, I illustrate unintended superpower cooperation in crisis management that succeeded largely because of structural factors. Chapter 6 focuses on attempts at intended cooperation in conflict resolution that failed largely due to the absence of necessary unit-level elements. The reason for the choice of the Middle East is that it has traditionally been a major arena of great power conflict and cooperation—both intended and unintended. Indeed, for the last two hundred years, the Middle East has been more consistently and thoroughly ensnarled in great power politics than any other part of the non-Western world (Brown 1984, 4). From the inception of the Eastern question[19] with the creeping decay of the Ottoman Empire through today's Arab-Israeli dispute, the Iran-Iraq War, the Lebanese crisis, and the Gulf War, an abundance of local problems has provided rich opportunities for external meddling in the Middle East. More specifically, there have been important attempts at conflict resolution by the great powers in this region during the Concert era, the Cold War,[20] and recently the post–Cold War initiative that resulted in the bilateral and multilateral Arab-Israeli talks. Moreover, the Eastern question has generated the danger of inadvertent escalation both during the Concert period, when the focus of the conflicts was in the Balkans, like in the Crimean War and World War I, and during the Cold War, when the focus has shifted to the Middle East, especially the Arab-Israeli conflict, as suggested by the recurrence of crises that have involved the superpowers.[21] Although it was in a completely different way, the Gulf Crisis showed the difficulties of crisis management in the Middle East in the post–Cold War era as well. Indeed, because of the intensity of the various conflicts in the Middle East and the linkages between them, the region remains a dangerous place that, because of its strategic and economic importance, could drag in external powers. The dangers might even increase in the post-Cold War era due to the rise of extremist forces such as Islamic fundamentalism and the growing problem of the proliferation of nonconventional weapons.

Consequently, in the Conclusions, I spell out the implications of the model for the post–Cold War period regarding intended and unintended conflict and cooperation of the great powers in general and in the Middle East in particular. Although the two subjects are interrelated, this book focuses on the sources or the factors affecting the likelihood of great power conflict and cooperation, rather than on the effects of these interactions on regional conflicts. Yet in light of the growing salience, and also the dangers, of regional conflicts in the post–Cold War era,[22] in the last section of the Conclusions, I offer some propositions for future research on the implications of different patterns of great power involvement and interactions for regional security.[23]

In addition to making a contribution to cooperation theory and the causes of wars, the proposed model is relevant to three general issues of international relations theory.

The first issue is the level of analysis problem. Rather than assuming that a single level best explains international politics (as a whole or at least in a certain historical period) or that all levels account for all outcomes in international relations, in this book I suggest that causal factors at different levels best explain different phenomena. Thus, the casual relations noted above between certain levels of analysis and types of wars and cooperation are specified.[24] Yet because of the difficulties, in social science in general and in international relations in particular, in identifying necessary and sufficient conditions,[25] I apply a weaker criterion for making the linkages between the causal factors at different levels of analysis and types of conflict and collaboration, namely that "the presence of a certain type of independent variable appears to 'favor' the occurrence of a certain type of outcome" (George 1982, 16).

The second issue is neorealism versus neoliberalism.[26] Instead of adopting one at the expense of the other, the model combines both power-related and normative-cognitive factors and thus proposes a way for integrating the insights of both structural realism and liberalism in a single theoretical argument. Some of the most relevant insights of neorealism include the constraints posed by anarchy on international cooperation, the effects of the global distribution of capabilities on international outcomes, and the importance of unintended consequences with regard to both conflict and cooperation. Important liberal insights include the effects of state attributes and factors related to them, such as values and norms, on intended wars as well as on high-level intended cooperation. Indeed, the analysis of great power collaboration and concerted diplomacy in conflict resolution integrates the realist insight on the crucial influence of the great powers in international politics with the liberal ideas about the possibilities for international collaboration, regimes and institutions, and peaceful settlement of disputes.

The third issue is structural theory. Although structural factors form an important part of the model, it goes beyond structural realism and provides a refinement of that theory by limiting and specifying its explanatory power with regard only to unintended crisis outcomes, namely, inadvertent wars and spontaneous-tacit crisis management. Thus, the book also makes a potential contribution to the old-time but recently revived debate on polarity and stability.[27] Other types of outcomes, such as intended wars and high-level cooperation in conflict resolution, are best explained by nonstructural factors, which consequently play an equally important part in the model. These factors may explain great power concerts that are considered an anomaly by structural theory.

The major effect of nuclear weapons, according to the proposed model, is to make premeditated wars obsolete. But since they are insufficient to prevent inadvertent wars, the likely future transition to multipolarity is dangerous with regard to possible failures in crisis management and wars of this kind. This situation creates the necessity for concerted great power diplomacy for the purposes of crisis prevention and conflict resolution. Indeed, when the structural conditions are not conducive to peace, there is a strong need not only for great power cooperation as such but also for powerful institutional and managerial cooperative arrangements to contain threats to global or regional stability and to prevent the outbreak of unintended wars. The most effective of such arrangements is a great power concert in conflict resolution. At the same time, the recent unit-level changes are promising with respect to the higher likelihood and feasibility of a great power concert in the post–Cold War era—a subject that I discuss in the Conclusions in light of the theoretical model of the book.

Chapter 1

# Intended and Unintended Conflict and Cooperation under International Anarchy

In this chapter, I suggest some of the implications of anarchy for international conflict and cooperation. In the first section, I introduce two competing conceptions of the nature of international anarchy: structural and international society. Both schools agree that, in the absence of a central government, the great powers play a critical role in the management of international conflicts. This management is most effective when the great powers cooperate, but international anarchy powerfully constrains interstate collaboration. Still, cooperation, broadly defined, is not impossible even in the area where it is least likely, that is, the political-security field. But to understand under what conditions cooperation will be successful, we need to distinguish between types of intended and unintended cooperation, as I do in the second section. I start by introducing some of the ambiguities in the international relations literature with respect to categories and forms of cooperation. Next, I deal with these ambiguities by differentiating between two ideal types of cooperation (spontaneous versus deliberate) and between two substantive types of conflict management (crisis management versus conflict resolution). These types of cooperation are closely related, in turn, to the two competing conceptions of the international order. Whereas spontaneous cooperation in crisis management is a reflection of the structural balance-of-power approach, deliberate cooperation in conflict resolution is a major expression of the international society perspective.

The absence of a central authority under anarchy encourages the resort to force as a common way to resolve international conflicts. In the third section, I make a parallel distinction between intended and inadvertent wars. Inadvertent wars are the other side of the coin of spontaneous cooperation in crisis, namely, these wars result from the failure of crisis management which, in turn, reflects the strength of the security dilemma under anarchy. Thus, in this chapter, I introduce the four major dependent variables of this book: unintended and intended cooperation in conflict management as well as intended and inadvertent wars.

## International Politics: Anarchic But Not Disorderly

The anarchic nature of the international system is the most fundamental trait of international political life.[1] Whereas domestic politics are centralized, the multiplicity of sovereign states leads to the absence of a central authority in the international system (Waltz 1979, 88–89). Anarchy encourages conflicts and constrains cooperation. Being anarchic, however, does not necessarily imply that the international system is totally chaotic and without order. The word *anarchy* has a number of possible meanings: the absence of government; the absence of law or of other kinds of rules; disorder; or confusion. The four are not identical. The absence of government may often generate disorder or lawlessness, but it need not have these outcomes (Nardin 1983, 35). Thus, for international politics, the most appropriate sense of anarchy seems to be the absence of government more than disorder or confusion (Bull 1966; Buzan 1983, 94), and possibly even more than the absence of rules (Bull 1977; Nardin 1983, 34–42; Wight 1978, 96–97), especially if the discussion is not limited to formal legalism or to explicit and negotiated rules but is broadened to encompass other forms of international order and of rules of state conduct, as I do.

Hence Waltz, who since *Man, the State and War* (1959) has stressed the importance of anarchy for our understanding of international political life, suggests at the same time that in international politics one has "to conceive of an order without an orderer and of organizational effects where formal organization is lacking" (1979, 89). Waltz recognizes, furthermore, the existence of some kind of rules in the states system. Even though the international system is anarchic, he asserts, states undergo "socialization" through which they accept the "so-called rules of state behavior" (1979, 127–28).

At least two differences between the state of nature and the states system can account for why order is possible in the latter setting but not in the former, despite the absence of government in both of them. First, since states are less vulnerable to violent attack than are individuals in the state of nature and, on the whole, are more self-sufficient (Jervis 1978, 172), they also have less need to establish a central authority to maintain order (Bull 1966, 45–46; Buzan 1983, 94; Nardin 1983, 40–41). Indeed, states seem to fear attempts to establish such an authority more than they fear the continuation of anarchy. Second, in contrast to the equality of people in the state of nature, the differences in states' capabilities allow the great powers to play a special role in establishing a degree of order in the international system. Both Bull (1966, 46; 1971; 1977; and 1980) and Waltz (1979, 132, chap. 9), despite their differences, stress this factor as a major contribution to the international order (see also Easton 1953, 138–39).

Even if theorists agree that anarchy does not mean disorder in world politics, there are competing conceptions of the character of this order. I contrast two such conceptions that are closely associated with the concern of this book about explaining intended and unintended types of conflict and cooperation.[2] The structural balance-of-power conception of order is that of spontaneous, unintended order, exemplified by unexpected success or failure in crisis management. The international society school conceives of a deliberate, purposive, and conscious type of order, as manifested, for example, in high-level great power cooperation.

### The Structural Balance-of-Power Approach

In the structural conception of order, the international structure, defined as the arrangement of the units (i.e., nations-states) in relation to each other, conditions and constrains the behavior and interaction of the units (see Waltz 1979, chaps. 4, 5).[3] As a result, the structure, particularly the distribution of capabilities among states, can impose an order of sorts irrespective of the motivations of decision makers or the attributes of states. Contingent on the structural circumstances, a spontaneous international order can emerge (Waltz 1979, 100). Like the economic order that is produced by what Smith in *The Wealth of Nations* (1776, 421) called the "invisible hand" of the market, the international order can be an unintended, self-generating outcome, the result of unilateral actions of competing, even rival, states that wish first of all to survive in an anarchic setting (Waltz 1979, 91).[4] This approach to international order informs the structural conception of the balance of power: according to this perspective, it is an automatic or self-generating mechanism, by which a threat to other states posed by a rising great power brings about the formation of a countervailing coalition to check and balance its power.[5]

This interpretation of international order and of the balance of power shares the classical realists' view of international politics as fundamentally conflictual and dominated by the security dilemma and the common resort to war.[6] But the structural perspective also highlights conditions that reduce the degree of disorder in the states system, albeit without transforming its anarchic nature. Hence, one of the striking differences between the Hobbesian state of nature and world politics is the unequal distribution of capabilities in the latter, as opposed to the equality among people in the former. Because of the inequality among states, the great powers emerge as potential regulators of world affairs.

Although it recognizes the benefits of inequality among states, the structural school appreciates, at the same time, the merits of an equilibrium among the major centers of power. Indeed, the automatic mechanism of the balance of power will tend to create an equilibrium among the great powers even if most or all of the great powers want superiority or hegemony rather than an equal balance of capabilities among them. Such an equilibrium is, in turn, a prerequisite of international order. Although unintended by the policymakers, such an order tends to have the following consequences.

1. the obstruction of the dominance of any single actor, in other words, maintenance of the states system
2. the preservation of the autonomy of small states (cf. Butterfield 1966, 142; Organski 1968, 280–81)
3. the reinforcement of the stability of the status quo (Claude 1962, 54–55; Jervis 1988, 345)
4. the promotion of peace (cf. Buchan, quoted in Blainey 1973, 110; Bull 1977, 107; Claude 1962, 55–57; Ferris and Wright, both cited in Patchen 1988, 39–40; Jervis 1976, chap. 3; Organski 1968, 404–27; Organski and Kugler 1980, 14–17)—even though this was not traditionally the primary function of the balance of power (see Gulick, cited in Blainey 1973, 111–12; Haas, quoted in Claude 1962, 52), its importance increased drastically in the modern era with the growing destructiveness of military technology, notably nuclear weapons.[7]

Because the primary function or consequence of this type of order is the first one, which may require a war (Bull 1977, 107; Claude 1962, 54; Jervis 1985, 60), this school can explain why antihegemonic wars occur: because there is a great power that seeks to establish its dominance in the international system and thereby threatens the security of other great powers.[8]

The structural perspective is also uniquely suited to explain the occurrence of unintended wars (resulting from the security dilemma), which is contrasted with the occurrence of intended wars in the last section of this chapter.[9]

### The International Society Approach

Classically, this perspective was associated with the Grotian tradition (cf. Bull 1977, 26–27).[10] More recently, the regime literature can, on the whole, be seen as a subset of the international society school, mainly in the field of political economy.[11] The international order according to the international society school (Bull 1977, 16–19) resembles in its consequences the balance-of-power order according to the structural school (the prevention of hegemony, the independence of individual states, and the advancement of peace).

The major difference between the two schools concerns the sources and the mode of the international order. In contrast to the unintended-spontaneous structural conception of order, the international society school stresses a purposive conception of order (Bull 1977, 5–18). Rather than conceiving the international order in the structural form of scientific laws and patterns observed by the outside analyst, the international society approach focuses on the actual ends and values of the participants that are sustained by such an order. Order in social life is thus defined as "a pattern of human activity that sustains elementary, primary or universal goals of social life" (Bull 1977, 5). It is not enough, according to this perspective, "for things to be done in an ordered way. It is also necessary that what is done should be such as to merit the word orderly. The essence or the effect of action is what counts, not the existence of recognized processes for its execution" (James 1973, 63). Thus, at least one element of this order goes beyond the structural approach and comes closer to the domain of international law. It refers to "the common goals of all social life: limitation of violence resulting in death or bodily harm, the keeping of promises and the stabilization of possession by rules of property" (Bull 1977, 19).

As opposed to the structural approach's emphasis on the competitive elements in an anarchic environment, this perspective views international politics as the continuous play of mixed-motive games that are partly distributive but also partly productive. States' consciousness of common interests or values, Bull (1977) argues, gives rise to shared rules and institutions; these, in turn, enable states to cooperate in accomplishing common objectives. Bull enumerates five institutions of the international society: the balance of power, international law, diplomacy, war, and the management of the international system by the great powers. Rules and institutions should supposedly constrain the independent behavior of states. However, Bull fails to make clear to what extent and in what ways international rules and institutions achieve this outcome and how they contribute to the international order beyond the restraining effects imposed by the balance of power (Rosecrance 1981).

One can deduce from this approach that the major causal factor in international politics is cognitive-cultural-ideological. Common ideas and values and a shared ethical code enable the definition of international rules, the evolution of joint institutions, and the reinforcement of a sense of common interests. The nineteenth-century Concert of five great European powers constitutes the most remarkable example of Bull's (1977) argument, especially with regard to the managerial responsibilities of the major powers.

According to the international society approach, not only cooperation but also conflict and war are foremost intended and are caused by the character and the motives of the actors. Luard sums up his extensive work on the causes of war in the international society by suggesting that "conflict has thus resulted from different types of issues in different ages. The questions which give rise to conflict at any one time depend on a number of factors. But they depend above all on the aspirations and attitudes of the dominant elites within society" (1990, 186). Especially in the modern age, ideological differences have played a critical role in causing conflict and war (Luard 1986b, chap. 5); at any rate, according to this perspective, wars are not inadvertent but are rather the result of calculated decisions by states (Luard 1986b, 232).

## The Importance of and the Limitations to Great Power Conflict Management under Anarchy

The two perspectives on the international order agree that under anarchy the great powers can manage international conflicts more effectively than other agents.[12] The reason for this role of the great powers is related to a combination of their lesser vulnerability; relatively high self-sufficiency; and superior diplomatic, economic, and military capabilities, including power projection into distant areas, as well as their global interests and system-wide concerns.[13] Yet the two schools disagree about the character of the regulatory role and the type of cooperation expected of the great powers to fulfill this function.

Structural theory postulates that it is "their extraordinary positions in the system," rather than their intentions and internal attributes, that lead the big powers "to undertake tasks that other states have neither the incentive nor the ability to perform" (Waltz 1979, 199). Thus, this theory would stress that the great powers might play their regulatory role even if, in fact, they intend to pursue solely individualistic goals (such as preserving their security) through unilateral means (notably balancing each other by armament and alliances). In other words, their contribution to conflict management might be an unintended outcome of their interaction. Mainly due to the constraints on cooperation posed by the international anarchy, the great powers might not be able on many occasions to go much beyond tacit-spontaneous cooperation. But that should be sufficient for effective crisis management under certain structural conditions, although not necessarily for the more ambitious aim of conflict resolution.[14]

By contrast, in the conception of a purposeful order, the world powers consciously pursue policies that enhance international tranquillity and settle interstate disputes. In this international society conception of the great powers, negotiated agreements among responsible powers rather than unilateral steps fulfill an especially important role in advancing international order.[15] Moreover, other states should, in this view, recognize the special responsibilities of the great powers. Indeed, even in the era of decolonization, when sovereign equality seems to be universally accepted, U.N. members have conferred a special status regarding international peace and security issues on the five permanent members of the Security Council (see Bull 1980, 437; Tucker 1977, 33–34).[16]

Because of their pivotal position in world politics, the absence or presence and the degree and type of cooperation among the major powers, especially in the area of conflict management, have critical implications for the international order. Yet anarchy poses severe constraints on international cooperation.

**Intended and Unintended Cooperation under Anarchy**

Anarchy and Great Power Cooperation

The anarchic, self-help nature of the international system makes international cooperation, especially among all the great powers of the day, extremely difficult.[17] As Jervis points out, "Because there are no institutions or authorities that can make and enforce international laws, the policies of cooperation that will bring mutual rewards if others cooperate, may bring disaster if they do not. Because states are aware of this, anarchy encourages behavior that leaves all concerned worse off than they could be, even in the extreme case in which all states would like to freeze the status-quo" (1978, 167).

Under the security dilemma, Waltz argues, states are more concerned with relative gains than with absolute payoffs. "When faced with the possibility of cooperation for mutual gain, states that feel insecure must ask how the gain will be divided. They are compelled to ask not 'Will both of us gain?' but 'Who will gain more?' If an expected gain is to be divided, say in the ratio of two to one, one state may use its disproportionate gain to . . . damage or destroy the other" (1979, 105).

Waltz's (1979) argument underlines the zero-sum character of the relations among rivals under the security dilemma.[18] Actors behave as negative altruists, that is, their payoffs vary inversely with the other's utility.[19]

The constraints on interstate cooperation are particularly powerful in the security realm. Indeed, there is wide agreement among students of international politics that collaboration is much more common in the economic than in the security realm.[20]

The differences between the economic and security issue-areas underline the strength of the obstacles to security collaboration.[21] For one thing, since national security involves the preservation of states, the stakes in this sphere are greater than in others. Even more important is the frequent irreversibility of mistakes in the strategic realm. The disincentive to cooperate is reinforced by the relative nature of military power. If one state is doing well economically, that need not adversely affect the prosperity of other states (although states might fear that a growing economic power can be translated at a later stage to military power). In contrast, the growing military capability of a certain power has traditionally posed a threat to others because the ultimate test of armed forces is in confrontation with other forces.[22] Arms control agreements have been less common than trade agreements because while both types might offer joint gains, the parties in arms limitations may be worried more about relative gains than about absolute benefits. In brief, zero-sum games, negative altruism or status games, and worst-case scenarios leading to purely competitive conduct have been much more characteristic in security relations than in other fields.[23]

Still, cooperation among adversaries is not inconceivable even in the security realm. Many situations in international politics are not pure zero-sum; instead, they resemble what Schelling has called "mixed-motive games" that are a mixture of "mutual dependence and conflict, of partnership and competition" (1960, 89). As Snyder and Diesing (1977) show at length, mixed-motive games also apply to the politicostrategic domain, including the presumably conflictual situation of international crises.[24]

Whereas conflict among competing great powers is taken for granted, there might also be shared interests among the adversaries (Axelrod and Keohane 1985, 231–32; Russett 1983, 112; Schelling 1960, 15). They are, moreover, "interdependent" because "each participant's 'best' choice of action depends on what he expects the other to do, and that 'strategic behavior' is concerned with influencing another's choice by working on his expectation of how one's own behavior is related to his" (Schelling 1960, 15).[25]

Indeed, in many cases the powers would prefer a cooperative arrangement to mutual defection, although they would not be ready to offer unilateral concessions. Similar to the economic sphere, unrestrained competition could damage all parties and thus create an incentive to collaborate. Since the military interdependence between adversaries is frequently not a single play but is continuous (but see also George, Farley, and Dallin 1988, 11), the effects of the "shadow of the future" (Axelrod 1984) could also be applied, in principle, to the political-strategic realm.[26]

It is true that the security dilemma makes security cooperation extremely difficult. However, precisely because of its strength, it also makes collaborative arrangements valuable since individualistic actions are not only costly but dangerous (Jervis 1983, 174). Indeed, if actors are "sensitive to costs" (Feldman 1982, 145) and insofar as military interdependence is not a single play, then we could, under certain structural conditions, expect at least some degree of cooperation also in the security domain.

Most important, since cooperation does not have to be conceived in dichotomous terms, like in game theory, certain types of collaboration might particularly apply to the security domain, even if they would be short of the international regimes and institutions that are more typical of political economy. In the security field, as compared to the economic realm, the common interest refers especially to avoiding or minimizing joint losses rather than to maximizing joint gains. Indeed, rather than rendering cooperation impossible in general, it is more accurate to propose that under anarchy different kinds of collaboration occur in different settings and are related to different causal factors (see the summary at the end of the chapter). Therefore, a crucial step in our understanding of the possibilities of great power cooperation is the identification of different types and degrees of it. This task is now in order.

## Some Ambiguities about Kinds and Levels of Cooperation

Although anarchy poses severe constraints on great power cooperation, it does not render it impossible. Accordingly, an increasing number of scholars have recently addressed not only interstate conflict but also the possibilities for international cooperation. The mushrooming literature on international cooperation since the late 1970s has put special emphasis not on "formal organizations with imposing headquarters" (Keohane 1984, 246; see also Keohane 1980) but rather on the general matter of cooperation in the absence of a world sovereign.[27] More particularly, the focus has been on explaining how international institutions and regimes are formed and what influence they exert.[28] On the whole, this literature seems better equipped than the traditional studies of international law and international formal organizations to deal with the problems of cooperation between states, because it takes more seriously the inherent effects of power and conflict on states' behavior in an anarchic environment.

The great contribution of this literature is that it showed the possiblities for cooperation under anarchy despite the many difficulties. Yet it failed to distinguish between types, levels, and forms of cooperation.

The concepts of *institution, regime,* and especially *cooperation* are very broad—at times too much so to be helpful.[29] Moreover, the usage of these terms tends to be dichotomous, as if these entities either exist in toto or not at all. Thus, in the regime literature there is a focus on the presence or absence of regimes, thus implying a dichotomous distinction between cooperation and noncooperation and, more specifically, between a full-blown regime and the absence of any cooperation. For example, some authors tend to associate regimes with negotiated formal agreements and explicit bargaining while deemphasizing other forms of cooperation.[30] Somewhat similarly, in writing about security regimes, Jervis (1983) asserts that while there was an elaborate regime in nineteenth-century Europe, there was nothing comparable in the security sphere during the postwar era. Yet, while a comprehensive and deliberate regime like the Concert of Europe has obviously not existed since 1945, that should not exclude the possibility of various forms of U.S.-Soviet security collaboration, even if short of full-blown negotiated settlements, on specific issues and in specific geographical regions even during the Cold War.[31] Likewise, structural and game theories also fail to define degrees and levels of collaboration. Most notably, in Prisoner's Dilemma, the players have only two choices: defection or cooperation. [32]

I propose that the usage of the term *cooperation* should not be dichotomous. Instead, we might more appropriately conceive of cooperation as a continuum. But so as not to multiply indefinitely the number of the dependent variables and thus make it impossible to generalize, a distinction between at least two fundamentally different modes of joint collaborative arrangements (spontaneous versus deliberate) should be drawn and then applied to different issue-areas, as I do in this book with respect to conflict management.

I deal with the apparent discrepancies regarding cooperation by differentiating among different forms or modes of collaboration in general. I link these modes, in turn, to substantive kinds of conflict management, as well as to causal factors at different levels of analysis.

### Contrasting Two Ideal Types of Cooperation: Spontaneous versus Deliberate

How does an applauding audience in a concert hall coordinate its action to agree whether to demand an encore or to taper off simultaneously? The phenomenon that takes place in situations of this kind is termed tacit communication and coordination. Whereas in everyday life it is possible to concert actions tacitly, it becomes more difficult for adversaries who have divergent interests. It would not be easy for rival armies that seek to occupy as much as possible of the same area of land, but still prefer to avoid an armed clash, to identify a focal point that could enable them to reach their seemingly contradictory goals.[33]

As Schelling demonstrates, however, in many real-world situations, as well as in game theory, there may be a "river" (1960, 71) or other salient outcomes and prominent points around which actors' expectations could converge.[34] Such tacit collaboration may spontaneously occur even when there is no deliberate design of cooperative arrangements and no direct communications, to the extent that the adversaries have converging interests in addition to their conflicting ones.[35]

Similarly, drawing on Ashworth's (1980) work on the trench warfare of World War I, Axelrod (1984, chap. 4) notes the emergence of tacit cooperation between British and German antagonists who had a shared interest in a live-and-let-live system despite the opposing objective of killing as many enemy troops as possible to weaken their forces in case a major battle was ordered.[36] Axelrod's study shows that cooperation can spontaneously emerge among self-seeking participants in Prisoner's Dilemma games depending on two necessary conditions: a high likelihood of continued interaction with each other and a salience of the future high enough in the players' calculations to overwhelm their temptation to defect on the present play. However, not all kinds of collaborative arrangements can be arrived at spontaneously and tacitly. Some arrangements, such as detailed negotiated settlements, depend on deliberate design and explicit communication.

Hayek (1973, 46) makes an important distinction between two kinds of order that presents a useful point of departure for thinking about the two ideal types or modes of collaborative arrangements. In contrast to spontaneous, self-generating collaboration, Hayek (1973, 37–38) notes that an organization is a human-made, artificially constructed and directed form of social order. Whereas organizations are the result of conscious design, automatic arrangements are spontaneous growths that do not require a deliberate plan and explicit awareness.[37] Furthermore, ad hoc collaboration can sometimes be arrived at unconsciously and even be unintended, at least initially.[38] Indeed, it is the unintended nature of tacit-spontaneous collaboration that is the central necessary characteristic of this ideal type for the purposes of the present study. Namely, while one may conceive of tacit-spontaneous forms of cooperation that are in full accord with the internal attributes and the intentions of the participants, the focus in this book is on tacit-spontaneous arrangements that are also unintended—i.e., opposed to the initial desires and domestic characteristics of the actors.

Since the term *regime* has become a fundamental one for students of international cooperation, how might we conceive of Hayek's (1973) two types of arrangements with regard to regimes? Krasner further elaborates the definition of regime offered above by stating that "Principles are beliefs of fact, causation, and rectitude. Norms are standards of behavior defined in terms of rights and obligations. Rules are specific prescriptions or proscriptions for action. Decision-making procedures are prevailing practices for making and implementing collective choice" (1983, 2).

Krasner (1983) goes on to argue that principles and norms are the fundamental defining attributes of a regime. Rules and procedures, on the other hand, are the instruments of a regime and are strongly affected by the power relations among the participants (Ruggie 1983, 200). If we relate this distinction to our two modes, it would seem that shared principles and norms would be conducive to the emergence of the deliberate form of cooperation. Thus, a full-blown regime based on principles and norms is an instance of this mode of cooperation. Conversely, a spontaneous arrangement might consist only of rules and procedures and not necessarily include principles and norms. Although such rules and procedures might suffice for effective coordination, the arrangement would lack the normative and cognitive basis of a full-blown regime and its attendant high-level of cooperation.[39]

Spontaneous arrangements tend to be reached, as Axelrod (1984) and especially Schelling (1960, 71, 75) make clear, through nonverbal communication. The tacit nature of the rules in a self-generating collaboration stands out in contrast to the explicitness of negotiated agreements that are achieved through formal talks.[40] By ranking rules according to the degree of explicitness with which they are communicated, Cohen (1980) found that at one end of the continuum are legally binding written agreements. A regime as a form of deliberate cooperation usually at least partly comprises such rules, as well as the closely related nonbinding, but still written, understandings, verbal gentlemen's accords, and the spirit of agreements, that is, their unwritten aspect. By contrast, Cohen found that in self-generating arrangements, the understandings on the tacit rules are contained "neither in a written document, nor in an explicit verbal promise, nor even in the spirit of a written agreement" (1980, 142).

In spontaneous cooperation, each of the parties may move unilaterally rather than reach an agreement with its opponents in advance. The parties might follow what Lindblom called "partisan mutual adjustment": "Such coordination as is achieved is a by-product of ordinary decisions, that is of decisions not specifically intended to coordinate. . . . A simple idea is elaborated . . . that people can coordinate with each other without a common purpose and without rules that fully prescribe their relations to each other" (1965, 28–29).[41]

It is the recurrence of similar situations that can turn unilateral actions and parallel behavior (or mutual adjustment) into tacit rules, even if that was not the actors' intention. Indeed, evidence for the existence of such rules can be gleaned from regularities in the participants' actual behavior; again, that does not indicate that the decision makers are necessarily aware of these rules (Bull 1977, 211).[42] But the tacit rules establish the range of acceptable conduct each state will tolerate of the other (in fact, although not necessarily in accordance with explicit principles) in the absence of a world authority. Thus, recurring patterns of behavior help to create expectations about the limits of permissible behavior and, concomitantly, help define what is intolerable and destabilizing (Gaddis 1986, 132–33; Keal 1983, 2–3; Williams 1976, 200).

Indeed, the nature of cooperation in a spontaneous-tacit arrangement tends to be negative in contrast to the affirmative character of a deliberate, negotiated regime.[43] In such an explicit regime, the actors have interests in common; whereas in a purely tacit arrangement, they would primarily like to avoid a certain outcome. Since the players in an affirmative type of cooperation would like to ensure that a particular outcome occurs, the regime must stipulate strict patterns of action and specify what constitutes cooperation and what constitutes defection. Cooperation entails agreed on rules to abstain from particular types of conduct, to behave jointly and positively for certain ends, and to invest the regime's institutions with powers to monitor behavior and to mediate conflicts. A related argument is that international organizations should not be equated with regimes, because the former do not necessarily regulate independent decision making or modify individualistic behavior (Keohane 1980 and 1984; Stein 1983, 133–34).[44]

On the other hand, arrangements for dealing with the dilemma of common avoidance need only facilitate coordination.[45] While prohibitions on behavior are accepted, coordination does not encompass central inspection and conflict settlement. Whereas in an explicit regime there is usually a measure of interdependence between the issues it regulates and other issues on the international agenda, in a spontaneous arrangement there is not necessarily any such linkage. Indeed, common principles and norms suggest the presence of common interests that go beyond a particular issue-area, whereas a negative cooperation is less likely to spill over into other areas. In other words, the scope of the cooperation[46] tends to be more comprehensive and general in an explicit regime. That does not mean that the substance of the issues covered in a self-generating arrangement is necessarily less important. Quite the contrary, since there are powerful constraints on the establishment of a security regime among antagonists, tacit, situation-related collaboration in so critical an area as international security is more feasible in some cases than a full-blown regime.

Each actor in a regime requires guarantees that the others will also take care to avoid their rational competitive choice (namely, defection). Thus, as Stein (1983, 128, 133) points out, such collaboration is more likely to need a measure of formalization and institutionalization than an avoidance type of cooperation. An ad hoc negative arrangement does not require formalization; hence, the difference in the degree of explicitness.

Ideally speaking, high-level cooperative arrangements such as regimes should both be more lasting and modify actors' behavior in a more meaningful way than tacit arrangements. Nevertheless, the anarchic structure of the international system may well limit the longevity and the independent effects of any collaborative arrangements, especially in the security realm. Thus, under the conditions of self-help and anarchy, tacit collaboration, despite the severe limitations of tacit rules, has a number of attractions. First, there might not be any better form of cooperation available, since explicit security cooperation among rivals is often infeasible.

Second, tacit understandings have certain advantages over explicit negotiated agreements in the domestic-ideological context. There is no need for direct talks—which makes them possible even among actors who lack diplomatic relations or are unwilling and unable to rely on normal channels of communication (Cohen 1980, 142). Implicit understandings are less costly in terms of bureaucratic time and energy (cf. Gowa and Wessell 1982, 4). They may also circumvent domestic and ideological problems. As Cohen points out,

> There is the sort of situation in which admission or articulation of the understanding would entail a loss of self-esteem on the part of one or both of the actors . . . or when the nature of the understanding is felt to be so discreditable and politically indefensible as to be inarticulable even in a purely verbal formula. This may occur when the infringement of some domestic taboo is involved or with an issue about which one is simply not

"supposed" to reach an understanding at all. (Cohen 1980, 142; see also MacFarlane 1985, 315–16; Vasquez 1991, 223 n. 13)

Third, implicit understandings are more adjustable to changing situations. They give the actors greater leeway in both strategy and tactics (cf. Gowa and Wessell 1982, 4).

However, despite the apparent usefulness of tacit rules in the post-1945 system, some analysts of conflict management have questioned their effectiveness (cf. Becker 1979, 253–55; Frei 1983, 140; George, with others, 1983, 377–78, 391–92 and 1985, 4; Gowa and Wessell 1982, 4; MacFarlane 1987a, 17 n. 1), stressing their narrowness and supposed fragility and unreliability for preventing the escalation of local conflicts to global crises and even to a world war. Moreover, many would not want to rely exclusively on spontaneous cooperation for preventing major wars. Such concerns then generate an interest in concerted diplomacy for the purpose of conflict resolution. Indeed, successful conflict resolution would supposedly not only reduce the likelihood of wars and crises but also make it possible for states to spend less on defense, allocate scarce resources to a great variety of other fields and needs, improve their relations on a wide range of issue-areas, and, overall, raise the quality of international life.

In the next section, I define the two substantive areas of great power cooperation in the field of conflict management that correspond to the two general collaborative modes: crisis management and conflict resolution.

## Substantive Types of Conflict Management: Crisis Management versus Conflict Resolution

The two major dependent variables dealt with in this section are tacit rules for crisis management and for regulating the threat and use of force in crises and concerted diplomacy for conflict resolution. Indeed, another major aspect of the distinction between spontaneous and conscious cooperation lies in the contrast between cooperation during crises versus cooperation that extends beyond the time of a certain crisis and takes place mostly in noncrisis settings, that is, during more normal periods of diplomacy. This contrast is based on a general distinction between crises and normal times. Such a contrast applies to a number of social science disciplines (psychology, labor-management relations, sociology, and political science). In international relations, it has been noted in the area of international political economy (see Gourevitch 1986), and was also implied in studies of international crises.[47] But the distinction has a special relevance for the theory of cooperation in security affairs, especially with regard to conflict management, since international cooperation is both so important and so difficult in this domain.

The theoretical literature on conflict management has failed to develop the distinction between crisis settings and normal diplomacy. Moreover, most of the existing literature on cooperation in conflict management has failed to highlight the conceptual and policy implications of the distinction between crisis management and conflict resolution. The reason might be the fixation with deterrence and crisis management (and, at most, local war termination) during the Cold War to the neglect of the more ambitious task of U.S.-Soviet cooperation in settling bilateral as well as third world conflicts. A more far-reaching distinction has been developed by George and colleagues (1983), who examined the differences between crisis management and crisis prevention.[48] In crisis management, the cooperation starts after the parties have already been drawn into a war-threatening confrontation. The collaboration is reflected in an effort to prevent the outbreak of a major war. In contrast, in crisis prevention, the collaboration should begin before the participants find themselves in a crisis situation, that is, they head off crises by controlling the escalation of their competition into dangerous confrontations. Yet crisis prevention and even George, Farley, and Dallin's discussion of "an enhanced role for diplomacy" and of "the importance of the basic political framework of relations" (1988, 594–97, 667–70) still fall short of cooperation in conflict resolution.

An international crisis is defined in this book as a change in the external situation that produces a threat to the vital interests of one or more states and an awareness of a finite time for response to the threat, so that the interaction between the participating states involves a considerable probability of the use of force. The critical element that characterizes a crisis and that differentiates it from a normal period is the dangerously high probability of resort to military force.[49] A great power crisis may arise either directly between the great powers, or as a result of great power involvement in local crises or wars between small states that are aligned with the external powers (Snyder and Diesing 1977, 7–8).

In an hour of crisis, the intensity of the rivalry and the time constraints preclude resolving the fundamental issue in conflict. At the same time, nonverbal tacit understandings and self-generating rules could be sufficient for avoiding war, even if the fundamental conflict was not settled and the parties could not explicitly agree on the rules and on the outcome. Thus, the United States and the Soviet Union succeeded in avoiding war in the Berlin crisis of 1961 through the West's tacit, de facto acquiescence to the establishment of the Berlin Wall and Moscow's dropping its deadline for resolving the Berlin conflict. Only after ten years were the powers able to reach an explicit agreement on the status of Berlin, and only in 1975 did they conclude the Helsinki accords on a general settlement in Europe. Even then the United States continued explicitly to insist on rejecting the division of Europe and to support the abolishment of the Berlin Wall and the eventual unification of Germany.[50]

Even at the moment of confrontation, of course, there may be explicit negotiations going on simultaneously with the shows of force and the threats of war. Thus, Kennedy and Khrushchev communicated quite often during the Cuban Missile Crisis and eventually reached an agreement on withdrawing the Soviet missiles in return for a U.S. pledge not to invade Cuba. As Schelling (1960, 53–81) points out, bargaining takes place even during wars, especially the post–World War II limited wars. Indeed, promises and not only threats are signaled during crises (Schelling 1960, 43–46, 131–37, 175–77). As Snyder and Diesing (1977, 243–80) demonstrate, there may even be attempts at accommodation and settlement in the hour of crisis. Yet following the logic of the definition suggested above, the dominant elements in a crisis, at least in its initial stage, would include threats to use force, manipulations of the risk of war, measures short of war, coercive diplomacy, and the fear of escalation;[51] and the main cooperative component would be of the negative nature of war avoidance or, at best, tacit, ad hoc arrangements such as the tacit rules for crisis management of the postwar era to be discussed in chapters 3 and 5.

By contrast, when parties attempt to resolve a conflict in noncrisis settings, they go beyond a negative type of arrangement to "formalize a settlement of the underlying issue in conflict"(see Snyder and Diesing 1977, 10, 18; see also Hampson and Mandell 1990, 192–93 n. 2). Not only is there an avoidance of a certain outcome, but the parties also seek to achieve a set of common goals.[52] This focus on affirmative cooperation is especially relevant for a concert or a security regime, although competition and conflict continue even in such high-level collaborative arrangements.

The distinction between crisis management and joint diplomacy in noncrisis periods, then, corresponds to the differentiation between the two ideal types of collaborative arrangement. Crisis management parallels the tacit, common-aversion, self-generating type of collaboration; conflict resolution fits the explicit, affirmative, and deliberate sort of arrangement.

In crisis management, states try to advance or protect their interests by coercive threats and maneuvers—which necessarily require posing the prospect of war—without actually raising the risk of war to an intolerable level (see Snyder and Diesing 1977, 451).[53] The unintended result of this dilemma is the emergence of the tacit rules that address the two dimensions of crisis management through the regulation of the threat and the use of force by the powers, their military intervention, and the nature and extent of their legitimate response to other powers' threats to use force. Such unspoken understandings about the regulation of force are particularly helpful when adversaries have intense conflicts of interests and are affected by the security dilemma but would still prefer to avoid war. Especially when the great power crisis derives from a local conflict, the powers share an interest in avoiding entanglement in the hostilities even though their foremost concern is still their own interests.

When we are dealing with great power involvement in local crises or wars, the managerial challenge to the big powers is twofold, although the two aspects are closely related: to avoid war between themselves[54] and to stop the regional hostilities through cease-fires, truces, armistices, and the like. Thus, the implicit rules have to regulate the threat or the use of force by the external powers as well as the nature of legitimate military behavior of the local powers. In other words, the unspoken understandings have to reconcile the conflicting roles of the great powers as system managers on the one hand and as alliance leaders and protectors on the other.[55] In general, crisis management in third areas reinforces the interdependence between the great power patrons, since they are not only able to harm each other but dependent on each other to control adventurous clients (Snyder and Diesing 1977, 506).

The other substantive dependent variable is great power cooperation in conflict resolution. When states concert their diplomacy for that purpose, they move beyond the management of the use of force to deliberate negotiations for explicitly settling the fundamental issues in dispute among them. Great power cooperation in conflict resolution may be further subdivided into several levels of cooperation, ranging from relatively short-term concerted diplomacy on a single issue to a great power concert or security regime, which is a relatively long-term, institutionalized, and multi-issue form of cooperation. Yet, even single-issue concerted diplomacy constitutes high-level, deliberate cooperation in comparison with tacit cooperation for crisis management. A great power concert attempts to resolve multilaterally major conflicts both among the concert members themselves and among third parties. I discuss the meaning of concerts and the conditions for their emergence in chapter 4.

Concerted diplomacy, let alone a full-blown concert, is not essential for successful crisis management, but it can be very helpful in *preventing* or at least minimizing the probability of crises among the great powers in the first place; thus, it minimizes the danger of failures of crisis *management*. But concerted diplomacy by itself cannot guarantee effective crisis management once a crisis erupts. Once the great powers (or some of them) are drawn into a war-threatening confrontation, the effectiveness of their crisis management under anarchy also depends at least in part on the structure of the situation; indeed, this dependence creates the possibility (obviously, not the certainty) of inadvertent wars under certain structural conditions.[56]

To sum up, two general modes of cooperation have been identified (spontaneous-tacit versus deliberate-explicit) and have been found to correspond to the two substantive types of cooperation in conflict management (crisis management versus conflict resolution). These two ideal types of cooperation also parallel the two conceptions of international order, in that the structural perspective highlights spontaneous, self-generating arrangements and the international society school puts forward a purposive, deliberately designed conception of order and collaboration. Whereas the post-1815 Concert of Europe approximated the conscious-affirmative-explicit type of cooperative arrangement (see chap. 4), U.S.-Soviet crisis management during the Cold War resembled the spontaneous-avoidance-tacit kind (see chaps. 3 and 5). These two ideal types also parallel the distinction between intended outcomes (deliberate, explicit mode of collaboration) and unintended ones (tacit-spontaneous mode of collaboration). In the following section, I demonstrate that the same distinction between intended and unintended outcomes also holds with regard to the conflictual outcomes—namely, types of great power wars.

### Intended and Unintended Conflict under Anarchy

### Anarchy and Great Power Conflict

Not only does anarchy pose severe constraints on international cooperation, but it also encourages conflict. Without a supreme law enforcement agency, the states system is a self-help system that has, moreover, a perpetual tendency toward interstate conflict (see Aron 1967; Carr 1964, 109; Waltz 1959, 159, 188, 205, 207, 227, 238; see also Nardin 1983, 38; Wight 1978, 101). As Waltz argues, "in politics force is said to be the ultima ratio. In international politics force serves not only as the ultima ratio, but indeed as the first and constant one" (1979, 112–13). Indeed, the state of war is one of the three principal attributes of Hobbes's state of nature[57] and seems the most salient characteristic of international politics.[58] Thus, with anarchy as the focal point, the central analytical question in international politics is not "Why do nations go to war?" but "Why do wars not always occur?" (Jervis 1985, 58; Waltz 1959). Anarchy may encourage wars in two major ways. First, it may permit states to initiate wars, as under anarchy there is no overall powerful authority to stop them and enforce a settlement. In this sense, although anarchy serves as a permissive factor (Waltz 1959), the causes of specific wars lie in the intentions and attributes of the initiating state. Yet anarchy may also have a more direct effect on the outbreak of wars through the operation of the security dilemma.

In the absence of a reliable law enforcement agency, states have to take care of themselves and worry about those states that could threaten their autonomy. In such a setting, the security dilemma emerges "not because of misperception or imagined hostility, but because of the anarchic context of international relations" (Jervis 1976, 76; see also Jervis 1983, 176). The security dilemma refers to a vicious interaction whereby measures that a state adopts to increase its own security constitute a threat to others who, as a result, take defensive steps of their own, which in turn reduce the sense of security of the first state.[59] In a self-help system, the quest to survive and the resultant security dilemma are sufficient to lead even status quo powers to pursue arms races, construct alliances, and occasionally even stumble into undesired and unintended wars (George 1984b, 4–5; Jervis 1976, 67, 94; 1979, 213, 217, 1985; Waltz 1959, 234). The two types of influence international anarchy exerts on the outbreak of wars parallels the following distinction between two ideal types of major war.

### Two Ideal Types of Major Wars

A basic distinction should be drawn between two ideal types of major wars: premeditated and inadvertent. Some scholars are skeptical of the idea of unintended war (see Blainey 1973, chap. 9; Luard 1986b, chap. 5).[60] Others tend to overlook or at least fail to use the distinction between intended and unintended wars as a springboard for the construction of a theoretical model of outbreak of wars.[61] Still, this distinction is critical for anyone who seriously considers the effects of anarchy and the security dilemma on international conflict. Moreover, this distinction can provide a useful and parsimonious explanation both of some major wars in the past and also of the Long Peace in the postwar era; it can also provide some clues for the future following the end of the Cold War (see chap. 3 and the Conclusions). This distinction is closely related to the distinction between types of settings (crisis versus normal times).

A major war is one that involves most or all the great powers of the day.[62] It may break out either directly among the great powers or as a result of the escalation of a regional conflict, with great powers taking opposite sides.[63]

Premeditated wars may be defined as wars by choice or deliberate intent, namely wars that break out as a result of a calculated decision of at least one party to resort to a massive use of force in the pursuit of its objectives. These objectives may be outright aggression (self-aggrandizement at the expense of other states) or prevention (blocking or retarding the further rise of an adversary to avoid the worsening of the status quo and the risk of war under less favorable conditions).[64] However, since even the most aggressive objectives are often put in a defensive guise, in practice they may be difficult to tell apart. Whatever the objectives may be, the war will be an intended one to the extent that a deliberate decision is made to initiate it in a context that allows the state a choice between war and nonwar. The decision does not necessarily have to meet the criteria of comprehensive rationality; it is sufficient that it is calculated. Intended wars usually break out without a preceding crisis. Ideally, the decision to initiate such a war is made in a normal peacetime environment, or more precisely, in the absence of an immediate threat to vital interests (which, as noted, is a characteristic of international crises). Although the initiating state may sometimes intentionally manufacture a crisis as a pretext for war, the war is a premeditated one to the extent that the decision to initiate it is made before and not during the crisis.

In contrast to premeditated wars, inadvertent wars[65] are usually preceded by a crisis. Wars of this type occur as a result of nonvolitional factors, that is, the escalation of an international crisis because of a failure or breakdown of crisis management. The crisis might be a direct great power crisis right from the outset or start as a third-party crisis or a local war that entraps the great powers at a later stage. An inadvertent war is distinguished by that at the outset of the crisis, all sides have limited objectives, and neither side wants or expects a war (George 1991, 8), or at least not a major war involving most or all the great powers of the day. Yet at some point during the course of the crisis, one side may reach the conclusion that the initiation of a war has become inevitable to secure its objectives or to avoid an unacceptable outcome. Typically, the sides in a crisis are not faced with a single decision whether or not to go to war but with a series of decisions at a succession of critical points as the crisis unfolds, each decision progressively narrowing their freedom of maneuver (Levy 1991b, 71). Thus, they are drawn into war by the course of events, as a result of an action-reaction process and a series of incremental decisions. It may be difficult to pinpoint the crucial decision that inexorably led to war, or at least to the major war in which the parties eventually found themselves engulfed. Even if we can identify such a decision, in all likelihood it either is based on miscalculation and misunderstanding of the consequences of one's actions or is the result of a loss of control over allies or pressures from the domestic environment. In either case, it is likely to be the culmination of a process whereby the parties have maneuvered themselves into a situation where war was the only acceptable outcome.

Inadvertent wars are one of the major adverse effects of the working of the security dilemma in the anarchic international system. This dilemma makes it hard for the actors to distinguish between defensive and aggressive intentions. The security dilemma leads to the spiral model (Jervis 1976, 62–83), an action-reaction process in which each state views its own behavior as defensive but its antagonists perceive the same measures as aggressive. Accordingly, in an inadvertent war, it may be difficult to identify the guilty or aggressive party. Rather, these wars may erupt even between status quo powers, despite their reluctance at the outset of the crisis to go to war—or, at least, to a major war.

Several scholars have identified some major sequences or paths to failure in crisis management and to inadvertent war (see Allison, Carnesale, and Nye 1985; Frei 1983; George 1991; Gottfried and Blair 1988; Lebow 1987). For the purposes of this book, I distinguish two major sequences to inadvertent war: miscalculation and loss of control.

In *miscalculation,* the hostilities escalate to large-scale violence because of a failure to adequately think through the consequences of actions (Kahn 1962, 44, cited in Frei 1983, 3). This type of inadvertent war may occur because of a misperception of the balance of interests, a misestimation of a rival's resolve and commitments, or a miscalculation of relative capabilities. These mistakes may result in a miscalculated escalation, when one of the powers crosses the other's threshold to war in the mistaken belief that the other will not respond by violent means (Lebow 1987, 26). This pattern may also be called "miscalculated fait accompli" (George 1991, 549–50). The rationale for such a fait accompli effort rests on a miscalculation of the opponent's probable reaction, and the outcome is a war that neither the instigator of the fait accompli nor the opponent wanted or expected. The pattern of *preemption* may also be categorized as an instance of miscalculation, to the extent that it is based on an erroneous strategic estimate. It is a direct result of the security dilemma, in that essentially defensive measures undertaken by the opponent are perceived as a sign of imminent attack. A major cause of miscalculations and misperceptions is crisis-induced stress and the attendant cognitive-psychological problems.[66] Another factor that may contribute to misperceptions in crisis is cultural and ideological differences.

*Loss of control* during a crisis as a cause of inadvertent wars can derive from three main causes: domestic pressures, the loss of control by a great power over its allies, and the loss of control by the political leadership over the military. In this sequence, the top decision makers are driven to an inadvertent war as a result of allied, military, or public pressures that they are powerless to resist, even though they may correctly perceive the external situation.

These two paths to inadvertent war,[67] although analytically separate, may converge in a single international crisis, thus further aggravating its management and contributing to its escalation. They are manifested in two major patterns of crisis behavior. Behaviorally, failure in crisis management (which may lead to an inadvertent war) is marked by either over- or underreaction. By contrast, successful crisis management is characterized by resolute caution. In fact, resolve and caution can be seen as the two complementary faces of successful crisis management. Ideally, a state demonstrates resolve once its stakes are greater than the opponent's, whereas caution is the order of the day when the reverse is true. Resolve ensures that there will be no erosion in one's own interests, whereas caution helps to avoid encroachment on the opponent's vital interests. In both these types of behavior, however, the focus is on the signaling, bargaining, and negotiating aspect of the use of military power, what George (1984a) terms "diplomatic logic" in contrast to "military logic."[68] Resolve, however, involves coercive threats or actions, including the threat to use force, whereas cautious conduct is more a matter of accommodative offers and concessions.

A distinction should be drawn between overreaction (or recklessness) and resolve on the one hand and between underreaction and caution on the other hand. In a crisis context, reckless behavior involves insensitivity to the stakes of a rival great power and encroachment on its vital commitments, based on a miscalculation of the opponent's resolve and the mistaken belief that it will not react militarily. This behavior may result in a violent reaction by the opponent and escalation to an inadvertent war.

Underreaction, by contrast, is a policy of inaction (disengagement) or concessions (appeasement) that may mistakenly signal to the opponent indifference to the issue in question and the unconditional abandonment of vital commitments and thus tempt it to act recklessly.[69] Thus, over- and underreaction may be interrelated in a crisis.

Apart from miscalculation, both these patterns of crisis behavior may stem from the loss of control, that is, from the pressures of allies, the military, or public opinion. Whereas small allies and the military usually push in the direction of overreaction, public opinion may work both ways.[70] Either it may be adverse to international involvement and support disengagement in a crisis, or, on the contrary, it may urge an intervention in a conflict that catches the attention of the media and sympathetic domestic groups. While under- or overreaction may both lead to an inadvertent war, a recurring behavior of resolute restraint can result in the evolution of tacit rules for crisis management that regulate the use of force in crisis and prevent an unintended escalation.

The differentiation between preventive and preemptive wars is related to the distinction between intended and inadvertent wars, in that preventive wars are one type of intended wars, while preemption based on an erroneous strategic estimate constitutes one of the paths to inadvertent war (see George 1991, 8–9, 31).[71] These types of war are often confused because both are based on a "better now than later" logic. Yet in a preventive war, the threat the initiator perceives is a long-term one, based on differential rates of great power growth and the changing balance of power in the opponent's favor, which makes a showdown more desirable now, before the opponent gets stronger. In contrast, the preemptor faces (or mistakenly believes that it faces) an imminent attack by the opponent. Therefore, the threat it perceives is "instant, overwhelming, leaving no choice of means and no moment for deliberation" (Webster, cited in Walzer 1977, 74). Indeed, in this context Levy (1987) notes that preventive wars are "wanted wars" in the sense that there is no compelling reason to act militarily now, but this action is the choice of the preventer who does not face an immediate military threat. It can attempt other methods to redress the situation, such as new alliances, negotiated settlements, etc., and in the worst case fight a preventive war later if conditions warrant it. By contrast, a preemptor feels, even if mistakenly, highly constrained by the circumstances to resort to force immediately because otherwise the opponent is going to attack first. As Schelling noted, "fear that the other may be about to strike in the mistaken belief that we are about to strike gives us a motive for striking, and so justifies the other's motive" (1960, 207). Thus, the preemptor has far less of a choice and may prefer to avoid war whereas "the preventer basically 'wants war,' in the sense that it would demand enormous concessions by the adversary and make few (if any) of its own in order to avoid war" (Levy 1987, 92 n. 23).

Premeditated and inadvertent wars are ideal types. In specific complex cases of major war, there may be controversies among historians, some of whom may regard the war as largely inadvertent and absolve all parties from responsibility, while others attribute it to the deliberate will of one side. Indeed, such controversies took place with regard to both World War I and World War II. In the case of World War I, Fischer (1967) challenged the prevalent interpretation of the war as inadvertent, presenting it instead as an aggressive war intended and planned by a Germany striving for world domination. In contrast, Taylor (1961) challenged the dominant view of World War II as an aggressive war caused by Germany, and his interpretation in fact emphasizes several inadvertent elements. Yet these difficulties in specific cases do not blur the general analytical distinction, which parallels, to some extent, the distinction between a premeditated murder and manslaughter in criminal law.

## Summary: Anarchy and Intended and Unintended Outcomes

I will now sum up the major relations between anarchy, conflict, and cooperation, which will inform the discussion in the next chapters.

*Anarchy and unintended cooperation:* In the absence of a central authority, the most effective substitute is an equal balance of capabilities among the great powers of the day. This situation can enhance order, stability, and peace irrespective of actors' intentions and attributes. The specific distribution of capabilities that is most conducive to tacit cooperation in times of crisis is bipolarity (see chaps. 2 and 3).

*Anarchy and unintended conflict:* The prevalence of the security dilemma under anarchy leads to conflict even among status quo actors. Multipolar structures are especially prone to failures in crisis management, which may lead to inadvertent wars (see chap. 3).

*Anarchy and intended conflict:* The absence of an authoritative mechanism for conflict resolution encourages attempts to resolve conflicts by the use of force. It is unit-level factors and actors' intentions that may cause the outbreak of premeditated wars under anarchy depending on the dominant military technology (see chap. 3).

*Anarchy and intended cooperation:* Anarchy poses severe constraints for international collaboration, especially explicit, high-level collaboration in regimes, concerts, and institutions. Thus, only restrictive unit-level factors may make such cooperation possible on an enduring basis in normal times (see chap. 4).

In the next chapter, I discuss the general linkages between structural factors and crisis management on the one hand and unit-level elements and cooperation in normal diplomacy on the other hand. In chapter 3, I develop the model with regard to the occurrence of intended and unintended wars.

Chapter 2

# Explaining Great Power Cooperation in Conflict Management

In this chapter, I present a model for explaining two of the four ideal types of outcomes introduced in the previous chapter: great power intended and unintended cooperation in conflict management. But the model is also relevant for a third type of outcome: inadvertent war. (The fourth type—intended war—is discussed in the following chapter.) I argue that (1) tacit regulation of the use of force (manifested most dramatically by great power crisis cooperation, i.e., *crisis management*) is conditioned by *structural* elements (most specifically, the distribution of capabilities in the international system), whereas (2) deliberate great power cooperation in *conflict resolution* (cooperation that extends beyond the time of a certain crisis) depends on *state-cognitive* factors (domestic regimes and leaders' beliefs). Such a theoretical model can account for some major puzzles for international relations theory, as well as provide some suggestive ideas for future conflict management.[1] Indeed, this model can begin to provide a parsimonious explanation for the four types of outcomes presented in the previous chapter; but for a fuller and more elaborate explanation for these outcomes as well as for the puzzles to be introduced in this chapter, we also need the analysis in chapters 3 and 4.

In the following section, I consider four puzzles derived from a comparison of the nineteenth-century Concert of Europe and the postwar era, and I present the basic model to explain them. In the second and third sections, I develop linkages between the types of outcomes and two levels of causal factors (structural and unit-level causes), to explain the emergence of different types of cooperation. More specifically, I argue that while structural factors are influential in times of crisis, especially for the purpose of crisis management, nonsystemic elements are critical during normal diplomacy, particularly for the purposes of conflict resolution.

This model challenges the domination of the crisis literature by decision-making analysis (see Allison 1971; George 1980b, especially 47–49; Holsti 1972 and 1989; Holsti and George 1975; Janis 1982; Jervis, Lebow, and Stein 1985; Lebow 1981 and 1987; Patchen 1988) and the more general disregard of systemic factors by inside-out theories. Crisis analysis is thus supplemented with structural factors. At the same time, however, this book addresses the failure of structural and game theories to specify the types of outcomes they best explain. I highlight the outcomes best explained by structural factors, such as the emergence of tacit rules for the regulation of the use of force in crisis and inadvertent wars (see chap. 3). These outcomes are closely related to the question of the failure or success of crisis management.

There are also important phenomena that structural theory fails to explain; these include high-level explicit cooperation in international regimes and especially their normative content and related learning (see George, Farley, and Dallin 1988, 6; Jervis 1988; Nye 1988a; Smith 1987).[2] To account for such outcomes, the analysis departs from an exclusive focus on system-level factors and includes unit-level elements as well. These unit-level elements constitute an equally important part of the model. Indeed, I find inside-out theories to be most useful for explaining great power concerts and cooperation in conflict resolution, that is, cooperation that takes place mostly in noncrisis periods.

## The Four Puzzles: Anomalies for International Relations Theory

For almost forty years, five great European powers managed international affairs together, yet the Concert of Europe collapsed in violence as a result of unintended wars. For over forty years, the two superpowers failed to cooperate in the management of international affairs, yet no world war, planned or unintended, broke out. Why?

Not only has international relations theory in general failed to formulate a parsimonious answer to these critical questions, but four puzzles deriving from them present serious anomalies for specific leading international relations theories.

1. Great powers that are relatively moderate (in their attitude toward the status quo) and similar (culturally and ideologically) fail to manage crises and indeed find themselves fighting inadvertent wars.
2. Relatively immoderate and dissimilar powers cooperate in crisis management and tacitly regulate their use of force in crisis.
3. Five competing powers establish a diplomatic concert and jointly manage the international system in normal (noncrisis) times.
4. The only two great powers in the international system fail to coordinate their diplomacy in noncrisis times even when their interests converge.

Where one should expect peace, according to unit-level theories, one finds a number of major wars (the first puzzle); and where there should have been, according to certain subsets of these theories, failure in crisis management, there was, by contrast, persistent success in regulating the use of force (the second puzzle). At the same time, in some cases, the level of cooperation in noncrisis situations is higher than what structural theories would lead one to expect (the third puzzle); however, in other cases, the degree of noncrisis cooperation is lower than what a subgroup of these theories seems to suggest (the fourth puzzle). Moreover, cooperation in normal diplomacy does not necessarily seem to prevent major wars, whereas the absence of such cooperation does not necessarily lead to such wars. On the other hand, successful crisis management is not automatically extended to conflict resolution and cooperation in normal diplomacy.

The first two puzzles present anomalies to unit-level theories, including aspects of the recent regime theories. Indeed, inside-out theories do not adequately explain unintended outcomes. In a more narrow sense, the second puzzle challenges the expectation, which one can deduce from the crisis literature, that because of subsystemic changes, crisis management should have been an especially difficult task in the postwar era.[3] Structural theory as well as the recent cooperation theory, for their part, cannot adequately account for the last two puzzles, as these theories supposedly expect cooperation to become easier as the number of actors declines.

International relations theories, then, are unable to explain the four puzzles parsimoniously; yet these puzzles deal with the fundamental problems of states' behavior and interaction in both crisis settings and normal diplomacy. The puzzles also involve such significant policy issues as the outbreak of wars, crisis management, collective diplomacy, and conflict resolution. Failure to cope with these problems could undermine the credibility of international relations theory in one of its classical domains.

But before I present my argument in greater detail, let me discuss further in what sense these puzzles are problematic.

The joint management of the international system from 1815 to 1854, or the Concert of Europe, involved all the great powers of that era.[4] Two kinds of collective action were most notable: concerted diplomacy and collective decision making through multilateral congresses and conferences, as well as joint use of force both within Europe and outside it. A dramatic case of the latter type of intervention occurred in 1840 when the great powers cooperated in enforcing the termination of the Egyptian-Turkish War.

The Concert of Europe was, nonetheless, severely undermined, if not brought to an end, by the extremely bloody—though unintended—Crimean War (1854–1856) (see Clark 1989; Craig and George 1983, 28–36; Elrod 1976, 172; Jervis 1983, 178; Kupchan and Kupchan 1991, 122 n. 23; Mandelbaum 1988, 26; Rosecrance 1963, 117; Schroeder 1972). If we accept the arguments of those who maintain that the Concert, even if in truncated form, actually lasted until 1914 (cf. Albrecht-Carrie 1968; Holbraad 1970 and 1971), then it ended in the even more destructive, bloody, large-scale—yet also, even if to a somewhat lesser extent, unintended—violence of World War I.[5]

On the face of it, U.S.-Soviet relations stand out in marked contrast to the Concert era. After all, the postwar era saw more than forty years of bipolar rivalry, keen competition in various parts of the globe, frequent crises, a costly arms race, and clashing aspirations for hegemony. Yet despite intense ideological antagonism in an anarchic setting, not only was there no nuclear war, but not even a single shooting incident took place between the superpowers. Moreover, Washington and Moscow succeeded in tacitly regulating their use of force in crisis situations. This regulation spilled over into cooperation in controlling and ending local wars in sensitive areas and, in effect, into implicit, unintended collaboration in maintaining the status quo in times of crisis.[6] Such implicit cooperation was seen most strikingly in a number of Middle Eastern wars since the 1956 Suez crisis, though it also occurred, to a lesser degree, in other armed conflicts in the Third World.

Moreover, this joint preservation of the status quo in crises took place despite the commitment of each superpower to promoting its own vision of world order at the expense of the rival camp. Likewise, while explicitly disavowing division into spheres of influence, Moscow and Washington recognized de facto each other's spheres of interest during times of crisis. Implicit joint management of international crises occurred, moreover, even though the superpowers faced severe ideological and domestic constraints on explicitly recognizing their adversary as a partner for such cooperation.[7] It is in these respects that the superpowers' tacit cooperation in times of crises was unintended. In historical perspective, U.S.-Soviet cooperation in times of crisis might look better than attempts at crisis management during previous eras, even including the usually much more cooperative Concert of Europe.

Nevertheless, until recent years, superpower tacit management of crises was generally not extended to explicit collaboration in normal (noncrisis) diplomacy. Until the late 1980s, bilateral arms control efforts have also failed to restrain the arms race and defense spending—although, apart from the unfortunate waste of resources, so long as both the United States and the Soviet Union possessed retaliatory capabilities that could absorb a first strike and still be able to inflict unacceptable damage, the likelihood of a premeditated strategic exchange was probably near zero. From the mid-1960s until the end of the bipolar era, one of the most likely scenarios of an outbreak of World War III was the escalation of a regional conflict into a global war.[8] This danger should hypothetically have provided a major incentive for superpower collaboration with respect to those third world disputes that were most likely to embroil both of them. The small number of great powers, as compared to previous international systems, should, in theory, have made diplomatic coordination between

Washington and Moscow easier. Yet though they succeeded in jointly terminating a number of regional armed conflicts, the superpowers did not do well—at least until recently, with the end of the Cold War—in concerting their diplomacy for the settlement of local disputes. Despite the unprecedented capabilities of the postwar superpowers and their relatively low dependence on weaker states, local actors succeeded in playing them off against each other while extracting considerable assistance from them. At the same time, the small actors persisted in their risky rivalries, presenting serious threats to the stability of their regions and sometimes even to the peacefulness of the world.

The most remarkable example of this pattern was the Middle East. There, the United States and the Soviet Union were engaged in costly and rival commitments. Massive weapons shipments, more than to any other third region, did not necessarily increase their control over local clients but instead dragged them into a number of superpower confrontations. Indeed, after the Berlin confrontation and the Cuban Missile Crisis of the early 1960s, most U.S.-Soviet crises occurred in the Middle East. At the same time, the global powers tried to cooperate in resolving what was the most intense, dangerous, and ongoing dispute in that area, namely, the Arab-Israeli conflict. However, all these efforts failed during the Cold War, and indeed, during that period the Arab-Israeli dispute remained unresolved and liable to escalation, with the possible involvement of the superpowers, in one form or another.[9]

Two of the puzzles (wars between similar and moderate powers and crisis cooperation between dissimilar and immoderate powers) are paradoxical both on commonsense grounds and in terms of a number of inside-out theoretical approaches that expect a correlation between similar internal attributes and the likelihood of cooperative outcomes. Why did a security regime such as the Concert of Europe collapse in violence? And why did ideologically antagonistic powers cooperate more effectively in crisis management than more similar and usually friendlier powers?

The most parsimonious answer links structural theory with crisis management. Following the realist tradition, this approach highlights the difficulties of sustaining high-level cooperation under anarchy of all the great powers of the day (no matter which), especially in the sensitive area of security. More specifically, in this book, I deduce from structural theory that a system-level change (i.e., the transformation from a multipolar to a bipolar international system following World War II) made it easier for competing great powers to manage crises and to avoid inadvertent wars.[10] Thus, structural theory can explain the emergence of tacit rules for regulating the use of force between antagonists in a bipolar world. By contrast, multipolarity made it difficult to manage crises even for members of a security regime or a diplomatic concert. The explanatory power of structural theory regarding postwar crisis management is reinforced by the fact that according to the inside-out perspective, subsystemic changes following World War II should have made it especially difficult to regulate the use of force.

But if systemic causes are especially powerful with respect to regulating the use of force in times of crisis, this is not the case in the context of normal diplomacy and conflict resolution. Indeed, unit-level analysis best accounts for the latter two puzzles: the formation of a five-power concert and the failure of noncrisis cooperation between the only two great powers in the system even when their interests converged.

This latter pair of puzzles presents two anomalies for structural theory. First, given the anarchic, self-help nature of the international system, how did the nineteenth-century great powers manage to transcend for about forty years the normal balancing behavior of states, especially of big powers, against each other by forming a concert in which all the great powers collaborated?[11] Second, why were the postwar superpowers, despite their low number, less capable than past powers (such as the Concert members) of coordinating their normal diplomacy, even when they had converging interests, whereas according to both structural and game theory, we should expect greater cooperation and joint management when there are fewer actors?[12]

To answer these questions, one must bring in subsystemic analysis. Structural theory alone cannot account for the differences in the attempts at establishing great power concerts following the three general wars of the last two hundred years. Clearly, something fundamental must have distinguished the post-Napoleonic Concert from the short-lived and ill-fated ones (if they were concerts at all) that arose after the two world wars. The formation of a true concert was made possible in the first case by the common (conservative) ideology of the elites of all the great powers after 1815 and by the shared internal-ideological threat they faced—of revolution and its concomitant dangers of war.[13] Such common ideology and type of shared threats were missing following the two general wars of the twentieth century; thus, no enduring concert could have emerged after 1918 and 1945. Only with the onset of the internal reforms in the Soviet Union in the late 1980s and the narrowing of the ideological polarization between the United States and the Soviet Union could cognitive and domestic constraints on concerted diplomacy considerably lessen. And only then could such cooperation emerge as has taken place in the late 1980s and early 1990s in southern Africa, Afghanistan, Cambodia, the Horn of Africa, and the Middle East.

At the same time, structural theory cannot account for the variations in superpower diplomacy in the postwar era, either regarding changes in their individual policies or the type of relations between them. Indeed, whereas superpower behavior and interaction in crisis settings (particularly regarding the tacit rules of crisis management) accorded well with structural expectations, the characteristics of their normal diplomacy corresponded to the types of outcomes that unit-level analysis is most useful at explaining.

**The Argument and Propositions**

Unlike the multitude of previous attempts at explaining the four puzzles individually, then, this book offers a theoretical model that provides a way of explaining all of them simultaneously. The core of the argument is that unit-level factors accounted for the joint diplomatic management of the European Concert but could not completely forestall the mismanagement of certain crises and the resultant outbreak of some inadvertent wars; on the other hand, system-level causes explain the evolution in the postwar era of tacit rules of crisis management that helped to prevent World War III. Overwhelmed by bipolarity, potentially destabilizing unit-level factors could not jeopardize crisis management in that era. And in reverse, systemic-level factors were insufficient for establishing concerted diplomacy, let alone a full-blown concert of the great powers in the face of powerful unit-level elements that constrained the superpowers' ability to collaborate in conflict resolution in normal noncrisis settings.

The two variables—system polarity and unit-level elements—can be combined to yield four possible worlds with respect to great power conflict management (see fig. 1).

The first ideal world (multipolar with considerable ideological convergence and cultural similarity of the great powers) produces a great power concert that jointly resolves international conflicts both among the great powers and in third areas. It thus reduces the likelihood of the onset of crises among the great powers in the first place, but there is still some danger of breakdown of the multiple, complex security regime if a crisis does erupt. This world is approximated by the nineteenth-century Concert of Europe.

The second world (multipolar in the distribution of capabilities and polarized along ideological and cultural lines) generates competition and conflict in normal times as well as a high probability of failure in crisis management. Moreover, crises are more likely to occur in this world because crisis prevention is much less effective than in the world of concerted diplomacy. The second world is approximated by the era of the 1930s. In the interwar period, the increased ideological and cultural differences among the powers and the mounting influence of domestic politics on foreign policy made joint diplomacy still less feasible than before World War I. Indeed, the world on the eve of World War I is located somewhere between the first and second ideal worlds. Changes in the character of unit-level elements since the first half of the nineteenth century (the rise of nationalism—resulting in less similarity and moderation—and the greater influence of domestic politics on foreign policy)

# When Opponents Cooperate

```
                    ┌─────────────────────────────────────────┐
                    │ Unit-Level Factors: Similarity and Moderation │
                    └─────────────────────────────────────────┘
                              ╱              ╲
                         High                  Low
                    (ideological         (ideological
                     convergence)         polarization)
```

|  | High (ideological convergence) | Low (ideological polarization) |
|---|---|---|
| **High (multipolar)** | **1** Cooperation in conflict resolution; Failure in crisis management (the Concert of Europe) (1914) | **2** Competition and conflict; Failure in crisis management (1930s) |
| **Low (multipolar)** | **4** Cooperation in conflict resolution; Effective crisis management (détente) | **3** Competition and conflict; Effective crisis management (Cold War) |

System Level Factors: Polarity (number of great powers)

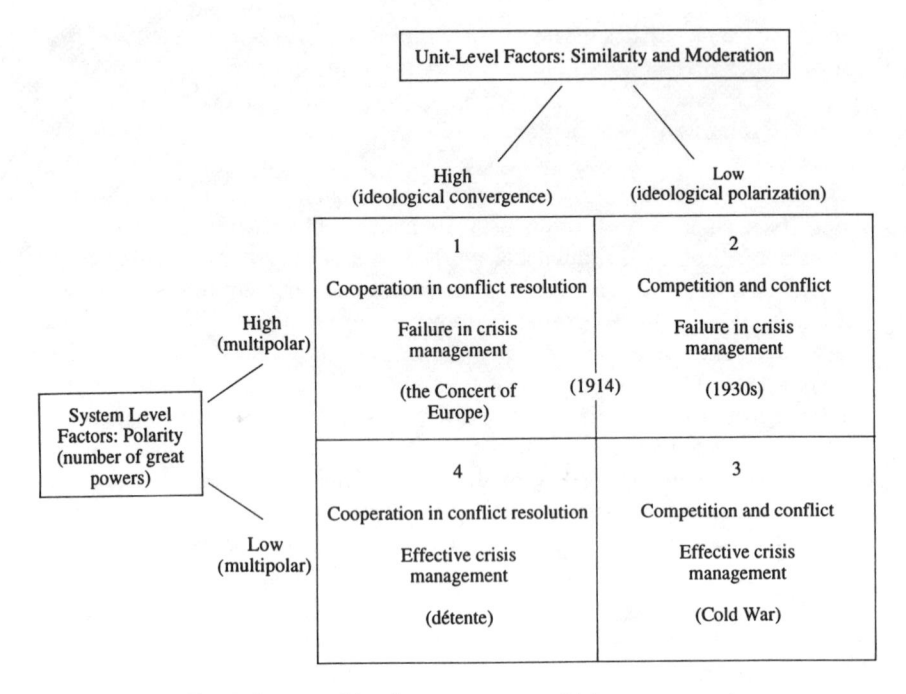

Fig. 1. Four worlds of great power conflict management

made crisis prevention in the early twentieth century less effective than it had been in the Concert era, yet some degree of concerted diplomacy survived almost until the outbreak of World War I.[14] Therefore, this war was much closer to the ideal type of an unintended war than World War II. On the eve of both world wars, however, the multipolar structure made crisis management difficult. In 1914, as we will see, the structure made it more likely that the powers would overreact, whereas in the 1930s, the structure provided incentives for the western powers to underreact to German aggression.[15]

In contrast, the bipolar structure encourages a delicate balance between resolve and caution and thus produces more effective crisis management in both world 3 and world 4. When the ideological gulf between the superpowers is great, however, like in world 3, they will not succeed in cooperating in conflict resolution. The likelihood of crises is thus high, and the competition remains keen. This world is approximated by the peak periods of the Cold War of the 1950s, the early 1960s, and the early 1980s.

In world 4, the ideological polarization is somewhat weakened or at least decision makers' perceptions of key international issues converge, which fosters a greater willingness to cooperate in settling disputes. This world is approximated by the U.S.-Soviet détentes of the 1970s and especially the late 1980s.[16] Indeed, these periods saw attempts at joint diplomacy with respect to both arms control and regional conflicts. Although these attempts failed on the whole in the 1970s, they achieved some success in the late 1980s, as the cognitive and domestic convergence became considerably more meaningful (that is, even before the collapse of Soviet power, the disintegration of the Soviet Union, and the end of bipolarity in the early 1990s). Indeed, I argue that even if the distribution of capabilities does not drastically change and hence the international structure remains essentially the same, subsystemic changes critically affect whether collective diplomacy is attempted. Moreover, to endure, emerging cooperative arrangements must be supported by cognitive and domestic factors.

Two further implications of my argument, then, are as follows:

1. Although systemic factors have a predominant influence on decision makers' behavior in times of crisis, the basic cognitive elements that underlie their decision making come to the fore during periods of noncrisis. In other words, decision makers are responsive to international pressures during crises, but they remain much more resistant to cognitive change during periods of normal diplomacy.

2. As a result, security regimes (which are based on trust and common normative elements) break down in crises if they run contrary to systemic-structural elements (this breakdown happens most notably in multipolar systems); on the other hand, security regimes cannot be established between rivals in times of noncrisis if they run contrary to cognitive-state elements (ideology, beliefs, and domestic politics).

The rationale of the model is, in brief, that in the hour of crisis, when external pressures on the state are unusually powerful, international factors (such as the distribution of capabilities in the international system) logically exercise a greater influence than usual on the behavior of states. However, causal factors below the system level (domestic constraints and ideological and cognitive beliefs) are more consequential for understanding the less intense noncrisis diplomatic collaboration, especially when it aims at resolving the fundamental issues in conflict. Indeed, the higher the level of cooperation, the lower the level of analysis (state and individual) at which supportive factors are required for the emergence and endurance of the cooperative arrangements (i.e., concerted diplomacy or a full-blown concert).

Let us now address in greater detail the rationale for the linkages between the dependent and independent variables of this model.

It should first be noted that the two schools of international order outlined in the previous chapter (the structural balance of power and the international society) have a bearing on this question, that is, they are relevant not only to the dependent variables of this book, but also to the independent ones and, indeed, to the linkages between them. The structural approach is linked to the system level and helps us understand unexpected success or failure in crisis management (see chap. 3). The international society school is linked to subsystemic factors and explains joint diplomacy in conflict resolution and also some of the conditions for intended wars. Historically, it may explain the successful management of international affairs by the nineteenth-century Concert of Europe (see chap. 4), while the structural approach accounts for the tacit regulation of the use of force in the crises of the postwar era as well as the failure in crisis management in the multipolar era (see chaps. 3 and 5). At the same time, the weakness of some of the factors associated with the international society school during the Cold War was reflected in the failure of concerted diplomacy by the superpowers, notably regarding the attempts to resolve the Arab-Israeli conflict (chap. 6).

**Structural Factors and Crisis Management**

What are the expectations of structural theory about states' international behavior,[17] and why should they be best met in times of crisis?

Before going into detail with regard to these expectations, let me suggest that although, on the whole, the following expectations are better met in times of crisis than in normal diplomacy, the degree or the nature of their manifestation in times of crisis is conditioned by the type of international structure (bipolar or multipolar). This point is elaborated in chapter 3.

The Dominance of the Situation and
Unintended Outcomes

As noted, the explanation of unintended outcomes is one of the major themes of this book. The international structure is expected to condition actors' behavior and constrain the processes in the international system (Waltz 1979, chaps. 5-6). Therefore, according to structural theory, the outcomes of states' interactions (results) often do not correspond to the actors' desires and characteristics (purposes). Structural analysis should therefore be best at explaining the occurrence of unintended outcomes in international politics, if it can be plausibly shown that the international structure is the cause of the low correlation between the intentions and attributes of the actors (derived from their beliefs and ideologies) and the international outcomes. Two types of unintended consequences, which can either stabilize or destabilize international systems irrespective of what states initially desire, should be distinguished: (1) destabilizing effects of the security dilemma, which raise the level of conflict in the international system beyond the initial intentions of the actors and can even result in inadvertent wars, and (2) cooperative arrangements between rivals. These cooperative arrangements are, at least initially, spontaneous, unintended, and tacit; they are explained by the *structure of the situation* (that is, they tend to be situationally determined)[18] rather than by the goals and characteristics of the actors. Indeed, both Axelrod and Schelling highlight the influence of the *situation* on tacit-spontaneous cooperation. As Schelling put it,

> Thus the empirically verifiable results of some of the tacit-bargaining games, as well as the more logical role of coordinated expectations in that case, prove that expectations can be coordinated and that some of the objective details of the situation can exercise a controlling influence when the coordination of expectations is essential. . . . When agreements must be reached with incomplete communication, the participants must be ready to allow the situation itself to exercise substantial constraint over the outcome. (1960, 71, 75)

Axelrod's (1984, chap. 4) analysis of the tacit truces of World War I also underlines situational sources of conflict and cooperation and, as a result, a situationally based resolution to the problem of cooperation (Gowa 1986, 180–81). The tacit, ad hoc arrangements persist so long as the situational factors that gave rise to them prevail; when these change, the nature of the coordination may be modified, or the arrangement may break down completely.

Unintended, situationally determined outcomes are more relevant to crises than to normal times. On the whole, it makes sense that the greater the level of the external threat, the more important are the effects of the international environment on the behavior of states in comparison with those effects during more normal periods. Thus, as noted, in the hour of crisis, when external pressures on the state are unusually powerful, international factors (such as the distribution of capabilities in the international system) should exercise a greater influence than usual on states' actions. As Wolfers puts it, "the closer nations are drawn to the pole of complete compulsion, the more they can be expected to conform in their behavior and to act in a way that corresponds to the deductions made from the state-as-actor model" (1962, 16). The point I am making is that, all other things being equal, external constraints play a greater role in crisis settings than in calmer periods. In the latter periods, internal factors (at both the individual and state levels) can express themselves more freely; thus, there is a more direct connection between intentions and outcomes. By contrast, in crisis situations, one would expect a higher frequency of structurally derived unintended outcomes, whether cooperative or conflictual.

Indeed, the system level is especially useful for explaining the unintended outcomes of crisis interactions, in particular, when ideologically moderate or status quo powers find themselves unintentionally at war with each other (all other things being equal, a multipolar world makes such an outcome more likely). The structure of the international system—and this pattern applies to a bipolar system—is also critically important when adversaries tacitly cooperate in managing global crises and terminating local wars. I elaborate and specify the influence of bipolarity and multipolarity on crisis interactions in chapter 3. I show that a bipolar structure has stabilizing effects in crises, while multipolarity exerts a destabilizing influence that makes crisis management more difficult.

### Patterns of Conduct: Similar and Recurring

According to structural theory, we should expect similar patterns of conduct from states that are similarly located in the system (namely, that share the same category of power capabilities) and that face similar types of external pressures, even if these states have different ideologies or domestic regimes. Hence, it makes sense to refer to *great powers* and to *small states* and to expect similar (though not necessarily identical) patterns of behavior in each class (see Mandelbaum 1988). The structural explanation of such similarity is international socialization and competition; that is, "competition spurs the actors to accommodate their ways to the socially most acceptable and successful practices" (Waltz 1979, 77).[19]

Such similarity is more typical of crisis situations, because of the dominant influence of the situation on behavior in crisis. As Wolfers asserts, the greater the external compulsion, the greater the similarity in actors' behavior:

> Imagine a number of individuals, varying widely in their predispositions, who find themselves inside a house on fire. It would be perfectly realistic to expect that these individuals, with rare exceptions, would feel compelled to run toward the exits. General fears of losing the cherished possession of life, coupled with the stark external threat to life, would produce the same reaction, whatever the psychological peculiarities of the actors. Surely, therefore, for an explanation of the rush for the exits, there is no need to analyze the individual decisions that produced it. (1962, 13)

Although psychologists generally tend to underline the effects of personality traits, some of them agree with the logic of situational determinism.[20] In the *Handbook of Social Psychology,* Snyder and Ickes (1985, 904) suggest that the more powerful the situation, the greater the uniformity of actors' behavior. As they put it, "because strong situations should shift the cause of behavior from a dispositional locus to a situational one, measures of traits and dispositions should typically predict behavior better in weak situations than in strong ones" (1985, 904). Gal and Israelashwili (1978) maintain that as conditions become more threatening and stressful, situational variables explain the observed behavior better than an analysis of personality dispositions. For example, while several psychologists have highlighted the influence of certain individual traits on acts of combat bravery, Blake and Bulter (cited in Gal 1983) and, to a lesser extent, Hallam and Rachman (cited in Gal 1985) underline the impact of particular situational constellations on these kinds of acts. Indeed, studies of some of the battles of the Yom Kippur War conclude that situational and circumstantial characteristics are more important than individuals' personal qualities in explaining the variety of gallant and courageous behavior in these battles (Gal 1983 and 1985).[21]

Structural theory should be especially useful for explaining persistent outcomes and long-term modes of behavior—including patterns of wars, arms races, alliances, balancing behavior, equilibriums, conflict, and competition—rather than specific events and decisions. Indeed, structural constraints are especially powerful (1) in explaining crisis interactions rather than the decision making of a single state during a crisis and (2) more broadly, in accounting for general patterns of crisis behavior and outcomes rather than for variations in the crisis behavior of specific leaders.[22] The international structure is particularly important for understanding patterns of crisis management among competing great powers, including their ability to cooperate and reach tacit understandings in times of tension.

More specifically, the number of the great powers can provide a parsimonious explanation for the emergence or nonemergence of tacit rules for regulating the use of force in crises. Because certain types of crisis situations are less ambiguous than settings of normal diplomacy, they also make possible tacit, unintended cooperation among rivals even if these antagonists are unable and unwilling to collaborate in normal diplomacy.[23] The conditions for this less ambiguous kind of crisis situation are best met in a bipolar world, for reasons that I discuss in the next chapter.

### The State as a Unitary Actor

The state is expected by structural theory to behave as a unitary actor; that is, a single preference function governs decision making.[24] A structural analysis would be especially useful where there is a high degree of consensus among the state's foreign policy elite. Such a consensus, where it exists, shows that neither domestic and bureaucratic politics nor individual-level factors necessarily explain outcomes and behavior (see Jervis 1976, 23–24). Rather, the state reacts to external threats and stimuli as a cohesive unit, carrying out coherent policies made by its top leadership.

Theoretically, the unitary actor model is most legitimate in studies of the most critical decisions made by states, those that deal with war and peace (cf. Bueno de Mesquita 1981, 16, 27–29; Huth and Russett 1984, 498–99; Patchen 1988, 19–22; Verba 1961, 115). Such decisions are most notably made in times of crisis, the most distinct characteristic of which was defined in chapter 1 as a dangerously high probability of resort to military force. Indeed, crises are pivotal situations that analysts see as either preludes to war (see Richardson 1960; Wright 1965, 1272) or, under certain conditions, surrogates for war (Bell 1971, 115–16; Waltz 1964, 883–84). As Snyder and Diesing point out, "it is useful to conceive of a crisis as an intermediate zone between peace and war. Almost all wars are preceded by a crisis of some sort, although of course not all crises eventuate in war" (1977, 10).[25]

Empirically, it is a widely held and well-researched supposition that in periods of crisis, decision making tends to be centralized in the hands of top leaders (Adomeit 1982, 48; Brecher 1980, 377; Frei 1983, 122; Hoagland and Walker 1979, 130; Snyder and Diesing 1977, 511; Verba 1961, 115; Williams 1976, 66).[26] Because crisis situations are times of threat, high stakes, a high likelihood of war, and often severe time constraints, the bureaucracy is consigned to a lesser role than it plays in routine matters.[27] Furthermore, high-level policymakers tend to reach a greater degree of consensus in crisis settings than in normal times. One observer points out that the "strain towards agreement" is strongest during times of crisis (Williams 1976, 69).[28] Although most of the research has been done on the American decision making process, Adomeit reports:

> One of the surprising realizations after studying a number of international crises is the degree to which Soviet behavior seems to follow engrained patterns of action—as if there existed a broad consensus about operational principles in foreign policy. This realization is even more surprising given important differences at all levels of Soviet domestic politics since World War II . . . whereas Soviet foreign policy in general is almost invariably affected by domestic controversy and conflict, Soviet decision-making in international crises will typically demonstrate a "rallying around the flag," the concentration of decisions in the hands of a select executive committee, the restoration of important elements of centralization, and a return to traditional reflexes and responses. (1981, 49)[29]

The greater consensus among officials in crises can be partly explained by Holsti's (1970) findings that differences in perceptions among decision makers decrease as tensions increase. Growing consensus is also related to the predominance of security interests in times of crisis.

## The Primacy of Security Interests

According to structural theory, security interests, however defined and however difficult to operationalize, are expected to dominate state behavior,[30] rather than the ideological aspirations and idiosyncratic world views of certain state leaders and political parties or the particularistic interests of certain groups and politicians (cf. Williams 1976, 63).

This expectation is more correct in times of crisis than at other times. It is reasonable to expect that national rather than parochial interests tend to dominate the policy-making process of a cohesive state more in times of severe external threat than in noncrisis settings.[31] Reflecting on his experience in crisis management, Kissinger remarks that "personality clashes were reduced; too much is usually at stake for normal jealousies to operate" (*Time Magazine*, October 15, 1979, 71). And as Verba suggests,

> The greater the sense of stress, the greater will be the legitimacy of the over-all norms of the system and the greater the illegitimacy of parochial norms. Furthermore, the greater the emergency, the more likely is decision-making to be concentrated among high officials whose commitments are to the over-all system. Thus it may be, paradoxically, that the model of means-ends rationality will be more closely approximated in an emergency when the time for careful deliberation is limited. Though fewer alternatives will be considered, the values invoked during the decision period will tend to be fewer and more consistent, and the decision will less likely be the result of bargaining within a coalition. (1961, 115)

And Morgan argues that in times of crisis more than at other times, we can expect leaders to put aside personal differences, career concerns, and bureaucratic and domestic interests, thus permitting a dispassionate analysis of possible courses of action "on their merits" (1983, 180). Facing severe external threats, it is more likely that state leaders in cohesive societies will act as the "custodians of the state's security" in times of crisis rather than in a noncrisis setting.[32]

A structural analysis expects that in a crisis, much more than in normal times, the state's security interests take precedence over the promotion of its ideology. Thus, even during the height of the Cold War, "the Soviet Union in crisis became Russian, and American policy, liberal rhetoric aside, came to be realistically and cautiously constructed. By the force of events, they and we were impelled to behave in ways belied both by their words and by ours" (Waltz 1979, 173).

Especially in the nuclear age, the avoidance of a major war has become a critical interest of the superpowers (although great powers in the past also occasionally attempted to avoid general wars because of their extremely high costs) (see Blainey 1973, 121). According to the conception of crisis management presented in chapter 1, decision makers are concerned during crisis periods not only with defending vital security interests but also with war avoidance. Indeed, Snyder and Diesing (1977, 280) have found that during a crisis, decision makers pay more attention to avoiding war than to maximizing the benefits to be gained from the use of force.

However, although the characteristics of the state as a unitary actor and the primacy of security interests on the whole fit crisis situations better than normal times, they may also fit certain crisis situations better than others, according to polarity. In other words, polarity conditions the degree of the influence of domestic politics, bureaucratic politics, and ideology in times of crisis, as I show in chapter 3. The same point also holds for another characteristic of crisis situations: sensitivity to external stimuli.

### Sensitivity to External Stimuli

According to structural theory, the state should be responsive to external stimuli, taking into account its essential security interests and showing sensitivity to new information from the international environment. It is sufficient here to assume that in responding to minimal security interests, leaders act according to modest definitions of rationality, rather than according to the comprehensive rationality and expected utility models.[33] Such modest definitions refer to Waltz's (1979, 118) assumption about the desire of states to survive in a competitive, self-help system; Snyder and Diesing's "bounded rationality" (1977, 342–48, 507); Morgan's "sensible decisionmaking" (1983, chap. 5); and Feldman's "sensitivity to costs" (1982, 145).[34] I define minimalist conception of rationality in this book as the extent of a state's sensible reaction to threats and opportunities provided by the external environment to protect its security interests, as opposed to a concern about bureaucratic needs, political aspirations, and ideological beliefs that are irrelevant to the situation at hand.[35]

On the whole, as discussed above, structural analysis should have especially great explanatory power in times of crisis because of the greater pressures exerted by the international environment.[36] More specifically, since the potential costs of overlooking international factors are greater in times of crisis than in normal times, high-level officials should pay more than usual attention to the international environment. Not only does the uncertainty accompanying crises stimulate a search for more information, notes Williams, but it ensures that

> Existing information is thoroughly and critically assessed. Indeed, the available data are usually subjected to the most detailed scrutiny in an

attempt to uncover every subtlety and nuance of the adversary's position. Although the information is partial and incomplete, therefore, maximum benefit is likely to be gained from it. In short, the task of processing and evaluating intelligence may be carried out more efficiently during crises than in non-crisis situations. (1976, 67–68)[37]

This tendency for gathering and evaluating information in times of crisis in no way entails that decision makers will meet the expectations of the comprehensive rationality model, as we see in the next chapter. Indeed, under frequently ambiguous, uncertain, and complex international circumstances, some degree of misperception and misjudgment arising from human fallibility is given.[38] But the greater than usual sensitivity to the international environment in times of crisis means that a major factor that influences the level and intensity of misperceptions, as well as their consequences regarding crisis behavior, is the clarity and simplicity of the international environment. Indeed, there are great variations in this respect among different international environments, according to their structure: some international structures foster misperceptions, whereas others minimize the likelihood, or at least the destabilizing effects, of misperceptions. In other words, the type of international structure conditions the level and intensity of misperceptions and miscalculations and affects their consequences in times of crisis. Thus, although this book advances the linkage between international structure and crisis behavior and outcomes, it does not exclude the effects of supposedly first-image factors such as misperceptions and information processing. However, my argument is that frequently the effect of these factors on crisis outcomes is mediated by the international structure. Misperceptions especially are, in many cases, conditioned by structural factors. Thus, I show that in times of crisis, bipolarity reduces the intensity of misperceptions whereas multipolarity enhances their adverse effects.

This proposition can reconcile the competing claims in the debate on rationality in crises. Indeed, there are both theoretical and empirical disagreements on the impact of crises on decision-making performance. Theoretically, realists, many students of deterrence,[39] and also some organizational theorists suggest that decision making in times of crisis tends to be more rational than decision making in noncrisis settings. By contrast, theories that focus on the individual and small group levels are much less optimistic about the quality of crisis decision making and suggest that it deteriorates in ways that it does not in normal settings.[40] There are also contradictory empirical findings on the effects of crises on rationality.[41] By linking international structures with crisis behavior, however, one can address these conflicts among both theories and empirical findings, as I do in the next chapter.

In chapter 3, I propose that, on the whole, the potentially destabilizing effect of postwar domestic changes (i.e., the growing influence of bureaucratic politics, of domestic politics, and of competing ideologies in Washington and Moscow) was overwhelmed in times of crisis by the transformation of the international system from multipolarity to bipolarity. This international change enabled superpower cooperation in crisis management; but it could not bring about explicit cooperation in normal diplomacy, a type of cooperation dependent on individual- and state-level factors.

## Unit-Level Explanation of Cooperation in Normal Diplomacy

The connection between unit-level elements and explicit high-level cooperation in normal times, especially in conflict resolution, is reinforced by four factors: the ambiguous effects of the structure, the prevalence of subjective factors, the wide range of values involved, and the necessity for converging beliefs.

### Ambiguous Effects of the Structure: Constraints and Incentives

In normal diplomacy, the structure provides both *incentives for* and *constraints against* cooperation; thus, nonsystemic factors are necessary to understand what occurred. To begin with the constraints, according to structural theory, because states are worried that cooperation for mutual gains may favor present partners, who may become potential opponents in the future, they are more concerned about relative gains than about absolute ones (Grieco 1988, 498–500; Waltz 1979, 105). Hence, given the slightest suspicion that others might gain relatively more, major states would prefer to deny benefits to their competitors, even if that might entail self-denial, rather than have all win in absolute terms.

Yet beyond the general constraints on cooperation, highlighted by structural analysis, in both bipolarity and multipolarity there is a mixture of constraints and incentives for great power cooperation in normal diplomacy. The ambiguity in structural theory is manifested by contradictory expectations concerning the effects of its main variable: system polarity. Thus, neorealist analysis suggests that cooperation in bipolarity is less likely than in multipolarity, but at the same time it also implies the opposite. As a result, it is unclear which system is more conducive to such cooperation. In other words, the polarity of the system is indeterminate with regard to diplomatic cooperation; consequently, it is largely irrelevant for understanding this phenomenon.

*Why Cooperation Should Be Less Likely in Bipolarity Than in Multipolarity*
Waltz argues that overall, in a two-power system we should expect more frequent crises (1964) together with severe constraints on superpower col-

laboration (1979, 175). Similarly, Snyder and Diesing (1977, 466), who follow Waltz's structural logic, propose that détente between the superpowers in bipolarity can never develop into a condominium—an agreement to police the world jointly—because basic structurally induced rivalry prevents this. Whereas in multipolarity détente smoothes the transformation from adversity to alliance, in bipolarity détente between the superpowers can never lead to entente or alliance, simply because there is no powerful third party to ally against. Jervis (1985, 69), for his part, contends that it may be harder to maintain a high level of cooperation when there are only two main actors in the system.

Indeed, in some important ways, a two-power world would supposedly appear less conducive to joint action than a multipolar one. Both Waltz (1964, 882–83 and 1979, 171) and Snyder and Diesing (1977, especially chap. 6) contend that great power rivalry in a bipolar world is keener than in a multipolar world. Specifically, great power diplomatic cooperation in third areas, some would maintain, is constrained by the logic of the Prisoner's Dilemma; that is, even if they may jointly benefit from cooperation in resolving a conflict between their respective allies, the fear remains that the other great power patron will defect first and support its ally in the local conflict. This leads to the temptation—or may even "force" a great power—to initiate a unilateral action, lest its client be weakened and the great power lose political influence as a consequence (Snyder and Diesing 1977, 505–6). Because of the intensity of this rivalry, smaller powers might be able to play off the two great powers, manipulating their fears to their own advantage and thus making joint great power action even less likely.

*Why Cooperation Should Be More Likely in Bipolarity Than in Multipolarity*

On the other hand, structuralists and game theorists have also claimed that great power cooperation is more likely in bipolarity. Waltz (1964 and 1979, chap. 8) provides persuasive reasoning about why a major war is less likely in a bipolar system. The ability of the great powers to manage world problems, moreover, increases as the number of members of the great power club declines (Waltz 1979, chap. 9). Snyder and Diesing (1977, 506–7) support Waltz's argument by applying the logic of the Prisoner's Dilemma to the problem of comanagement by the principal powers. The Prisoner's Dilemma, they argue, is more severe in a multipolar system than in a bipolar one because the potential costs of collusion loom larger, relative to the potential benefits. On the other hand, according to game theorists, the Prisoner's Dilemma and the collective goods problem are in fact lessened as the number of players decreases.[42] The reason is that as this number decreases, the probability of autonomous defection and of recognition and control problems is reduced while sanctioning defectors becomes easier. At the same time, the identification of common interests is easier in bipolarity because transaction and information costs are relatively low. Indeed, in the special volume of *World Politics* on "Cooperation under Anarchy," Oye states the seemingly agreed-on conclusion that "game theorists and oligopoly theorists have long noted that cooperation becomes more difficult as numbers increase" (1985, 4). Likewise, Gowa observes that "cooperation is generally considered to be more difficult to achieve in an n-person group or PD game than in a group or game limited to two members" (1986, 172).[43] Thus, it is persuasively argued that a bipolar structure produces powerful incentives and opportunities for cooperation.

And as for the drive to achieve relative gains, Waltz (1979, 195) suggests that in comparison with multipolar systems, the superpowers in a bipolar world are actually concerned less with relative gains and more with making absolute ones. This, he argues, is because of two characteristics of two-power structures: (1) a stable balance of capabilities between the leading powers and (2) a large gap between them and the next most powerful states, which removes the danger of third states catching up. These factors, according to Waltz, dispose the Big Two to collective efforts, even though other states may gain disproportionately from them. Diplomatic coordination is also easier in a bipolar world, that is, easier between two powers than between many.

Nevertheless, although the small number of great powers and the related structural factors are critical to crisis management, and for reaching spontaneous, de facto understandings concerning the use of force, these factors are insufficient by themselves to induce cooperation in conflict resolution. Thus, it is instructive that purely structural analyses that focus on the relations between the number of actors and cooperation tend to highlight those kinds of collaborative arrangements that are limited either to crisis management (Oye 1985, 18–20; Snyder and Diesing 1977, chap. 6; Waltz 1964, 884; and 1979, chap. 8)[44] or to a de facto, tacit division of spheres of influence between the powers (Waltz 1979, chap. 9). In short, the structure by itself cannot determine the feasibility of diplomatic cooperation. The ambiguity inherent in the structural analysis can be resolved, however, by differentiating beween degrees and types of cooperation. Although the feasibility of spontaneous-tacit collaboration is closely related to the number of actors, explicit-conscious collaboration depends mainly on factors below the system level.

Subjective Factors

In normal diplomatic bargaining there is a greater subjectivity and sometimes even ambiguity as compared with the relative clarity of interests, alignments, capabilities, commitments, and risks in major military crises, especially in a bipolar system. To be sure, in a crisis it is very difficult to gauge a rival's military capabilities and especially its real objectives; but in normal times it is even harder to estimate its overall capabilities (including nonmilitary and nonquantifiable elements such as diplomatic skills, ideological appeal, alliance cohesion, allies' domestic stability, leverage over allies, and domestic support of international engagements), let alone its long-run intentions. Not only are objectives relatively narrow and specific in a crisis (cf. Morgan 1983, 180), but the whole intelligence community is focused on understanding the rival under such conditions and tries to gather as much hard evidence as possible.[45] Moreover, in a crisis there is usually a phase of intense bargaining that may clarify the relative bargaining power of the opponents (see Patchen 1988, 298–300; Snyder and Diesing 1977, 248–49). Normal bargaining is, by contrast, less intensive and dramatic and thereby more likely to be influenced by bureaucratic politics and cognitive biases.[46]

Wide Range of Values

Noncrisis settings involve a wider range of values than crisis situations. During crises, the focus is on security; in normal periods, states are also interested in other goals such as economic prosperity, social welfare, diplomatic prestige, and ideological imperatives. It is easier to achieve consensus within the decision-making elite when the objective is the preservation of the state's security—although, of course, there often may be intensive debates on the best means of achieving this end. On the whole, it makes sense and is relatively easy to structure actors' preferences in crisis settings according to game-theoretical payoffs such as the Prisoner's Dilemma (see Brams 1985; Patchen 1988, 46; Snyder and Diesing 1977). But in normal times there is a much greater variation of needs and preferences both within and between states that is influenced by beliefs and ideologies and is not easily captured by the framework of cooperation under anarchy. Indeed, as theorists suggest, differences both within the elite of a certain state and between states with respect to foreign policy choices (differences that subjective factors reinforce in normal diplomacy) indicate the explanatory power of unit-level causes.[47]

Converging Beliefs

For high-level cooperation in normal diplomacy, appropriate conditions at the unit level are indispensable. Although during a crisis the number of actors can decisively affect the ability of rivals to communicate tacitly and to reach situation-related agreements (because the clarity of the situation is so critical under the conditions of high tension and pressure), the structure of the situation cannot, by itself, lead to explicit joint action in normal times if there are domestic or ideological constraints to cooperation. Whereas common beliefs or, at least, converging perceptions are not essential for the relatively simple (inasmuch as the conducive structural factors are present) task of crisis coordination, they are necessary for the much more complex task of conflict resolution. Indeed, high-level cooperation between all the great powers, like in a security regime or a concert, requires a minimum degree of moderation and common values, or at least converging beliefs and perceptions.

Because spontaneous cooperation is best explained by the structure of the situation, the termination of the rivalry, the settlement of disputes, shared beliefs, and common morality or at least converging perceptions are not essential for the emergence of the tacit rules. Yet deliberate collaboration in joint actions is accounted for by unit-level factors; thus, to understand such conscious collaboration, we must look at the actors' attributes, images, and beliefs. Since it is consciously designed and intended, this kind of collaborative arrangement presumably rests on common cognitive elements and on shared beliefs and norms. For example, Ruggie (1983) suggests that principles and norms, reflecting a congruence of social purpose among the leading powers, constitute a regime's normative framework.[48] Thus, shared social purposes and the ideological agreement among the leading Western nations on what Ruggie calls embedded liberalism determined, in the aftermath of World War II, the normative framework of the Bretton Woods system of international trade and monetary regimes. The persistent consensus on the regime's social objectives, Ruggie further argues, accounts for the continuation of its normative framework despite changes in power distribution that, in turn, have led to changes only in the instruments of the trade regime but not in its principles and norms.[49] Indeed, in contrast to situationally determined arrangements, once regimes are entrenched, as Krasner (1983) argues, they may alter the egoistic interests and power distributions that led to their establishment in the first place.[50] Even more importantly, as Ruggie demonstrates, high-level cooperation can outlast changes in power relations as long as the normative consensus continues.

Explicit, formal agreements are more likely than tacit rules to require trust among the parties (Schelling 1960, 53) as well as a common cultural-ideological framework and similarities in beliefs, attitudes, and values (Deutsch 1973, 374). Moreover, formal, explicit agreements do not constitute a regime even if they use an apparent regime language unless they reflect a degree of cognitive consensus that would enable the parties to operationalize common norms and act jointly. Thus, the U.S.-Soviet Basic Principles Agreement (BPA) of 1972 did not produce a full-blown security regime or a concert, even though some of its rhetoric resembled regime terminology.[51]

The two modes of cooperation introduced in chapter 1 (tacit-spontaneous and deliberate) parallel the two types or levels of learning—simple learning (or adaptation) and complex learning.[52] The learning of the tacit rules can be conceived as just simple adaptation to changed circumstances. Waltz advances, in fact, the notion of simple or structural learning by arguing that "the close juxtaposition of states promotes their sameness through the disadvantages that arise from a failure to conform to successful practices. It is this 'sameness,' an effect of the system, that is so often attributed to the acceptance of so-called rules of state behavior" (1979, 127–28). In regimes, however, a higher-level or more complex learning occurs that "involves recognition of conflicts among means and goals in causally complicated situations, and leads to new priorities and trade-offs" (Nye 1987, 380).

High interdependence and mutual vulnerability among the participants would be conducive to the two types of cooperation.[53] Yet whereas situationally based, objective interdependence might be sufficient to lead to tacit-spontaneous cooperation, there needs to be subjective interdependence, perceived by the decision makers, if they are to attempt to construct explicit, higher-level regimes.

A common cultural-ideological framework and similarity in beliefs made high-level cooperation easier for the nineteenth-century European powers, although their absence in superpower relations in the postwar era did not mean an absence of any cooperation. Rather, as I show in the subsequent chapter, this cooperation tended to be spontaneous and manifested in tacit rules.

## Summary

While introducing four historical patterns of events as puzzles to international relations theory, I have proposed in this chapter a theoretical model that links tacit cooperation in crisis management with structural factors and explicit cooperation in normal diplomacy with unit-level elements. In the next two chapters, I further develop and specify the model with regard to the four types of outcomes introduced in chapter 1. I specify and illustrate the linkage between unit-level factors and cooperation in conflict resolution in chapter 4. Indeed, the two puzzles related to the success of the nineteenth-century Concert of Europe and the failure of concerted diplomacy in the postwar era is addressed in that chapter. I address the two other puzzles—concerning the Long Peace of the postwar era and the inadvertent wars during the Concert era and the early twentieth century—in the next chapter. In that chapter the focus is on the effects of systemic factors on crisis management and the occurrence of wars. Thus, we now turn to a specification of the causal linkages with regard to intended and unintended wars.

Chapter 3

# Polarity, Nuclear Weapons, and Major War

This chapter focuses on one of the puzzles presented in the previous chapter: the postwar Long Peace, but it emerges that for resolving this question, there is also a strong need to address another of the four puzzles—that of the occurrence of inadvertent wars among status quo powers. To answer the puzzles, I further develop the general model of the book with regard to the conflictual outcomes. Thus, the two types of wars distinguished in chapter 1—intended and inadvertent—play a key role as the two dependent variables of the model I present in this chapter.

Why and how was a general great power war avoided during the postwar era? Why did the Cold War not escalate to a hot war but instead turn out to have been the Long Peace between the great powers (see Gaddis 1986, 100)?[1] Three of the most important questions involved in the hitherto unresolved debate on the causes of the Long Peace are the following:

1. Have nuclear weapons been the major cause of the postwar peace? Whereas many analysts have underlined the restraining effects of nuclear weapons on superpower conduct (see Bundy 1988; Gaddis 1986; Jervis 1989a; Mandelbaum 1981; Mearsheimer 1990; Waltz 1990), some have sharply disagreed, considering nuclear weapons irrelevant to this issue (see Mueller 1989; Vasquez 1991; Wagner 1993).
2. What, if any, were the effects of the bipolar structure on war avoidance during the Cold War? Here the old debate on the relative stability of bipolarity versus multipolarity is relevant.[2]
3. Is it possible to distinguish between the effects of polarity and nuclear arms on the outbreak of wars? Some of those who have underlined the moderating role of nuclear weapons have also emphasized the stabilizing role of bipolarity while failing to clearly distinguish the effects of the two factors on the Long Peace (see Gaddis 1986; Mearsheimer 1990; Waltz 1979),[3] and thus begging the question. In the postwar era, which witnessed the combination of these two pacifying factors, the Long Peace was in fact overdetermined. Yet this question assumes a special importance for the post–Cold War era. Should we be pessimistic about the chances of avoiding a major war after the passing of

bipolarity, or do nuclear weapons compensate for it and neutralize its negative effects?

The three unresolved questions emphasize the importance of specifying the effects of polarity and those of military technology on the outbreak of wars and differentiating between these effects (see also Levy 1989a, 235). This is the major objective of the model I present in this chapter.

*I propose that while polarity affects the likelihood of failure in crisis management and inadvertent wars, the nature of military technology influences the possibility of intended wars.*

The chapter focuses on the deductive logic of the effects of polarity and military technology on the outbreak of wars. I also illustrate the historical applicability of these effects. The first section briefly reviews the nuclear peace thesis and its limitations—one of the unresolved controversies in the literature on the Long Peace—and also considers the major weakness of this literature—the underspecification of the effects of polarity and nuclear weapons on war avoidance in the postwar era. In the second section, I present the main propositions and the resultant model concerning the distinctive effects of polarity and military technology on the likelihood of inadvertent and premeditated wars, respectively. The model distinguishes between four possible worlds according to a combination of polarity and military technology. In the third section, I analyze each of the four propositions arising from the model, whereas in the following section, I briefly review the three worlds derived from the model that existed historically: conventional multipolarity, conventional bipolarity, and nuclear bipolarity. I discuss the fourth future world of nuclear multipolarity in the Conclusions of the book, thus making it possible to examine the likelihood of a major war in the post–Cold War era in view of the model.

However, to many analysts the explanation of the postwar peace is self-evident; therefore, the proposed model may seem redundant. According to this view, the Long Peace was induced by nuclear weapons. In other words, they constitute both a necessary and a sufficient condition for its explanation. Before proceeding to discuss the proposed model, it is therefore necessary to show briefly why the nuclear explanation of the Long Peace is at best insufficient.

## The Limitations to the Nuclear Peace Thesis and the Need to Disentangle the Effects of Nuclear Arms and Bipolarity

Many analysts argue that "nuclear weapons can explain superpower caution: when the cost of seeking excessive gains is an increased probability of total destruction, moderation makes sense" (Jervis 1991, 71; see also Waltz 1990). Therefore, wars between the great powers in a nuclear world are unlikely. Yet some major limitations to the nuclear peace thesis have been noted.

For one thing, some observers contend that nuclear weapons do not necessarily eliminate the option of a conventional superpower war. Thus, Snyder's (1965) stability-instability paradox suggests that even if nuclear arms can maintain strategic stability, they do not preclude—and, indeed, may even make more likely—lower levels of violence. Because the balance of terror makes the implementation of nuclear threats extremely costly, they are not credible and are therefore supposedly useless for deterrence at the conventional level (Jervis 1984, 31 and 1991, 71; Levy 1989a, 292; Snyder 1965; Wagner 1993).

For another thing, some analysts have argued that nonnuclear causes were much more important than nuclear weapons in bringing about the Long Peace.[4] Mueller (1989) argues that major war has become obsolescent irrespective of nuclear weapons. Vasquez (1991), for his part, suggests that the pacifying effects of nuclear deterrence were much less influential than the effects of factors such as tolerance of the status quo, the creation of the rules of the game, crisis management, and arms control.[5] (Yet it is questionable whether these were independent or intervening variables. I argue that the stabilizing effects of at least some of these factors spring from the bipolar structure of the postwar international system.)

Most importantly, nuclear arms did not prevent superpower crises. Each superpower was willing to take risks and to threaten the use of force even in situations involving the other superpower. Data from the International Crisis Behavior Project shows that the postwar era was characterized by repetitive crises, including twelve international crises in which both the United States and the USSR took part (Brecher, James, and Wilkenfeld 1990; Brecher and Wilkenfeld 1991, especially 101). Indeed, mutual vulnerability has created incentives not only to avoid conflictual outcomes but also to attempt to exploit the rival's fear of escalation to extract diplomatic gains (Levy 1989a, 292).[6] The recurrence of such a pattern of behavior in a substantial number of crises could result in an inadvertent escalation to armed superpower conflict.[7] An especially dangerous tendency in this regard was the superpowers' frequent use of a wide range of short-of-war tactics for diplomatic signaling in crises.[8] These show-of-force measures might be misinterpreted in times of crisis as offensive, and such misjudgments could precipitate an inadvertent escalation.

These limitations show the insufficiency of the nuclear factor for explaining the Long Peace and the resultant necessity of bringing polarity back into the discussion of this question. The argument developed in this chapter is that system polarity exercises critical effects on the likelihood of inadvertent wars.

Thus, the major factor that facilitated crisis management and the avoidance of inadvertent escalation in the postwar era was the bipolar structure. As for intended wars, their likelihood is affected by the type of military technology. Thus, a conventional world makes premeditated wars possible, although the realization of this possibility would depend on unit-level elements (such as domestic politics, military organizations, and ideology). In other words, conventional military technology is a necessary but not a sufficient condition for a premeditated war. By contrast, the likelihood of intended wars between nuclear powers is extremely low because of the wide gap between the value of the interests in conflict and the potential cost of war (cf. Brodie 1973, chap. 1). An inadvertent escalation might still be possible between adversaries in a nuclear world, and all other things being equal, its likelihood would depend on structural factors. Regarding the effects of different international structures on crisis patterns and inadvertent wars, I argue that multipolarity is prone to failures in crisis management and inadvertent wars, whereas bipolarity is conducive to tacit rules for regulating the use of force in crises, thus facilitating successful crisis management and making inadvertent wars unlikely.

This kind of argument can help to advance the unresolved debate on the relative stability of bipolar and multipolar systems.[9] It can also address the arguments that polarity does not exercise important effects on system stability and that it is not the critical variable affecting the likelihood of war and peace (see Hopf 1991; Kegley and Raymond 1992; Van Evera 1990–91).[10] Most significantly, the present argument might allow us to disentangle the distinctive effects of bipolarity and nuclear weapons on great power peace during the Cold War and thereby make more specific predictions about the likelihood of major wars in the post–Cold War era following the decline of bipolarity. Predictions of this kind are impossible to make based on the overly general and underspecified arguments made by Gaddis (1986), Waltz (1979, 1981, and 1990) and Mearsheimer (1990), who confound the effects of polarity and military technology on the outbreak of major wars.

The dependent variables of this argument—intended and unintended wars—were presented in chapter 1. Let us now present the main propositions of this part of the study.

## Modeling the Effects of Polarity and Military Technology on the Outbreak of Major Wars

In this section, I present the overall model of the chapter. In the next sections, I go into detail with regard to the logic of each proposition and provide appropriate historical illustrations for the explanatory power of the model.

*Proposition 1:* The nature of military technology affects the likelihood of intended wars:
    a. Conventional military technology makes intended wars possible (although the realization of this possibility depends on unit-level elements).
    b. Nuclear military technology, especially MAD (mutual second-strike capability), renders intended war highly unlikely.

*Proposition 2:* The structure of the international system affects the likelihood of inadvertent wars:
    a. Bipolarity is conducive to successful crisis management and renders inadvertent wars unlikely.
    b. Multipolarity is prone to failure in crisis management and to inadvertent wars.

Structural factors are critical for understanding the two types of crisis outcomes: failure in the management of crises and inadvertent wars and successful crisis management manifested in tacit rules for regulating the use of force in crises. According to the general argument of the book, the explanatory power of the international structure should be especially strong with regard to these outcomes as these are unintended outcomes. Multipolarity may lead to inadvertent wars, that is, to a higher level of conflict than the actors desired at the outset. In contrast, bipolarity can make possible a greater degree of cooperation in times of crisis (even if only tacit) than the players initially intended.

The presence of nuclear weapons in the postwar era drastically reduced the probability of calculated aggression and premeditated wars between the superpowers because of the disproportionately high costs that could be expected to be paid for any attempt at a violent change of the status quo, especially so long as both parties possessed a second-strike capability. Yet it was bipolarity that minimized the probability of inadvertent wars and made crisis management easier than it would otherwise have been.

Accordingly, a combination of the two factors discussed in this chapter— the dominant type of military technology and the international structure— yields four worlds with regard to intended and unintended wars (see fig. 2). The first world of nuclear bipolarity is the most stable and the least war prone: neither intended nor inadvertent wars are likely. Even if the powers are engaged in a keen geostrategic or ideological competition, tacit rules emerge for regulating their use of force in crises. Moreover, the superpowers successfully cooperate in terminating local wars and prevent their escalation to superpower level, even though their cooperation is spontaneous and tacit rather than consciously designed. During the postwar era this indeed was the case with regard to regional conflicts, which were related in one way or another to the global rivalry, such as the Arab-Israeli wars (see chap. 5).

|  | Bipolar | Multipolar |
|---|---|---|
| **Nuclear Weapons** | 1<br><br>Both intended and inadvertent wars unlikely | 2<br><br>Intended wars unlikely; inadvertent wars possible |
| **Conventional** | 4<br><br>Intended wars possible; inadvertent wars unlikely | 3<br><br>Both intended and inadvertent wars possible |

Type of international structure (Bipolar / Multipolar); Type of military technology (Nuclear Weapons / Conventional)

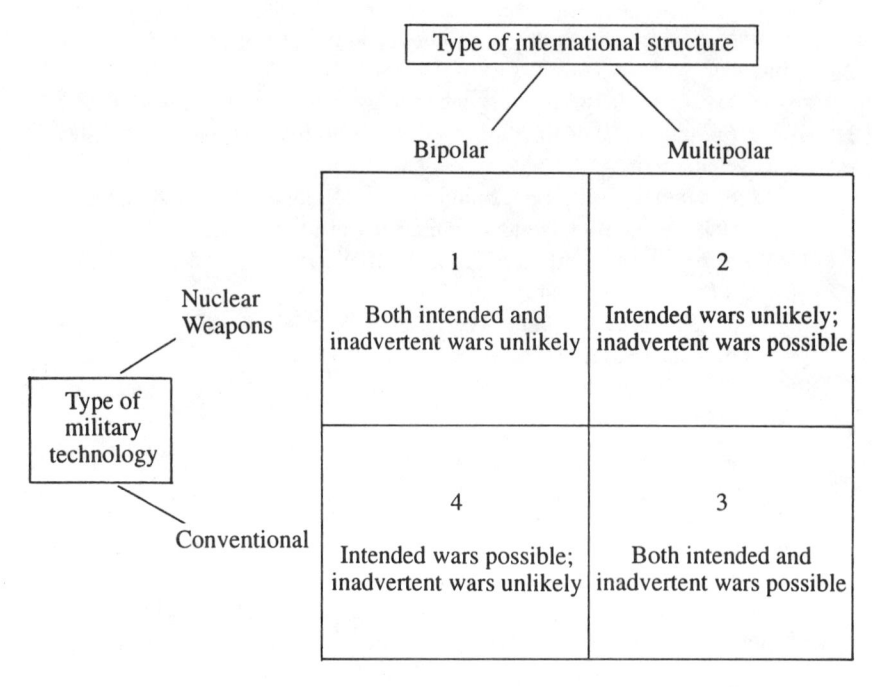

Fig. 2. The probability of intended and inadvertent wars according to international structure and military technology

In the second world of nuclear multipolarity, the presence of nuclear weapons minimizes the probability of planned wars among the great powers, yet the multipolar structure could lead to failures in the management of third-party crises, notably with regard to the early termination of regional wars. In extreme cases, such crises could escalate to inadvertent wars involving some of the great powers. As I discuss in the Conclusions, this scenario might have some relevance for the post–Cold War world.

In world 3—conventional multipolarity—inadvertent wars among the powers are quite likely, as was the case in the Seven Year War, the Crimean War, and World War I. Indeed, world 3 is the least peaceful because both types of major wars are possible: intended (due to conventional technology) and inadvertent (because of multipolarity).

In world 4—conventional bipolarity—intended wars are possible because of the absence of nuclear weapons. But the emergence of tacit rules for regulating the use of force in crises even between extreme rivals is also possible because of the bipolar structure. In other words, inadvertent wars resulting from the failure of crisis management are less likely.

## Propositions

### The Limits to Structure: Conventional Military Technology and Intended War

"In a conventional world, states going to war can at once believe that they may win and that, should they lose, the price of defeat will be tolerable" (Waltz 1990, 743).[11] Conventional war can be rational, in that a state could be better off fighting than not fighting. A state can make a cost-benefit calculation before going to war. It can try to gather as much relevant information as possible to assess the likely gains and costs and thus make a "sensible" decision (Morgan 1983) whether to initiate war or not, depending on its ends and means. A critical factor in this decision is the relative military balance. If a country is stronger than its adversary and can defeat its military forces, it can translate its military superiority into political benefits through the use or threat of force. The more powerful state can also minimize the military costs of carrying out the war and maintain a tolerable level of domestic, economic, and social dislocation. At the very least, in a conventional balance, a state can have some grounds to believe that by initiating war, it can make some important gains at affordable costs.

Conventional military technology is a permissive factor that allows for both aggressive and preventive wars. A superior military power may calculate that by initiating war, its benefits will exceed costs (aggressive motivation). It can also calculate that it is better to use its superiority before other countries catch up (preventive motivation). The key word here is permissive. Conventional military technology does not cause intended wars to occur but permits them, while nuclear MAD, as I show in the next section, prevents them from occurring.[12] In other words, conventional military technology is a necessary but not a sufficient condition for intended war. A conventional world makes premeditated war possible, although the realization of this possibility would depend on unit-level factors producing aggressive states (such as domestic regimes and bureaucracies).

Thus, intended wars have been possible, and have indeed occurred, in conventional systems regardless of polarity. Intended wars in multipolar systems include most of the great power wars cited by hegemonic theories, whether aggressive or preventive (see the brief review in Levy 1985b, 345–46, and the cases in Levy 1987). In bipolar systems we may cite the Peloponnesian War (a preventive war) and Israel's invasion of Lebanon (which occurred in the bipolar regional context of the Israeli-Syrian conflict over Lebanon).

## Nuclear Weapons and the Obsolescence of Intended War

The nuclear revolution has made intended war unlikely because it has enormously widened the gap between the value of the interests at stake in any given conflict (however high) and the potential costs of nuclear war. This is especially true under MAD because this situation has caused the great powers to lose their capability to defend their highest value—their major population centers—irrespective of the outcome on the battlefield.[13] In contrast, in a conventional world, it was still possible, especially for the great powers, to defend their civilian centers. The bombing of cities notwithstanding, only a decisive military defeat made their populations highly vulnerable to enemy forces. Because of the nuclear revolution and the development of long-range delivery systems, that is no longer true for the great powers. As Schelling suggests, "nuclear weapons make it possible to do monstrous violence to the enemy without first achieving victory" (1966, 22). MAD means that the loser from a purely military viewpoint can inflict as much destruction on the side that is winning as vice versa (Jervis 1989a, 5). In other words, the direct link between military power and defense capability has drastically declined, and even the most powerful state can be destroyed by war. Thus, relative military advantages do not tempt a superior power to use its power, because under MAD "no one can promise the full success of a disarming first strike" (Waltz 1990, 734). Even if the initiating power intends to use only conventional forces, under MAD there can be no certainty that the opponent will not retaliate with nuclear weapons or that the war will not escalate to the nuclear level at a later stage. Given the magnitude of this threat, even conventional wars between nuclear powers are too dangerous to be initiated. As a result, a calculated initiation of war based on a cost-benefit analysis does not make any sense, and an intended war becomes highly improbable irrespective of polarity.

At this point, two potential criticisms must be addressed. First, in the previous section I argue that the realization of the possibility of intended wars depends on unit-level factors, such as aggressive leaders, bureaucracies, or regimes. Conceivably, these may arise even in a nuclear world, making nuclear arms less able to prevent intended wars. The answer to this argument is that even though aggressive leaders such as Hitler may appear in a nuclear MAD world, assuming that they are not wholly psychopathic and act according to the most minimal conception of rationality (namely, self-preservation), they will behave differently and more cautiously than in a conventional world and refrain from aggressive acts that are likely to bring about a nuclear response. Thus, unit-level factors are overridden by nuclear MAD with regard to the initiation of an intended war.

Second, one might ask whether the influence of nuclear weapons does not strech to inadvertent wars as well. In other words, the caution induced by nuclear MAD may prevent crises from occurring in the first place or at least from escalating. If this were indeed so, nuclear proliferation, especially if it were well managed, could provide a simple remedy to all major wars (as advocated, in fact, by Waltz 1981 and Mearsheimer 1990).

In response, it may first be asserted that nuclear arms can work both ways in crises. On the one hand, the fear of nuclear escalation may induce greater caution; on the other hand, it may tremendously increase stress and the attendant psychological problems decision makers face: "The stress generated by a nuclear crisis would almost certainly surpass that of the most acute crises in the past" (Lebow 1987, 147).[14] As a result, misperceptions and miscalculated escalation are more likely to occur.

As for the other major path to inadvertent war, nuclear weapons are insufficient for the prevention of inadvertent wars that occur as a result of the loss of control during crises. Nuclear weapons cannot by themselves resolve or eliminate such problems as control over allies or the military.

Thus, the nuclear revolution did not at all free analysts from worries that an inadvertent nuclear war may break out as a result of miscalculated escalation or loss of control in time of crisis.[15] In fact, these concerns increased in the postwar era despite nuclear MAD, due to the unit-level characterisitics of the postwar superpowers (discussed below), which could increase even more the likelihood of miscalculated escalation and loss of control in crises.

To sum up, due to the indeterminate influence of nuclear weapons on the crisis behavior of decision makers (caution versus stress), and thereby on miscalculated escalation, and due to their irrelevance to the problem of loss of control in crises, the likelihood of inadvertent wars in a nuclear setting is conditioned by another critical factor, namely system polarity.

Even more fundamentally, admitting that nuclear weapons played an important role in encouraging cautious behavior on the part of the superpowers in the Cold War era, we must bear in mind that inadvertent wars are a major manifestation of unintended outcomes in international politics (see chaps. 1–2). Given the nature of these outcomes, good intentions cannot prevent them by definition. Therefore, the fear of war and the caution induced by nuclear weapons, although highly relevant to the abstinence of great powers from intended wars, are insufficient and might even be irrelevant to inadvertent ones. In other words, it is not always enough to fear an inadvertent war to prevent it, and intentions to avoid war do not necessarily result in peace.[16]

The military technology by itself could not prevent failure in crisis management through either overreaction or underreaction in postwar crises. It was bipolarity that minimized the likelihood of these possibilities by encouraging a delicate balance between resolve and caution, reducing the collective goods problem, facilitating control over unruly allies and the military, insulating the decision makers from the pressures of domestic groups, and moderating the destabilizing effects of miscalculations and misperceptions in times of crisis. Thus, the bipolar structure was the major factor that enabled the translation of the desire to avoid war into recurring tacit rules for regulating the use of force in crises.

### Polarity and Inadvertent Wars

In general, polarity has two types of effects on crisis management (or mismanagement) and the likelihood of inadvertent wars: directly derived effects and more indirect ones. Each type is related in particular to one of the two major paths to inadvertent war. The effects directly derived from polarity refer especially to the degree of simplicity and clarity of the international system. These factors especially affect the likelihood of misperceptions and miscalculated escalation. The more indirect effects of the international structure condition the potentially destabilizing influence of unit-level factors such as the military and domestic politics, and thus they mainly affect the likelihood of loss of control as a path to inadvertent war.[17] In other words, the international structure will affect the degree of influence of potentially destabilizing domestic factors on crisis decision making. I argue that bipolarity tends to minimize the destabilizing effects of various unit-level factors, whereas multipolarity aggravates them. This argument goes beyond Waltz in specifying how and when polarity conditions the relative influence of unit-level factors. (See table 4 on international structures and crisis management.)

*Bipolarity and the Improbability of Inadvertent Wars*
The argument that bipolarity is less war prone than multipolarity has recently gained some strong deductive and inductive support.[18] Yet in light of the recent criticism of the explanatory power of bipolarity (see Hopf 1991; Kegley and Raymond 1992; Van Evera 1990–91; Wagner 1993), and the overgeneralized nature of the debate on polarity and stability, this argument badly needs important specifications and qualifications.

Rather than just repeating the Waltzian argument, as supporters of bipolarity usually do, that this system is more stable or peaceful in general than multipolarity, I make a more specific claim, namely, that bipolar systems reduce the likelihood of a certain type of wars—inadvertent wars. Intended wars are possible in a bipolar world (when the military technology is conventional), but the greater ability of the great powers in such a system to develop tacit rules for regulating the use of force should help them to manage crises and thus to reduce the likelihood of unintended escalation. Conversely, I show how various characteristics of multipolarity may bring about the two major paths to inadvertent war—miscalculation and loss of control. Thus, a connection is

**TABLE 4. International Structures and Crisis Management**

| Bipolarity | Multipolarity |
|---|---|
| Simplicity and clarity | Complexity and discontinuity |
| Relatively weak effects of stress and misperceptions on crisis decision making | Tendency to stress and misperceptions during crises |
| Control over allies and the military | Tendency to loss of control over allies and the military |
| Relative autonomy from domestic constraints during crises | Growing domestic constraints during crises |
| Tendency to resolute restraint | Tendency to overreaction or underreaction |
| Successful crisis management | Inadvertent war |

war and crisis management, which has traditionally concentrated on unit-level factors.

Let us elaborate the rationale for the proposition.

*The Inclination for International Engagement and the Conduct of Restrained Resolve*
made between the polarity-stability argument and the literature on inadvertent The combination of two central attributes of bipolar systems reduces the danger of either overreaction or underreaction, at least in times of crisis. These attributes refer to the focused nature of the major threat and the availability of a clear-cut leadership for defense against it, which means the certainty of response by a countervailing force to any attempts at violent changes of the status quo. Because only the other superpower can cause a major harm, there is a single source of potential threat for each of the superpowers. The focused nature of the potential threat disposes each of the powers to intensive engagement regardless of initial inclinations, to contain potential expansion by the opponent, and prevents underreaction and disengagement. The presence of a single leader in each of the camps in bipolarity, who is in charge of response to external threat, reduces the likelihood of buck-passing and of free ridership, typical of the collective goods problem in multipolar systems, because there is no one else, apart from the superpowers, who may defend the camp members. The result is resolute behavior by the superpowers. But this resolve in times of major crises is restrained because each of the superpowers is faced with a countervailing force whose basic ability and willingness to defend its interests cannot be mistaken. It is when there is no such manifest countervailing force that one may expect overreaction and reckless behavior.

Precisely because of the keen competition in bipolarity that leads the superpowers to demonstrate the strength of their commitment to defend their important interests, the end result is a delicate balance between caution and resolve in their crisis behavior. In other words, under bipolarity the party that has the advantage in the balance of interests shows resolve whereas its opponent behaves cautiously. Such crisis conduct makes possible the emergence of tacit rules even between rivals; these rules reflect the relative balance of interests of the superpowers.[19]

*Simplicity and Clarity*
In the absence of formal agreements between antagonists, the relative clarity of the balances of capabilities and interests minimizes the chances of misjudging the rival's resolve to defend its vital stakes. The superpower show of sensitivity to the interests of the adversary is facilitated by the relative clarity of the balance of stakes in a bipolar system. Once there is a single leader in each camp who is responsible for promptly responding to threats to its values, mutual expectations about the other's reactions are more likely to evolve. Moreover, the presence of only two great powers facilitates nonverbal bargaining, which is especially critical in crisis periods. Through various show-of-force options, the superpowers signal their "red lines,"[20] that is, the point beyond which the stakes of the signaling superpower are clearly greater than those of its rival. Because of the relative clarity of two-player games, the red lines are more easily identified. Since trespassing the red lines may trigger a military reaction by the rival superpower, each superpower has a strong incentive to be cautious and to restrain its allies. In short, the clarity and simplicity of bipolarity make it easier for the superpowers to follow the tacit rules.[21]

*Control over Allies*
In light of the structural advantages of great powers in bipolarity, they are more able to restrain their allies once push comes to shove, that is, when there is a high likelihood of escalation into a major war. For one thing, there is a relative absence of options for realignment in the rigid alliance system of bipolarity.[22] Even if the lesser powers realign, however, it will be insignificant for the overall balance of power, since that will still be determined by the preponderant weight of the two superpowers. The realignment of even a relatively big state would not change the basic bipolar structure. Indeed, there is an extreme asymmetry in strategic interdependence in bipolarity (Gilpin 1981, 236; Snyder and Diesing 1977, 443–44, 505; Waltz 1979), and a low security dependence of the superpowers on their allies, including the most important of them (Midlarsky 1991, 106–7). Thus, even if a realignment by a smaller state matters to the superpowers for reasons of domestic politics and ideology, it would not be so crucial for maintaining the global balance (Johnson 1985–86, 37–38, 51) that it would compel the superpowers to provide a "blank check" to unruly allies. Indeed, the relative self-sufficiency of the bipolar superpowers means that the damage they can inflict on each other is far greater than any

damage they might suffer as a result of the loss of any ally or allies. Not only are allies unimportant in terms of the global balance under bipolarity, but the limited options for realignment provide the great powers with a positive leverage over their allies in times of crisis, because of the latter's dependence on the superpowers for deterrence against the intervention of the rival superpower and for weapons resupply. Only the superpowers can deter each other and embark on a massive resupply effort in a relatively short time through sealift and especially airlift during intense local wars (see Neuman 1986 and 1988). As a result of these attributes of bipolarity, there is a relative freedom from alliance constraints in a world of two great powers. One of the implications of this is that the great powers under bipolarity are much more capable of restraining their lesser partners in crises than their counterparts in multipolarity (Snyder and Diesing 1977, 506-7; Waltz 1964). In other words, the danger of entrapment in allies' wars is lower in bipolarity (Midlarsky 1991, 106-7; G. Snyder 1984).

*A Relatively High Degree of Control over the Military and a Relative Autonomy from Domestic Pressures by Top Decision Makers in Crises*
Bipolarity restrains the potentially destabilizing effects of domestic public opinion, which may be inclined to either over- or underreaction in crisis, and of the military, which for organizational-bureaucratic reasons is likely to pull in the direction of overreaction. These effects are restrained because of the clearcut and overwhelming nature of the structural constraints and incentives in bipolar systems, which, in turn, are especially influential in times of crisis. In other words, under the clarifying and restraining effects of bipolarity with its clear and focused threat, public opinion is less likely to misperceive the international situation and support either disengagement or overreaction. To the extent that it does, decision makers more easily resist public pressures. Because of the overshadowing structural constraints, they also more easily control the military in crisis. As a result, under bipolarity leaders enjoy an enhanced leeway to pursue policies that are either more dovish or more hawkish than what the public or their bureaucracies advocate.

## Multipolarity and the Likelihood of Inadvertent Wars

*Complexity and Discontinuity*
In bipolarity there is one dominant great power dyad, so the only two powers must continuously interact. Even if the interaction is competitive, the same two powers get many chances over time to identify the interests of their opponent and to learn to respect its resolve. In multipolarity there are a number of great

power dyads, and they may be changing over different places, issues, and periods. Thus, the ability of opponents to get to know the others' interests in times of crisis is constrained by the discontinuity and complexity of the interactions. Moreover, the identity of allies and rivals might be changing over different regions, periods, and issues. Such structural problems pose severe constraints for spontaneous cooperation in times of crisis and for the evolution of persistent tacit rules between potential rivals.

*Misperceptions and Crisis-Induced Stress*
The unclarity of the balances of interests, capabilities, responsibilities, and commitments and the uncertainty about the identity of allies and the sources of threats in a multipolar world (Waltz 1979, chap. 8) might lead to misperceptions and misunderstandings that would, in turn, make the task of crisis management very difficult. In extreme cases, such difficulties can result in inadvertent wars through miscalculated escalation.

Some analysts, drawing on cognitive psychology, are concerned about the pathological effects of crisis-induced stress on policymakers, including increased cognitive rigidity, impaired attention and perception, and resultant misperceptions and miscalculations.[23] Yet the degree of stress depends on the simplicity and clarity of the situation, which stems in turn from system structure. In other words, the international structure conditions the ambiguity of the situation and the information overloading of decision makers. Thus, the structure shapes the range of leaders' miscalculations (see chap. 2), which means that the complex multipolar setting is more conducive to stress and its adverse effects on crisis management.

In comparison, bipolarity reduces the ambiguity of the situation and the overloading of policymakers. That lessens the destabilizing effects of crisis-induced stress. Hence, to the extent that the two leading powers have strong incentives to avoid a general war, a bipolar structure facilitates tacit cooperation in crisis settings.

*The Loss of Control over Allies and the Instability of Alliances*
The major balancing mechanism in multipolarity is external: alliance formation rather than internal expansion of the military and economic power base (Waltz 1979, 163, 167–70). This mechanism gives the small allies powerful leverage vis-à-vis their patrons. Moreover, the relative equality between alliance partners makes them highly interdependent in their security. In multipolarity there are also more options for realignment than in bipolarity, and should the smaller allies realign, it would influence the general balance of power. As a result, the great powers are less capable of restraining their lesser

allies in multipolar crises (Snyder and Diesing 1977, chap. 6; Waltz 1964), and the danger of the loss of control over them and entrapment in allies' wars is higher than in bipolarity (G. Snyder 1984). At the same time, the instability of alliances in multipolarity (Gowa 1989), and therefore the inability to trust one's allies, may generate insecurity among both the great powers and their smaller allies. Such feelings of vulnerability might lead to overreaction and preemption in crises.

*The Inclination of Status Quo Powers to Disengage*
A multipolar structure makes a disengagement strategy possible for status quo powers because the presence of a number of great powers might lead at least some of them to believe that they can pass the buck to others, that is, to ride free on other states' balancing efforts and thus to save costs (Posen 1984, 232-33; Waltz 1979, 165). Thus, there is no single leader who is clearly committed to defend the status quo. Moreover, the diffusion of sources of threat in multipolarity tends to discourage intensive and costly international engagement on the part of status quo powers.

The great advantage of a disengagement strategy from the viewpoint of the external powers is, of course, the reduction in the likelihood of entanglements in local wars and also saving scarce resources that would be spent in a costly competition in remote places. Yet a strategy of disengagement may result in inadvertent war either because of miscalculated escalation or the loss of control. The first sequence might take place because disengagement can tempt other powers, especially revisionist ones, to a miscalculated fait accompli. Concluding from prior experience (of their own or of other challengers to the status quo) that the status quo powers are not going to resist challenges, revisionist powers might try to take advantage of this lack of resistance by piecemeal expansion until the crossing of a threshold to war triggers an armed response by the status quo powers. The outcome might then be considered an unintended escalation because the challenger would have avoided the escalatory step if it could anticipate such a response. The complexity of the multipolar structure contributes to the miscalculation by making it difficult to identify the adversaries' red lines and to develop accurate expectations about their responses; thus, it raises the probability of miscalculated escalation as one of the paths to an inadvertent war.

In addition to providing a temptation to revisionist great powers, disengagement may also deprive turbulent regions of the stabilizing presence of status quo powers and thereby lead to difficulties for crisis management at the regional level.[24] A questionable willingness or ability to protect the status quo on the part of status quo powers may make smaller states feel insecure and thus lead them to overreact to external threats. Effective external agents able to restrain local clients or to deter potential regional aggressors are also missing. Thus, in the absence of great power involvement, regional crises and protracted local wars are more likely. These crises or wars may escalate to great power level, however, if a regional balance of power is drastically disrupted, if great power interests are infringed on, or if major atrocities are committed. In such a case, it would be difficult for the powers to resist the urge to intervene, because of domestic pressures or fears about potential international implications, especially if the upheaval catches the attention of public opinion, the media, sympathetic domestic groups, and local allies. The powers then have the worst of both worlds: they are unable to prevent the crisis before it escalates and compelled to intervene when events are out of control and thus face a potentially costly and dangerous confrontation. Hence, paradoxically, a strategy of disengagement may in fact increase the likelihood of an inadvertent major war.

*The Loss of Control over the Military and Growing Domestic Constraints*
Because of the complexity of multipolarity, the international structure is unable to play the simplifying and restraining role as effectively as in bipolarity. Thus, the effects of destabilizing unit-level factors are less likely to be controlled by the clarifying and constraining international setting, and as a result, there is more leeway for the influence of bureaucracies and domestic politics on crisis decision making and a greater probability that the decision makers will give in to these pressures.

In general, the international structure conditions (either restrains or aggravates) the effects of unit-level factors on crisis management (see chap. 2). Therefore, in bipolar systems, even immoderate actors can manage crises successfully because of the reduction in the destabilizing effects of ideology, domestic politics, and misperceptions during crisis periods. In contrast, in multipolarity, even relatively moderate actors might inadvertently find themselves at war. This is because such systems encourage either overreaction (due to misperceptions of interests and capabilities as well as difficulty in controlling the influence of allies, the military, and the domestic public on crisis decision making) or underreaction (due to free ridership and uncertainty about the sources of threat). Indeed, great power crisis decision making under multipolarity may be characterized by extreme oscillations between under- and overreaction. Overreaction and underreaction, in turn, are more dangerous for crisis stability than the somewhat delicate balance between resolve and caution that prevails in bipolar crises.

The next section discusses the three worlds that have existed thus far: conventional multipolarity, conventional bipolarity, and nuclear bipolarity. The fourth (future) world (nuclear multipolarity) is discussed in the Conclusions.

## The Worlds In Practice

### Multipolar Conventional World: Intended and Inadvertent Wars

This kind of world is expected to be permissive for intended wars (because of the conventional technology) and also to encourage the occurrence of unintended wars. While most of the deliberate attempts at hegemony and preventive wars took place in this setting,[25] the major analytical challenge is to show that multipolarity had a crucial effect on the outbreak of some major cases of inadvertent wars. Several wars fought in a multipolar setting fit the definition of an inadvertent war. Two of the examples I present in this section are major wars (the Crimean War and World War I), and the third is a regional war (the 1967 Six-Day War). The Middle East in 1967 was a multipolar subsystem and the war was a major one, involving several of the major regional actors.[26] As I noted in chapter 2, both the Crimean War and World War I are intriguing cases of unintended wars because these are failures in crisis management among powers that were relatively moderate in their attitude to the status quo and similar ideologically and culturally. The Crimean War is an especially suggestive case of an inadvertent war because it erupted between powers that were still members of the usually cooperative Concert of Europe, even if the crisis took place after the Concert was greatly weakened due to the 1848 revolutions.

The definition of the Crimean War and of the Six-Day War as inadvertent wars is largely unproblematic.[27] However, the classification of World War I as inadvertent[28] is somewhat more ambiguous, given the thesis of historian Fischer (1967) and his followers who assert that Germany was the deliberate aggressor in World War I. Yet the definition of an inadvertent war as presented in chapter 1 does allow us to reconcile the prevalent view of World War I as a classical case of inadvertent war with Fischer's interpretation. As noted, one of the sides to a crisis leading to an inadvertent war may plan or be willing to risk a limited local war, but to the extent that it does not want or expect a major war, the resulting war may be considered inadvertent. In July, 1914, Germany may have wanted and have been willing to risk a local or conceivably even a continental war. Yet "even Fischer and Imanuel Geiss, the strongest supporters of the German war guilt argument, do not go as far as to argue that Germany sought a world war" (Levy 1991b, 69), that is, a war with the participation of Britain. None of the great powers have wanted a world war, "yet they ended up with the war that none of them wanted and have deliberately sought, and, in this sense, World War I was inadvertent" (Levy 1991b, 87). The crucial misperception that led to the escalation of the war was the German assumption of British neutrality. Thus, "a hypothesis based on a belligerent Germany is not necessarily inconsistent with a crisis management/inadvertent war perspective" (Levy 1991b, 62). Indeed, even Fischer's supporters accept that Germany did not want a world war but that it stumbled into it as a result of misguided attempts to ensure German security (Christensen and Snyder 1990, 148 n. 25).

In each of the three cases, it may be briefly demonstrated that war broke out as a result of the characteristics of multipolar systems, which made it more difficult to manage crises than would otherwise have been the case.

*Complexity*

Smoke characterizes the crisis that preceded the Crimean War as an "intricate maze" and notes that "the politico-military events surrounding the Crimean crisis and war are the most complicated of any period in the nineteenth century" (1991, 38). The same could be said of the "exceedingly complex" crisis of July, 1914, preceding the outbreak of World War I (Gottfried and Blair 1988, 28). The 1967 crisis involved not only Egypt and Israel but also the complex and tense relations within the Arab world, both between the radical regimes (such as Egypt and Syria) and between them and the conservatives (such as Jordan and Saudi Arabia). Another complicating factor, at least at the early stages of the crisis, was superpower involvement: the Soviets spread rumors about an imminent Israeli attack on Syria and thus exerted pressures on Egypt to act; the unclear U.S. commitment to Israel meant that the United States was able neither to deter the Arabs nor to reassure Israel.[29]

*The Lack of Control over Allies*

In each case, alliance politics and commitments, exacerbated by the multipolar structure, played a role in the drift toward war. The greater ability of small allies to play off their great power patrons in multipolarity made it easier for Turkey to play off Britain against Russia in the Crimean War. Britain and France stumbled into the war as a result of the actions and the inactions on the part of Turkey (Smoke 1991, 55–56).

The Austrians drew the Germans through the "blank check" into their conflict with Serbia (Orme 1987, 106) because of the German security dependence on their weaker ally in 1914 (Midlarsky 1991, 107); and the Russian support of the southern Slavs meant that in a multipolar system, the French would be entrapped in a Russo-German war because of their fear of being abandoned by Russia in some new Franco-German crisis (G. Snyder 1984, 474).

The onset of the 1967 crisis was directly related to Nasser's (largely misplaced) fear, fed by the Soviets but also by Israeli statements, that Israel was going to attack Syria, which had been sponsoring raids on Israeli territory. As an aspirant to the leadership of the Arab world and because of his worry that a Syrian defeat would considerably change the balance of forces in Israel's favor, Nasser felt compelled to come to the defense of Damascus and to deter

Israel by sending his forces to the Sinai. Therefore, an attempt at extended deterrence, by providing some sort of a "blank check" to his Syrian ally, initiated the escalation of the May crisis.

Thus, in each case it was the involvement of a smaller ally that drew one or several powers into the war.

*Misperceptions and Miscalculated Escalation*
The June war was essentially caused by Egypt and Israel reacting to each other's defensive moves, a process of action and reaction that led to escalation and eventual hostilities. Although Nasser probably miscalculated in believing that his moves would not lead to an Israeli attack, the establishment of the pan-Arab pact boosted his confidence and encouraged him to escalate his threats toward Israel. The initiation of war by Israel was a case of preemption, based on an overestimation of the probability of Egyptian attack (Stein 1991, 141–42). Indeed, when Nasser barred Israeli shipping through the Straits of Tiran on May 23, Israel became convinced that war was inevitable. Thus, after the failure of international diplomacy to open the straits, it felt compelled to resort to military means. At the same time, the emergence of the pan-Arab alliance sharpened Israel's security dilemma, and it felt encircled and thus obliged (by June 5) to preempt before it would be too late and the costs of war would be intolerable.[30] Thus, the decision to preempt was also made under considerable stress.

The unclarity of the balance of interests, and of related commitments to intervene, typical of multipolarity, made it more likely for the British to overestimate the extent of Russia's ambitions toward Turkey, which led Britain to overreact, and thus to contribute inadvertently to the escalation of the Russian-Turkish crisis (Smoke 1991, 46). Britain perceived as aggressive moves Russia intended as defensive, thus illustrating the effects of the security dilemma under multipolarity. The unclarity inherent in multipolarity also led to the Russian miscalculation of the British commitment to Turkey in 1853–54, and this miscalculation resulted in the escalation of the Crimean War (Smoke 1977, 147–94).

The lack of clarity of interests and commitments in the pre–World War I multipolarity heavily contributed to the inadvertent escalation of a local conflict not only to continentwide hostilities but also to a world war. Several escalatory moves by parties to the crisis sprang directly from misperceptions. Austria, abetted by Germany and wishing to repeat the diplomatic success of the 1908 Bosnian crisis, severely underestimated the probable Russian response to the Austrian declaration of war on Serbia (Levy 1991b, 79–80). Likewise, Russia underestimated the effect of its general mobilization on Germany (Joll 1984, 21). Yet the most critical misperception of the July crisis was the German misjudgment of the British commitment to the Triple Entente in the summer of 1914, which was a major factor in the escalation of a continental crisis to a world war (Levy 1991b). A major cause of these misperceptions, especially in Germany, was crisis-induced stress. The Stanford Studies show its adverse effects, resulting in the reckless behavior of some of the key actors in the summer of 1914 (Holsti 1972; Holsti, Brody, and North 1969). For example, it was found that information overloading, which is more likely in a multipolar world than in bipolarity (Deutsch and Singer 1964), generated greater hostility and resulted in overreaction, escalation, and war (Holsti 1972, 81). The adverse effects of crisis-induced stress on the kaiser and the chancellor increased both their tendency to overeaction and the predominant influence of the military on crisis decision making in Germany (Lebow 1981, 119–47; and 1987, 145). An additional factor that contributed to the German miscalculation of British neutrality was the British policy of underreaction during the crisis, manifested in indecision and a failure to commit itself to support France and Russia.

*The Loss of Control and Overreaction*
Still, another part of the explanation for the overreaction of the parties to the three crises lies in the loss of control. In addition to the lack of control over allies, the military and domestic public opinion also exercised a major destabilizing influence on crisis decision making.

In the July 1914 crisis, the civilian decision makers, especially in Russia and Germany, let the military leaders have the dominant voice in decision making, substituting the military logic of war fighting for the diplomatic logic of crisis management. Thus, the escalation of the crisis was largely dictated by the military plans of the great powers (Lebow 1987; Taylor 1992, 524). This accounts for two major escalatory acts: (1) the Russian general mobilization, which was adopted because of military considerations and the rigidity of mobilization plans, not allowing for partial mobilization (Levy 1991b, 83–84) and (2) the German declaration of war on France, which sprang from the Schlieffen plan—Germany's only war plan—which envisaged a war on two fronts and therefore brought France into what was until that point a Central-East European crisis, thus escalating it to continental proportions (Levy 1991b, 85–87). The mobilization orders issued during the crisis, and the prospect of war they posed, brought about an outpouring of nationalist emotions in the major powers—an additional factor that made deescalation more difficult (Lebow 1987, 110).

Israel's decision to preempt in June 1967, was also influenced by military considerations, namely the inability to maintain a general mobilization for a considerable time because of economic dislocation. Nasser's loss of control over the aroused Arab public opinion, both in Egypt and in the Arab world in general, was a major factor influencing his escalatory policy (Stein 1991).

Nasser was severely constrained in his later moves by his concern that steps toward deescalation would lead to an allegation in the Arab world that he had deserted Syria and the Arab cause and yielded to Israeli pressure. Thus, in some sense he lost control over the situation and continued the escalatory moves, culminating in the signing of a pact with Jordan on May 30 that was expanded to include Iraq in early June.

Bellicose public opinion played a destabilizing role in the Crimean crisis as well. The outrage of Western (especially British) public opinion at the Sinope massacre (the annihilation of the Turkish flotilla in the harbor of Sinope by the Russian navy) created a popular demand for a strong counterstroke and contributed to the Western powers' decision to send an expeditionary force to the Crimea (Smoke 1991, 47, 53).

*Disengagement in Multipolarity and World War II*

Because of the aggressive nature of the Nazi regime, World War II was not an inadvertent war similar to World War I, let alone the Crimean War. To the extent that Hitler had aggressive intentions and was willing to risk a major war to achieve his expansionist objectives, World War II was an intended war.[31] Yet multipolarity aggravated the problem of miscalculation in the protracted crisis of the late 1930s as well, and thus the outbreak of World War II has some inadvertent elements. Multipolarity made it difficult to identify sources of threat and to be prepared accordingly. Thus, Britain and the United States were very late in recognizing the German threat and did not pursue appropriate military buildup, which could have enhanced deterrence vis-à-vis Germany (Mearsheimer 1990).[32] Indeed, the multipolar structure encouraged strategies of underreaction by the status quo powers. In addition to American isolationism, Britain was unwilling (or unable because of its imperial engagements) to commit itself to the defense of Eastern Europe, the most problematic region of the interwar order (cf. Craig and George 1983, 54–57). This situation left France as the only major status quo power ready to make such a commitment, yet French resources were insufficient for sustaining a credible commitment and for deterring aggression, especially in the face of the growing power of the revisionist powers and the ideological-domestic constraints on cooperation between the Western powers and Bolshevik Russia against Nazi Germany.

A major factor that facilitated the pursuit of disengagement, however, was the absence of clear-cut leadership and responsibility to defend the status quo in the multipolar interwar system. This absence resulted in the tendency for buck-passing between France and Britain with regard to the production of the public goods of collective security and stable balance (Posen 1984). The Soviets, for their part, could hope that the Germans would become bogged down in a war of attrition similar to World War I on the Western front.

Politicians and domestic opinion in the United States and Britain supported disengagement policies because of short-run benefits associated with saving defense expenditures, avoiding seemingly undesirable alignments (such as with the Soviet Union), and shunning what appeared to be unnecessarily dangerous entanglements in faraway places and expensive commitments against the fascist powers. Besides, Britain and France attempted to avoid war by an active policy of appeasement. Yet such disengagement and appeasement at best only delayed the war and might have considerably aggravated its eventual scope or even contributed to its outbreak (Taylor 1961). Because of Western appeasement, made possible by the complexity of the multipolar balance, Germany failed to anticipate the British and French reaction to its invasion of Poland and the eventual U.S. entry into the war. Such misperceptions encouraged German aggression.

## Conventional Bipolarity: Intended Wars Possible but Unintended Wars Unlikely

Critics of bipolar stability tend to cite the Peloponnesian War as an example of the outbreak of a major war in a bipolar system. In fact, there are differences of opinion among experts whether the structure of the ancient Greek system at the time of this war was indeed bipolar.[33] A more important point for the purposes of this book, however, is the nature of this war as a preventive war rather than an inadvertent one. Such a characterization of the war does not contradict the present model. Admittedly, the causes of the Peloponnesian War have provoked another controversy among historians. Thus, Lebow notes that "the origins of the Peloponnesian War are characterized by an unresolvable ambiguity. So too are many modern conflicts" (1991, 137). Yet in this book I adhere to the prevalent interpretation of the war as preventive. Indeed, Thucydides's account that the causes of the Peloponnesian War could be found in "the growth of Athenian power and the fear which this caused in Sparta" (1954, I/23) serves as the classic statement of the preventive motivation (Gilpin 1981, 191; Howard 1983, chap. 1; Levy 1987).

Our confidence that bipolarity is conducive to the emergence of tacit rules between adversaries can be reinforced if we witness a similar phenomenon in a bipolar conventional setting, that is, without the intervening influence of nuclear weapons. Indeed, the Israeli-Syrian antagonism in Lebanon suggests the possibility of the emergence of tacit rules even between fierce rivals in conventional settings, or at least in the absence of MAD, once the structure of the conflict is bipolar, that is, there are two dominant actors, each of them much more powerful than any combination of the other participants.

In contrast to the overall multipolar structure of the Middle Eastern system (which indeed gave birth to the inadvertent escalation of the 1967 crisis), the structure of the continuing conflict in Lebanon since 1976 was bipolar. At least until recently, Lebanon lacked a central authority but rather resembled an anarchical system with a multiplicity of armed actors that were in one degree or another in a state of war with each other. Yet the clearly superior capabilities of two of these actors—Syria and Israel—made the structure of the conflict over Lebanon, in fact, bipolar. The rivalry between the two dominant actors was very intense, the cultural-ideological differences very wide and suspicions of each other's long-term objectives very high. Still, as Evron (1987, 170–74) shows in his comprehensive study of the Israeli-Syrian deterrence dialogue, the antagonists succeeded in developing a "red lines system" of tacit rules for the regulation of their military engagement in Lebanon (see also Bar 1990; Rabinovich 1987). The established red lines concerned the geographical limitations on the Syrian and Israeli deployment and ground operations in Lebanon, both sides' air activity in the Lebanese air space, and the nondeployment of Syrian surface-to-air missle (SAM) systems in Lebanon. Evron (1987) points out that the major reason for this success was the relatively limited number of misperceptions of the other side's military capabilities and vital security interests. These interests, in turn, were closely related to the "objective strategic situation" (Evron 1987, 220) and should be differentiated from fundamental, long-term ideological objectives. The relative weakness of misperceptions, despite the great differences in value systems, seems to be closely related to the structure of the conflict: the presence of only two major players. Thus, the Israeli-Syrian experience seems to confirm the linkage established in this book between structural factors related to polarity, levels of misperceptions, and tacit cooperation in the regulation of the military behavior of rivals. In other words, the lower the number of major players, the weaker the effects of misperceptions and, as a result, the greater the probability of the emergence of tacit rules for crisis management.

The 1982 Israeli invasion of Lebanon was a clear-cut case of an intended war rather than failure in crisis management; thus, it does not challenge the argument that inadvertent wars are unlikely in bipolarity. As opposed to the preemptive Israeli strike in 1967, the Lebanon war was partly a preventive war initiated by Israel against the long-term threat posed by the rising power of the Palestinian Liberation Organization (PLO) in Lebanon. Another part of the motivation was more aggressive: the war was initiated by some Israeli leaders to establish a "new order" in Lebanon by bringing to power pro-Israeli Maronite elements that would sign a peace treaty with Israel and expel the PLO and Syrian forces from Lebanese territory. Prime Minister Begin stated that this was a "war by choice" on the part of Israel, in contrast to some other Arab-Israeli wars that were wars of "no choice" for Israel (cited in Yariv 1985, 9).[34]

### Nuclear Bipolarity: Low Likelihood of Both Intended and Inadvertent Wars

*Nuclear Weapons and the Obsolescence of Intended Wars in the Postwar Era*

The record of the postwar era serves to confirm that the nuclear revolution has transformed the traditional attitude of the great powers toward intended war as a major rational means of statecraft. There has been a convergence of positions on this question on the part of political leaders in both Washington and Moscow. Soviet leaders told their Chinese counterparts in 1963 that "The atomic bomb does not observe the class principle" (cited in Zimmerman 1969, 5, 255–59). A year later, Lyndon Johnson stated, "There is no real comparison between the attitudes of most of the world's governments today and twenty-five years ago on the role of warfare as an instrument of national policy. War is obsolete, obsolete because there can be no winner" (cited in Osgood and Tucker 1967, 15).

Not only did aggressive wars become unthinkable between the superpowers in the nuclear era (Lebow 1987, 23, especially n. 9), but the other type of motivation for intended wars—preventive wars—became much less likely than in the conventional era (Levy 1987). Thus, Truman and Eisenhower consistently rejected the option of a preventive war against the Soviet Union despite the overwhelming U.S. nuclear superiority at the time.[35] Indeed, the two expectations of hegemonic theories concerning a growing likelihood of intended wars as a result of changes in the relative balance of great power military capabilities toward greater parity (aggressive war by the rising challenger or a preventive war by the declining hegemon)[36] were not fulfilled because of the restraining presence of MAD. On the one hand, the relatively declining military hegemon (the United States) did not initiate a preventive war because of Soviet deterrence vis-à-vis Europe as well as the U.S. homeland.[37] On the other hand, the growing military (strategic and power projection) capabilities of the rising challenger in the late 1960s and 1970s did not lead even a supposedly revisionist state such as the USSR to initiate a military adventure under the emerging full-blown MAD of that period.[38] Indeed, one of the major effects of MAD is that nuclear weapons as an "absolute weapon" (Brodie 1946) make the precise military balance much less relevant than in the conventional era; thus, in contrast to the prenuclear age, changes in the relative military equation in the direction of parity do not bring about major hegemonic wars (which are intended wars).

*Bipolarity, the Avoidance of an Inadvertent War, and the Tacit Rules for Crisis Management*

The absence of an inadvertent war between the superpowers in the Cold War era confirms the proposition about the effects of bipolarity on crisis management in that it was not a coincidence or just the result of luck but rather reflected the emergence of mutual restraint and tacit rules. Thus, in contrast to the pre–World War II failures of crisis management that resulted in inadvertent wars, the superpowers continuously succeeded in managing crises during the postwar era. This successful crisis management took place in spite of the prevalence in the postwar era of some of the major unit-level factors that could conceivably have had especially destabilizing effects on great power crisis management and could have brought about misperceptions and miscalculations and especially loss of control. These factors include the ideological antagonism in the postwar era; control over the military could be problematic; and the growing domestic pressures in the policy-making process of democratic states.

The ideological antagonism in the postwar era, which was more intense than in previous eras, could generate misperceptions and misunderstandings due to the different outlooks of the superpowers. These misperceptions could lead to an overestimation of hostility beyond what is warranted by real events and intentions[39]—especially in crisis situations (cf. Frei 1983, 114), increase the decision makers' tendency to overreaction, and create difficulties for managing crises. Another potentially destabilizing influence of ideological antagonism was its ability to arouse domestic public opinion and thus increase the risk of loss of control by decision makers over policy making in crises. Furthermore, the keen ideological competition between the United States and the Soviet Union during the Cold War led to the perceived importance of the gain or loss of smaller allies (cf. Holsti, Hopmann, and Sullivan 1973, 15–16; Kahler 1979–80, 384), even if objectively they were not significant for the global balance of power. This competition could presumably make it more difficult for the superpowers to control the actions of allies than in earlier, less ideological periods (especially before World War I). The great danger was that as a result, the patrons might have inadvertently become entrapped in one of the numerous local wars in the Third World (Shoemaker and Spanier 1984, 70–78), especially in a conflict-ridden but critically important region such as the Middle East.

Control over the military, especially in times of crisis, could be problematic in the postwar era (see Lebow 1987, chap. 3) because of the vast expansion, growing complexity, and worldwide deployment of the military. Another type of potential complication was related to the frequent use of short-of-war tactics for diplomatic signaling in crises in the postwar period, which increased the likelihood of loss of control by the decision makers over their military machines.

The growing domestic pressures of legislatures, public opinion, the mass media, and interest groups in the foreign policy-making process of democratic states (cf. Craig and George 1983, chaps. 5, 8) could complicate the American policymaker's task of balancing the demonstration of resolve with self-restraint in times of crisis and especially slowing down or freezing a given crisis, which, according to Craig and George (1983, 215) and George (1984a), constitutes an important requirement for crisis management. More specifically, the growing influence of public opinion on foreign policy in the postwar era was expected to undermine crisis management in two opposite ways: Hawkish or nationalist publics might impel state leaders to behave recklessly. On the other hand, the fear of war, especially nuclear war, could lead to public calls for concessions, and such pressures could impel policymakers to underreact by appeasing the adversary (like in the interwar era). Domestic support for small allies, especially in the pluralist U.S. system, could also make it more difficult to handle the task of controlling the reckless conduct of clients.

The loss of control over small allies and the military, as well as misperceptions and reduced autonomy vis-à-vis domestic public opinion, could result in unintended escalation. Thus, during the Cold War, such unit-level factors should have led us to expect severe problems in superpower crisis management. Yet despite the intensity of U.S.-Soviet rivalry and the common image of the conflictual nature of their relations, Moscow and Washington tacitly cooperated in managing crises and in terminating regional wars. Indeed, such a contradiction between a range of unit-level influences and postwar crisis patterns reinforces our confidence that structural factors best explain these unintended patterns. The potential obstacles to successful crisis management were overridden by the simplicity and clarity of the bipolar setting, which allowed the superpowers to formulate and follow tacit rules and prevent escalation in crises in spite of the domestic difficulties. Following a brief review of the tacit rules for crisis management, I discuss how the international structure directly discouraged misperceptions, facilitated control over small allies, and, more indirectly, conditioned and moderated the destabilizing effects of the unit-level constraints on crisis management.

**The Tacit Rules**

A growing number of students of U.S.-Soviet relations have reported their findings concerning the emergence during the Cold War period of "tacit rules of superpower competition" (Allison and Williams 1990, 249–57), "tacit norms" or "understandings" (George 1990, 112–13), "rules of prudence in U.S.-Soviet relations" (George, Farley, and Dallin 1988, 583–85), "unspoken rules" (Keal 1983), or the "implicit rules of the superpower game" (Gaddis 1986, 132–40; see also Vasquez 1991).

What is common to all these rules, however, is that they apply foremost to crisis situations and that they are essentially equivalent to "patterns of restraint" for regulating the use of force (George, with others, 1983, 377–78). Thus, the tacit rules accord well with the proposition regarding the resolute yet cautious behavior of the superpowers in crises so long as the restraining effects of bipolarity are in place. The combination of resolve (in defense of one's important interests) and caution (toward the other's important stakes) should lead us to expect that the substantive content of the rules will reflect the relative balance of interests of the superpowers in different regions,[40] even if the legitimacy of these balances is recognized only in times of crisis and only tacitly. Indeed, generally speaking, one may identify three types of rules that existed in the Cold War era, according to the superpowers' interests and degrees of involvement in different regions.

The first type of rules is respect for each other's sphere of influence (Allison and Williams 1990, 250–51; Gaddis 1986, 133; Keal 1983). Indeed, George observes that the superpowers showed great restraint in their policies and actions toward areas of vital interest to the other superpower (George, Farley, and Dallin 1988, 585). Whereas this restraint was relatively simple in areas with high-interest asymmetry favoring one of the superpowers, that is, Central America and Eastern Europe (George 1990, 108–9), the other two types of rules went even further than that.

The second type of rules is asymmetrical intervention outside the spheres of influence. If one party became militarily involved in a regional conflict, the adversary tended to remain on the sidelines (Allison and Williams 1990, 251). Examples included Vietnam, Korea, and Afghanistan. Yet the most complex were rules of a third kind.

In regional conflicts in which both superpowers had important interests and close allies but they disagreed on their balance of interests, they tacitly cooperated in managing crises and terminating local wars according to certain implicit rules. The Middle East, especially the relatively early termination of Arab-Israeli wars, constituted the foremost example of the operation of the tacit rules regulating superpower interventions in this kind of conflict (these rules are discussed in chap. 5).[41] These tacit understandings were informed by the balance of stakes, even if they held only in times of crisis.

In the next section, I show that the explanation of all these types of rules is structural, by suggesting that bipolarity controlled the destabilizing effects of unit-level factors that could obstruct crisis management in the postwar era (ideology, bureaucratic politics, and domestic politics).

## The Stabilizing Effects of Bipolarity on Domestic Constraints

### *Control over the Military*

Political control over military operations was much tighter in the postwar era than in earlier periods (George 1991, 15–16),[42] as was shown in major Cold War crises such as the tense 1961 Berlin crisis (Betts 1977, 146), the Quemoy-

Matsu crisis of 1958 (Eisenhower 1965, 299 n.), and Middle East crises (see chap. 5). Sometimes the political control over the military may even have been too tight.[43] Analysts have also criticized the best-known account of loss of control over the military during the postwar era, namely, Allison's (1971, 129–30) account of the Cuban Missile Crisis (especially regarding the loss of presidential control over the navy).[44]

Indeed, one study that examines the interaction of military forces in four Cold War crises concludes that crises can be politically controlled (Bouchard 1991). Yet as a review of the book suggests, bipolarity was the critical factor that made possible such control because of its relative simplicity and stability: "the situation grows more complex as the number of powers involved in a crisis increases, which makes maintenance of political control more difficult" (Viotti 1992, 837). Thus, the lack of inadvertent escalation of the short-of-war options used by the superpowers in times of crisis was made possible, or at least easier, by the relatively simple and clear-cut bipolar structure.

*Domestic Constraints and International Responsibilities*

In the case of Washington, a particular difficulty for the emergence of consistent superpower rules lay in the fragmented and incoherent nature of American foreign policy because of the multiplicity of domestic influences on the process of its formulation (Nye 1984). Traditional U.S. isolationist inclinations vis-à-vis Europe (such as during the pre–World War II era, see Schneider 1984, 12) could encourage underreaction and thus pose a problem for the evolution of persistent and effective rules for regulating the use of force in crises.

Yet the international structure conditions the effects of domestic constraints on crisis management. Thus, the transformation of the U.S. public's attitude from isolationism to support for international engagement was related to the transition from multipolarity with its diffusion of threats and tendency of buck-passing to bipolarity with its clarity of threats and responsibilities, as became clear in the early Cold War crises (see Gaddis 1982, 22–23; Oneal 1982).

The U.S. departure in the postwar era from its traditional isolationist approach (especially vis-à-vis Europe, the Middle East, and some other parts of the Third World) cannot be explained by nuclear weapons. By themselves, nuclear weapons could encourage a policy of disengagement, both because of the enormous costs in case of escalation as a result of the global engagement and the attendant public fear of a nuclear war, and the supposed decline in the value of control over territory and of overseas bases in the age of long-range missiles and MAD (see Mueller 1989; Wagner 1993). Rather, the pursuit of an active international engagement and the ability to mobilize domestic support for such a policy is explained by the focused and clear-cut nature of the major threat in bipolarity and the strong need to contain it[45] to maintain the global balance of power and prevent Soviet hegemony. The United States willy-nilly had no choice but to lead the West and its allies, because in bipolarity it could not pass the buck to other powers if it wanted the USSR to be contained.[46] This bipolar structure helped to address the collective goods problem and brought about a clarity of responsibility for the defense of the status quo.

*Domestic Temptations and International Restraints*
However, in the postwar era there were also powerful domestic incentives and interests in favor of a hard-line approach toward the other superpower. In addition to the intense ideological rivalry between the superpowers, the "scapegoat theory,"[47] for example, would lead us to expect that the Kremlin's insecurity (Gaddis 1986, 118–19) and the serious domestic problems of at least some U.S. presidents (Lebow 1981) could produce domestic incentives for aggressive policy toward the other superpower.

Yet the presence of a clear-cut countervailing force guaranteed that politicians facing domestic vulnerability would not be tempted to manipulate the popular support of aggressive foreign policy to boost their own domestic standing and pursue adventurous conduct abroad,[48] at least not beyond those red lines that could trigger inadvertent escalation to the global level.[49]

Many critics of U.S. foreign policy argued, and not without justification, that the United States occasionally overreacted, most notably with regard to Vietnam. However, that did not happen in major bipolar crises. Thus, the active engagement by Washington did not become, on the whole, an aggressive or reckless policy of trying to change the status quo by violent means. That it did not can be explained, at least partly, by the certainty of response by the countervailing force of the Soviet Union. However assertive the declarations of U.S. leaders in normal times, in times of crisis they belied their own words and behaved cautiously, notably with regard to rollback in Eastern Europe, which was proclaimed by Dulles but never implemented, including in the Hungarian uprising of 1956. Even if the United States was unable to explicitly recognize Eastern Europe as a Soviet sphere of influence because of ideological and domestic constraints, its behavior in times of crisis implied such a recognition. There was a somewhat similar gap between Soviet revolutionary ideological tenets and its cautious crisis behavior, which also implied a tacit recognition of the U.S. sphere of influence in the Western hemisphere.[50]

Indeed, the United States was constrained by the bipolar structure even before the major Soviet military buildup in the 1960s and 1970s (see Nye 1990, 97–104, and the references he cites), while, on the other hand, the Soviets continued to be restrained by systemic factors after their buildup (see chap. 5). Thus, in a bipolar world, the growing military capabilities of even a supposedly revolutionary state would not bring that state to behave recklessly in times of crisis, especially where important interests of the other superpower are involved, although it might become more assertive in noncrisis periods or where peripheral interests are engaged. Thus, the likelihood of miscalculated escalation and a resultant inadvertent war are low so long as the structure remains bipolar.

Indeed, the clarity and certainty of the postwar era led to resolute caution in times of crisis in accordance with certain tacit rules. The rules evolved as a result of the stabilization of mutual expectations about the opponent's response or, at least, about a range of likely reactions to certain steps; this stabilization minimized the probability of an inadvertent escalation. Substantively, the rules reflected the balance of superpower interests in relation to the status quo and to spheres of influence, despite the opposition to these same ideas in noncrisis situations. The opposition was derived, in turn, from unit-level elements within both superpowers (such as domestic politics and ideology). But in times of crisis, the influence of these unit-level factors was overshadowed by the stabilizing and clarifying effects of the bipolar structure.

## The Direct Effects of the Bipolar Structure

In addition to stabilizing the detrimental effects of unit-level factors on crisis management, the attributes of bipolarity directly affected the level of misperceptions and the degree of control over allies in the Cold War era.

### *Stress and Misperceptions*

The presence of nuclear weapons tremendously increased the significance of the values at stake in superpower confrontations. As a result, the theory of crisis-induced stress would lead us to expect greater cognitive and emotional impediments to crisis management in nuclear crises than in conventional ones. Yet superpower crisis management (as indicated by the tacit rules) was more successful, and decision makers behaved more rationally in U.S.-Soviet crises than in many of both prewar crises and nonsuperpower postwar crises. Thus, few adverse consequences of crisis-induced stress were found in studies of the most important Cold War crises, including U.S. policymaking during the Berlin blockade of 1948–49 (Oneal 1982; Shlaim 1983); Soviet decision making in the two Berlin crises (Adomeit 1982); the U.S. decision to intervene in Korea (Paige 1968, 81–93, 292); U.S. decision making during the Middle East crises of 1958, 1970, and 1973 (Dowty 1984); and in the Cuban Missile Crisis (Blight 1992).[51] In contrast, the psychological effects of crisis-induced stress adversely influenced decision making in World War I and also in nonsuperpower postwar crises.[52] If we can safely assume that U.S. and Soviet leaders were not necessarily more rational or smarter than other leaders, we must consider that a critical factor was the simplifying and clarifying effects of the bipolar structure. Thus, bipolarity helped to clarify the balance of superpower interests. It also raised the certainty of response by the countervailing force of the other superpower to any attempts to go beyond the red lines.

*Control over Allies*

The dominance of the structural logic in crisis settings made it possible to control allies that tended to be unruly in normal times because of the asymmetric interdependence between the superpowers and their allies in bipolarity (Midlarsky 1991). Such control took place despite the Cold War and decolonization, which should supposedly have complicated superpower control over their small allies. Thus, the Soviets maintained a tight control over the Cubans and the East Germans during the two most dangerous postwar crises—the Cuban Missile Crisis (Midlarsky 1991, 106) and the 1961 Berlin crisis (Williams 1976, 130–31). Moscow also moderated Chinese behavior at the time of the 1958 Quemoy crisis by confining its support to the defense of the mainland rather than extending it to a Chinese invasion of the offshore islands or Formosa (Snyder and Diesing 1977, 444; Williams 1976, 133). The Kremlin has also withheld its support from Third World allies when the latter challenged the status quo and behaved as aggressors according to the tacit rules of the game (Karsh 1985; see chap. 5). Washington, for its part, exercised effective pressures during crises not only on small allies such as Taiwan (in 1955 and 1958) but also on two of its major postwar allies, Great Britain and France, which it succeeded in restraining in the 1956 Suez crisis (see Midlarsky 1991, 107; Snyder and Diesing 1977, 441–45; Waltz 1964, 900; see also chap. 5). Although West German interests were directly engaged, the United States also played the leading role in the Western alliance in the Berlin crises[53] as well as in the more direct superpower confrontation in Cuba. An especially intriguing case is Israel, because while the United States frequently failed to control Israeli foreign policy behavior in noncrisis situations, it was much more successful in times of Arab-Israeli wars that threatened to escalate to the superpower level (see chaps. 5 and 6). Thus, whatever the situation in normal times, in crises the superpowers preferred the avoidance of war over their commitments to allies. Control over allies in postwar crises was thus more effective than in earlier multipolar crises.

## Conclusions

This chapter has advanced the proposition that whereas intended wars were prevented during the Cold War by nuclear arms, these arms could not prevent an inadvertent war. Indeed, such a war could have erupted because of the nature of the unit-level factors discussed in this chapter, misperceived changes in the balance of forces, entanglement in allies' local wars, and, above all, miscalculations and loss of control in times of crises resulting from all these factors. Yet because of its clarity and simplicity, bipolarity helped to prevent an unintended war by facilitating the evolution of tacit rules for crisis management and the termination of local wars and by reducing the destabilizing effects of the unit-level factors. In chapter 5, I further examine these propositions with regard to superpower crises in the Middle East during the Cold War.

Chapter 4

# Explaining the Emergence and the Form of Great Power Concerts

The purpose of this chapter is to provide a theoretical analysis of the conditions affecting the emergence of a great power concert, and to gain a better understanding of this phenomenon as it was presented in one of the puzzles of chapter 2. In contrast to some important theoretical works that have underlined the role of various systemic factors in the formation of a concert (see Jervis 1985; Weber 1990; see also Mandelbaum 1988, chap. 1; Schroeder 1986), and in accordance with the model presented in chapter 2, I argue that it is unit-level factors that make the difference with regard to great power concerts. In this chapter, I develop the general model of the book with regard to concerts and also provide historical illustrations of the influence of the explanatory factors on the emergence or nonemergence of concerts. The only historical case of a great power concert to date is the nineteenth-century European Concert.[1] I compare this period and the Cold War, when a great power concert manifestly did not take place; thus, I also address the last of the four puzzles of chapter 2.

The chapter has four sections. In the first one, I define a concert and distinguish it from a condominium. In the second section, I examine the effects of three alternative types of factors on the emergence of great power concerts. First, drawing on the analysis in chapter 2, I suggest that system polarity is indeterminate with regard to the formation of a concert. Second, I analyze the effects of relative capabilities and, more specifically, the proposition that inferior or vulnerable powers have a greater inclination to collaborate with other great powers than superior or more secure ones. With regard to the emergence of concerts, such structural factors are at best insufficient and superseded by unit-level factors. Indeed, these are the third type of factors to be examined, and the analysis suggests that they are the major elements that affect the emergence of a durable concert. In accordance with the argument some other scholars have advanced (see, most notably, Kupchan and Kupchan 1991), I maintain that the more similar the great powers (culturally and ideologically) and the greater their willingness to legitimize the status quo (or peaceful change) and the coequal status of the other powers, the greater the feasibility for the emergence of a concert. Yet the analysis highlights another necessary factor neglected by previous studies. Namely, common fears of revolutions or inadvertent wars, based on cognitive and ideological factors, also have to be shared by all the great powers for a concert to be formed. The combination of the two propositions explains why a concert necessarily emerged in the post-Napoleonic era in Europe but neither earlier nor later. More precisely, great power similarity and moderation differentiates the Concert from later periods (probably apart from the post–Cold War era), whereas the absence of common fears accounts for the nonemergence of a concert in an earlier period such as the eighteenth century.

In the third section, I specify the cognitive background to these conditions for the emergence of concerts, namely the decision makers' images of the following three elements: the dynamics of international politics, the relations between global politics and regional conflicts, and the image of the opponent.

In this chapter, I also address the form of the great power concert with regard to small states and distinguish between the coercive and the accommodative forms. In the fourth section, I show that state attributes also influence the great power approach to the form of the concert, in particular, the readiness of great powers to engage in a coercive form of concert (termed *condominium*). On the whole, the weaker the domestic constraints on foreign policy, the greater the ability to take part in a condominium; more specifically, pluralist powers are both less willing and less able than centralist ones to embark on a condominium that might involve a joint coercion of small states and are rather more inclined toward an accommodative approach.

**Defining a Concert and a Condominium**

A concert is an international institution or a security regime for high-level diplomatic collaboration among all the great powers of the day.[2]

It is a relatively durable, wide-scope, multi-issue, and institutionalized framework of cooperation. This cooperation is the result of a convergence of long-term, stable, and deliberate collaborative approaches or strategies on the part of the great powers. This conception of a concert should be distinguished from single-issue concerted diplomacy,[3] and multi-issue but lower-level and less institutionalized forms of great power diplomatic cooperation such as détente and entente.[4] All these forms of great power cooperation are influenced by basically the same unit-level factors. However, as an especially high-level and demanding form of cooperation, a concert requires the presence of all these factors in a considerably higher degree. Another major distinction should be made between a concert, which includes all the great powers in the international system, and an alliance of several great powers balancing against others.[5]

With regard to the nature of great power diplomatic cooperation in a concert, theoretical work on concerts[6] has failed to define the term clearly enough, especially regarding two critical differentiations betwen types of collaboration—between a passive-negative and an active-affirmative conception of collaboration—and between two forms of affirmative collaboration—accommodative and coercive (which parallels the distinction between a concert and a condominium).

Thus, Jervis, a leading theorist of concerts, does not make clear whether the major criterion for defining the post-Napoleonic era as a concert and as an era of an "unusually high and self-conscious level of cooperation" (1985, 59) relates to war avoidance among the great powers, to crisis prevention, to generally restrained behavior, or to joint diplomacy, the settlement of disputes, and comanagement of the international system. The terms in which Jervis characterizes the Concert are too vague and ambiguous for a meaningful comparison with the postwar era. Thus, Jervis asserts that in the post-Napoleonic age, states showed self-restraint and "made more concessions than they needed to" (1983, 179); he cites Elrod's observation that there were several examples "of states forgoing gains which they could probably have gotten" (1976, 168). But Jervis leaves open the question of how one can test the cases in which states forgo gains "which they could probably have gotten" or how one can measure self-restraint and show that states "made more concessions than they needed to" (1983, 179).

More importantly, Jervis (1983, 1985) overlooks a major element of a great power concert. The nineteenth-century Concert was not only a matter of restraint in the relations among the great powers but also of conscious cooperation of an exclusive great power club in managing international conflicts in general. Indeed, these are the two major conceptions or functions of a concert, though they are intertwined rather than mutually exclusive. Most of the literature on the nineteenth-century Concert refers, at least implicitly, to both functions but does not explicitly distinguish between them. The objectives of the two functions are, moreover, similar: to guarantee stability, to preserve the status quo, to prevent wars among the great powers, and to maintain the balance of power by preventing unilateral attempts at domination by aspiring hegemons. Yet it is important to make a conceptual differentiation between the two.

One conception focuses on the relations among the big powers themselves, specifically the mutual self-restraint that is characteristic of a concert.[7] Such relations dramatically depart from the power politics conception of world politics. Instead of pursuing only selfish goals, the major actors also define their own interests, to some degree, in terms of a larger common good.

The other conception focuses on the great powers as the regulators of the international system, that is, it also stresses their relations with the lesser states in the system. In this conception, their comanagerial responsibilities for maintaining peace and stability and for resolving disputes are highlighted.[8]

In terms of ideal types, one can envision that in the former conception, each of the big powers still behaves as an individual actor, albeit in greater moderation than is usually the case in international politics. An illustration might be arms control among the great powers. By contrast, in the latter conception, the great powers act together as equal members of a "board of directors" that consults and decides on great international questions. Obviously, in both formulations, third states are in the background; yet there are some differences. In the first perspective, which is more passive and negative, the great power actors may avoid unilateral gains in general, including in smaller countries, without necessarily reaching agreements and coordinating their actions with the other powers. The second role is more active and affirmative and thus more demanding: the actors consult and exchange views on problems that involve lesser states; they may also coordinate joint actions to solve these problems diplomatically or even, if warranted, by collective coercive measures. Hence, in this conception the great powers' policing and managerial role is more salient.

In fulfilling this function, a concert attempts to resolve multilaterally major conflicts both among the great powers themselves and among third parties and thereby makes possible peaceful change (see Clark 1989, 121, 126–27; Hinsley 1963, 225). Indeed, in a concert, in Bull's formulation, the great powers "join forces in promoting common policies throughout the international system as a whole" (1977, 225). To this end, the great powers hold regular discussions for defining common objectives and determining how best to achieve them (Bull 1977, 227). The emphasis in a concert is on collective consultation, decision making, and action with respect to the diplomatic agenda.[9]

In accordance with the distinction between types of collaboration in chapter 1 and the model in chapter 2, the focus of this chapter is on the second, affirmative function or dimension of a concert, manifested in joint action or cooperation in regional conflict resolution. Indeed, while a negative-avoidance type of cooperation may be achieved tacitly and spontaneously, the affirmative type is what distinguishes and characterizes the ideal type of deliberate, conscious cooperation.

One must also differentiate between two major forms of affirmative collaboration in a concert toward small states: accommodative or coercive. The accommodative mode of great power cooperation emphasizes negotiated multilateral diplomacy for regional conflict resolution; the local actors actively participate in the negotiating process and can voice their concerns and bargain among themselves and with the great powers. The talks between the great powers and the small actors tend to be based on persuasion and characterized by compromise and give-and-take rather than sheer diktat by the big powers to the smaller states. Indeed, accommodative diplomacy in a concert attempts to advance peace and stability while minimizing the encroachment on the local states' sovereignty. In contrast, in the coercive[10] mode of collaboration in a concert, great powers jointly impose some sort of an international order.[11] A coercive great power concert may be termed condominium. In the context of regional conflict resolution, a condominium refers to a collusive definition of great power interests, geared toward jointly imposing on weaker states terms for peaceful regional settlement that the great powers have worked out on their own (Breslauer 1983b, 330; see also George, Farley, and Dallin 1988, 594). Another manifestation of a great power condominium is an agreed division of certain areas into spheres of influence of the great powers.

Was the post-Napoleonic Concert of Europe an accommodative kind of collaboration or a condominium (that is, joint coercion)? Opinions vary;[12] the Concert was probably, on balance, an amalgam of these types that incorporated a mixture of coercion and persuasion by the Big Five (Britain, France, Prussia, Russia, and Austria) toward the small states over matters that concerned them. The coercive element included agreed divisions of some areas into spheres of influence (Lauren 1983, 43–46). Moreover, there were also divisions of opinion within the Concert concerning coercive collaboration.

**Explaining the Emergence of Great Power Concerts**

In the next sections, I advance and analyze several alternative factors that may affect the emergence of great power concerts, so as to assess their explanatory power. The first possible approach to the formation of concerts is structural theory. However, in accordance with the model of the book, in the next section, I address the reasons for the limited explanatory power of structural theory with regard to the emergence of great power concerts, beyond pointing out some important constraints on their formation. So the explanation of their emergence depends, in the final analysis, on nonsystemic factors.

The Limitations of Structural Theory regarding the
Formation of Great Power Concerts

Drawing on the analysis in chapter 2, there are three main theoretical reasons for the limited explanatory power of structural theory with regard to the emergence of concerts.

*Systemic Constraints*
Structural theory highlights the constraints on concerted action of all the great powers of the day. In accordance with balance-of-power theory, states, especially the great powers, are expected to compete and balance each other (Walt 1987; Waltz 1979) rather than concert their diplomacy or work together at the

expense of smaller states. Closely related is the structural expectation that at the end of major wars, war-winning coalitions will break down (Waltz 1979, 126). Although this expectation is useful for explaining why concerts have been a relatively rare historical phenomenon (Holbraad 1971, 4–10), in cases in which a concert has emerged, it creates an anomaly for structural theory and a need to turn to nonstructural factors for explanation.

## The Ambiguity of the Neorealist Analysis of Polarity and Cooperation

Beyond the general skepticism about the feasibility of enduring concerts, there is an indeterminacy in neorealist analysis. Indeed, despite the crucial importance that structural theory attributes to the effects of polarity on international outcomes, it is not clear from that literature whether one should expect more great power cooperation in bipolarity or multipolarity. These discrepancies attest to the indeterminacy and the consequent irrelevance of polarity to the emergence of concerts.

## Levels of Analysis and Types of Cooperation

Although structural theory is useful for explaining certain types of cooperation (notably, tacit crisis management), unit-level factors play a critical role in affecting the type of cooperation that concerns us here—deliberate cooperation for conflict resolution.

Accordingly, in the following sections, I analyze other factors that may affect the inclination of great powers to form or join a concert.

## Relative Capabilities, the Degree of Vulnerability, and the Choice of Unilateral versus Multilateral Path

Before turning to unit-level factors, another kind of power-related explanation of the emergence of concerts must be addressed, namely the relative capabilities of the great powers. Even between great powers that are roughly equal in overall capabilities, there may be differences in resources in certain issue areas or regions. We may thus distinguish between relatively superior and inferior powers. Great powers may also be more or less vulnerable based on geopolitical considerations. In cases of such inequality in great power capabilities and vulnerability, there might be differences between the superior and the inferior or the more and less vulnerable powers with regard to the inclination to pursue concerted diplomacy or to take part in a concert.

> *Proposition 1:* All other things being equal, the dominant great power tends to exclude the other powers from international diplomacy in the regions or issues involved and prefers unilateral management, believing

that its resources enable it to play the role of an exclusive broker. In contrast, the weaker powers prefer a multilateral framework in which they are able to take part alongside the leading power in the management of regional problems. Their inclusion also conveys a recognition on the part of the dominant power of their equal great power status, at least on the issues involved. As for the factor of vulnerability, the less vulnerable power has less incentive to take part in concerted efforts to resolve local conflicts, being less threatened and less affected by them. It is more likely to prefer noninvolvement in the regional conflict.

The historical record of two different periods (the post-Napoleonic era and the post-1945 era) seems to accord with this proposition. Thus, in the Concert era, Great Britain was less in favor of a tight and centralized Concert system than any of the other post-Napoleonic Concert members.[13] For instance, Britain opposed joint intervention by the Concert in Spain in 1820, in Italy in 1820–21, and in Greece in 1821 (see Hinsley 1963, 204). By contrast, Metternich and Czar Alexander of Russia sought to elevate the Concert into an international enforcement agency that would preserve the order created in Vienna in both its domestic and international aspects (Hoffmann 1965, 103). The maintenance of the status quo would be enforced by the automatic intervention of all the great powers in the politics of any country in which there was a threat to the established order (Albrecht-Carrie 1968, 10–11; Craig and George 1983, 31; Hinsley 1963, 201), although such intervention would twist the independence, territorial integrity, and free consent of small powers (Hoffmann 1965, 105, 107).

Britain opposed such attempts by the Eastern powers (Austria, Russia, and Prussia) and called for the functioning of the Concert only as a framework of political consultation (Hinsley 1963, 204; Rosecrance 1963, 61). Since the Eastern powers were not dissuaded from collective meddling in the domestic politics of lesser countries, the British had to reduce the level of their participation in the Concert from the 1820s onward (Craig and George 1983, 32; Hinsley 1963, 203–12; Mandelbaum 1988, 22–23), although they continued to contribute to the Concert's joint management of international affairs, notably regarding the Eastern question.

One possible explanation for the difference in attitude between the continental powers and Great Britain with regard to the question of joint interventions in Europe is that the British were the most powerful and especially the least vulnerable actor in this era of Pax Britannica. They could afford to resist a tight Concert system in Europe because they were more secure than the continental powers, owing to the relative insularity of an island and to the British Fleet. Thus, they were less threatened by uprisings in small continental states than the other powers.

This kind of explanation seems to hold even more in the case of the postwar superpowers. In the postwar era, the United States was even more forceful than Great Britain in resisting occasional Soviet offers for cooperation, which according to some observers amounted to no less than a superpower concert or a condominium (see Kissinger 1979 and 1982; Sestanovich 1987, 18; see also George 1980a; George, with others, 1983, chaps. 2 and 5).[14] At different times the Soviets showed interest in a division of key regions into spheres of influence (especially under Stalin), in multilateral diplomacy for conflict resolution in a number of regions (see George, with others, 1983, chaps. 2, 5; MacFarlane 1987b; Simes 1986, 154–55) such as the Middle East (see chap. 6), and in joint intervention to impose peace (Adomeit 1973, 37), especially in situations involving third nuclear states such as China (Kissinger 1982, 275). Moscow also sought a formally recognized, equal superpower status (Jonsson 1984, 24–25), but on the whole, the United States rejected such demands (Calleo 1987, 17).

The Soviet Union's strategic nuclear inferiority during the first two decades of the postwar era, its persistent economic-technological disadvantages versus the West (see Kennedy 1987, 488-514; see especially Nye 1990, 115–30), and a greater degree of vulnerability compared to America[15] remind us of the continental powers in the nineteenth-century Concert and their desire for a condominium because of their higher degree of vulnerability compared to Great Britain. In fact, the Soviet offers of cooperation may be traced to relative Soviet weakness or vulnerability in various periods and regions. At the same time, there is a certain similarity between the two hegemons in their rejection of offers of concert or condominium and instead their supposed preference for leading a Pax Britannica and a Pax Americana, respectively.[16] The U.S. disinclination to cooperate with the Soviet Union was especially apparent in the Middle East. Because the United States has enjoyed superior diplomatic and economic resources in that area, it was able to play the unilateral role of an honest broker and to exclude the Soviets from the international diplomacy of such an important region (see chap. 6). To sum up, while the main factor in the British disinclination to cooperate with the continental powers in Europe was its lesser vulnerability, the parallel factor in the American disinclination, notably in the Middle East, was its relative superiority.

However, the explanation based on relative capabilities has important limitations. According to its logic, a concert should not emerge at all between relatively superior-inferior and more-less vulnerable powers. The superior power would prefer to manage local conflicts on its own, while the less vulnerable power may prefer not to be involved in the region at all. In both cases, they are not inclined to cooperative efforts with other great powers. Yet in spite of Britain's reservations and lesser vulnerability, it did participate in the European Concert after the 1820s, even if at a lower level than the continental powers. As we will discuss in the Conclusions, the much greater willingness of the United States to cooperate in conflict resolution with the Soviet Union since the late 1980s can be best explained by changes in unit-level factors rather than in relative capabilities. The critical importance of unit-level factors, rather than of relative capabilities, is also suggested by the U.S. inclination to cooperate with its weaker democratic allies (notably, the Europeans and the Japanese) in the postwar international political economic regimes and especially its apparent preference for collaboration with them in multilateral enterprises in the post–Cold War era, that is, even after the disappearance of the common Soviet threat.[17] A disinclination to cooperate on the part of the dominant power may be overridden or superseded by more critical unit-level factors that positively affect its willingness to join a concert.

On the other hand, although a willingness to collaborate on the part of an inferior power can be helpful, it is insufficient for the emergence of a concert so long as it is based on weakness as the major motive for cooperation. However, the reason is not only that the dominant power will reject the concert due to its superior capabilities but also that an inclination based on inferiority in capabilities is insufficient to overcome mutual distrust among rival great powers under anarchy and to create a positive "image of the opponent."[18] Yet mutual trust and such a positive image, which are necessary for the formation of a concert, are unlikely to last for an extended period in the absence of unit-level elements such as moderation and similarity. As noted, a concert constitutes a relatively durable, institutionalized, and long-term framework of collaboration, which takes place across regions and issues. The inclination of an inferior power to collaborate, on the other hand, tends to be confined to a specific issue or region where it is in fact relatively weak. Such an inclination is based on immediate and specific self-interests and does not amount to a willingness to pursue a general, durable collaborative strategy. It also lacks the normative component that is necessary for the great powers to define their interests, at least to a certain extent, in terms of a larger common good. Accordingly, many Western policymakers and observers have distrusted general Soviet intentions in spite of its willingness to pursue concerted diplomacy in specific issues and regions. In addition, a large part of the differences in attitude between Britain and the Eastern Concert powers, as well as between the United States and the Soviet Union, had to do not with a willingness or a disinclination to collaborate at all but rather with the form of this prospective cooperation. Such differences are also explained by unit-level factors.

## Unit-Level Factors and Great Power Concerts

The severe limitations of power-related explanations (whether based on polarity or relative capabilities) establish the primacy of unit-level factors for explaining the emergence of great power concerts. Being an especially high-level and demanding form of affirmative cooperation, concerts require very restrictive unit-level conditions. Thus, a durable concert can take place only if two types of unit-level factors are present: positive elements—what all the participants have in common—and negative elements—what all the participants wish to avoid. The positive components involve ideological similarity and moderation that are, in fact, noted by many students of great power concerts (see Kupchan and Kupchan 1991, and the sources they cite). This book adds to this scholarly consensus the equally necessary negative component: common fears of revolution or of inadvertent escalation, which derive from cognitive and ideological factors.

These combined factors produce converging cooperative orientations and are strong enough to override the disinclination of a great power to cooperate based on its superior resources or lesser vulnerability. These converging inclinations enable the great powers to establish an institutionalized framework for high-level cooperation, based on common principles, norms, and rules. On the whole, the positive elements differentiate the European Concert from later periods, at least until the end of the Cold War, whereas the negative factors distinguish it from earlier eras because of the lessons that the Concert statesmen learned from the French Revolution and the Napoleonic wars. Thus, the combination of both these types of factors explains why a concert was formed between 1815 and 1854 and neither earlier nor later.

*Proposition 2:* Only powers that are similar (ideologically) and moderate (with regard to the acceptance of the status quo or of peaceful change as the only legitimate method for international change) can establish a concert.

*Similarity*
The social psychologist Deutsch summarizes his extensive research on conflict resolution by arguing that "Similarities in beliefs, attitudes, and values—i.e., in basic perspectives—are usually conducive to compatibility and hence to cooperative resolutions of conflict. . . . Dissimilarity in outlook often leads to antagonistic relations because it is experienced as a fundamental threat to one's conception of reality and thus to one's security." (1973, 374)[19]

In international relations theory, cognitive and Grotian variants of the regime literature focus on how common purposes and beliefs affect interstate cooperation in international political economy.[20] Even before the emergence of regime theory, the research of Deutsch and his colleagues (1957, 123–37) on international integration highlighted the idea that states with similar societal attributes are most likely to develop "security communities" in which there is a peaceful resolution of conflicts without resort to war. Such similarity involves not only political ideology and its institutional manifestations but also shared values, tradition, language, culture, and way of life.

Under the conditions of an extreme ideological dissimilarity, the great powers harbor negative images of each other as well as a severe distrust of the opponent, resulting in an unwillingness to cooperate with it. Similarity in societal attributes and ideological like-mindedness, on the other hand, may produce stable converging cooperative inclinations and even override the disinclination of a dominant power to cooperate with inferior ones.

Accordingly, Bull underlines the connection between great powers' shared vision of the international order and their ability to concert their diplomacy. The presence of such a common theory or ideology of world order, Bull asserts, made the Concert of Europe possible (1977, 226–27), whereas its absence in the post-1945 era has prevented the emergence of a U.S.-Soviet concert (1980, 439–42). Indeed, since the United States and the Soviet Union were both more different and more consciously ideological than most of the previous great powers, there has been widespread agreement among scholars that behind their "antithetical conceptions of national security lie antithetical ideological goals and images of reality which have given the U.S.-Soviet rivalry a dimension of righteous passion and paranoia that exceeds the psychological dynamics of traditional geopolitical rivalry" (Osgood 1981, 4).

At the same time, many authors cite ideological similarities as a major factor that united the Concert members despite their competitive inclinations in an anarchic system. Rosecrance explains the great power resort to collective diplomacy as motivated by "a new ideological harmony of self-conscious conservatism to assure the peace" (1963, 56).[21] Also important was the cultural homogeneity of the nineteenth-century European elites (Craig and George 1983, 245; Garrett 1976, 400; Gulick 1955, 5–10; Holbraad 1979, 144; Lauren 1983, 53), which stands in marked contrast to the absence of a common culture between the major powers in the postwar era (Bull 1977, 115, 316–17; Craig and George 1983, 165). More specifically, transnational ties between professional diplomats made communication easier during the Concert's multilateral conferences, even when there were conflicts of interests between the states they represented.[22]

*Moderation*

Nevertheless, cultural-ideological homogeneity in itself is insufficient for a great power concert. The members of a concert must also entertain moderate intentions, especially with respect to the status quo, whose legitimacy they accept; they must share the objective of maintaining the existing international order.[23] Although force may be used to preserve the status quo, changes must occur peacefully through multilateral diplomacy in which all the members participate.

Legitimacy, in turn, has two components: normative and cognitive.[24] The normative element refers to the desirability of the international order and to a consensus that its moral value is consistent with the fundamental values of the participants. The cognitive component is the members' belief in the long-term endurance or feasibility of the existing order.[25] The actors embrace the principles and norms of the international order through a process of learning and socialization. A further necessary dimension of moderation requires the great powers to respect the domestic legitimacy of the other powers and to be ready to grant them equal status.

Many scholars agree that moderate intentions and shared objectives characterized the post-Napoleonic Concert (see e.g., Craig and George 1983, 34; Elrod 1976; Hoffmann 1965, 104; and 1980, 39; Jervis 1983, 178–81; Kissinger 1964; Lauren 1983, 33). The explicit agreement of the European powers about the legitimacy of the status quo contrasts sharply with the absence of such a consensus between the superpowers in the post-1945 period (Bull 1980, 439–42; Hoffmann 1980; Mandelbaum 1988, 29–31), with respect both to their proximate spheres of influence (see George 1980a; Keal 1983; Johnson 1985–86, 47–48, citing the Kissinger Commission) and to the Third World (see Garthoff 1985; Johnson 1985–86; Matheson 1982, 65–83). A further contrast is between the Concert powers' acceptance of mutual legitimacy and equal status as great powers and the lack of such acceptance by the superpowers in the Cold War, especially the rejection by the United States of an equal status for the USSR.

More generally, the combination of similarity and moderation clearly sets the Concert era apart from later periods because of the rise of nationalism following the 1848 revolutions (Kupchan and Kupchan 1991, 142–43 n. 81) and the wars of the Italian and the German unification in the late 1850s and in the 1860s. Also related is the growing impact of domestic politics, which was accelerated after World War I (Craig and George 1983). Moreover, cultural heterogeneity increased in the twentieth century as the essentially European states system became truly global, while there was also a greater ideological diversification in the aftermath of the Russian Revolution of 1917.

How similar do the great powers have to be for a concert to emerge? This question is related to the linkages between similarity and moderation. Indeed, for a concert to emerge, the great powers have to be ready to accept the other powers as equal managers of international conflicts. The types of regime that are most conducive to such an attitude toward other powers are conservative monarchies and liberal democracies, but only when they face like-minded regimes.[26]

A key distinction here is between unifying and divisive ideologies (Walt 1987, 35–37). Among regimes with unifying ideologies (which include conservative monarchies and liberal democracies), similarity helps to foster moderation. In contrast, great powers with divisive ideologies (which include totalitarian regimes informed by revolutionary, messianic, or hypernationalist ideologies) cannot establish a concert even with similar powers because they do not tend to respect the equal status and the autonomy of the members of the same movement. At the same time, a concert between revolutionary-radical regimes and democracies or even moderate conservatives is highly unlikely. Revolutionary ideologies may not prevent these regimes from pursuing short-term cooperation or an ad hoc arrangement on a certain issue or region out of inferiority or vulnerability (although they do preclude the adoption of a stable, long-term strategy of cooperation), yet conservative monarchies are likely to reject their offers for cooperation because of the threat they pose to their traditional legitimacy. Liberal democracies are even more likely to oppose a concert with nonliberal regimes because "liberal states assume that nonliberal states, which do not rest on free consent, are not just . . . their foreign relations become for liberal governments deeply suspect" (Kant, according to Doyle 1986, 1161).

What then about the feasibility of a concert between democracies and conservative monarchies? Temporary concerted diplomacy (as well as détente) between them is much more likely than between either one of them and totalitarian-revolutionary states because the latter are suspected of desiring to transform the international order, even by the use of force. Yet a full-blown and long-run concert between democracies and absolutist monarchies is less likely than either among democracies or among monarchies alone. The reason is powerful differences about the sources of domestic legitimacy. Conservative monarchies would worry about the threat posed to their traditional legitimacy by the spread of democratic ideas whereas democracies tend to see as fully legitimate only regimes that rest on the free will of the people.

Such differences created divisions even among the fairly conservative members of the post-Napoleonic Concert. Although the main difference was regarding the form of the Concert rather than its mere existence, the Concert could continue to operate until 1854 mainly because of the weakness of domestic constraints in nineteenth-century international politics (see Albrecht-Carrie 1968, 6; Craig and George 1983, 32–33; Hoffmann 1965, 104; and 1972; Mandelbaum 1988, 65–69). Indeed, in the first half of the nineteenth century, even British democracy was still very qualified (Albrecht-Carrie 1968, 6; Hinsley 1963, 226; Rosecrance 1963, 58). Although differences about the sources of domestic legitimacy were powerful enough to limit joint interference within Europe, the common ideological denominator was strong enough to make joint action possible when European stability was threatened by events on the periphery. Accordingly, from 1815 to 1822, when conservatism was at its height in Britain as well, the Concert was able to reach its zenith. Nonetheless, as the British government moved toward internal reforms (1822), it could not sustain the same level of cooperation with the Concert (Rosecrance 1963, 58–59). For a contemporary full-blown democracy with active participation of public opinion in the formation of foreign policy, it would be much harder to maintain such high-level cooperation with authoritarian monarchies in the framework of a long-term institutionalized concert.

*Common Fears*

The linkage between similarity and moderation is insufficient to explain why a great power concert did not emerge before 1815, as the great powers of the eighteenth century (before the French Revolution) were also sufficiently moderate, at least in the minimal sense that none of them was a revolutionary power, and in fact possessed an even higher degree of ideological and cultural similarity than their nineteenth-century counterparts. This may show that even ideological similarity and the related moderation might not be enough for engaging in joint diplomatic and military actions in a concert. Such joint engagement is quite demanding with respect to the level of cooperation needed and can be costly in terms of blood, treasure, and the time of top decision makers. Therefore, a negative element of common avoidance must also be present.

> *Proposition 3:* Common fears of revolutions or inadvertent wars shared by all the great powers have to be present for a concert to emerge.

According to balance-of-power logic, to join forces, great powers need to feel a common threat. Almost by definition, however, a concert of all the great powers of the day cannot face a substantial external challenge by another state (or coalition of states). Instead, one or both of two other major sources of threat must be present to bring the great powers to act together. While the first source of threat derives from internal regime attributes and ideological similarity, the second stems from cognitive factors. Indeed, the common perception of both these sources of threat by all the great powers in the post-1815 era, as opposed to its absence in earlier eras, explains why a concert could be active and enduring only in that era and not earlier.

The first source is a common threat to the domestic legitimacy of their regimes (which, in turn, requires that the great powers share some degree of ideological sameness). Thus, a common fear of revolutionary movements (see Hinsley 1963, 220–23; Jervis 1985, 65; Rosecrance 1963, 56; Schroeder 1972, 404) by all the great powers of the Concert period, including the more liberal France and Britain, made cooperation among them possible. These revolutionary forces were either domestic or transnational and were not represented by the power of one or more states. Hence, it was not France as a state that posed a threat to the European powers in the classical meaning of the balance-of-power perspective. Instead, the threat was that of revolution, that is, an ideological menace to the conservative European elites, including the French. In fact, especially from 1816 to 1830, France had a very conservative government and thus could join the Concert. The common fear of revolution made possible joint management of international conflicts, which was intended to prevent any challenge to the existing international order.

The second element of avoidance involves the danger that the great powers will get entangled in a major war because of either internal unrest or third-party conflicts. Such a danger could bring all the great powers to act together, especially in the aftermath of a devastating general war. The recent memory of the destruction and turmoil of the Revolutionary and Napoleonic wars[27] motivated the powers to cooperate in managing regional disputes. Since they feared that unilateral actions by any one of them in third areas (those areas that were not the exclusive sphere of influence of a single power) at the expense of the others might escalate to a great power war, they decided to avoid exclusive advantages and pursue collective actions to resolve regional conflicts or at least to prevent their escalation (see, e.g., Craig and George 1983, 29–35; Elrod 1976, 166; Garrett 1976, 415–20; Lauren 1983, 46–50; Schroeder 1986), especially with regard to the Ottoman Empire and the Eastern question.[28]

On the whole, the perceived interrelationship between the two sources of danger (revolution and a general war) was a major motivation for the formation and maintenance of the European Concert (Holbraad 1979, 142–43; Jervis 1985, 65; Lauren 1983, 57). In Jervis's words, "at that time, states were interdependent in their internal security" (1985, 66).[29] In other words, the European powers were concerned that a revolution anywhere would compel all of them to use force, because it would be likely to spread and threaten the domestic legitimacy of all of their regimes. Moreover, revolution could result in the emergence of an anti–status quo power that might challenge the existing international order. At the same time, a war could foment further domestic unrest and revolution, which might then spread from one country to another. A weakening of any one of the great powers as a result of war could bring about a revolution in that country that might then pose a threat to all the powers. Hence, they had an incentive to avoid unilateral advantages at the expense of the other members of the Concert and to adopt crisis prevention measures.[30]

Since neither of the two sources of common fear was perceived by all the great powers prior to the French Revolution and the Napoleonic wars, a concert could not be formed in the eighteenth centrury even if common ideology and culture were even more striking in that era. In other words, the lessons that the Concert leaders derived from the Napoleonic wars were essential for the emergence of the preference for concerted action as the most effective counterhegemonic strategy rather than balancing behavior characterized by rivalry and competition (see Hinsley 1963, 196).[31]

Neither the memories of a recent major war nor fears of stumbling into a new one, however, are sufficient to produce high-level affirmative cooperation unless the positive elements of similarity and moderation are also in place. The presence of these elements in the aftermath of the Napoleonic wars, in contrast to their absence following the two world wars of this century, goes a long way toward explaining why a concert emerged in the first case and not in the other two. This is so even though, according to Jervis's (1985) structural–game-theoretical account of a concert, one should have emerged in all three cases.

Clearly, there has to be a fundamental difference between the nineteenth-century Concert and the post–World War I and post–Word War II ill-fated and short-lived concerts, if they were concerts at all. Jervis (1985) admits that the breakdown of the post–World War I cooperation was accelerated by factors of domestic politics, which lie outside the realm of his structural theory. However, he claims to account for the difference between the post-1815 success and the post-1945 failure in great power security collaboration. But the explanation that he advances—the division of Germany after 1945 as opposed to French strength after 1815—should be conceived more properly as an effect than as an independent cause. Germany was partitioned because of the general rivalry and failure of collaboration between the United States and the Soviet Union rather than the other way round. On the other hand, in the aftermath of the Restoration, France could join the Concert because of the common conservative ideology of the European elites after 1815 and the shared domestic-ideological threat of revolution and unrest that they faced.

**Cognitive Factors and Concerted Diplomacy**

In this section, I focus on the cognitive factors affecting the emergence of concerts, namely, the perceptions and beliefs of decision makers. These factors do not constitute a new, additional set of conditions for a great power concert but rather specify the cognitive dimension or background underlying the conditions discussed above.

Tacit rules for crisis management can be unintended, that is, can emerge regardless of the cognitive dispositions of state leaders. In contrast, high level cooperation in conflict resolution is contingent on the perceptions and beliefs of decision makers as well as their cognitive learning. In other words, the presence of common interests, observed by objective analysts, is insufficient for cooperation in conflict resolution to emerge. State leaders have to perceive the community of interests, and such perceptions, in turn, depend on their beliefs and learning as well as on the state-level factors mentioned above in this chapter. In this section, I focus on the effects of specific images[32] on policy-makers' orientation toward diplomatic cooperation in conflict resolution.

A great variety of relevant beliefs can be suggested, but I highlight three images that are especially pertinent to my concerns in this book, namely, images of (1) the dynamics of international politics, (2) the relations between the center and the periphery, and (3) the opponent.

Two of the images are conducive to the emergence of the basic conditions for a great power concert. A specific image with regard to the dynamics of international politics encourages moderation (more precisely, its cognitive component), while a second specific image concerning center-periphery relations underlies common fears of regional instability, escalation, and inadvertent wars. Thus, these images are necessary for conscious cooperation in conflict resolution. The other conditions for the formation of concerts—namely, similarity and the normative component of moderation—are not derived from cognitive factors but rather from state-level domestic attributes of ideology and regime. These attributes, in turn, influence the content of the third, and most critical, of the images discussed below—the image of the opponent. Thus, in the absence of the state-level conditions, a concert does not take place, and only the combination of the appropriate factors on the two levels of analysis—domestic normative-ideological factors on the state level and cognitive factors on the individual level—results in its emergence.

These images also influence deliberate cooperation in conflict resolution on a more down-to-earth level, by shaping the preferences of individual decision makers for a multilateral-cooperative versus a unilateral-exclusionary strategy. Thus, they are a useful tool to explain disagreements within a decision-making elite with regard to cooperation, as well as differences between decision makers concerning the degree of their support for cooperation and variations in policy over time.

Divisions of opinion among American or Soviet state leaders with respect to the three perceptions, and the effects of such divisions on different positions toward concerted diplomacy, indicate the importance of first-image factors for high-level cooperation in conflict resolution.[33] In chapter 6, I analyze these factors to explain the attitudes of American and Soviet decision makers regarding the initiation of and reaction to attempts at concerted superpower diplomacy in the Middle East.

Even if there is no logical connection between the three images, in stateleaders' minds there are linkages between them because of the psychological tendency to maintain cognitive consistency between beliefs (Jervis 1976, 117–24, chap. 10; and 1981, 57–59). On the whole, what seems feasible is also perceived as desirable and vice versa. Hence, as a first step, I identify the positions of two main purist groups of policymakers with respect to cooperation in conflict resolution. The members of each group tend to hold similar stances (although with considerable variations) about the three images irrespective of the rational connection between them. These stances lead them either to support or to oppose a cooperative-multilateral strategy. However, it emerges that this twofold distinction, which parallels the distinction between hard-liners and soft-liners, is too all-encompassing and cannot capture the differences in the positions of some policymakers.[34] Therefore, as a second step, I refer to two versions of the unilateral-exclusionary view; thus, we get three orientations with regard to cooperation in conflict resolution, each orientation informed mainly by one of the three images.

The Image of the Dynamics of International Politics:
Balancing versus Bandwagoning

> *Proposition 4:* Believers in the balancing dynamics of international politics are more inclined toward a cooperative-multilateral strategy than believers in bandwagoning.

My usage of these terms in this book is somewhat different from the way they are used in balance-of-power theory (Waltz 1979). As a systemic pattern of behavior, *balancing* means that states use unilateral means (armament or alliance formation) to offset a threat to their autonomy. States resort to these means irrespective of ideologies or intentions; securing survival is a necessary as well as a sufficient motivation for such automatic balancing. Moreover, according to balance-of-power theory, even if states seek power maximization and domination, the unintended outcome of their egoistic, self-seeking policies is mutual balancing and the emergence of an equilibrium.

By contrast, the first-image (individual) perception of balancing suggests that leaders who subscribe to this belief consciously seek to preserve the existing international order by maintaining an equilibrium of forces between the great powers and preventing the emergence of a hegemon (including a rejection of hegemonic inclinations by their own state). Thus, this belief is necessary for the quality of moderation, more specifically, for the perception of the feasibility of the existing international order. But they also want to avoid an exclusive use of unilateral means for these purposes, because they consider such options too costly. This preference springs from the basic belief that immoderate actions trigger counterbalancing strategies and that hegemony is infeasible. Hence, they think that a resort to hegemonic policies is futile but, at the same time, that reliance on the automatic balancing mechanism of the system to contain aspiring hegemons is too costly and results in arms races, competitive alliances, crises, and wars. They prefer, instead, reliance on multilateral means and a pursuit of conscious cooperation among the great powers.

Inspired by memories of the Napoleonic wars and the lessons of the power politics of the eighteenth century, statesmen in the post-1815 period tended to hold these beliefs. Widespread agreement among senior diplomats on this point was one of the factors that led to the emergence of moderate intentions and to the formation of the Concert (Clark 1989, 119–21; Hinsley 1963, 195–96, see also 224–25; Jervis 1983, especially 185–86; Kaplan 1979, 67, 135, 139; Lauren 1983, 32–34). As Hinsley remarks,

> The key to the Congress settlement is that the governments who made it, who were all reeling under the impact of Napoleon, were obsessed by the need for a balance . . . but revolted by the thought of returning to balance of power politics as between themselves. The Congress system was essentially the first attempt in history . . . consciously to find an alternative both to the old aim of domination by one Power, of which the latest practitioner had just been laid low, and to the balance of power as it operated in the eighteenth century, from which all felt it imperative to escape. (1963, 196)

Applied to the international politics of important regions, the belief in balancing implies that unilateral-exclusionary policies cannot succeed in attracting all the local states to the camp of an aspiring hegemon. Closely related to this is the perception that another great power with vital interests in a region cannot be excluded, at least not in a way that is affordable.

On the other hand, believers in bandwagoning are afraid of falling dominoes, that is, they believe that defeats will accumulate if states do not show enough resolve (see Jervis 1979, 220–21; Jervis and Snyder 1991). At the same time, these decision makers hope that their state's comparative advantages in particular regions can lead to the establishment of its hegemony there. This is the other side of the accumulation of defeats: victories also add up. That is, an advantage (frequently only a perceived advantage) in resources makes it both feasible and desirable, according to this view, to exclude other powers from certain issues or regions, since the presence of a single leader is perceived as the most conducive to advancing an international or, for that matter, a regional order. Because in addition to all the ideological-political differences, postwar state leaders tended to believe in bandwagoning,[35] as opposed to the belief in balancing by the Concert's statesmen, it is not surprising that even limited concerted diplomacy in areas of converging superpower interests (let alone a concert) was much less achievable following World War II than in the Concert period.

### Global versus Regional Images of Third-Area Conflicts

> *Proposition 5:* Regionalists tend to support a multilateral-cooperative strategy more than globalists do.

What are the sources of problems in third areas? To what degree are regional forces autonomous? What are the relations between global rivalries and local conflicts? Different decision makers have different answers to these questions depending on whether they have a global or a regional focus with regard to third areas.[36] The answers, in turn, affect state leaders' inclinations to cooperate or to compete with other world powers in third areas.

Globalists focus on threats rival great powers pose. Local unrest and turmoil are seen, to a large extent, as the outgrowth of external agitation, mischief, and intervention. Indeed, local disputes are tightly connected, in the minds of globalists, to the world rivalry and are not indigenously generated. Hence, to address regional threats, one has in the first place to contain or even to roll back the influence of the external antagonist.

In the eyes of those U.S. decision makers and analysts who have held such views during the Cold War, the East-West axis was long seen as dominating most, if not all, other international affairs.[37] Soviet assistance to radical forces and Moscow's "penetration" into the Third World were viewed as the main causes of the turbulence in those regions (MacFarlane 1985, 299 n. 8). If Washington failed to show determination in stopping the spread of Soviet-sponsored radicalism and in supporting anticommunist forces, dominoes would fall one after the other and pro-Soviet elements would take over in country after country. (Thus, the globalist perception is connected with the bandwagoning image.)

A sophisticated variant of the globalist approach calls for the unilateral resolution of local conflicts to enhance one's own influence at the expense of the rival power. Such a use of exclusionary diplomacy can be feasible if there is a (perceived) gap in capabilities in one's favor that could, presumably, allow the pacification or stabilization of third areas under the exclusive sponsorship of the dominant great power (the hegemon). This was indeed Kissinger's strategy in the Middle East (see chap. 6).

A regionalist image differs in that it recognizes the autonomy of local issues, regional conflicts, and indigenous forces. The sources of the regional problems are perceived as independent of great power rivalry, derived instead from local conditions (poverty, exploitation, population pressures, disease, unequal distribution of resources) and regional disputes, and they should be decoupled from the global contest. A great power, according to this logic, could either disengage from a region or address its problems through nonsecurity-related means (usually socioeconomic measures rather than alliances and arms supply). Or if the interests of several powers are intensely involved in a region, a great power could embark on a cooperative path. This option is considered feasible especially if great powers' leaders see the main problem in third areas not in the expansion of their competitors but in the danger of uncontrollable escalation of local quarrels that might entangle the big powers. The common fear of regional instability and escalation, informed by such perceptions, is a necessary factor in the formation of a concert.

Indeed, the main concern of the Concert of Europe, at least when it was at its peak, was how to avoid a general war as a result of the anticipated scramble over the spoils of the declining Ottoman Empire. Hence, nineteenth-century statesmen tried to avoid unilateral actions that could lead to a spiraling escalation. Instead, they used multilateral diplomacy to maintain the integrity of the Ottoman Empire (Elrod 1976, 166; Jervis 1983, 186) or, if it seemed necessary, resorted to collective use of force (Lauren 1983, 47–48) to quell local wars (Turkey-Egypt, 1838–40) or to make controlled disintegration possible (the independence of Greece, 1821).

The regionalist approach gained support in U.S. elites during the 1970s, in the aftermath of the Vietnam War and the 1973 oil embargo. Growing turmoil and radicalism in the Third World and its demands for a New International Economic Order were increasingly seen as North-South matters that could and should be separated from U.S.-Soviet competition. Some analysts and practitioners paid greater attention to socioeconomic problems in the Third World and to the autonomous nature of the numerous regional conflicts there.[38] The regionalist approach was especially powerful during the Carter administration, at least in its initial stage (see, e.g., Ben-Zvi 1986; Feinberg 1983, 26–28; Garthoff 1985; Hoffmann 1984, 257–59; Spiegel 1985a). At that stage, the administration was ready to cooperate with Moscow, particularly where the latter had both important interests and significant power resources. In the postwar era overall, however, the globalist image tended to dominate U.S. foreign policy thinking (see especially Garthoff 1985, 674–75; see also Feinberg 1983; Johnson 1985–86). Such a conception of third world conflicts constrained the possibilities for U.S.-Soviet cooperation in regional conflict resolution.

The Soviet ideological-rhetorical view, on the other hand, appeared as regionalist because it highlighted the domestic sources of progressive change in the Third World.[39] By not linking the Strategic Arms Limitation Talks with U.S. behavior in the Vietnam War, Soviet diplomatic practice also endorsed the compartmentalization between détente and regional conflicts (Smith 1980, 136–37, 382–83).[40] However, rather than enhancing cooperation, the Soviet decoupling of support for third world liberation movements from U.S.-Soviet relations was one of the causes of the breakdown of détente, because of its incompatibility with the U.S. linkage approach (Breslauer 1983b, 326–27). Furthermore, in spite of its regionalist appearance and in accordance with its long-standing revolutionary ideology, Moscow in fact underlined the globalist nature of conflicts in the Third World, where the United States was seen as the main culprit. Thus, the Soviets argued that "the way to peace in the Third World is for the West to get out of the way of revolutionary transformation. There would be no 'hotbeds' if the imperialists, through their attempt to suppress national liberation and reestablish hegemony, did not create them" (MacFarlane 1985, 302).

The Soviets, in other words, held a mirror image of the American globalist position. As the newcomer to the Third World, they saw their national interest as lying in the weakening of U.S. dominance there. This interest and the Soviet ideological commitment to support anti-Western national liberation movements were mutually reinforcing and together posed an obstacle to superpower collaboration in the Third World.

### The Image of the Opponent

> *Proposition 6:* A positive image of the opponent is essential for the emergence of concerted diplomacy.

In discussing the concept of the "operational code," George (1969) suggests that

> A political actor's belief system about the nature of politics is shaped particularly by his orientation to other political actors. Most important of these are one's opponents. The way in which they are perceived—the characteristics the political actor attributes to his opponents—exercises a subtle influence on many other philosophical and instrumental beliefs in his operational code. (in Hoffmann and Fleron 1980, 174)[41]

Although great powers can jointly manage crises even if they do not have positive images of each other, that is not the case with high-level cooperation. As Liska has pointed out,

> The attempt to achieve far-reaching concert requires the development of positive assumptions about both the rival and the relationship that, if valid, would be capable of maturing into genuine concord. Such positive assumptions are precisely what have been missing from any version of détente. . . . Foremost among the U.S. assumptions currently blocking progress is that the United States is in all respects different from Soviet Russia. This conviction has been fed since 1917 by analyses that stress an aspect of Soviet society and foreign policy that, superficially at least, is novel—an ideology of world revolution. . . . (1986b, 5)

One of the conditions for the formation and maintenance of a security regime, Jervis argues, is that "the actors must believe that others share the value they place on mutual security and cooperation—if a state believes it is confronted by a Hitler, it will not seek a regime" (1983, 177). Jervis adds that "in several cases security regimes may have been ruled out not by the fact that a major power was an aggressor but by the fact that others incorrectly perceived it as an aggressor" (1983, 177). By contrast, during the era of the Concert of

Europe, "others were seen as partners in a joint endeavor as well as rivals, and unless there were strong reasons to act to the contrary their important interests were to be respected" (Jervis 1983, 180).

On the whole, the willingness to cooperate heavily depends on whether one believes that the other is ready to be cooperative or unalterably antagonistic (Jervis 1985, 76; Spechler 1978, 63–73). Intentions are more soft and intangible than capabilities;[42] thus, while the problem of assessing Soviet capabilities became somewhat more manageable over the years (though it was not fully resolved),[43] international events since 1945 definitely did not—at least until the recent major changes in the former Soviet Union—resolve the question of Soviet intentions. In fact, in the twenty years or so preceding the late 1980s, the U.S. foreign policy elite had become even more polarized than before over this issue.[44]

Consequently, the willingness to cooperate with the Soviets, to recognize the legitimacy of their interests, and to confer on them the status of a co-manager of regional conflicts in normal (noncrisis) diplomacy depended during the postwar era, to a considerable extent, on such closely related factors as the image of the Soviet Union as a normal or a revolutionary great power; the perception of Soviet intentions; and their perceived attitude toward the status quo, including in third areas. Indeed, one of the important effects of belief systems is that beliefs about a particular state strongly influence the interpretation of its specific policies (Jervis 1981, 58). Thus, the Soviet quest for equality has been interpreted, according to the content of the observer's image of the Soviet Union, either as an end in itself or as a first step on the way to world domination.[45]

Competing U.S. images of Soviet intentions have, in turn, been shaped to a considerable extent by ideological and domestic factors on both the American and the Soviet sides of this equation. On the U.S. side, such images not only have been influenced by general world views (Snyder and Diesing's [1977] hard line and soft line) but probably also have been related to competing views about the desirable character of American society.[46] And they have been even more closely linked to ideas about the U.S. leadership role in the world (Holsti and Rosenau 1983; Osgood 1981, 6), which are, in turn, at least partly related to the images of balancing and bandwagoning.

On the Soviet side, what gave much room for conflicting U.S. beliefs and perceptions of Soviet intentions was the "marriage of the Russian empire and a universalistic ideology." Nye suggested that this marriage

> has produced a state that looks to some people like a defensive status quo power and to others like an expansionist revolutionary power. The fact that defensive motives can be combined with aggressive policies further confuses our perceptions, and a repressive and secretive political system

frustrates efforts to fathom Soviet intentions. It is small wonder that Americans often have divided views about the nature of the Soviet state. . . . (1984, vii)

Because of cognitive consistency and because of the primacy of the image of the opponent, underlined by first-image theorists, it tends to influence the other two beliefs, that is, the dynamics of world politics (balancing versus bandwagoning) and the loci of primary problems and threats (global versus regional). Thus, those who have perceived the Soviets as expansionist have tended to believe both that it is possible to exclude them from the resolution of regional conflicts (bandwagoning) and desirable to do so insofar as the Kremlin was seen to constitute the major threat to regional and international stability (globalists). On the other hand, those who saw the Soviets as essentially a status quo or normal power claimed that it was both necessary to include them in the settlement of disputes in regions where they had vital interests (balancing—i.e., it is impossible to exclude the Soviets, who can obstruct a unilateral Pax Americana) and also desirable to do so (the main problem being regional escalation, not Soviet expansion, whereas the Soviets could be helpful in moderating their clients and legitimizing regional arrangements).

The image of the Soviets has played a key role in shaping U.S. officials' views of cooperation and has been the most important independent variable on the cognitive level for explaining variance with respect to cooperation with the Soviets in normal diplomacy. The other two cognitive beliefs, however, must also be included as independent variables because they have played an especially important role in influencing the positions of officials who have not had a clear-cut and rigid image of the Soviets as either aggressive or defensive. Moreover, with the disappearance of the Soviet threat, the other two images, especially the image of the dynamics of international politics, might play a much more critical role in the post-postwar era than during the Cold War.

## Orientations toward Cooperation in Conflict Resolution Based on the Three Beliefs

So far, only two orientations toward great power cooperation in regional conflict resolution were distinguished: multilateral-cooperative and unilateral-exclusionary. Beyond the dichotomous differentiation of hard-line and soft-line views that throughout the postwar period did much to determine U.S. policy toward the USSR, there have been two distinct versions of the unilateral-exclusionary view.[47]

Each of the three images informs one major orientation toward great power cooperation, although each orientation is also influenced by the other

**TABLE 5. Orientations toward Great Power Cooperation in Regional Conflict Resolution**

|  | Unilateral-Exclusionary |  | Cooperative-Multilateralism |
|---|---|---|---|
|  | Confrontation | Competition |  |
| Critical image | Image of the opponent | Dynamics of international relations | Loci of problems |
| Image of the opponent | "Evil empire"; unalterable antagonist | Limited adversary | Relatively benign; potential partner |
| Dynamics of international relations | Bandwagoning | Bandwagoning | Balancing |
| Loci of problems | Global | Global (but sensitive also to regional conflicts) | Regional |
| Policy means | Unilateral military measures | Unilateral diplomacy (and some limited cooperation) | Concerted diplomacy |
| Historical application | Peaks of Cold War (1950s, early 1980s) | Détente (1970s) | Concert of Europe |
| U.S. Cold War strategy | Global containment and roll back | Mix of competition and limited cooperation | Accommodation with the rival |
| Post–Cold War U.S. strategy[a] | Isolationism/ disengagement | Pax Americana | Joint actions via international institutions |

[a]The effects of the post–Cold War on the three orientations are elaborated in the Conclusions.

two images (see table 5). Thus, we get the following three orientations: multilateralism, confrontation, and competition. Each of these orientations has been dominant in a different era depending on the beliefs of key decision makers in that period: multilateralism during the Concert of Europe (and it also appears to dominate thus far the early post–Cold War era); confrontation during the peak periods of the Cold War; and competition in the détente of the 1970s.

Multilateralists hold a relatively benevolent image of other powers as status quo oriented and subscribe to the beliefs in balancing and in the autonomy and centrality of local problems. The crucial factor affecting the multilateralists' orientation is their perception of regional conflicts primarily as a potential for escalation (rather than for unilateral gains to be made at the expense of other powers). These policy makers believe that responsible great powers can and should restrain their allies and confer international legitimacy on regional arrangements. They can be expected to grant an equal status to the other great powers and to attempt to resolve conflicts jointly.

The confrontational approach is advocated by pure hard-line ideologues who are primarily motivated by their image of the opponent as an evil empire, though they also tend to be globalists and believers in bandwagoning. Such ideologues do not see their rival great power as a normal state but perceive it as an agent for revolutionary change that challenges the legitimacy of the international order. Hard-liners are not inclined to collaborate with their rival because they see it as the main problem in the international system rather than as part of the solution. They aim at global containment of their enemy and even rolling back its influence by unilateral military means such as armament or military alliances around the globe.

A third group is somewhat less ideologically oriented and holds a mitigated hard-line view of the opponent. Although these officials focus on the global geopolitical competition, they are more sensitive to regional problems than the pure ideologues. The major element in determining their orientation is the belief in bandwagoning in the sense that they are pessimistic enough to worry about falling dominoes owing to the machinations of the rival power but are optimistic enough to believe in the capacity of their own state to unilaterally broker regional conflicts. Since these policymakers also tend to be suspicious of their adversary's intentions, they cooperate with their rival only when it is essential to do so to prevent crises and to maintain the costs of regional involvement at a reasonable level. When it seems to be possible, they exclude the rival power, at most paying lip service to its privileges as a great power, and attempt to establish the dominance of their state by using its comparative advantages (in the diplomatic, economic, or other domains) for stabilizing conflict-ridden areas.

Despite the sharp disagreements among policymakers regarding the image of the Soviets, during the Cold War overall, the extreme dissimilarity of the Soviet Union to the United States and its strangeness in American eyes quite frequently tended to produce a negative image of it. Yet those decision makers who held mitigated views of the opponent and who were also influenced by the other two images in determining their position toward concerted diplomacy tended to be somewhat more disposed toward cognitive learning than the pure ideologues.[48] The reason is that the less confident people are in their belief systems, the more open and responsive they are to the environment (Jervis 1976, 195–201). Indeed, the degree of ideological purity (either hard-line or soft-line) is closely related to the degree of openness to inputs from the international environment. Pragmatists are sensitive to contextual information, whereas crusaders are less open to it.[49] Thus, to understand the ideologues' behavior, we must focus on their beliefs, but regarding the pragmatists, international factors and learning play a relatively greater role in shaping their behavior.

During the Cold War, the relative pragmatists, who have been affiliated mostly with the orientations of competition and, to some extent, also multilateralism, were indeed able to pursue some degree of learning concerning the need at least for a limited cooperation with the Soviets. Yet the ability of the parties to learn the positive value of international cooperation and to perceive their subjective interdependence (or to develop an awareness of their mutual dependence), which reflects complex learning (see chap. 2), is conditioned by the degree of similarity and moderation of their domestic attributes. In other words, dissimilarity and immoderation lessen such an ability to learn and to perceive, and vice versa. Thus, the capacity to learn the value of cooperation with the other superpower was severely constrained during the Cold War by the absence of similarity and moderation on both sides.

## Explaining Great Power Differences with Regard to the Form of a Concert

The discussion so far has been concerned with the inclination of great powers to pursue a collaborative-multilateral versus a unilateral-exclusionary strategy. Yet great powers that adopt a cooperative approach (whether due to inferiority and vulnerability or to similarity, moderation, and common fears) might still differ with regard to their preference for a certain form of cooperation, that is, the inclination of certain states to pursue coercive collaboration while other states tend to oppose it. While the inclination to take part in a concert concerns the strategy toward the other great powers, the approach to the form of cooperation relates to the great power's attitude to small states—whether to respect their autonomy (accommodative approach) or to infringe on it in some major ways (coercive strategy). Such disagreements over the form of cooperation may constrain the smooth operation of the concert and even undermine it.

## Pluralist versus Authoritarian States and the Formation of a Condominium

I propose that the capability and willingness of great powers to enter a condominium that involves a joint coercion of smaller states also depends on unit-level attributes. The logic of the second (state or unit-level) image suggests that there is a congruence between the domestic environment of states and their behavior in international affairs. When it comes to a coercive collaboration of the great powers, two factors internal to the state exert an influence. The first is the dominant *ideology,* political culture, or world view of a great power, which affects its *willingness* to form a condominium. Even more important is the second, namely, the domestic political *structure,* which affects the *capability* of a great power to take part in an enduring coercive collaboration at the expense of small states.[50] I look first at the differences and similarities among the members of the Concert of Europe with respect to joint intervention in small states. I then look at how domestic attributes affected the willingness and ability of the superpowers to take part in a condominium-like arrangement in the postwar era. The relevant unit-level distinction in this context is one between liberal democracies and authoritarian states.

### Democracies' Belief in Self-Determination as a Constraint on Joint Coercion

> *Proposition 7:* All else being equal, liberal democracies are relatively more concerned about the right of small nations to self-determination and are relatively less likely to favor a coercive regulation of the domestic and foreign affairs of other nations. Such an acceptance of pluralism in the international arena reflects the maintaining of pluralism at home.[51]

This proposition largely explains the disinclination of Britain and the United States to cooperate with their authoritarian counterparts. Although this applies particularly to the United States, with its long-standing resentment of the European balance-of-power system and particularly the notion of spheres of influence, in the nineteenth century one can already discern a growing, though still limited, British inclination in this direction.

Thus, the sense of security and the lack of vulnerability in the British case stemmed not only from the external geopolitical circumstances but also from the internal attributes of legitimacy and political stability. Being a constitutional monarchy with an evolving representative government, Britain did not have to fear social revolution as did the other European powers (Jervis 1978, 173–74; and 1985, 65; Rosecrance 1963, 61–63). Being less subject to this fear, it had less incentive to take part in the Concert, at least regarding interventions in Europe. Yet this domestic factor affected not so much Britain's inclination to take part in the Concert as its preference regarding the form of the Concert.

Thus, the nature of the evolving British constitutional political system played some role in affecting the British orientation toward a condominium.[52] Castlereagh, the chief British diplomat, knew that Great Britain, as a parliamentary state with its own institutions based on peaceful domestic change, would oppose interference by the Concert in the internal affairs of other states (Hinsley 1963, 206). Indeed, it was under pressure from the public and the cabinet (Hinsley 1963, 205; Kissinger 1964, 221–23; Rosecrance 1963, 61) that Castlereagh had to oppose the condominium suggested by the Eastern powers.[53]

However, the growing British sensitivity to the right of small nations to self-determination applied at that period mainly to European peoples, so that there was no ideological or domestic hindrance to joint meddling in the affairs of the Near East (or to the subsequent division of Africa into explicit spheres of influence). Thus, although Britain opposed joint interventions in Europe, it was ready to participate in joint coercive collaboration in the Near East, most notably in the Greek revolt (1827) and in the termination of the Egyptian-Turkish war (1839–40) (see Albrecht-Carrie 1968, 102–28; Brown 1984, 41–43, 46–47, 219–21; Craig and George 1983, 193–95, 201–3; Hinsley 1963, chap. 10; Lauren 1983, 46–47; Rosecrance 1963, chap. 5). In other words, when a Near Eastern crisis seemed to threaten the stability of Europe, the British were more than willing to take part in an intervention to restrain the local actors and thus keep the peace.[54]

As for the United States, an enduring theme in American idealism has been a belief in national self-determination "as a fundamental principle of foreign policy and as the necessary basis of a proper world order" (Waltz 1974, 10; see also George 1980a, 239; Hoffmann 1980, 9; Johnson 1985–86, 43–45; Seabury 1978; Tucker 1968). This attitude has gone hand in hand with a distaste for the old-fashioned spheres-of-influence arrangements between the European great powers (cf. Cohen 1980, 138, and the sources he cites; George 1980a, 242, 246; Hunt 1987). Two examples suggest that even if the U.S. leadership was interested in some kind of a coercive great power arrangement, it was constrained by the public commitment to these ideals.

Thus, as George (1980a) shows, this commitment constrained Roosevelt from constructing a condominium with the Soviets based on an old-fashioned spheres-of-influence arrangement. Roosevelt realized at the outset that such an agreement would be unacceptable to the U.S. public as a violation of the principle of self-determination. Even his more benign "grand design" of the "Four Policemen"—an idea resembling the European Concert of great powers cooperating in the maintenance of peace—was too much for American idealists. Whereas Stalin was seemingly inclined to cooperate in such a concert (George 1980a, 242, 247) and probably to accept a division of Europe into spheres of influence, the American president was unable to mobilize domestic support for any form of great power collaboration with the Soviet Union, especially one that might appear to violate the idealists' principles of states' sovereign equality. Once the war ended, the U.S. public and the Congress increasingly interpreted Soviet behavior in Eastern Europe both as breaching the right of self-determination and as a harbinger of more aggressive goals. As a result, it became more and more difficult to establish any kind of collaboration and to arrest the drift into cold war.

The Nixon-Kissinger détente of the 1970s was also constrained by the Americans' devotion to the rights of small states and opposition to any arrangement that seemed to smack of a great power condominium at their expense. It is not surprising that hard-liners opposed the relatively more collaborative policy toward the Soviet Union pursued by Kissinger, since they regarded détente as an appeasement of Moscow's expansionism and its military buildup. More interesting is the resistance of some liberals who, one might think, should have supported a more cooperative framework with the rival superpower. However, as a leading specialist on American public opinion noted, "Liberals were suspicious of Nixon and Kissinger's bipolar and power-oriented view of world politics; they saw détente as a cartel arrangement between the two great superpowers that ignored or endangered the interests of the Third World" (Schneider 1984, 32).[55] Thus, while the hard-liners opposed any form of collaboration with the Soviet Union because of a distrust of Soviet intentions, liberals opposed a coercive form of collaboration.

Indeed, the difference between a democratic and an authoritarian regime with respect to the principle of self-determination conditions their attitudes toward small states. As a result, all other things being equal, a democratic great power is somewhat less inclined to collude with other great powers in coercing small states. Yet the democratic great power is even less inclined to do so if the small state is also democratic. That is because democratic states regard each other's governments as a manifestation of the will of its people and thus as more legitimate than nondemocratic regimes.[56]

In contrast, an authoritarian power should be more favorably disposed to negotiate with the other great powers behind closed doors, over the heads of its small clients, once it perceives that this approach best serves its interests. That is especially true for a communist great power because communist ideology has traditionally preferred the establishment of centralized-hierarchical movements and called the members to obey a single authoritative leadership. Consequently, all the members of the communist alliance faced threats to their autonomy from the leader (Walt 1987, 35–36, and the sources he cites).[57]

Even if the United States has sometimes also violated the rights of small states (notably in the Western Hemisphere), it did so to a considerably lesser extent than the Soviet Union (which not only exercised coercion vis-à-vis the small states in its sphere of influence in Eastern Europe but also annexed the Baltic states).

At any rate, great power ability to engage in coercive collaboration may be more significant than its willingness. The major factor affecting ability is the domestic structure and its effects on the capacity of small states to oppose external coercion by mobilizing support for their cause within the polity of the great power.

## Strong States, Weak States, and Condominium

Krasner's (1978, chap. 3) distinction between "strong" and "weak" states is a good starting point for discussing how domestic political structure affects the likelihood of a great power condominium. Domestic structure refers to the relationship between a state and its society and to the organization of the state and societal groups. If a state is weak, it is unable to manipulate the behavior of domestic groups, interest groups are often successful in attaining their objectives, there is a multiplicity of access points to the government, and state power is fragmented.

*Proposition 8:* Weak states are less able than strong states to pursue a condominium that might involve a joint coercion of their small allies.

Thus, an authoritarian power's ability to reach agreements at the expense of small allies is greater than a democratic power's because of the weaker domestic political structure in a pluralist society. Accordingly, those small partners of the United States that could mobilize powerful domestic resources within the American political system were capable of influencing its policy-making process and especially of seriously limiting its ability to collude with Moscow—even when the American leadership was convinced that such cooperation would serve U.S. interests.

## U.S. Inability to Join a Condominium

In terms of the strong-weak distinction, the United States is a weak state (and a strong society) whereas the USSR was until recently a strong state (and a weak society) (Krasner 1978, chap. 3). In foreign policy specifically, the U.S. Constitution establishes an open "invitation to struggle" through the division of powers between the president and Congress (Corwin 1940, 200; and additional references cited in n. 4 in Nye 1984, 3; Nye 1986). There is also a diffusion of power within the executive branch in the foreign affairs domain. The growing linkage between domestic politics and international affairs in the modern era, enhanced in the United States by an increasingly protracted presidential nomination process (cf. Polsby 1983), has vitiated the insulation of the foreign policy elite from internal pressures, an insulation that existed in all the great powers at the time of the Concert of Europe (cf. Craig and George 1983; Hoffmann 1972, 69; Mandelbaum 1988, 69). A rising number of government agencies, congressional committees (and subcommittees), interest groups, and think tanks have a stake in the making of American foreign policy. The growing role of the media in American politics has also had an impact on foreign affairs.

The multiplicity of access points to the government in the U.S. political system has meant that a great variety of domestic groups can affect U.S. foreign policy on various issues, including relations with the Soviets.[58] Strategies of cooperation were especially vulnerable to pressures from anti-Soviet constituencies (cf. George 1984c, 154). The influence of these groups can take two forms that are relevant to our concern with great power collusion over the heads of small nations: a straightforward domestic influence on foreign policy and the role played by transnational linkage groups. Both forms of influence differentiate a penetrated, pluralist, and open system such as the United States from a closed society like the postwar Soviet Union, in which the decision making process, especially in foreign affairs, was until recently centralized-hierarchical. Thus, postrevisionist historians (Dallek 1979; Gaddis 1972) underline the constraints domestic politics (rather than the economic causes emphasized by revisionists) posed on U.S. capacity to conciliate the Soviets in the early postwar era.

The anti-Soviet sentiment of some ethnic constituencies (notably from Eastern Europe), on top of the ideological objection to communism of broad segments of American society, made anticommunism an electoral asset and constrained collaboration with the Soviets as comanagers of the international system (see Destler 1984; Destler, Gelb, and Lake 1984, 38–58; Gelb 1971, 143–44; Wolfe 1979, 36, 38),[59] notably with regard to the acceptance of Eastern Europe as a Soviet sphere of influence. Another prominent example of domestic influence was the congressional restraints on trade cooperation with the Soviets imposed by the Jackson-Vanik amendment to pressure the Soviets to allow more Jewish emigration.

As for the second type of influence, in an open society the weakness of the state structure makes possible the penetration of external ideas and agents. Furthermore, transnational linkage groups can be formed between U.S. allies on the one hand and agencies of the American government or interest groups in the U.S. political system on the other.[60] The establishment of these coalitions leads to "demands for aid to small allies . . . filtered through domestic groups and spoken with an American accent" (Keohane 1971, 166). Indeed, such linkage groups have proved effective in influencing U.S. foreign policy, especially when influential constituencies in the American political system have been sympathetic to the concerns of the small ally.[61]

Lesser allies are particularly able to penetrate the great power political system through sympathetic ethnic, religious, or cultural groups.[62] To the extent that allies, with the help of their ethnic supporters, are able to mobilize public and congressional support for their positions, they become participants in the domestic democratic game. The internationalization of this game via the presence of linkage groups increases the bargaining power of the small ally vis-à-vis the U.S. government (Keohane 1971).

As a consequence of transnational linkages, the lesser state can get more diplomatic, economic, and military aid from Washington than what one might expect according to a realpolitik analysis of tangible resources, strategic value, and defection options. Because lobbies have, as a whole, more access to

Congress than to the administration, especially where foreign policy is concerned, such interest groups are more likely to affect foreign aid levels, and sometimes arms sales, than the intricacies of diplomatic initiatives (see Spiegel 1985a, 389–90). But linkage groups are important because they can also constrain collaboration with ideological rivals and especially because they can affect the ability of different polities to form a condominium.[63] Since in the postwar era, U.S. cooperation with the Soviets was, at any rate, vulnerable to domestic criticism, opposition by transnational linkage groups could preclude joint superpower actions from getting very far even if supported by the administration. Thus, for example, pro-Israeli groups (with the help of anti-Soviet elements) have obstructed two ambitious attempts at superpower cooperation in resolving the Arab-Israeli conflict—attempts that were seen at the time as anti-Israeli and collusive: the Rogers I plan of December, 1969, and the joint statement of October 1, 1977 (see Spiegel 1985a, 186–89, 338; see chap. 6).

Lobbies are not always successful, nor do they determine policy even on the subjects that most concern them. Yet the active role of transnational linkages in the foreign policy process of a pluralist state stands in striking contrast to the weakness of such linkages in a centralist system, especially on the mass public level.

### Soviet Inclination and Ability to Form a Condominium

Although a totalitarian model may not reflect Soviet decision making in the post-Stalin era (cf. Spechler 1978, 2–8),[64] it is fair to characterize the Soviet Union as a strong state in Krasner's terms until the late 1980s (see Krasner 1978, 69, citing Leonhard). The policymaking process, until recently, was much more centralized and hierarchical than in the U.S. system. Although elements of bureaucratic politics might have applied to certain policy processes, there were still far fewer access points for nongovernmental (i.e., nonparty and nonbureaucratic) interest groups and public opinion. That was especially true for foreign policy (see Dallin 1980, 38)[65] and even more so for transnational penetration by allies and linkage with domestic groups.

Thus, during the postwar era, the Soviets were more able than the United States to control aid and supplies to allies when they believed it was in their national interest to do so. If any arrangement in the postwar era has approximated a great power condominium, it has been cooperation between Washington and Moscow to control the spread of nuclear weapons.[66] Indeed, it was found that the Soviets enforced tighter controls on nuclear supplies to their allies than did the United States (see *New Republic,* December 17, 1984, 18–23, especially 19)[67] Moreover, Moscow was more able to embark on coercive collaboration with the United States both because of its lesser regard for the self-determination of small nations and its centralized domestic structure. Because of his freedom from such normative and structural constraints, Stalin was more able to accept a spheres-of-influence division or Roosevelt's idea of a great power concert, even though his long-term willingness to cooperate may be doubted.[68] The Soviet interest in a condominium-like agreement, or at least some degree of joint action with the United States, continued under Khrushchev, and later Brezhnev, in the context of the rising Soviet rivalry with China. Chinese fears of U.S.-Soviet cohegemonism (establishing a joint consortium to rule the world) were, however, entirely fanciful—for reasons having rather more to do with the American political system and the public rejection of power politics than with an absence of interest by the Soviets (Ulam 1983, 43).

The Soviets were apparently interested in more than an anti-Chinese coalition. In short, they asked for some kind of a condominiumlike arrangement (Kissinger 1979, 1146; and 1982, 277, 285),[69] that is, a great power collaboration to jointly impose peace in third areas or divide them into spheres of influence between the powers, notably in the Middle East (see Ben-Zvi 1990, 92–104; Kissinger 1982, 583; Nixon 1978, 2:430; see chap. 6).[70]

Indeed, as Ulam observes,

> Behind the Marxist-Leninist idiom in which the language of Soviet diplomacy was couched, it operated very much in the manner of old-fashioned imperialism, with its penchant for secret agreements, bargains struck with another power at the expense of other parties, and spheres of influence. Such practices clashed with the moralistic and legalistic strain of the American approach to foreign relations, and quite apart from other considerations, made negotiations, and even the process of communication between the two superpowers, very difficult (1983, 58).

Thus, in terms of the advocacy of a great power condominium, and particularly the ability to propose such an arrangement, the Soviet Union reminds us of the nineteenth-century Concert members, especially the continental-authoritarian states of central and eastern Europe. The similarity between the Soviets and the continental powers is both with regard to the authoritarian domestic structure and the related lack of respect for the right of self-determination of smaller nations. This explains the ability to engage in coercive collaboration. Yet the greater sense of vulnerability, common to both the Soviets and the continental powers, provided an important incentive for a condominium.

There is a basic difference between the two periods, however. In the post-Napoleonic era, the main problem was disagreement on the character of the Concert and not so much its mere existence. When the Concert powers were able to overcome their disagreements in this respect, the Concert operated

**TABLE 6. Summary: Factors Affecting the Inclination of a Great Power to Cooperate in a Concert**

| Exclusionary-Unilateral Inclination | Cooperative-Multilateral Inclination | |
|---|---|---|
| Dominance | Inferiority/Vulnerability | |
| Immoderation (and related bandwagoning image) | Moderation (and related balancing image) | |
| Ideological dissimilarity (and related negative image of the opponent) | Ideological similarity (and related positive image of the opponent) | |
| Lack of common fears (and related globalist image) | Presence of common fears (and related regionalist image) | |
| | Accommodative form of cooperation | Coercive form of cooperation |
| | Pluralist/liberal great power | Authoritarian/illiberal great power |

smoothly. In the post-1945 era, underlying the differences in attitude between the superpowers regarding the form of joint management of international conflicts, there were basic obstacles to any form of high-level collaboration that prevented the emergence of a concert, namely the absence of similarity and moderation. Indeed, the differences between the United States and the USSR regarding both the essence and the form of cooperation constrained their ability to pursue more limited concerted diplomacy even when their interests converged (notably concerning regional conflicts such as the Arab-Israeli dispute; see chap. 6).

Table 6 summarizes the major argument of this chapter by presenting the factors affecting the inclination of a great power to join a concert and also great power differences with regard to the form of a concert.

## Conclusions

In this chapter, I show that systemic factors do not determine the nature of great power diplomatic cooperation in conflict resolution. Thus, despite the higher number of players and because of unit-level (domestic, ideological, and cognitive) factors, the five-power Concert of Europe could cooperate more effectively in joint diplomacy than the two superpowers in the postwar era. Hence, it appears that subsystemic causes explain the emergence of a concert better than structural theory, which would predict that the likelihood of a durable and explicit concert of all the great powers of the day would be low (especially in a multipolar system) because they would tend to compete and to balance each other rather than join forces for the purpose of resolving international conflicts.

In sum, the analysis provided in this chapter suggests the terms under which the two theoretical conditions necessary for a concert to emerge are met. The two conditions are as follows:

1. The great powers have to overcome systemic and domestic *constraints* against international cooperation by all the powers of the day.
2. The great powers have to share powerful *incentives* so that they will be willing to provide collective goods such as peace and conflict resolution.

The first conditon is best met when all the great powers are similar and moderate; the second condition is met by the presence of the common fears of inadvertent escalation, revolutions, and instability. Accordingly, the post–Cold War era might be the first period since the 1815–54 era in which these conditions seem, even if remotely, to be met.

The implications of this analysis for the current and future eras are discussed in the Conclusions. Let us turn now to an examination of the theoretical propositions in case studies of superpower crisis management and conflict resolution in the Middle East during the Cold War. Whereas in chapter 5 I explore some of the propositions of chapter 3 regarding crisis cooperation, in chapter 6 I investigate the arguments introduced in this chapter concerning the attempts at superpower concerted diplomacy for conflict resolution.

Chapter 5

# The Superpowers and Middle East Crises during the Cold War: Tacit Cooperation

In this chapter, I provide a detailed case study of one of the propositions of the model in chapter 3: the conduciveness of bipolarity to successful crisis management, to the prevention of inadvertent escalation, and to the conduct of restrained resolve, manifested in the emergence of tacit rules for regulating the use of force in crisis. This proposition is, in turn, derived from the general model of this book, which stipulates the connection between systemic factors and crisis management (see chap. 2).

The case study concerns the crisis behavior of the superpowers during Arab-Israeli wars in the postwar era, beginning with the 1956 Suez crisis. The proposition serves to explain two major puzzles presented by the historical record that are closely related to the Long Peace puzzle addressed in chapter 3. First, the superpowers' engagement in these crises never escalated to a global armed conflict; moreover, in contrast to past experience of earlier great powers in similarly intense regional conflicts, the superpowers not only avoided any actual use of force against each other[1] but tacitly cooperated in restraining their regional clients and in terminating the local wars.

Second, despite the superpowers' intense political-ideological rivalry and the popular wisdom about the Cold War, the Arab-Israeli crises were part of a larger pattern of cooperation between Moscow and Washington in regulating local crises. Moreover, this pattern took place despite the prevalence of potentially destabilizing unit-level factors (such as domestic politics, bureaucratic politics, crisis-induced stress, and ideology). In addition, the superpowers' mutual restraint persisted despite changes in the balance of their military forces, in contrast to the expectations of hegemonic theories. In previous eras, such changes, especially the growing military capabilities of a revisionist power, have led to instability and major wars. Most interestingly, not only did this crisis cooperation occur in an era characterized overall by keen great power competition, but this competition should supposedly have made it possible for small states to manipulate the United States and the Soviet Union and to play them off each other. Yet despite the absence of an explicit agreement on the superpowers' balance of interests in the Middle East, in times of crises, that balance, as a matter of fact, informed the tacit rules for regulating the use of force.

However, to advance a structural explanation of this pattern of tacit cooperation based on the attributes of bipolarity, it is necessary to demonstrate that the superpowers did in fact consistently behave in crises with restrained resolve. Some scholars have advanced different interpretations of superpower behavior in Middle Eastern crises.

In tackling these problems, I begin, in the first section, by briefly introducing the basic elements of superpower competition in the Middle East, their interests and alliances, which made superpower cooperation especially difficult. In the second section, I discuss the two common arguments concerning Middle East crises that run counter to the present argument: the supposed reckless behavior of the Soviet Union and the United States in these crises and the thesis regarding the alleged stabilizing effects of superior U.S. power on the management of these crises. In the third section, I suggest, however, the limitations of these two arguments; instead, I highlight the balance of interests, rather than the precise balance of military capabilities, as the major determinant of superpower crisis management. In the fourth section, I analyze the tacit rules of superpower crisis management in the Middle East. In the conclusions of the chapter, I focus on the explanatory power of systems theory for understanding these rules. Whereas *nuclear deterrence* provided powerful incentives for avoiding intended wars, *bipolarity* made it relatively easy to coordinate superpower behavior for purposes of crisis management and thereby to avoid inadvertent escalation. Since I am dealing with crisis management in this chapter, I focus on the effects of bipolarity. Indeed, under bipolarity, the balance of interests determined patterns of great power crisis management.

## Superpower Rivalry in the Middle East during the Cold War: Disputed Interests and Antagonistic Alliances

Third areas—those areas that are neither the central arena of great power interaction nor the exclusive spheres of influence of either one of the global powers—have some dangerous attributes (see Miller 1988, chap. 1), and some of the most acute great power crises take place there. If the great powers have important interests in an area but do not agree about their relative balance of interests there, that locale is especially risky (see George, with others, 1983, chap. 15). Indeed, because of the geographical, and frequently also ideological, distance between the world powers and their clients on the periphery and because of the domestic weakness of many local regimes, the regional alliances of great powers are often unstable and elude the powers' full control. Moreover, external powers are often allied with states that are engaged in intense conflicts with each other and thus can potentially draw the big powers into their local wars.

These characteristics fit the Middle East more than any other region; indeed, since the Berlin confrontation and the Cuban missile crisis of the early 1960s, most U.S.-Soviet Cold War crises have occurred in this area, and even in the post–Cold War era it remains a potential trouble spot, as the 1990–91 Gulf Crisis shows. Thus, the Middle East is a region where U.S.-Soviet cooperation has been fraught with extreme difficulties yet at the same time was potentially very valuable—for helping to settle local conflicts, notably the Arab-Israeli dispute (but also the conflicts in the gulf), and for preventing the escalation of local disputes to a world war.

What have been the interests of the superpowers in the Middle East?[2] Basically, they fall into four categories: crucial geostrategic location; relative proximity to the Soviet Union, especially to the industrial Black Sea-Ural region; vast oil fields; and the special U.S.-Israeli relations—categories that, as we shall see, are interrelated.

In the Cold War period, these conflicting interests ostensibly gave rise to a zero-sum competition. Because of the geostrategic importance of the region, both superpowers tried hard to increase their own influence with key states in it and to deny influence to the other superpower as part of their global rivalry. In third areas, such alliance-building was closely bound up with and, in fact, constituted a precondition for the acquisition of strategic assets (see Breslauer 1985).[3] Overall, each superpower was inclined to regard any increase in the influence of the other superpower in this region as a setback for itself and feared that any such increase would further destabilize the region and contribute to a further weakening of its own overall position (George 1986, 8).

Thus, the United States, for instance, was interested in bases for Strategic Air Command (SAC) in the Northern Tier (Iran and Turkey) in the 1950s, and the Soviet Union was very much concerned about these bases (Fukuyama 1981, 595; Rubinstein 1980, 324). Although the development of intercontinental ballistic missiles (ICBMs) and submarine-launched ballistic missiles has supposedly reduced the significance of such deployments proximate to Soviet frontiers, events in southwest Asia in the late 1970s (particularly, the removal of the pro-U.S. regime in Iran and the Soviet invasion of Afghanistan, on top of a growing Soviet naval posture in the Indian Ocean) have renewed the American interest in access to military facilities in the Middle East-Indian Ocean region for the Rapid Deployment Force in case of threats to the flow of oil from the Persian Gulf (see, e.g., McNaughter 1985, chap. 1; Noyes 1982, 127–28). The Soviets, for their part, sought since 1964, and until the end of the Cold War, to counter the deployment of the U.S. seaborne nuclear systems in the Mediterranean by deploying the Fifth Eskadra there. Thus, the Soviets needed port facilities to serve their naval squadron and air bases for the aircraft necessary for the protection and functioning of the fleet. Egypt, and later other Arab states, became the focal point of this quest (see Fukuyama 1988, 161; Golan 1979, 106–7).[4]

The characteristics of third areas aggravated the superpower competition in several ways. For one thing, the superpowers were unable to agree on their balance of stakes in the Middle East. During the Cold War, there was a symmetry of vital superpower interests in Europe and a symmetry of limited interests in many parts of the Third World. In what used to be the exclusive spheres of influence (Central America and Eastern Europe), for a long time the balance of interests clearly favored one or the other superpower. The Middle East, however, was characterized by what George called "disputed interest symmetry" (1986, 7).[5] The United States has claimed to possess paramount interests because of two particular objectives it has in the Middle East.[6] The first is to guarantee the free flow of oil from the region, especially in light of the high dependence of major U.S. allies—Western Europe and Japan—on Gulf oil. The second is the U.S. moral commitment to the survival of the state of Israel. Based on (or rationalized by) these ostensibly superior interests, but in many cases explained, in fact, by the kind of unit-level factors discussed in chapters 4 and 6 (notably, ideologically motivated hard-line images of the Soviet Union held by many policymakers and influential segments of public opinion), the United States tended to reject conferring an equal status on the Soviets in managing Middle Eastern conflicts.

The Soviets, for their part, persistently rejected the American claim of superior stakes, asserting that they had special security interests in a region that almost adjoins the USSR's own southwestern borders, its "soft underbelly"; indeed, much of the Middle East is far closer to the (former) Soviet border than Grenada is to the United States (Luard 1986a, 1018; Primakov 1986, 30).[7] But most U.S. administrations did not recognize the equality or even the legitimacy of Soviet security interests in the Middle East,[8] perceiving Soviet motives as offensive rather than defensive.[9] Accordingly, many, though by no means all, U.S. policymakers denied that Moscow deserved an equal voice in Middle East diplomacy.

In contrast to the central arena (Europe), there also was no distinct division of the Middle East into spheres of interest between the United States and the Soviet Union. Indeed, the superpowers competed hard in all parts of the region and tried to acquire influence in almost all key states.[10] In the decade after World War II, the focus was on the Northern Tier. From 1954 to 1967, the Arab "cold war" provided a major arena for superpower rivalry. Since the mid-1970s, the Gulf-Indian Ocean area has ranked high on the agenda of the global powers. But, as we shall see, it was the perennial Arab-Israeli conflict that triggered the most dramatic superpower confrontations in all of the Third World.[11]

The security dilemma has also had exacerbating effects on the great powers' regional rivalry, most clearly evident in the extension of the containment strategy from the Northern Tier to the Arab world. In the aftermath of World War II, the Russians seemingly returned to the prerevolutionary practice of expansion at the expense of Iran and Turkey. The United States, which did not play the Middle Eastern game before the war, replaced the weakened Great Britain as the counterweight to Russian power in the area. The containment policy of the new world power was expressed by the Truman Doctrine of 1947, initially directed toward Greece and Turkey but later including an implicit Iranian extension. The policy of commitment to assist in safeguarding the independence and territorial integrity of the local states, announced by the doctrine, proved effective, and by the early 1950s Moscow renounced its demands on Turkey and Iran. These states had long-standing security fears of their giant northern neighbor; that was not the case, however, with the more remote Arab world, which had experienced Western (especially British and French) rather than Russian imperialism.

The Eisenhower administration (in close collaboration with Britain) extended the containment policy into the Arab world through the establishment of an anti-Soviet alliance, the Baghdad Pact (1955), and later through the Eisenhower Doctrine (1957) and the resultant military interventions in Lebanon (by the United States) and Jordan (by Britain) in 1958.[12] But under the security dilemma, this policy produced unintended consequences. Even if the West intended to be defensive—to contain expected Soviet aggression in light of earlier offensive Soviet moves in the Northern Tier—the Soviets interpreted the U.S. steps as part of the West's attempt to pursue an offensive strategy, that is, to encircle the Soviet Union. The newly emerging revolutionary regimes in the Arab world also viewed U.S. actions in cooperation with "imperialist" Britain as offensive, that is, designed to help Arab conservatives in their "cold war" with the "progressive" regimes. Washington was thus associated with the old legacy of Western imperialism in the Arab east. As a consequence, a new alliance emerged between the Soviet Union and the radical nationalist and anti-imperialist Arab states.[13] Its first major manifestation was the Czech arms deal with Egypt, which, in fact, made it possible for Moscow to leapfrog the Northern Tier and to "penetrate" Arab countries, thus jeopardizing what was the rationale for Dulles's containment policy in the Middle East in the first place—the prevention of Soviet "penetration" to the core of the Middle East.[14]

The events of the mid-1950s produced some of the basic superpower alignments in the Middle East for at least the next two decades. Superpower interests in the Middle East tended to be conflicting, disputed, or unclearly divided, and their respective alliances there were generally antagonistic, unstable, and difficult to control.[15]

The superpowers tended to associate their own position in the region with the standing of their local proxies, even when the latter were engaged in local conflicts not directly related to the global rivalry. This view was derived from the strategic importance of allies and the credibility of the superpowers as global patrons. However, there was some degree of ideological affiliation between the superpowers and their regional allies. Although many Soviet specialists agree that state (strategic) interests and not fundamental ideological goals (in the sense of world revolution and party-to-party relations) determined Soviet Middle East policy (Breslauer 1985; Golan 1979, 108–9; Quandt 1986b, 24), Moscow was inclined to stand by the "progressive" forces in the Arab world (most notably, Egypt until 1974, Syria, Iraq since the 1958 revolution, and the PLO).[16] At the same time, the United States has lent support to the Arab conservatives (most notably, the monarchies of Saudi Arabia and Jordan) and to democratic Israel (and also to presumably democratic Lebanon in 1958) against the assaults of the Soviet clients. (Or, others could claim, the United States has sustained the Israeli military machine and thus enabled its encroachment on Arab neighbors, especially the Palestinians.)[17]

Nevertheless, at least some of the superpower alignments in the Middle East have been neither stable nor controllable. Defections have occurred both on the U.S. side (mainly because of revolutions such as in Iraq in 1958, Libya in 1968, and Iran in 1978–79) and on the Soviet side (chiefly through reorientations of existing governments such as Sudan in 1971, Somalia in 1977, and most notably Egypt in 1974–76; Iraq has also moved somewhat away from the Soviet orbit since the late 1970s). In addition, it was often difficult for both world powers to rein in local allies.[18] Yet it was less difficult in times of crisis than noncrisis.

### Superpower Conduct in Middle East Crises

In the eyes of some observers, the claim that superpower crisis behavior in the Middle East was cautious would seem a strange one. Arms shipments by the United States and the Soviet Union allegedly made it possible for the quarreling Middle Eastern nations to engage in large-scale modern warfare in the first place or, at least, to raise the level of intensity of the local wars (cf. Becker 1979, 253–54). Clearly, in some cases, most notably the 1973 Arab-Israeli war, superpower arms resupply helped the fighting states to prolong the armed conflict. During most of the Arab-Israeli wars, the global patrons also engaged in shows of force, such as alerts of airborne forces and especially naval movements. Most dangerously, they reached the brink of direct conflict several times in the Middle East, far more frequently than in any other region in the last thirty years.

Because of the geostrategic importance of the Middle East in the superpower global rivalry, as well as the commitment of the United States and the USSR to their respective allies in the Arab-Israeli conflict, almost every war that was related to that conflict also triggered a superpower crisis. In this context, a *superpower crisis* refers to a situation in which there was a threat of the use of force or actual use of it by at least one of the superpowers that could reasonably have also led to a military intervention by the rival superpower and thus to a potential armed conflict between them.[19]

Moscow's crisis behavior may seem to be especially competitive or even confrontational; its advisors became engaged in military activities in the War of Attrition and the 1973 war, and it threatened to intervene militarily at the end of six Middle Eastern crises: the 1956 Suez crisis, the 1957 Syrian-Turkish crisis, the 1958 Lebanese-Iraqi crisis, the June 1967 War, the 1970 War of Attrition, and the October 1973 War. Furthermore, the Soviets deployed their own combat troops on three occasions: 1970, 1973, and 1983 (in Syria). Overall, observers have pointed to elements of reckless Soviet conduct in six Middle Eastern wars: the 1956 Suez crisis, the Arab-Israeli wars of 1967 and 1973, the War of Attrition, the Jordanian civil war of 1970, and most recently in 1983, following the Israeli invasion of Lebanon in the preceding year. Hence, let us look at the Soviet crisis record first.

### Reckless Soviet Conduct in Middle East Crises?

Following the Israeli occupation of Sinai and the Anglo-French invasion of the Suez Canal Zone in early November, 1956, Moscow issued four types of threats, some of them quite harsh. In order of decreasing severity and increasing explicitness, the threats were the following:[20]

1. Premier Bulganin's messages to London, Paris, and Washington included a vague warning that the hostilities in Egypt might "spread to other countries and develop into a third world war"(Holbraad 1979, 22–25 citing *Documents on International Affairs*).
2. In a message to the Israeli prime minister, Bulganin warned that by collaborating with Britain and France, Ben-Gurion's government had put "in jeopardy the very existence of Israel as a state" (Jonsson 1984, 154, citing *Documents on International Affairs*).
3. Moscow tacitly threatened the major American allies, Britain and France, with an attack by atomic weapons. Bulganin asked British Prime Minister Eden, "In what situation would Britain find herself if she were attacked by stronger states, possessing all types of modern destructive weapons? And such countries could, at the present time, refrain from sending naval or air forces to the shores of Britain and use

other means—for instance, rocket weapons" (Holbraad 1979, 24, citing *Documents on International Affairs*). France was issued a similar threat. As Betts notes (1987, 62–63), these threats were the first case of Soviet nuclear saber rattling in a crisis.

4. There was also a threat to use conventional force. Its main expression was a TASS (Soviet news agency) announcement threatening intervention by Soviet "volunteers" if Israel, Britain, and France did not withdraw all their forces from Egypt (Holbraad 1979, 25, citing *United States Policy in the Middle East, September 1956–June 1957, Documents*). The Soviets also spread rumors that they were taking steps to send forces to the Middle East and that some of them might already have arrived (Bar-Zohar 1978, 1279; Bohlen 1973, 433–34, cited in Mangold 1978, 116).

The United States responded by declaring its intention to oppose any unilateral Soviet action in the Middle East, and Eisenhower made it clear to the Kremlin that a nuclear attack on the Europeans would draw American retaliation. The Sixth Fleet, the Strategic Air Command, and the Continental Air Defense Command were alerted. Planes were fueled and loaded with weapons, and some units were deployed to forward bases. A naval force, including aircraft carriers, was dispatched toward Europe (Betts 1987, 64; Holbraad 1979, 29; Jonsson 1984, 156; and the sources they cite). Thus, the Soviet threats brought the superpowers, and not for the last time in the Middle East, to the brink of confrontation.

There is a widespread agreement among analysts that the Soviets also played a critical role in inflaming the May, 1967, crisis that eventually led to the Six-Day War, with its far-reaching consequences for the Arab-Israeli dispute (see Ben-Zvi 1988, 346; Glassman 1975, 39–40; Golan 1979, 124n. 15; Jonsson 1984, 161; Safran 1969, 275–78).[21] Beginning in late April, the Soviets had issued allegations that Israel was planning to attack Damascus. The most important target of this apparent disinformation campaign was Egypt; Moscow informed Cairo that "Israel was massing its forces on the Syrian frontier and an attack was planned for some time between May 18 and May 22" (Heikal 1978, 171). At the same time, the Soviet ambassador in Tel Aviv turned down an Israeli offer to see for himself the alleged Israeli troop concentrations on its northern border (Eban 1977, 318–19). The important point is that whereas Egypt did not attribute much credibility to Syrian reports of a similar nature, "their approval by the Soviets caused Nasser to proclaim a state of emergency on May 16 and to send troops into the Sinai" (Heikal 1978, 174–75),[22] although "it is quite impossible that Moscow could have believed what it was saying" (Eban 1977, 320).[23] The Egyptian move, which the Soviets supported (see Jabber and Kolkowitz 1981, 424–25; Wells 1979, 159, and sources he cites in n. 5), triggered an escalating cycle that resulted in the outbreak of the war on June 5, 1967. The Soviets allegedly made little effort to restrain Nasser and obstructed attempts by other powers to prevent the war in the weeks preceding its outbreak (Wells 1979, 159, drawing on Howe 1971, 73).

The USSR made its most threatening move in the war on the last day of the fighting, June 10. As the Israelis were completing their takeover of the Golan Heights, Moscow threatened to intervene militarily. The threat was communicated in a hot line message Premier Kosygin sent to President Johnson. According to Johnson's memoirs, Kosygin spoke of the possibility of an "independent decision" by Moscow; Kosygin also foresaw the risk of a "grave catastrophe" and stated that unless Israel unconditionally halted operations within the next few hours, the Soviet Union would take "necessary actions, including military" (1971, 302). Johnson acknowledges that the threat was received with "great concern and utmost gravity" (1971, 302). This impression is supported by interviews with key U.S. officials who were involved with the conflict, including Secretary of State Rusk who said that "his feeling at the time was one of despair if the cease-fire had not held and the Israelis not halted when they did" (Wells 1979, 166; see also Dayan 1977, 379–80). One source, quoting the joint chiefs of staff, reports that the Soviets had moved beyond verbal threats and alerted their paratrooper divisions (Bar-Zohar 1970, 260, cited in Bar-Joseph and Hannah 1988, 457).[24] Indeed, the United States responded by moving the Sixth Fleet much closer to the eastern Mediterranean coastline.

Less than three years later, in the midst of the Israeli-Egyptian War of Attrition along the Suez Canal, the Soviets went beyond just issuing threats of intervention.[25] Starting in the spring of 1970, Moscow deployed into Egypt large numbers of highly capable air defense missiles and aircraft as well as 15,000 to 20,000 military personnel, including technicians, advisors, air defense crews, and, most dramatically, Soviet pilots (cf. Rubinstein 1981, 474). In fact, Soviet forces assumed responsibility for Egyptian air defense. This was the first substantial deployment of Soviet combat troops into a third world country. "While the direct involvement of these forces in combat against the Israelis turned out to be negligible in the end, they were clearly prepared to fight a major battle if circumstances had required" (Dismukes 1979, 221).

Indeed, beginning in early summer 1970, Soviet-staffed SAM units reinforced the Suez Canal air defense and caused rising Israeli air losses. Moreover, in July Soviet-piloted MiG aircraft that "during their first weeks in Egypt had restricted their patrols to the Nile Valley, extended their operations forward to areas on the flanks of the Canal front" (Glassman 1975, 78; see also Dismukes 1979, 232; Whetten 1981, 60). This Soviet move increased the probability of direct Soviet-Israeli clashes and of the situation getting out of control. Fortunately, when Israeli-Soviet combat finally took place on July 30

(Israeli pilots shot down five Russian-piloted jets south of Suez City), it was just on the eve of a cease-fire. Still, the Soviets cooperated with the Egyptians in a blunt violation of the terms of the cease-fire by deploying SAMs along the canal after the warring nations had stopped shooting (Evron 1979, 30; Rubinstein 1981, 476). Nixon and Kissinger, in particular, believed that the USSR was partly responsible for these breaches (Kissinger 1979, 585–91; Quandt 1978, 260). Indeed, Moscow's military intervention and apparent complicity in the violations led Nixon to state "that the Soviets are the main cause of Middle East tensions" (Nixon 1978, 1:598; see also Quandt 1978, 265).

That same year, in September, a civil war broke out between the pro-Western King Hussein of Jordan and radical Palestinian guerrillas who challenged his authority. The Jordanian army's success in driving the Palestinians out of Amman triggered an invasion by Syrian armored forces into Jordan, beginning on September 18. The Syrians initially were successful; but after a few days of fighting, the Jordanians defeated them and Hussein maintained his grip over the country.

Nixon and Kissinger held the Soviets responsible in general for the violent challenge to Hussein and in particular for encouraging Syria's intervention in Jordan (Kissinger 1979, chap. 15). Kissinger drew a connection with the War of Attrition, stating that "the Soviet military thrust into Egypt and its incitement of radical Arabs spawned the crisis in Jordan" (1979, 594). Even if the Soviets could not be blamed for instigating any specific threatening actions in the initial stage of this crisis, "they could, however, still be charged with general culpability for the state of affairs that engendered the crisis, and most decision makers assumed that they would in every event try to capitalize on the situation as well as they could" (Dowty 1984, 118). When the Syrian incursion into Jordan took place, however, there was little doubt in Kissinger's mind that the Soviets were abetting the Syrians. As he conveyed to Nixon, "the Soviets are pushing the Syrians and the Syrians are pushing the Palestinians" (Nixon 1978, 1:598).

As for the 1973 Yom Kippur War, it provided fertile ground for allegations by American politicians and observers about the Soviets' irresponsible conduct in the Middle East.[26] These critics charged, moreover, that the Soviet Union failed in this crisis to meet its obligations under détente, specifically relating to the 1972 and 1973 agreements on crisis prevention, namely the BPA and the Agreement on the Prevention of Nuclear War (Garthoff 1985, 385–93).[27] Hence, the Soviet failure to prevent its Arab clients from resorting to force, along with Soviet behavior during the hostilities, considerably harmed public and congressional attitudes toward détente, thereby helping to jeopardize the entire détente process (Garthoff 1985, 405–8; Glassman 1975, 2; George, with others, 1983, 148, 150; Porter 1984, 114; Spechler 1986, 439). Indeed, both in the months preceding the October War (starting from February, 1973—see Porter 1984, 123; Spechler 1986) and shortly after the war broke out, the Soviets delivered massive shipments of arms to their clients that enabled the latter first to initiate the fighting and then to prolong it.[28]

Most importantly, the Soviets again threatened military intervention on two occasions. Toward the end of the first week of the war, the Soviet ambassador to Washington warned Kissinger that "the Soviet Union could not be indifferent to threats to Damascus. If Israel continued its advance, matters might get out of hand" (Kissinger 1982, 508). Pursuant to this, on the evening of October 10, the Soviets alerted three airborne divisions (and possibly an additional four),[29] and about three days later the staff of an airborne division was transferred to Syrian military headquarters near Damascus (see Hart 1984, 216, also cited in Bar-Joseph and Hannah 1988, 457; McConnell 1979, 272–73).

Then, on October 24, toward the end of the war when there were ceasefire violations on the Egyptian front, Secretary-General Brezhnev conveyed a message to Nixon in which he said, "if you find it impossible to act jointly with us in this matter, we should be faced with the necessity urgently to consider the question of taking appropriate steps unilaterally. Israel cannot be permitted to get away with the violation" (Kissinger 1982, 584; Nixon 1978, 2:497–98). This message, Nixon asserted, "represented perhaps the most serious threat to U.S-Soviet relations since the Cuban Missile Crisis eleven years before" (Nixon 1978, 2:497). The letter proved especially damaging to superpower détente. A leading critic of the Moscow-Washington thaw, Senator Henry Jackson, first to expose that Brezhnev's note had been sent, publicly described it as "brutal" and "threatening" (Kissinger 1982, 531, 595).[30] Kissinger, for his part, argued in his memoirs that the note was "in effect an ultimatum. . . . It was one of the most serious challenges to an American President by a Soviet leader" (1982, 583); he added that "we had tangible reasons to take the threat seriously" (1982, 584).

There were, indeed, a number of Soviet military moves that made Brezhnev's verbal threat appear credible. By October 24, all seven Soviet airborne divisions, totaling some fifty thousand troops, were on alert. Moreover, a stand down in the airlift of Soviet arms supplies also took place on that day; the reason might have been to concentrate and prepare the airlift for the transport of Soviet troops (Blechman and Hart 1984, 278–79; Garthoff 1985, 377; Glassman 1975, 161; Jonsson 1984, 186; Whetten 1981, 75).[31] The Soviet naval fleet in the Mediterranean had gradually been reinforced to reach the unprecedented size of eighty-five ships (Kalb and Kalb 1975, 552; see also Blechman and Hart 1984, 278; Whetten 1981, 75). Finally, a nuclear dimension was added when a Soviet freighter, passing the Bosporus on October 22 en route to Alexandria, gave off neutron emissions, indicating the potential presence of nuclear weapons on board, possibly for a brigade of Soviet Scud missiles (Blechman and Hart 1984, 278; Garthoff 1985, 378 n. 69; Glassman 1975, 163; Jonsson 1984, 186). These ominous steps, combined with

Brezhnev's message, caused much alarm in Washington; the feeling was that the Soviets might be on the verge of a large-scale unilateral intervention in the Middle East (Blechman and Hart 1984, 280; Garthoff 1985, 377 n. 68; Glassman 1975, 163).

The administration claimed that the United States was forced to respond by ordering a worldwide Def Con–3 (Defense Condition–3) alert of its conventional as well as nuclear forces to deter the Soviets from intervention (Kissinger 1982, 587–88). Thus, the superpowers had seemingly reached the brink of a dangerous showdown. Although the crisis was quickly defused in the following two to three days (Garthoff 1985, 380–82; Jonsson 1984, 188–89; Kissinger 1982, 591–99), this superpower confrontation delivered a major blow to the prospects of improved U.S.-Soviet relations.

Finally, like in the 1970 War of Attrition, Moscow introduced sophisticated air defense systems (notably the SAM-5s, manned by Soviet personnel) into Syria in 1983 following the Israeli invasion of Lebanon. As Ross (1990) points out, the deployment of an additional five thousand Soviet advisors meant that, in fact, the Soviets assumed responsibility for the Syrian air defense. They also provided the Syrians with modern ground-to-ground missiles capable of hitting Israeli population centers. Moreover, since the SAM-5s covered Israeli air space, they generated a high risk of a preemptive Israeli strike and thus a potential for dangerous escalation.

In sum, both the 1970 and 1983 deployments could have generated an escalation that would have been difficult to control and would have required the Soviets to up the ante further. In the Jordanian crisis, the Soviets appeared to support aggression by their allies against a U.S. ally. Certainly, the threats of intervention in 1967 and 1973 seemed risky, triggering American military responses and thereby creating two of the most dangerous confrontations in the Third World in the postwar era.

However, charges have been leveled not only at the Soviets for their behavior in Middle East crises; other analysts have focused on what they regard as American recklessness in the form of overreactions, especially in two crises: the 1970 Jordanian civil war and the 1973 Yom Kippur War.

### Reckless U.S. Behavior in Middle East Crises?

Allegedly, Nixon and Kissinger misperceived the 1970 Jordanian crisis as a critical global showdown.[32] It has been suggested that they overemphasized "the global U.S.-Soviet dimension of the crisis" (Quandt 1977, 124) and overrated the Soviet role and their control of their clients (interviews conducted by Dowty 1984, 151 n. 13). At the same time, the administration is thought to have overlooked the regional elements of the crisis, which were related to the Palestinian problem and to the Arab-Israeli conflict.

As a result of these misperceptions, Washington supposedly overreacted by both tough anti-Soviet rhetoric (stated by Nixon, see Garfinkle 1985, 123; Quandt 1977, 114) and unnecessary and overblown military moves, intended to influence Soviet behavior and thus also to restrain clients assumed to be under Moscow's control. Thus, in 1970 the Eighty-Second Airborne Division and five divisions in West Germany were put on alert; even more risky, in light of the proximity to considerable Soviet naval forces, was the buildup of the Sixth Fleet from two to five carrier task forces, which sailed toward the eastern Mediterranean.

Indeed, the Soviets deployed the elements of two additional anticarrier task groups to counter the U.S. reinforcement, and these could have posed a significant military threat to the Sixth Fleet (Shulsky 1979, 171–75). To shadow the U.S. naval units, the Soviets intermingled their ships with the U.S. task force (Garfinkle 1985, 125). As Shulsky points out, "the sustained presence of two powerful fleets in close proximity during a period of international tension tends to produce an inherently unstable situation" (1979, 175).

However, since the Soviets behaved in an unprovocative manner (Garfinkle 1985, 126; Hersh 1983, 240–41), the prospects of escalation were substantially reduced. Still, under such tense circumstances, actions by third parties, whether accidental or malicious, could always lead to the situation getting out of hand. That seemed to be especially true for the United States, "since by concentrating almost exclusively on the U.S.-Soviet relationship, Nixon and Kissinger let themselves be manipulated by the local parties" (Quandt 1978, 288).

Through both its verbal and unspoken behavior, the United States committed itself almost unconditionally to the defense of Jordan, the administration having made that country a cornerstone of its position in the Middle East. However, since the United States lacked sufficient interventionary forces at the crisis locale (Garfinkle 1985, 125–26), it had to encourage an Israeli intervention; in turn, Washington committed itself to come to the help of Israel in case of Egyptian or Soviet reactions. Thus, it appeared that both Jordan and Israel could potentially have dragged the United States into military engagement, whereas the United States was unable to control the activities of these two clients. Under these circumstances, presumably only a fortunate development on the ground could have saved the United States from a dangerous escalation or an embarrassing backdown. Indeed, it was the absence of the Syrian air force from the fighting that enabled Hussein's army to defeat the Syrians and the PLO decisively.

More severe but also seemingly more straightforward are the charges in the second case of alleged U.S. recklessness. Ostensibly, the Washington Special Action Group overreacted to Brezhnev's message of October 24, 1973, not only by ordering a worldwide Def Con–3 but also by alerting the Eighty-

Second Airborne "for possible movement" and by sending additional aircraft carriers to the eastern Mediterranean (Kissinger 1982, 587–89). In addition, fifty to sixty B-52 strategic bombers—an important element of U.S. nuclear forces—were moved from their base in Guam to the United States; aerial refueling tankers assigned to SAC were dispersed to a greater number of bases and began nonroutine actions; and marginal changes were made in the status of the strategic submarines and ICBMs (Blechman and Hart 1984, 281).

The 1973 crisis coincided with one of the peaks of the Watergate affair (the Saturday Night Massacre occurred on October 20). Thus, some have argued that U.S. behavior, especially the nuclear alert, was influenced by domestic politics (cf. Betts 1987, 126). In addition, some suspected that Nixon, acting under the high stress and pressures of Watergate-related matters, was not entirely rational and was inclined to overreact, as was manifested particularly in the nuclear alert. Hence, according to these allegations, the superpower confrontation did not result from Soviet threats but was manufactured by U.S. decision makers for internal political consumption.[33] The logic of these accusations could, in fact, be reinforced by the quick diffusion of the superpower confrontation and by the contention that the Soviets were just posturing and, at any rate, did not seriously consider intervention (Fukuyama 1981, 588–89).

### Destabilizing Effects of Changes in the Relative Military Balance?

The confrontational interpretation of superpower crisis conduct postulates a constancy of great power behavior over time, as well as similarity in the behavior patterns of different great powers. In the aftermath of World War II, however, the United States enjoyed strategic nuclear superiority over the Soviet Union and also advantages in power-projection capabilities into such third world areas as the Fertile Crescent. Only in the mid- to late-1960s did the Soviets reach rough nuclear parity (cf. Jonsson 1984, 79; Larson 1978, 178–87)[34] as well as impressive airlift and sealift capabilities (cf. Dismukes and McConnell 1979, chaps. 1–2; Fukuyama 1981, 596; and 1988; Garthoff 1985, 685–89; Larson 1978, 191–96).[35]

Indeed, a second common interpretation of great power crisis behavior in the Middle East focuses on such differences and changes in the military balance.[36] Thus, a division of superpower crisis management in the Middle East into two subperiods according to changes in the relative military equation seems to make sense. Until the Six-Day War, the United States was the dominant external actor in Middle Eastern crises, such as those of 1956 (Suez), 1957 (Jordan), and 1958 (Lebanon and Jordan). In the 1950s, the Soviets could not transfer forces to the Middle East heartland (Fukuyama 1981, 596) and still possessed limited strategic nuclear capabilities (Glassman 1975, 16). According to this interpretation, in this period the United States presumably behaved as a responsible leader in the Middle East and upheld international order. Hence, in the Suez crisis, the United States checked what was widely seen as an aggressive move by two of its closest allies, France and Great Britain, who had conspired with Israel to attack Egypt (cf. Glassman 1975, 17). This responsible crisis management by the United States was not obstructed in this period by its still relatively weak challenger.

By the mid- to late-1960s, however, the USSR had acquired a substantial second-strike capability and had built up airborne divisions and a blue-water navy (cf. Karsh 1985, 15–20, 87–90; Porter 1984, chap. 3) including the permanent deployment of a naval squadron in the Mediterranean since 1964. Indeed, the challenger seemingly became emboldened; thus, we have noted the allegedly reckless Soviet behavior in 1967 and 1970, culminating in the threat to intervene in 1973. The declining power, for its part, seemed either to succumb to Soviet coercive pressures or to escalate its response. Some, as we will see, have subscribed to the first part of the proposition with respect to U.S. behavior in 1973. Other observers, as we have just seen, believe in the validity of the second part, as demonstrated by U.S. conduct in the Jordan crisis and especially by the worldwide alert at the end of the 1973 war, which supposedly represented a very dangerous point for world peace (see Nixon's interview in *Time,* July 29, 1985). Ten years later, the proximity of U.S. troops in Lebanon and Soviet military personnel in Syria again created a risky situation where a war between rival clients could conceivably have entangled their patrons (see Saunders 1988, 572). Hence, it seems that the growing equality in superpower military capabilities made the world supposedly more dangerous. Third areas apparently became potential superpower battlegrounds as the Soviet Union gained a capability to intervene that it had lacked during the period of U.S. predominance. Washington, for its part, had to respond more assertively; otherwise, its actions would ostensibly be misinterpreted as indicating the weakness of a declining hegemon. Essentially, unilateral crisis management by a responsible hegemon appears to be more stabilizing than the confrontation of two roughly equal adversaries, each trying to outcompete the other.

However, I refute these apparently plausible interpretations of the superpowers' crisis conduct in the Middle East in the next section.

## Restrained Resolve and the Balance of Interests as Determinants of Superpower Crisis Management in the Middle East

Despite the impressive battery of evidence concerning both Soviet and American apparent aggressiveness in Middle East crises, analysts drawing conclusions on the basis of this evidence tend to overlook a factor that better explains patterns of superpower crisis management. The most serious shortcoming of their analysis is that it overlooks the relative *balance of interests* between the superpowers in each crisis as a major determinant of their behavior and of outcomes. To the extent that a great power demonstrates resolve in crisis only when its important interests are threatened, while being restrained once the adversary has greater interests at stake, one may conclude that the likelihood of the crisis escalating into an armed conflict between the great powers is low.

Indeed, as we will see, it is the balance of interests, rather than the precise military balance, that is the decisive element in affecting the balance of resolve,[37] and it goes a long way toward explaining U.S. and Soviet conduct in Middle East and in other third world crises. Our confidence in the explanatory power of the balance of interests is reinforced if we can discern recurrent patterns of restraint (which might even amount to tacit rules), regardless of the relative changes in the military balance between the powers.

Under bipolarity, as I noted in chapter 3, the superpower defending the status quo, an interest that is in its possession, tends to have an advantage in the balance of resolve in relation to an opponent challenging the existing balance. Since the status quo is a highly subjective and ambiguous concept, especially in the Third World, I define it in this book as the preservation of an existing regime of a local client, rather than the avoidance of relatively marginal territorial changes or of a tactical military defeat.[38] The implication for third world crises is that a patron defending the survival of its client has the edge in the balance of resolve over the protector of a client that is trying to change the status quo and thereby disrupt the regional balance and, as a result, also affect, even if only to a limited extent, the great power balance.

Hence, most apparent U.S. and Soviet overreactions in Middle Eastern crises can be accounted for by their commitment to defending the survival of their key allies. Since in most of the crises, Soviet clients were on the defensive strategically (see also Karsh 1985, 37; McConnell 1979, 249), it should not be surprising that the Soviets showed a greater willingness than the United States to become engaged in Arab-Israeli wars. But the Soviets threatened to intervene militarily only when a regional ally faced a major danger. At the same time, they, as well as the Americans, refrained from any military engagement in the offensive activities of a client that took place on the territory of the client's rival, and both powers showed some willingness to restrain aggressive clients.

### Resolute Caution in Soviet Behavior in Middle East Crises

The Anglo-French-Israeli attack on Egypt in 1956 was widely regarded as a colonialist act of intervention that received almost universal condemnation in world opinion and U.N. resolutions. One of the new champions of anti-imperialism in the Third World was under heavy military pressure from Israel and two major (though declining) colonial powers. In this light, the Soviet threats during the Suez crisis can be seen as consistent with an attempt to defend an internationally legitimate postcolonial status quo. Indeed, in a letter to the Security Council on November 5, Soviet Foreign Minister Shepilov proposed either a UN or a joint superpower military action to defend Egypt if the three invading powers failed to cease fire and withdraw (Holbraad 1979, 21–22, citing *Documents on International Affairs*). The proposal for a joint U.S.-Soviet action was spelled out even more explicitly in a note from Soviet Premier Bulganin to Eisenhower on the same day:

> The Soviet Union and the United States of America are both permanent members of the Security Council and great powers possessing all modern types of weapons, including atomic and hydrogen weapons. We bear a special responsibility for stopping the war and restoring peace and tranquility in the area of the Near and Middle East. We are convinced that if the governments of the U.S.S.R. and the United States firmly declare their determination to ensure peace, and come out against aggression, then aggression will be ended and there will be no war. Holbraad 1979, 22–23, citing *Documents on International Affairs*)

In a move that resembled subsequent American reactions to similar Soviet offers, the Eisenhower administration rebuffed the Kremlin's proposal and tried to deter the Soviet intervention by counterthreats backed by a variety of precautionary military moves.

The likelihood of actual use of force by the Soviets was quite low from the outset, and the threats are widely viewed as having been less credible than Soviet intervention threats in later crises, because of the limited Soviet military capabilities in 1956 (with respect to power projection to the Middle East and nuclear second-strike forces) compared to the patron of the European powers—the United States.[39] Indeed, there are a number of indicators that the Soviets did not seriously consider military intervention. The first is the timing of the threats. They came after the peak of the crisis: on the morning of November 5, Israel had already unilaterally halted operations and accepted the UN cease-fire resolutions, and the British and French were also about to stop fighting (Bar-Joseph and Hannah 1988, 453). The Soviets were also assured by that time of the strong U.S. opposition to the actions of its allies through Washington's statements and UN votes. The threat to dispatch "volunteers" to Egypt was not made publicly until November 10, four days after the cease-fire had come into effect (Fukuyama 1981, 583; Glassman 1975, 16–18; Holbraad 1979, 25–26).

The second indicator is the vague content of the threats (Mangold 1978, 116). The Kremlin never stated that it would implement them if its demands were not met, only that it could. The demands to Britain and France to cease fire—while avoiding the more far-reaching demand of troop withdrawal—did not stipulate a time frame within which France and Britain would have to comply (Jonsson 1984, 155). And although it called on Israel to withdraw from Sinai, Moscow refrained from demanding an immediate pullout. In contrast, in their communications about the proposed joint action with the United States, the Soviets suggested more specific military actions and more precise deadlines.

Third, there was a lack of any accompanying military moves that would have signaled resolve and preparedness to use force if Soviet demands were not complied with. Indeed, Soviet advisers stationed in Egypt were withdrawn to the Sudan during the war, much to the relief of the invading forces who had feared that these advisers might be used to man Egyptian MiG 15s and Ilyushin 28 bombers, for which not enough Egyptian pilots had been trained (Dayan, cited in Mangold 1978, 116). In fact, Soviet leaders admitted at the time of the crisis that they were unable to help the Egyptians militarily. Thus, when Syrian President Quwatli asked for Soviet aid to Egypt during a visit to Moscow, Marshal Zhukov, the Soviet minister of defense, reportedly responded, "How can we go to the aid of Egypt? Are we supposed to send our armies through Turkey, Iran, and then into Syria and Iraq and on into Israel and so eventually attack the British and French forces?" Khruschev told the Egyptian ambassador in Moscow that "there is no way in which we can help you militarily" (Heikal 1978, 70–72).

However, the low likelihood of Soviet resort to force in the 1956 crisis does not mean that there were not dangerous elements in its behavior in that crisis or that the Soviet threats were completely ineffective in bringing about the desired outcome of an early cease-fire and a withdrawal of the tripartite forces from Egyptian soil. Moreover, U.S.-Soviet interaction in the Suez crisis established some of the general patterns of their relations in Middle East crises: Soviet intervention threats are issued when a major ally faces a military defeat by a U.S. ally; the Soviet threats are followed by a twofold U.S. reaction—the deterrence of the Soviets and restraining pressures on its allies.

The USSR threatened to intervene in the 1967 war only when the road to the capital of a client state appeared open and there seemed to be a danger of an attack on that capital (Jabber and Kolkowicz 1981, 434; Wells 1979, 165), which could have brought down a pro-Soviet government. Before that stage of the Six-Day War, however, the Soviets did not threaten to intervene and did not provide much help to their Arab allies, despite the humiliating defeats that they suffered (Fukuyama 1981, 584; Heikal 1978, 181, 185, 191; Wells 1979, 165; Whetten 1981, 55) and despite the Arabs' outrage at the Soviets' nonintervention (Jabber and Kolkowicz 1981, 436). On the Egyptian front, the Israelis stopped at the Suez Canal and did not make any threatening move toward Cairo. But on the Syrian front, on June 10 Israel could easily have advanced on Damascus since Syrian defenses on the nearby Golan Heights had collapsed (Jabber and Kolkowicz 1981, 434; Wells 1979, 165). There were also indications that the Israelis were more inclined to overthrow the radical Syrian regime (Aronson 1978, 388 n. 85; Riad 1981, 17; Whetten 1981, 47). The United States, for its part, "would probably not have acted on her own to prevent Israel cutting the three main highways to Damascus (the presumed operational plan) and thus humiliating the Syrian regime . . . it was only when the Soviet Union threatened independent action that the U.S. decided, if she could, to exercise a moderating influence on Israel" (Whetten 1981, 54). Indeed, U.S. pressures probably helped to stop the Israeli advance (Ben-Zvi 1988, 351; Whetten 1981, 54 n. 31).

Thus, the superpowers in fact tacitly agreed that the overthrow of Middle Eastern governments through external military pressure should be avoided. By restraining Israel, moreover, the United States implicitly recognized the legitimacy of the Soviet threat.[40] On the whole, both superpowers demonstrated caution. Whereas the United States showed sensitivity to Soviet interests in Syria, the USSR did not back up its intervention threat with any military moves; nor did the Fifth Eskadra behave as if a Middle East war was under way (Jabber and Kolkowicz 1981, 436–37; Whetten 1981, 54).

Indeed, the late timing of the Soviet threat in the 1967 war—after the United States had been actively pressuring Israel to cease fire and Israel was already halting its activities—led one prominent analyst to conclude that the Soviets were, in fact, bluffing (Fukuyama 1981, 584). But although Soviet conduct was indeed very restrained, the claim of a bluff seems somewhat exaggerated. Fukuyama admits that, at the time Kosygin issued his threat, "the Soviets could not have known for sure that the Israelis were not about to push on to Damascus" (1981, 589). Since the Soviet objective was fulfilled—Israel complied with the cease-fire and the danger to Damascus disappeared—"the seriousness of the Soviet threat was never put to the test" (Wells 1979, 166). U.S. policymakers took the Soviet threat seriously.[41] The White House believed that Moscow was on the verge of using its airborne troops; the secretary of state and the president "had never assumed any [different]"(Wells 1979, 166, interviewing Rusk).[42] As a result, the Soviet threat exercised some influence, at least, on the intensity and timing of U.S restraining efforts toward Israel and consequently also on Israel's behavior and on the final outcome of the Six-Day War: the preservation of the Soviet client's regime.

As for the Soviet provocative behavior in May, 1967, that is, in the crisis period before the outbreak of the war, the most plausible explanation is the apparent Soviet calculation that they would be able to control Egyptian moves, so that these would remain at the level of deterrence but would not provoke Israeli military action. The Soviets were interested in an Egyptian show of force to deter a widely expected Israeli attack on Damascus (cf. Neff 1988b, 60; Whetten 1981, 47). This expectation was related to the mounting tensions between Israel and Syria since the radical Ba'athist coup of February, 1966. This Ba'athist regime supported Palestinian guerrilla raids from Syrian bases against Israel (Wells 1979, 159, and the sources cited in n. 3). Syrian shelling also led to increasing artillery duels between the two armies that even escalated on April 7, 1967, to an aerial dogfight in which Israeli jets downed six Syrian MiGs (cf. Aronson 1978, 61; Neff 1988b, 57). At the same time, with the encouragement of the Soviets, its two main allies in the Middle East, Syria and Egypt, were drawing together (Safran 1981, 387). On top of all of this, the Syrians issued bellicose and provocative anti-Israeli statements.[43]

As this Syrian behavior continued, Israel (most notably, its chief of staff, Yitzhak Rabin) began issuing public warnings that there was a limit to its patience (Aronson 1978, 61, 388 n. 85; see also Riad 1981, 17). On May 12, United Press International reported from Jerusalem that "a high Israeli source said today Israel would take limited military action designed to topple the Damascus army regime if Syrian terrorists continue sabotage raids inside Israel." The next day, the *New York Times* reported on its front page that Israeli leaders had "decided that the use of force against Syria may be the only way to curtail increasing terrorism. . . . The comments being heard in recent weeks in Tel Aviv, and especially since last weekend, are stronger than those usually heard in responsible quarters" (cited in Neff 1988b, 58–59). As an Israeli observer notes, "Fearing a massive Syrian artillery attack after the April air battle, the Israelis deployed some troops along the Syrian border. The Israeli troop concentrations were not very large, but, taken together with the earlier fighting, they could be interpreted as evidence of Israel's sharp change of course and an intention to attack Syria and bring down the Ba'athist regime" (Aronson 1978, 62).[44]

Such an attack could easily have devastated the unstable pro-Soviet Syrian government (Fukuyama 1981, 584) and thus could have caused the loss of a major Soviet ally and undermined Soviet standing in the Middle East.

While supporting the Egyptian show of force (i.e., its deployment of troops in the Sinai) at the outset of the May crisis, the Soviets failed to support subsequent Egyptian steps that could more easily have generated an escalation, notably the closure of the Straits of Tiran (Glassman 1975, 40–44; Holbraad 1979, 79–80; Jabber and Kolkowicz 1981, 431; Jonsson 1984, 162; Wells 1979, 159; Whetten 1981, 49). Not only is there no evidence that the Soviets pressed Egypt to go to war (Aronson 1978, 62), but the lesson of the unintended escalation appears to have been quickly learned. Only a few days after spreading false rumors, Moscow already tried to collaborate with Washington in restraining their respective clients. In Holbraad's words,

> With the likelihood of a strong reaction from Israel and its friends, the Russians must have feared not only a defeat of Egypt, about whose state of preparedness they were better informed than most, but also a confrontation with the United States. This would explain why, when the Americans told the Russians that they had received information from Israel indicating that Egypt might be planning to attack on 27 May, the Soviet government had its ambassador in Cairo call Nasser out of bed at 3:30 in the morning with an earnest warning to exercise restraint. . . . Descriptions of the Soviet attitude between then and the outbreak of war vary from mild concern to alarm. It does seem that Moscow, unhappy about the call for a "holy war", addressed several words of warning to Arab leaders before 5 June. (1979, 79–80)

During the June war, like during all the subsequent third world wars, the Soviets behaved very cautiously and did not support aggressive military moves by their clients. Most important, already in the June crisis and in all the later armed conflicts, the Soviets were extremely circumspect in terms of their own military actions, even if that behavior frustrated their Arab allies time and again (Heikal 1975, 1978; Sadat 1977).[45] The Soviets attributed their caution in the Six-Day War, despite the decisive Arab defeats, to the possibility of nuclear escalation,[46] a possibility that reflects the two major systemic factors of the postwar era, namely, the nuclear revolution and bipolarity.[47]

The Soviet decision to intervene in the 1969–70 War of Attrition seems to have been related to the major blows Israel inflicted on Egypt in that war, which could have threatened the survival of the Nasser regime. Tacit U.S. blessing of the Israeli moves tended to reinforce the Soviet inclination to become militarily engaged in Egypt.

In the light of these two factors, one can identify a number of stages in the Soviet intervention. In the fall of 1969, Israel achieved total air superiority in the canal front and thus was in a position to inflict heavy damage on the Egyptian military. The delivery of U.S. Phantom planes to Israel in September could, moreover, be interpreted as tacit approval of Israel's policy and as a major fortification of Israeli might (Breslauer 1983a, 79; Quandt 1977, 88; Riad 1981, 105). This seems to have been the background for the Soviet decision around that time (autumn 1969) to commit forces, if required, to reconstruct Egyptian defenses. The Soviets, however, were cautious enough to postpone the final decision, pending political-military developments (Breslauer 1983a, 79; Rubinstein 1981, 473). On January 7, 1970, Israel initiated deep penetration raids on the heartland of Egypt; the Israeli leadership hoped that the in-depth bombing would cause the weakening and even the overthrow of Nasser. Since the Israelis assumed that Nasser was a main factor in the continuation of the conflict, it seemed likely that his overthrow would pave the way for a political settlement acceptable to Israel (Aronson 1978, 117; Bar-Siman Tov 1980, 104–5, 121–25; Riad 1981, 118–19; see also Breslauer 1983a, 76; Quandt 1977, 95).[48] Once again, the United States seemed to be supporting Israeli behavior, if not Israeli intentions (Aronson 1978, 116–17; Riad 1981, 121; Whetten 1981, 60–61).

In his trip to Moscow at the end of January, Nasser threatened to resign if the Soviets would not restore Egypt's capacity to defend its skies. Nasser's resignation could have meant the loss of the Soviets' most trusted and important ally in the Middle East, and this was a key factor in the Soviet decision to let their own crews take charge of Egypt's air defense (Heikal 1975, 83–90; Riad 1981, 113, 119–20, 124–25; Sadat 1977, 197).[49] But rather than immediately carrying out their pledge, the Soviets first issued a threat of an intervention that would be implemented in case the Israeli air offensive was not halted. The somewhat vague threat was conveyed in a letter from Kosygin to Nixon (Kissinger 1979, 560–62). The United States rebuffed the warning, and the Soviets introduced their air defense system in late February, 1970. By not countering this Soviet intervention and by, initially, even suspending arms transfers to Israel, the United States, in fact, tacitly acknowledged the legitimacy of the Soviet engagement and the significance of Soviet interests in Egypt (Evron 1979, 30; George, with others, 1983, chap. 9 and 1986, 9).

The expansion of Soviet involvement after May, 1970, was probably designed to establish military parity or stalemate between Israel and Egypt as the most conducive condition for political negotiations.[50] The Soviets did not aim, however, to help Nasser acquire offensive capacity to regain occupied Sinai (Rubinstein 1981, 485). For one thing, Soviet combat engagement on the canal front started only at the last minute—in July, 1970, when the negotiations for a cease-fire had already gained considerable momentum (Fukuyama 1981, 585)—and the engagement was very limited (Dismukes 1979, 234). The Soviets adhered to the U.S. request not to deploy closer than thirty kilometers to the canal (Bar-Siman Tov 1980, 161). At the same time, because his requests for increased Soviet military support were turned down, Nasser was, in fact, forced to accept the second Rogers plan, which called for a cease-fire (see Heikal 1978, 199; Fukuyama 1981, 592; Sadat 1977, 128, 198).[51]

Soviet complicity in the Egyptian violation of the cease-fire on the canal following the War of Attrition seems, indeed, to conform to power politics conduct—an effort "to consolidate gains in a moment of ambiguity" (Breslauer 1985, 143). Still, the Soviets persisted in their caution by distinguishing between the periphery and the center and between defensive and offensive postures. While continuing to deploy their troops in the heartland of Egypt until July, 1972 (when Sadat expelled them), the Soviets, by contrast, were quick to withdraw their few crews from the canal front as soon as Egyptian replacements were available. By making this distinction, "the Soviets showed a keen sensitivity to the limits of activism, beyond which U.S. counteraction was likely to be stimulated" (Dismukes 1979, 234; see also Karsh 1985, 41).

In contrast to the contentions of the critics of détente, the USSR behaved cautiously in the 1973 War and in the months preceding it.[52] The Soviets did not support Arab plans to go to war,[53] mainly because of the fear of a superpower confrontation. Such a confrontation could have occurred regardless who was the local winner: an Arab victory would have led to U.S. intervention; an Arab defeat would have forced direct Soviet engagement. Moreover, a second decisive Israeli victory over Soviet arms and clients (after the 1967 war), which the Kremlin probably saw as the most likely outcome of an Arab-Israeli war, would have dramatically reduced Soviet influence in the Middle East.

The Soviet arms supply in the months before the war was probably a response to growing American unilateralism in the region (see chap. 6) and to the Egyptian expulsion of the Soviet advisors in July, 1972 (George, with others, 1983, 145; Shamir 1980, 282; see also Golan 1977, 41; Porter 1984, 123). One of the major reasons for the expulsion, in turn, was the restraints the Soviets imposed on their arms shipments to Egypt in the preceding years. Worried that they would lose their position in the centerpiece of their Middle East strategy, the Soviets became more responsive to Egyptian arms demands. At the same time, Moscow urged Cairo to turn away from the idea of war to negotiations (Garthoff 1985, 362–68; Golan 1977, 39–42; Karsh 1985, 39–40; Porter 1984, 116–25). Indeed, some argue that the arms supply in the months before the war was not intended to encourage Egyptian aggressiveness but to deter a preventive Israeli attack, thereby inducing the local parties to move toward a diplomatic solution (Jabber and Kolkowicz 1981, 464–65). At most, one could claim that the Soviets hoped to preserve some restraining control over a policy of war that Egypt had already decided on, irrespective of the provision of Soviet materiel (Golan 1977, 41; Roberts 1979, 193; see also Breslauer 1985; Porter 1984, 120–23; Sadat 1977, 238).

Similarly, since the Soviets had anticipated an Arab defeat, the wartime arms delivery represented "more an attempt to minimize their expected defeat than an attempt to help them achieve an overwhelming victory" (Sagan 1979, 162).[54] Their use of military tools, such as naval deployments, during the war was restrained (Jabber and Kolkowicz 1981, 458–62).[55]

Once the war broke out, moreover, the Soviets sought to bring an early halt to the fighting (Sadat 1977, 252–54).[56] Premier Kosygin again pressed for a cease-fire during his visit to Cairo (on October 16–19; see Sadat 1977, 258–

65) and eventually succeeded in persuading the Egyptian president to comply (Porter 1984, 127–28).[57] Even more critical and coercive was the pressure Moscow exerted on the Syrians to accept a cease-fire on October 22, which they did a day later.[58]

Like in the 1967 and 1970 wars, Moscow threatened to intervene in 1973 once its ally faced a strategic defeat that could have brought about the collapse of its regime. The three airborne divisions were alerted only on the night of October 10 when Israel, having recovered from its losses in the first days of the war, had advanced to the post-1967 border and was on the verge of a decision whether to invade Syrian territory. The Soviet warning was issued on October 13 when Israel had reached the defensive lines shielding Damascus and the Syrian heartland (McConnell 1979, 272–73). Indeed, the Soviet threat played some role in influencing the Israeli decision not to attack the Syrian capital. There were other considerations as well, but when to these, as an Israeli strategist commented, "were added the Soviet interest in the security of Damascus and the Soviet threats, it was obviously not in Israel's interest to advance beyond a point from which Damascus could be threatened by Israeli artillery fire" (C. Herzog 1975, 136). This evaluation was reinforced by the extremely low likelihood of U.S. aid to Israel in case of such a flagrant breach of the status quo (McConnell 1979, 273).

On October 22, the UN Security Council endorsed Resolution 338, which was jointly sponsored by the superpowers and called for a cease-fire. Nevertheless, the problem of enforcing the cease-fire was not an easy one. Although the question who had first broken the cease-fire is irrelevant, the Israelis, evidently, were taking advantage of the violations to complete their encirclement of the Egyptian Third Army. Since the surrender of the Third Army could have politically undermined his regime, President Sadat asked both the United States and the Soviet Union to dispatch a joint peacekeeping unit to enforce the cease-fire. Although the United States immediately dismissed the plan, the Soviets supported it. Indeed, the threatening message from Brezhnev to Nixon proposed, in the first place, to respond to Sadat's appeal for a joint U.S.-Soviet intervention to oversee the cease-fire, which both superpowers had sponsored. Only if the United States rejected the idea would the Soviets "consider the question of taking appropriate steps unilaterally" (Kissinger 1982, 583). Brezhnev did not explicitly state that these unilateral steps would be military ones, as Kosygin had in 1967, nor did Brezhnev in fact pledge to implement them, but only to "consider the question."[59] The Soviets also knew from their talks with Kissinger in Moscow on October 21, and from the two U.S. votes in favor of the cease-fire in the UN, that the United States supported the status quo of October 22. Moreover, Washington and Moscow shared at the moment the same operational objective, though for different reasons—to prevent a humiliating Egyptian defeat.[60]

Soviet certainty about the American position and the late timing of Brezhnev's ultimatum led Fukuyama (1981, 588–89) to conclude that, like in 1967, the Soviets were again bluffing. Indeed, even Soviet military activities "were sufficiently ambiguous to cast serious doubts on their status either as deliberate signals of a will to intervene or as bona fide preparations for impending unilateral action" (Jabber and Kolkowicz 1981, 458).[61] Still, it would be erroneous to suggest that the Soviets did not take any risks in making the threat[62] or that their moves did not have any effect on the termination of the war. At the time it issued the threat, the Kremlin could not be certain about Israeli intentions and especially about U.S. determination and capacity to control its ally. An absence of immediate Israeli compliance with the UN resolutions could then have presented the Soviets with a very uncomfortable choice between a major blow to their credibility as a patron (in the eyes of their clients and also in relation to the United States) and some kind of unilateral intervention with all its escalatory dangers.

The best way to think of the Soviet threat is neither as a bluff nor as a reckless move toward confrontation with the United States; rather, the Soviet signaling most likely aimed at increasing the pressure on the United States to control Israel (Glassman 1975, 164; Golan 1977, 124–28; Sagan 1979). Indeed, the main effect of the Soviet show of force was to accelerate the U.S. pressure on Jerusalem. Washington would have attempted to restrain its client in any case, in its own interests; but with time critical and facing such a disobedient ally as Israel, the Soviet ultimatum provided Kissinger with an invaluable card in his efforts to rein Israel in (Garthoff 1985, 384–85; Jonsson 1984, 188–89; Spiegel 1985a, 265; Whetten 1981, 75). Since the Soviet diplomacy of force made the stakes much broader than Israeli interests and U.S.-Israeli relations (Kissinger 1982, 576), Kissinger could afford to exert very heavy and effective pressure on a client (Dayan 1977, 551–52; Eban 1977, 537; Kissinger 1982, 602–5) that in normal times has commanded a powerful constituency in the American body politic.[63]

Whereas the Soviets were ready to confront Washington when the balance of interests was in their favor (that is, when their allies faced a strategic defeat like in 1967, 1970, and 1973), they behaved cautiously when a U.S. ally was threatened by their client—as was the case with Jordan in September, 1970. There is widespread agreement among analysts that Nixon and Kissinger were wrong in believing that the Soviet Union had instigated the PLO and Syrian violent actions against Jordan's King Hussein in that year (Garfinkle 1985, 136; Quandt 1978, 278–79; Shulsky 1979, 169–71). The Soviets expressed their disapproval of the Syrian invasion by withholding Soviet military advisors from the Syrian units that crossed the border (Shulsky 1979, 171), and Moscow reported the removal to Washington as a sign that it disagreed with the invasion (Kalb and Kalb 1975, 239). This removal is consistent with Soviet conduct in cases when its clients have invaded other countries—a type of action that the Soviets have not tended to support by military engagement (Karsh 1985, 37–41).[64] Such disengagement can be considered a signal of disapproval because it stands in marked contrast to the Soviets' tendency to support their allies when they have been on the defensive and especially when they have faced a strategic defeat. The Soviet fleet, though it was reinforced, did not interfere with the Sixth Fleet's movements (Hersh 1983, 241; Quandt 1978, 281). Moreover, Moscow was trying to restrain the Syrians through public announcements but mainly by quiet diplomacy in Damascus (Garfinkle 1985, 136; Quandt 1978, 280; Shulsky 1979, 177). In addition, the USSR urged "utmost restraint" on the Egyptians (Heikal 1975, 98–100; for a similar report, see also Riad 1981, 165).

The most plausible explanation of this Soviet caution is to be found in the superpower balance of stakes: clearly, the Soviets had a much smaller interest in Jordan than the United States had in the preservation of a long-standing ally facing the radicals' attack (Garfinkle 1985, 136; Quandt 1978, 281). Thus, for Moscow, "it did not take much of a combined U.S.-Israeli threat to make the crisis seem unduly risky" (Quandt 1978, 281).[65]

### Resolute Caution in U.S. Behavior in Middle East Crises

Does that mean that the Soviet Union would not have behaved much differently had there been no U.S.-instigated pressure in September, 1970? Is the implication, then, that the United States simply overreacted in the Jordan crisis by its show of force and by encouraging Israeli intervention and thus that Washington was the reckless actor in that episode, as critics of the Nixon administration have claimed? The answer is negative, for five reasons.

First, the United States was cautious with respect to providing an umbrella for Israeli intervention and probably did not pledge specific and unequivocal support against possible Soviet or Egyptian counterintervention (Garfinkle 1985, 130). Second, since there had not been any formal or explicit superpower agreement on the balance of stakes, given the superpower competition, the United States could not be sure about the Soviet position and had to demonstrate its resolve by nonverbal military means that would clarify its commitment to Jordan and thus minimize the prospects of miscalculation. That was a useful reminder to the Soviets at a time when sizable American forces were committed in Vietnam and the Soviets might be tempted to press for advantages in other regions. Third, the Soviets themselves admitted that their attempts to restrain Syria and Iraq "were aided to a considerable degree by the American military buildup in the Eastern Mediterranean" (quoted in Shulsky 1979, 177 n. 29). Fourth, the U.S. signaling also reassured King Hussein much more than he could have been encouraged by verbal promises alone. Hence, the

Jordanian monarch was emboldened enough to commit his full military power to the decisive battle, which removed the need for U.S. or Israeli action. Finally, American diplomacy coordinated the Israeli reaction with Amman and thus helped to avoid miscalculations in the absence of direct Israeli-Jordanian communication during the crisis (Quandt 1977, 125). To the extent that Jordanian power and Israeli deterrence were instrumental in containing the Syrian invasion, the United States played a useful role in stopping the Syrian attack, even if its show of force, directly or through the Soviets, was not the primary factor in Damascus's pullout.[66]

It is noteworthy that although Moscow tacitly accepted that the United States had greater stakes in Jordan, the Soviets' naval show of force and their propaganda also made clear Moscow's commitment to the defense of its Syrian protégé in the event of a U.S.-Israeli attack against Syria proper—that is, beyond helping Hussein to expel the invaders from Jordanian territory.

Indeed, the Soviet obligation to Syria would in all likelihood have deterred an Israeli action against Damascus, especially in light of the lack of a specific U.S. umbrella, had Israel found it necessary to intervene militarily. Thus, much as the U.S. commitment to Jordan influenced Soviet restraining efforts toward Syria, U.S. caution and the Soviet obligation to Damascus restrained an Israeli action against its northeastern neighbor.

The restrained resolve in U.S. crisis behavior in September, 1970, does not, however, obviate that Nixon and Kissinger overemphasized the global dimension of the Arab-Israeli conflict and overlooked regional concerns.[67] Yet such misperceptions have less to do with U.S. crisis conduct than with the administration's mishandling of the diplomatic effort to resolve the conflict up to the 1973 war. This mishandling, discussed in chapter 6, derived not so much from the Jordanian crisis but from the beliefs and perceptions that Kissinger held, at least since coming to office in January, 1969 (Kissinger 1979, chap. 10).

Although the coincidence in the timing of the Def Con–3 alert (at the end of the 1973 war) with the culmination of the fight over access to the presidential tapes in the Watergate affair seems to provide some basis for the contentions that the alert constituted an overreaction for domestic purposes, this was probably not the case. For one thing, whereas Watergate evidently increased the stress on Nixon, for that very reason his role in the crisis policy-making, particularly at the peak of the crisis on October 24–25, was largely confined to ratifying conclusions reached by others (Dowty 1984, 261; Garthoff 1985, 379 n. 71; Kissinger 1982, 593). For another thing, seen in the context of the time at which it was issued and in light of other U.S. responses to crisis situations, the alert seems to have been more a deliberate reaction to an external threat than to a domestic challenge. The Soviets had the motive for an intervention in that a military collapse of the Egyptians would have entailed a major strategic loss and put "their prestige as a superpower on the line" (Quandt 1977, 196; see also Dowty 1984, 256; Kalb and Kalb 1975, 553; Kissinger 1982, 585, 587).[68] The Soviets also had the capability, at least for a limited intervention (Dowty 1984, 257; Spiegel 1985a, 264),[69] which would have been sufficient to have "explosive political, and perhaps even military consequences" (Quandt 1977, 196–97). Hence, a Soviet unilateral move was perceived as likely (Blechman and Hart 1984, 286–87; Dowty 1984, 257; Kalb and Kalb 1975, 554–55, 563–64; Spiegel 1985a, 263–64).

Top U.S. decision makers believed that a failure to oppose a Soviet intervention in a vital region such as the Middle East would have a major adverse impact on the U.S. position worldwide. Under these circumstances, the alert was viewed as an unambiguous and prompt device to signal the seriousness with which the United States regarded the situation and its willingness to react to any Soviet resort to force, with military power if necessary (Blechman and Hart 1984, 286; Sagan 1985, 124). The shift to Def Con–3 was viewed as especially effective because it was expected to be picked up immediately by Soviet intelligence without being publicized in any country's media; thus, there would be no public challenge to the Soviet Union and no domestic political turmoil in the United States (Blechman and Hart 1984, 286; Dowty 1984, 258; Kissinger 1982, 587, 591; Sagan 1985, 124–25, 128) (which, incidentally, provides another powerful argument against the thesis that the alert was manufactured for domestic purposes). A solely conventional response would not have been powerful enough to quickly convey U.S. determination. "Only escalation to the nuclear level, symbolically of course, was seen as dramatic and threatening enough to make absolutely clear the gravity with which the U.S. perceived the situation and [its resolve] to do whatever was necessary to stop it" (Blechman and Hart 1984, 286–87; see also Sagan 1985, 124–25, 128). Even those who thought a Soviet intervention was unlikely still believed that the United States must demonstrate that it could act resolutely (Spiegel 1985a, 264). "In short, in its nuclear moves and statements, the U.S. was demonstrating and making credible the vital interests it perceived in the situation." (Blechman and Hart 1984, 288; see also Betts 1987, 125–26).

No less salient in the superpower behavior in Middle Eastern crises than the demonstration of resolve has been the showing of restraint and sensitivity to the other superpower's vital interests. As well as signaling that it would have escalated if the Soviet Union had used force, the United States helped keep the situation in hand by showing sensitivity to Soviet concerns. Simultaneous with the alert and similar to the twofold reaction of the Johnson administration at the end of the 1967 war, Kissinger exerted extremely heavy pressure on Israel. He demanded that Jerusalem comply with the cease-fire and permit the resupply of the Egyptian Third Army, which Israel had surrounded after the cease-fire the superpowers had sponsored. He thereby addressed the Soviet concern that had led Moscow to threaten intervention in the first place. Indeed, the U.S. pressure was effective and the Israelis succumbed to it.[70] In addition, Washington provided Moscow a face-saving formula by agreeing to the deployment of a limited number of Soviet (alongside American) observers to supervise compliance with the cease-fire, as a part of a UN peacekeeping force mainly composed of non–great power personnel.

However, if the United States had tried only to remove the reason for the Soviet threat by pressuring Israel but without deterring Soviet unilateral actions, the Kremlin could have interpreted that action as a sign that coercive threats influence U.S. behavior. Failure to counter the Soviet threat could have conveyed an impression of weakness before other audiences such as the Europeans, the Third World, and especially the Arab countries. Moreover, without countervailing actions, it would have been more difficult for the United States to convince Israel to spare the Third Army and for the administration to avoid angering pro-Israeli constituencies in the United States because of the perceived submission to Soviet menaces.[71]

In light of the rationale for the alert and the respect shown for Soviet sensitivities, it is hard to characterize the U.S. response as reckless. Washington behaved primarily in response to external stimuli. Hence, in his extensive research on U.S. decision making during the 1973 war, Dowty concludes, in contrast to the expectations of the crisis-induced stress school,[72] that "the greater the crisis, the greater the felt need for information, the more thorough the quest for information, and the more open the receptivity to new information." He also reports that "the greater the crisis, the more information about it tends to be elevated to the top of the organizational [decisional] pyramid quickly and without distortion," whereas "as crisis-induced stress declines, receptivity becomes permeated by more bias" (1984, 307).[73]

To the extent that the domestic crisis of Watergate had any effect on U.S. policy, it was only in the more limited sense of the need to demonstrate that the U.S. government was still able to function adequately and act decisively in the domain of national security despite internal distractions (Betts 1987, 126; Blechman and Hart 1984, 289; Dowty 1984, 261; Kissinger 1982, 589; Quandt 1977, 203; Spiegel 1985a, 264).

### From Suez to Lebanon: The Minimal Effects of Changes in the Balance of Forces on Superpower Crisis Behavior

According to hegemonic theories, periods of movement toward greater military parity between a hegemon and a challenger are dangerous and destabilizing. Many observers have indeed feared the destabilizing effects of greater military parity between the superpowers. The Middle Eastern crises of 1956 and 1982, respectively the first and last superpower crises in the Third World, should be especially helpful in evaluating the effects of changes in the military balance on superpower crisis behavior over time. In this section, I show that the influence of these changes during the Cold War was, in fact, exaggerated. On the one hand, the United States was constrained by the bipolar structure even before the major Soviet military buildup of the 1960s and the 1970s while, on the other hand, the Soviets continued to be restrained by systemic factors after their buildup.

Although the United States enjoyed a clear military superiority over the Soviets at the time of the Suez crisis, the bipolar competition in the Third World served as a major factor in inducing Washington to restrain its allies when they were the aggressors. Explanations of U.S. behavior in this crisis that are based exclusively on the good intentions of a responsible hegemon who is committed to maintaining the international order are necessarily subjective, being contingent on the inclinations of particular leaders and elites. Even if the latter are inclined to preserve order and stability, such inclinations could be undermined by the security dilemma inherent in the anarchic nature of the international system. In some cases and regions—Vietnam, Cambodia, Chile, Central America—where both Soviet capabilities and interests were less salient than in the Middle East, the United States behaved more recklessly than in that region.

In contrast, as Zacher points out, in a bipolar world "the close allies of an aggressing state would tend to oppose its actions for fear of driving the victim state and possibly other nonaligned states into closer collaboration with a rival coalition" (1979, 219). The fear of driving Egypt and the rest of the Arab world toward the Eastern bloc seems, indeed, to have been a prominent motivation in the American moderating acts vis-à-vis its allies in the Suez crisis. Eisenhower and Dulles were worried that the use of force by U.S. allies might make the leader of the Western alliance appear imperialist and therefore less credible as a bulwark against Soviet expansion (Spiegel 1985a, 71). In addition to superpower competition, the fear of superpower confrontation provided an important incentive for the United States to rein in its allies (Glassman 1975, 17). Eisenhower was furious at the British and the French in that the United States would have had to bail them out had they gotten "into real trouble with the Soviets" (Spiegel 1985a, 76). Thus, the effect of the Soviet threats on the invading states was both direct (especially in the case of Israel, but also, to some extent, for the European powers)[74] and indirect—that is, through the effect on Washington, which led to the latter's pressure on its allies. The effect on Washington was also double edged—the fear of confrontation with Moscow but also the provision of leverage to the United States over its allies. In other words, the Soviet threats to Paris, London, and Jerusalem made it more important but also easier for Washington to control its partners. Rumors about potential Soviet intervention triggered American precautionary measures and "as in 1973, Soviet-American preparations for a possible confrontation put pressure on the Israelis" (Spiegel 1985a, 77; see also Glassman 1975, 17). Only after the exchange with Bulganin on November 5 did Eisenhower find it imperative to check the allies urgently and put a stop to their operation. He made it clear to the British and French governments that although they were covered against the Soviet nuclear threat, they were on their own if the Kremlin decided to send "volunteers" to the Middle East. Following November 5, the United States exerted extremely heavy diplomatic and economic pressure on its allies; this pressure was critical in influencing decision makers in Paris and London to accept the cease-fire and withdraw from Egypt (Holbraad 1979, 32).

As Moscow narrowed the gap in its military capabilities vis-à-vis Washington, it should supposedly have engaged in more challenging and assertive crisis conduct. Indeed, U.S. fear of Soviet intervention in an Arab-Israeli war reached a peak at the end of the 1973 war and was expressed in the nuclear alert.

Since 1973, however, only one more Arab-Israeli war has taken place, namely, the war in Lebanon beginning with Israel's invasion in June, 1982.[75] Again, Moscow's clients, Syria and the PLO, were roundly defeated.[76] Yet despite the massive material and political support that the Soviets had provided to both these parties in the past, Moscow remained virtually passive during the summer of 1982 (Jentleson 1988, 324–25; Ross 1990; see also Dawisha 1982–83; Golan 1982; Sella 1982). However, the USSR did become more assertive in 1983, in fact assuming responsibility for the Syrian air defense (Ross 1985, 162 and 1990). Soviet willingness to run such risks over Syria suggests that it was premature to argue that there had developed a "marked Soviet disinclination to get involved" in the region (Dawisha, 1982–83, 449). Rather, as Breslauer (1985) maintains, the Middle East still held a relative priority in Soviet foreign policy. There was, moreover, a basic continuity in Soviet risk-taking propensity during the Cold War, at least up to the late 1980s, irrespective of the improvement in their interventionary capabilities but in high correlation with the importance of their interests at stake in different crisis situations.

Soviet inaction in 1982 can best be explained, then, by their relatively low stakes during the Peace for Galilee operation as compared to previous Arab-Israeli wars. This time no key allied Arab government was threatened. The PLO is a national liberation movement, not a nation-state; the lack of help for the PLO was consistent with past Soviet behavior in relation to such movements in general and to the PLO in particular (Ross 1990). The Syrians, on the other hand, have been the key Soviet ally in the Middle East since Egypt's realignment. Nevertheless, although the blow inflicted on the Syrians in 1982 constituted a major tactical defeat, it did not threaten Damascus. Moreover, the hostilities took place on Lebanese and not Syrian soil, and the Soviets had disapproved of the Syrian entry into Lebanon in 1976 (Golan 1982, 4; Karsh 1985, 38–39; see also Saunders 1988, 572).

One can certainly make the argument that despite the expansion of its sealift and airlift capabilities, Soviet military power was still a far cry from being able to control developments on the battlefield. This observation makes sense, given the considerable distance of the Arab-Israeli theater from the Soviet Union, U.S. naval deployment in the region,[77] and Israel's local superiority and overall impressive military power (in absolute terms and not only in relation to its neighbors).[78] Yet we have seen the earlier Soviet willingness to issue threats of intervention and to demonstrate an inclination to use force even when their military forces (strategic-nuclear and power projection) were weaker. The difference, then, concerns not the capabilities but the interests at stake. Hence, in 1982 the Soviets were essentially passive. But in 1983, as the question became (like in 1967, 1970, and 1973) one of the preservation of a central ally, the USSR became more assertive and indeed deeply involved—though still restrained (Ross 1985, 162–64). Its assumption of Syrian air defense and delivery of advanced ground-to-ground missiles were meant to deter future Israeli actions that could directly threaten Damascus.

### The Balance of Capabilities versus the Balance of Interests

We may conclude that relative changes in the balance of superpower military capabilities did not basically affect the recurrent patterns of restraint and tacit cooperation during times of crisis. Hence, Fukuyama (1981, 589) points out the consistent extreme caution in Soviet crisis behavior since 1956.[79] Indeed, Moscow's policy in 1973, let alone its inaction in 1982, was no more threatening than in 1967 and 1956, despite the increase in its military power (cf. Spiegel 1985a, 264).

Structural theory goes a long way toward explaining U.S. and Soviet restraint. In other words, the presence of only two great powers in the postwar period made it easier for Moscow and Washington to identify, and thus to be able to respect, each other's important interests in times of crisis.

That does not mean, however, that the presence of superpower forces at the local theater and the acquisition of power-projection capabilities had no effect on crisis conduct. Thus, whereas some could argue that Soviet threats in 1956 were not taken very seriously by their Western rivals, beginning with the 1967 war Moscow became a more credible participant in third world crisis management. Indeed, the growth of Soviet military forces led to "the evolution of mutual expectations about behavior, coupled with self-restraint" (Evron 1979, 21).

This link between the achievement of superpower military parity and the emergence of tacit rules seems a major manifestation of Waltz's (1979, 203–4) idea about the "maturation" of the bipolar world. Rather than resulting in growing instability (as hegemonic theories have expected), the emergence of full-blown bipolarity with two roughly equal (militarily) superpowers had the following consequences.

First, the most dangerous U.S.-Soviet crises (Berlin in 1948, 1958–59, and 1961 and the Cuban Missile Crisis in 1962) occurred when the United States enjoyed military superiority at the strategic level and, in the case of the Cuban Missile Crisis, also at the conventional level. At the very least, one can argue that U.S. preponderance did not prevent the outbreak of confrontations. In the case of the Cuban crisis, moreover, its origin seems to lie precisely in the American superiority. Indeed, although "several hypotheses have been advanced to explain why the Soviets placed missiles in Cuba . . . [b]y far the most widely accepted is the perceived Soviet need to redress the strategic balance."[80] If we compare the severity of the Berlin and the Missile crises with the post-1962 confrontations, we may conclude that an era of hegemony cannot guarantee the absence of severe crises more effectively than a period of equilibrium.

Second, after the Cuban crisis, the superpowers avoided direct confrontations, preferring instead conflict by proxy (cf. Holbraad 1979, 110–11; Jonsson 1984, 191). Although that must have been the chief lesson of Cuba (Holbraad 1979, 110), it was the expansion of Soviet military (power-projection) capabilities that made it possible to transfer the superpower competition to relatively remote third areas rather than the central arena (Europe). At the same time, the rising parity, manifested in the growing Soviet strategic capability, made it less necessary to compete in the established and proximate spheres of influence. This is because it became less necessary for the superpowers, especially the Soviets, to deploy nuclear missiles in great proximity to the other superpower to reach strategic parity. Although there still remained a potential danger of stumbling into volatile local conflicts, especially in the Middle East, on the whole, crises in the periphery were less dangerous than direct superpower confrontations in Europe or in the Caribbean, where the stakes were higher.

Third, the danger of the escalation of local wars was further reduced through the evolution of implicit understandings for crisis management in the Third World. The growth in Soviet airlift and sealift capabilities was a precondition for the development of such tacit rules and related procedures. The end result of the evolution of tacit rules and procedures was a decline in the probability of miscalculation and loss of control as compared to 1956 and 1962. As Jonsson (1984, 191) points out, the hollow Soviet nuclear threats in

1956 generated a greater war scare than the actual nuclear alert by the United States in 1973. The latter was interpreted as a diplomatic signal, whereas the 1956 Soviet threats succeeded in raising the specter of nuclear war.[81] Indeed, the Soviet nuclear saber-rattling in the Suez crisis was one of the few instances in which the tacit Soviet threat was to take the nuclear initiative and not, like in most other cases, to counter U.S. initiatives. Even if the world was very far from a nuclear exchange in 1956, by the 1970s the increase in Soviet military capabilities had made it less necessary for them to resort to the type of harsh threats they used in 1956. Under crisis circumstances, threats of this kind are destabilizing, and under the adverse effects of the security dilemma, they might lead to miscalculations and preemptive strikes, even if one or both parties are not interested in going to war.

Fourth, the more equal the superpowers became militarily, the greater became their ability to communicate nonverbally. Over the last two decades, both the Soviet airborne divisions and the Soviet navy have been able to serve as trip wires. The growing Soviet naval capacity, in particular, facilitated unspoken diplomatic communication in hours of crisis. Thus, Wells (1979, 167–68) observes the diplomatic utility of the combatant "tattletales" that shadowed the Sixth Fleet in the post-1967 crises. The Soviets could both convey their own interests in a crisis and also make significant inferences about U.S. policies from the location and conduct of U.S. forces. The Soviets (and the rest of the world), Wells argues, had been denied this information during the Suez war, when

> U.S. forces disappeared from their normal operating areas and the resulting uncertainty aggravated an already dangerous international situation. In 1967 the Soviet tattletales . . . ensured that any symbolic moves by the Sixth Fleet would be observed. They also ensured that in negotiations the Soviets could not claim to believe erroneous reports concerning Sixth Fleet activity, such as the report early in the war that U.S. carrier aircraft were engaging in combat operations in support of Israel. Ironically, the Soviet "tattletales" could be as valuable to the U.S. in crisis management as to the Soviets, in that they made it possible for the two governments to communicate with each other in the language of naval action as well as through more familiar channels of diplomacy. (1979, 168; see also Shulsky 1979, 177)

Fifth, the rising Soviet power helped, through the tacit rules, to terminate local wars before one of the local parties collapsed completely. This relatively rapid ending of regional wars could, at the same time, occur without having to rely on a single hegemon's sense of responsibility or its capacity to control unruly allies. In addition, the mounting capability of the Fifth Eskadra made it more difficult for the Sixth Fleet to provide assistance to U.S. allies; thus, the Soviet countervailing force posed a constraint on U.S. military behavior. Nevertheless, the overall U.S. military power, including the strength of its presence in the Mediterranean together with that of its allies, guaranteed that the Soviet willingness to use its forces would be a factor only when Moscow's friends faced potential aggression or strategic defeat, rather than when they were on the offensive. It is important to note that the Soviet buildup of its navy occurred at the end of both the Jordan crisis and the October War, that is, after Soviet clients had already been defeated (Dismukes and McConnell 1979; Jabber and Kolkowicz 1981).

Superpower theater forces did not have to be precisely equal for the Big Two to cooperate tacitly in crisis management. Even Gowa and Wessell's suggestion of "rough parity" (1982, 101–2) might not be essential for superpower mutual restraint in a bipolar world. However, a minimal but credible superpower capability to intervene militarily is a prerequisite for the emergence of implicit understandings (see McConnell 1979, 243). When the superpowers have powerful incentives to be cautious and when there are only two world powers that intervene in the periphery, the ability to deploy trip wires is sufficient to indicate commitment to allies, to signal resolve, and thus also to clarify and signal that the stakes are high. The credibility of the commitments to defend important interests, in turn, does not depend on the details of the balance of forces; more important is the historical pattern of behavior of the superpowers with respect to the particular issue in the particular region. In bipolar crises, show-of-force signals by the cautious actors usually reflect the persistence of their interests in the given area. This persistence of high stakes is manifested by the determination demonstrated in previous crises as well as by continuous arms supply, economic aid, and diplomatic engagement during noncrisis periods in the region in question. Another important indicator of resolve, however, is the sustained deployment of superpower forces in a certain region, and the size of these forces is important as an index of commitment. The multidimensional (military-economic-diplomatic-ideological) and persistent involvement of the United States (since the Truman Doctrine of 1947 and reinforced by the Eisenhower Doctrine of 1957) and the Soviet Union (since the Czech arms deal of 1955) in the Middle East clearly accords with these conditions.

Hence, despite their conflicting objectives in the Middle East and their dispute over the balance of interests between them, Washington and Moscow were able not only to avoid any shooting incidents between their forces there but also, because of the restraining and clarifying effects of bipolarity, to reach tacit agreements in times of crisis on the relative balance of their stakes and on regulating their use of force. These agreements constituted the rules of the U.S.-Soviet game in the Middle East during the Cold War.

## The Rules of the Game

Superpower interaction in Arab-Israeli wars during the Cold War showed patterns of restraint that might approximate tacit rules of the game, or unwritten understandings.[82] These rules established when it was legitimate for a superpower to intervene militarily on behalf of its local ally, how the intervention was to be carried out, and what ought to have been the other superpower's reaction. The tacit rules responded to the need to find a delicate balance in superpower behavior between resolve and restraint or, more specifically, between the commitment to an ally on the one hand and the desire to avoid an armed conflict with the rival superpower on the other. In Snyder and Diesing's terminology, this dilemma corresponds to the problem of how "to find the optimum mix or trade-off between coercion and accommodation" (1977, 207; see also 207–81).

In the initial stages of these Arab-Israeli wars, the great powers demonstrated their resolve mainly by diplomatically supporting their clients, tailoring their positions with respect to cease-fires to the fortunes of their clients on the battleground (see Stein 1980 and 1982). Occasionally, like in 1973, they also resupplied their protégés militarily. At this stage of the game, moreover, the superpowers neutralized each other (McConnell 1979, 249) through mutual deterrence, both of them behaving cautiously and neither of them threatening to intervene militarily.

This symmetry changed, however, once red lines were trespassed (Evron 1979). The most significant red line in third areas was the high probability of a complete military defeat of a key regional ally of a superpower, which jeopardized, in turn, the existence of the losing regime. Since in terms of the global superpower rivalry, the collapse of an allied government meant a loss to its patron, the balance of motivation—or stakes—clearly shifted, at this point, in favor of the patron supporting the loser. The rules of the game suggested that this asymmetry in the balance of interests made it both legitimate and credible for the patron of the loser to threaten to use force to prevent the loser's collapse. The patron of the winner, for its part, was expected to restrain its client while, at the same time, deterring the other superpower from actual military intervention. The threat of the intervention of the loser's patron, however, was more credible, so that if the winner's patron was unable or unwilling to restrain its client, one could expect that the loser's patron would have actually intervened. As long as the intervention remained defensive, it should have been acceptable to the winner's patron. Thus, the United States could tacitly accept the legitimacy of the Soviet intervention in Egypt during the War of Attrition as long as it was confined to saving Nasser's regime. The more Soviet forces became involved on the canal front, however, the greater became the U.S. willingness to provide sophisticated electronic countermeasures to the Israelis and thus to signal nonverbally the U.S. disapproval of the expanded and more offensive form of the Soviet engagement.

The cautious conduct of both the U.S. and the Soviet Union does not fit popular images about the high risk-taking propensity of the superpowers during the Cold War. More specifically, instead of a tendency to try to maximize gains, the rules manifested an inclination by the superpowers to minimize losses (McConnell 1979, 277; Stein 1980, 495). In fact, they have defended the status quo—the loser's patron by preserving its client, and the other superpower by tacitly accepting the legitimacy of the intervention, as well as by being on guard to keep the first superpower from going beyond reducing losses. Hence, as McConnell puts it, "this is no zero-sum game" (1979, 277). Their failure to prevent local wars notwithstanding, by observing the tacit rules and by being restrained in crises, the United States and the Soviet Union have shown little inclination to provide "blank checks" to their allies. Instead, they have demonstrated a strong desire to avoid armed hostilities between themselves that has induced them to cooperate in the limitation and relatively early termination of these local wars.

Each of the superpowers played a role in preserving order during Middle East crises. Crisis management in this region was not a single-star show. Even if it could plausibly be argued that the United States contributed more to crisis management than the Soviet Union because of its superior capabilities (being the patron of the militarily most powerful actor in the Middle East) and because of its supposedly greater willingness to preserve the status quo, the Soviets still fulfilled an important role in containing Arab-Israeli wars.

For one thing, the Soviets restrained their own allies. They withheld support from clients who invaded other countries (Syria in Jordan in 1970 and in Lebanon in 1982—due to the Soviet opposition to the Syrian invasion of that country in 1976).[83] The USSR also exerted moderating pressures on the Egyptians to accept an early cease-fire in both the 1967 (Johnson 1971, 297; Stein 1980, 490–92) and 1973 wars (Garthoff 1985, 369; Heikel 1975, 232; Sadat 1977, 252–53; Stein 1980, 500–501).

Obviously, the Soviets did not fully control the behavior of their Arab clients. There were lapses of time until their clients accepted the Soviet position; moreover, developments on the battleground played a greater role in inducing the Arab acceptance of cease-fires than the Soviet pressures. As their primary arms supplier, however, the Soviets could exercise restraining influence (cf. Garthoff 1985, 388) and, more specifically, could limit the ability of their protégés to fight protracted wars.[84] Thus, a lack of Soviet support for the continuation of the fighting probably helped lead to an earlier termination of the wars than would otherwise have been the case. It is true that Moscow failed in its efforts to prevent the outbreak of the 1967 and 1973 wars. Such failures indicate the limits of superpower influence on determined clients who have greater stakes, at least initially, in the outcome of local conflicts than the external powers. Still, Ben Porat reports that the Soviets succeeded in averting the planned Arab assault in May, 1973, hoping that the scheduled superpower summit in the following month would preclude the need for the Arabs to resort to force to recover the occupied territories (Ben-Porat 1985; see also chap. 6).[85]

One of the motivations for these restraining efforts was Soviet concern that another Arab defeat would undercut their standing in the Arab world. An even more important worry, however, was of destabilization in relations with the United States as a result of an Arab-Israeli war that would get out of hand.[86]

For another thing, through their diplomacy of force, the Soviets also exerted a restraining influence on the military conduct of American allies. Occasionally this was done directly, as when their involvement in the War of Attrition halted the Israeli deep penetration raids. More important, however, was the indirect effect of the Soviet threats, that is, through exerting pressure on the other patron. Soviet intervention was instrumental even in those cases in which the United States shared the same operational goal of containing the hostilities. At the very least, the Soviet threats increased the effectiveness of U.S. restraining efforts vis-à-vis its own allies. Hence, Moscow's threats lent greater credibility to American pressures on the Israelis in 1956 and 1973 (and also on the British and the French in 1956) to stop their advances, for fear they would trigger World War III. On the other hand, in 1967 and in the War of Attrition, and to a lesser extent in 1983, the Soviets fulfilled an even more important role in defending regimes that the United States and Israel might have wanted to topple. On a more general level, by conferring identical rights and duties on both superpowers, the unspoken rules connoted a sense of great power equality, and fostered international order through this parallelism of great power responsibilities in crises (although in normal diplomacy, the United States resisted granting an equal superpower role to the USSR in the international system in general and in the Middle East in particular—see chaps. 4 and 6).

At this point, a qualification is in order. Although, on the whole, the rules, indeed, were tacit, unspoken, and manifested in unilateral moves (as the model of the book leads us to expect), the superpowers also managed, to some limited extent, to coordinate their crisis behavior through explicit communication. Thus, in several Middle East crises, the United States and the Soviet Union showed some readiness to synchronize their restraining efforts through direct negotiations with each other. They did so regarding both their own activities as well as their pressures on third parties directly involved in the conflict (Holbraad 1979, 100–106).

Hence, as soon as large-scale violence broke out in 1967 and in 1973, the superpowers managed to communicate to each other their intention not to intervene directly. Kosygin's reply to Secretary Rusk's message on June 5,

1967, was the first use of the hot line in a crisis. In the ensuing exchange, the Soviet premier and the U.S. president agreed, in fact, on mutual nonintervention (Holbraad 1979, 106-7; Johnson 1971, 297-98; Jonsson 1984, 165; Quandt 1977, 62; Stein 1980, 488-89). And, on October 7, 1973, a day after the Yom Kippur War had started, Nixon sent Brezhnev a letter urging reciprocal caution; Brezhnev's reply was conciliatory and encouraging (Glassman 1975, 143; Jonsson 1984, 181; Kalb and Kalb 1975, 524; Quandt 1977, 173).

An interesting example of prompt crisis communication to avoid escalation involved an American intelligence ship, the USS *Liberty*, that was operating off the Sinai coast during the Six-Day War. On the fourth day of the war (June 8, 1967), the ship was attacked by unidentified aircraft and torpedo boats, which later proved to be Israeli.[87] What is most relevant here is the great sensitivity that the administration exhibited toward Moscow in handling the affair. Initially, Johnson and McNamara were worried that it might have been a Soviet attack, "and dark predictions of 'World War III' were briefly heard in the White House situation room" (Quandt 1977, 62). As soon as the administration learned the identity of the attackers, however, Johnson cabled Kosygin on the hot line to inform the Soviets of the incident and of the dispatch of aircraft from the Sixth Fleet to the scene of the attack. The incident indicates, as Quandt comments, "the extraordinary degree to which Johnson was attuned to Soviet behavior once the war actually began. If during the May crisis he had been prepared to see the conflict primarily in terms of Arabs and Israelis, once hostilities were under way the main focus of his attention was the Soviet Union. With Israel secure from defeat by the Arabs, only Soviet behavior could trigger a direct American military response. The regional dispute paled in significance before the danger of superpower confrontation" (Quandt 1976, 63). Thus the same administration that was blamed by many for irresponsible behavior in escalating the U.S. involvement in Vietnam showed great restraint and caution in an arena where Soviet capabilities and interests were heavily involved. Indeed, rather than differences of personality, a systemic factor—namely, bipolarity and the balance of interests, as manifested by the degree of Moscow's engagement in a certain area—goes a long way toward explaining the differences in American behavior in Vietnam and in the Middle East. Eugene Rostow, then the undersecretary of state for political affairs, stated in late 1968 that the president "feels in many ways it's [the Middle East] a more dangerous crisis than Vietnam, because it can involve a confrontation with the Russians, not the Chinese" (cited in Spiegel 1985a, 151).

Beyond coordinating their own military disengagement, the superpowers sometimes synchronized their efforts to moderate the behavior of their clients. Hence, on May 25-26, 1967, the United States and the Soviet Union coordinated the delivery of notes by their diplomats to both Egypt and Israel, calling for self-restraint (Holbraad 1979, 103; Johnson 1971, 291; Jonsson 1984, 164;

Whetten 1981, 49). The communication on the hot line on the first day of the Six-Day War also referred to joint attempts to moderate the local actors. Cooperative crisis diplomacy reached its peak during the 1973 war with Kissinger's trip to Moscow on October 21 following Brezhnev's request for urgent consultations. In their talks, Kissinger and Brezhnev reached an understanding on how to end the war. They agreed to a simple cease-fire "in place," together with a call to begin the implementation of UN Resolution 242. A day after the superpower talks, the Security Council unanimously adopted Resolution 338, which was almost identical to the U.S.-Soviet cease-fire agreement, thus ratifying that agreement (Garthoff 1985, 371–72; Kissinger 1982, 552–59; Spiegel 1985a, 260–61).

However, this explicit superpower cooperation in postwar crises had severe limitations. The superpowers faced recurrent dilemmas, and frequent trade-offs, between their fear of escalation and their regional role as alliance leaders and protectors (Snyder and Diesing 1977, 447; Stein 1980, 488–89, 513). They tried to reconcile the resulting inevitable conflicts by maintaining a delicate balance between resolve and restraint, by coercing prudently or accommodating cheaply, or by some combination of both (Snyder and Diesing 1977, 207–8; see also Williams 1976, 52–55; Young 1968). But as patrons they were committed to minimizing the losses of their clients, even if that entailed coercive diplomacy that might lead to confrontations with the other superpower.

Thus, despite certain elements of coordinated crisis diplomacy in 1967 and 1973, Washington and Moscow stumbled into confrontations toward the end of both wars; confrontations in which shows of force played a key role. Indeed, threats of intervention backed by short-of-war procedures were essential to activate the unspoken rules (see George 1986, 9). In other words, only when the patron of the loser raised the risk of escalation through a threat of intervention did the other patron exert sufficient pressure to restrain its victorious ally and thereby force an end to the fighting (see Stein 1980, 496).

The most recent example took place during the Lebanese War of 1982, even though in this crisis Soviet involvement was less intense than in previous cases. But after the severe blows that the Israelis had inflicted on the Syrian air-defense system on June 9, Assad's instinctive reaction was to turn to the Soviet Union. The Soviets were ready to provide hardware and personnel but not direct intervention. Yet as the first comprehensive account of the Lebanese War reports, Moscow "began preparing for possible Israeli invasion of Syrian territory. Massive quantities of equipment began to be stockpiled at airfields in the southern part of the Soviet Union, ready to be rushed to Syria at a moment's notice. It was all alarmingly reminiscent of the prelude to the Soviet airlift in 1973—and that was enough to spur the United States into action. Steps had to be taken to prevent a further escalation and the spread of the war" (Schiff and

Ya'ari 1984, 168). Indeed, as "the Russians were starting to show signs of edginess . . . [f]or Washington that meant the time had come to rein Israel in before the whole affair got out of hand" (Schiff and Ya'ari 1984, 169).[88]

But the role of military force in U.S.-Soviet crisis management and the recurring superpower confrontations and threats of intervention do not invalidate the characterization of each side's behavior as cautious. Threats to intervene, guided by diplomatic rather than military logic (George 1984a, see chap. 1), were used primarily for bargaining purposes. During crises, the superpowers usually focused on the signaling, bargaining, and negotiating aspect of the use of military power and not on the actual negation of the rival's military capabilities. Signaling for political purposes was, indeed, an important function of the superpower nuclear and power-projection forces.[89]

Thus, the Soviet threats in 1967 and 1973 were designed to activate U.S. pressure on Israel to comply with the cease-fires. In other words, the threats were, as Williams (1976, 109) points out, designed specifically to ensure that intervention would be unnecessary. The Soviet alert of four airborne divisions on October 24, 1973, which "appeared as vigorous preparation for military action, was probably intended as a substitute for it" (Williams 1976, 109; see also Ben-Zvi 1988, 349–50). This is also true for the Soviet threats in 1956 and 1967, and probably in 1970 (before the actual Soviet deployment in Egypt during the War of Attrition). Similarly, the U.S. show of force in September, 1970, was intended to avoid the necessity of the use of force, as was the case with the 1973 alert.

Because both superpowers had an important role in the operation of the rules, the regional order did not depend on a single good hegemon. Instead, while one protector activated the rules, when the asymmetry of motivation developed in its favor, the second patron played a significant restraining role. As the structrual balance-of-power perspective would lead us to expect, the second patron induced caution in the first protector (the one that issued the threat of intervention), by making it "think through the matter carefully and make sure that real interests are in jeopardy and that the effect of his intervention, however defensive in intent, will not be such as to give his client a subsequent advantage. He [the second power] has an even more important role if and when intervention actually takes place: to make sure the defensive intervention remains defensive" (McConnell 1979, 249).

The United States played this role of balancer, the restraining force, in 1956, in 1967, in the War of Attrition, and in 1973. The USSR played it in 1970 (Jordan) and in 1983 (Syria).

In sum, the type of cooperation that emerged during U.S.-Soviet crisis interaction fits the predictions of the structural balance-of-power school about great power crisis conduct in a bipolar world: resolute but also restrained, competitive but cautious, security-conscious rather than power maximizing. In addition, as the structural balance-of-power approach leads us to expect, this crisis collaboration, especially in the critical moments of regional war termination, was mostly tacit and primarily unintended—the outcome of unilateral moves and of what Holbraad characterized as "parallel but unconcerted and uncoordinated steps" (1979, 100).

The resultant tacit rules limited the duration, outcome, and scope of regional wars that had broken out, even if it took some time to reach a cease-fire and then to implement it on the battlefield (six days in 1967, eighteen days in 1973).[90] Moreover, by lending more effective and credible support to the defensive operations of their clients than to their aggressive designs, the superpowers unintentionally helped to preserve the status quo in the Middle East, especially the independence of the small states in this region. The United States and the Soviet Union were most successful in regulating their own military engagement in the regional wars, thereby minimizing the chances of the globalization of these conflicts. But in the process, they also tacitly and unintentionally recognized the stakes of the rival superpower, its sphere of interest, and its equal status.

## Conclusions: A Structural Explanation of Superpower Crisis Cooperation

The crisis behavior described in this chapter fits the expectations of systems theory regarding great power crisis cooperation in bipolarity. We have seen how, in the case of superpower involvement in the Arab-Israeli conflict, even seemingly aggressive, unilateral moves by the superpowers lead to "partisan mutual adjustment," tacit bargaining, and unintended cooperation.[91]

Indeed, unintended outcomes are a central theme in structural theory, which asserts that intentions and results sometimes do not coincide and that the structure of the international system conditions how actors behave. Due to external pressures, the outcomes of states' interactions often do not correspond to the actors' initial desires and domestic characteristics. The analysis of the superpower involvement in Middle East crises has indeed shown that the bipolar structure of the postwar era generated outcomes that were more moderate and stabilizing than one might have expected from the ideologies and internal characteristics of Moscow and Washington.

Thus, the bipolar structure restrained the behavior of the superpowers during crises. Despite their intense ideological and geopolitical rivalry in normal times, the United States and the Soviet Union were able to tacitly cooperate in times of crisis, more from *necessity* than by *choice*. As structural theory would lead us to expect, the absence of a shared vision of world order did not jeopardize the emergence of tacit arrangements for crisis management, once the appropriate systemic conditions were in place. More specifically, the tacit rules constituted unintended outcomes in that whereas during normal periods the superpowers desired to revise the status quo in their favor, their crisis behavior, in fact, helped to consolidate it. Similarly, while both the United States and the USSR fundamentally rejected the idea of spheres of influence, the tacit rules did acknowledge in practice the legitimacy of such spheres. Ideological rivalry and cultural heterogeneity, in contrast, were able to constrain the construction not only of long-term security regimes with explicit norms and principles, as envisioned by the international society school, but also more limited concerted diplomacy, as shown in the next chapter.

The presence of survivable second-strike capability in both superpowers could induce even ideological rivals to avoid premeditated war. More specifically, the fear of World War III in the nuclear age created the need for a means of exercising power in a crisis that would be more powerful than mere verbal threats yet short of large-scale violence. The various show-of-force signals, which became more common in the postwar era, provided these means, as we have seen in Middle East crises. Indeed, short-of-war options enabled the United States and the Soviet Union to demonstrate resolve in defending their interests and yet avoid war by showing self-restraint. Hence, crises became a surrogate for war in the post-1945 era and a means for demonstrating resolve (Bell 1971; Snyder and Diesing 1977; Waltz 1964).

But the lack of inadvertent escalation to the global level of such shows of force, and of the Middle East crises during which they were used, can be accounted for by the stabilizing features of bipolarity suggested in chapter 3.

## Clarity and Simplicity

The clarity and simplicity of the bipolar structure facilitated the communication of the show-of-force signals and helped to make them more credible and effective and thus made possible the emergence of tacit rules. In a bipolar world, there is greater clarity about commitments and about the balances of capabilities, interests, and threats, all of which facilitates crisis management. In Middle Eastern wars, as we have seen, the superpowers focused on each other; and the single source of threat (and of potential cooperation) has enabled effective coordination between them and successful crisis management.

## Control over Allies

When push came to shove, the limited significance of allies for the global balance of capabilities in bipolarity encouraged the superpowers to be restrained in their support of clients. In a world in which so powerful a state as China could switch alliances twice since 1945 without bringing about a major change in the global balance of forces, no loss in the Middle East could have caused a decisive shift in the East-West balance, despite the significance of such states as Iran, which the United States "lost" in 1979, or Egypt, which the Soviets "lost" between 1974 and 1976. Moreover, the high dependence of clients on the superpowers' economic assistance, arms transfer, and diplomatic support made it easier for Moscow and Washington to restrain their allies, at least at the time when such structural asymmetries in relative capabilities should play the most critical role—times of crisis.

Indeed, that realization was shared by many regional leaders and spokespeople, perhaps because they were particularly aware of the high dependence of their states on the superpowers and the considerable leeway of the latter toward their clients in bipolar crises. For example, the Israeli defense minister at the time of the 1973 war and an Egyptian confidant of Presidents Nasser and Sadat had the following to say, respectively, about superpower cooperation in terminating the war:

> After we cut off and surrounded the Egyptian Third Army, crisis followed. At first it seemed that the two Super Powers alone were involved. But it was soon evident that the United States and the Soviet Union had resolved matters between themselves, and the crisis turned into one between the U.S. and Israel. (Dayan 1977, 551)

> The incident of the 25 October alert was revealing in many ways. It demonstrated how the two super-powers had become at the same time partners as well as antagonists. It demonstrated their determination at all costs to avoid being dragged into a real confrontation with each other. . . . It showed that . . . they always find it easier, when it comes to the stage of making concessions, to put pressure on their friends rather than to do it themselves. (Heikal 1975, 225)

### Autonomy from Domestic Pressures

U.S.-Israel relations are especially pertinent for evaluating the autonomy of top decision makers from domestic politics in bipolar crises. Indeed, despite Israel's considerable influence in U.S. domestic politics (see chap. 4), the United States succeeded in controlling Israeli behavior in times of Arab-Israeli wars (see Organski 1990, 190–201), although not necessarily in times of normal diplomacy (see chap. 6).

The contrast between U.S. Middle East policymaking in crisis and noncrisis settings clearly conforms to the structural expectation (presented in chaps. 2 and 3) about the relatively minor influence of domestic politics in bipolar crises. As Quandt generalizes from his comprehensive study of U.S. Middle East diplomacy, "crisis periods, especially, tend to isolate policy makers from domestic pressures. Decisions are often made rapidly, before public opinion can be mobilized. Information is closely held, depriving interest groups of the means for effective action. The stakes are high and the public tends to be deferential to presidential authority, even when that authority has been weakened, as Nixon's had been" (1977, 203).[92]

## Control over the Military

Although there is a potential danger of loss of control over the military during a tense crisis, the Middle East record confirms the expectation that under bipolarity, as crises become more intense, the control by the political leadership will increase rather than decline (see chap. 3; see also Mangold 1978, 165). Kissinger, for example, reports that during the 1973 war, he insisted on determining the exact location of navy units sailing off the shores of Israel and Egypt (cited in Frei 1983, 144). Kalb and Kalb (1975, 232) observe a similar pattern in Kissinger's behavior during the Jordanian crisis. Similarly, Dowty's conclusions on U.S. crisis behavior in 1958, 1970, and 1973 directly challenge the application of the bureaucratic politics model to crisis situations: the evidence from all three Middle Eastern crises indicates that "the more intense the crisis, the less the influence of 'standard operating procedures'; the more intense the crisis, the greater the role in decision-making of officials with a general rather than a 'parochial' perspective; the more intense the crisis, the less the influence of vested interests in the bureaucracy ('bureaucratic politics')" (1984, 348).[93]

## Effects of Crisis-Induced Stress

The record of U.S. and Soviet conduct in Middle East crises, notably their adherence to the tacit rules, is consistent with the proposition advanced in chapter 3 that few adverse consequences of crisis-induced stress should be expected in bipolarity.

Indeed, Stein concludes that during Middle East crises, "Soviet and American leaders approximated rational modes of negotiation. A distinguishing characteristic of rational bargaining, a characteristic that occurs all too infrequently, is recognition of the inevitability of trade-off among competing values. Both in 1967 and in 1973, Soviet and American leaders met this test" (1980, 513).

In his study of U.S. behavior in three Middle Eastern crises, Dowty concludes that "it is clear that increasing stress did not lead decision-makers to become more closed to new information [, though] other aspects of cognitive performance are more complex to judge" (1984, 339). Moreover, the evidence from U.S. decision making in Middle Eastern crises regarding the search for and receptivity to information accords well with the conception of "minimal rationality" advanced in chapter 2.[94] In other words, fundamental values and policy goals remained rigid, but

> perceptions of the environment and immediate policy choices proved to be . . . sensitive to external change and flexible in operation. Policy-makers proved willing to accept evidence that challenged prevailing perceptions on many issues, such as . . . the likely costs of U.S. action in 1970, and the military balance during the 1973 war. . . . There was also sensitivity to negative feedback from policies carried out. . . . On the whole, then, there was no cognitive rigidity, but rather considerable adaptability, in analyzing situational factors and preferred strategies. (Dowty 1984, 340)

A modest form of rationality also prevailed concerning the search for and evaluation of alternatives. The narrowing of focus on military options and immediate concerns "was accompanied by a clear tactical rationality. . . . Policy-makers did not, at the height of crisis, reexamine their basic beliefs, but their choice of options was based on analysis of costs and gains rather than on purely affective reactions or bureaucratic bargaining and compromise" (Dowty 1984, 343–44).

### Persistent Engagement and Restrained Resolve

Not less important for the avoidance of an inadvertent escalation, however, was the persistent military and diplomatic engagement of the superpowers in the Middle East during the Cold War. Accordingly, they were repeatedly ready to demonstrate resolve (as distinguished from recklessness and overreaction) in defending their important interests and commitments in the region. At first glance, this determination seems to have been destabilizing since it brought about frequent superpower crises. Nevertheless, the frequency of crises in the initial period of the Cold War, such as the Suez crisis, gave the global antagonists the opportunity to delineate their red lines and to learn the implicit rules through a process of signaling threats and promises. Hence, precisely because of their recurrent willingness to protect their vital assets, it became easier for each superpower, in a world of only two great powers, both to identify and respect the interests and spheres of influence of their rivals in crisis situations.[95]

However, the type of cooperation discussed in this chapter was primarily tacit and spontaneous—the unintended outcome of unilateral moves and of simple learning by the superpowers. The systemic factors that were so helpful for the emergence of the tacit rules were not, however, sufficient for producing a higher level cooperation and more complex learning.[96] Indeed, factors below the system level exert a critical influence on normal diplomacy and joint attempts not only to manage crises but also to resolve conflicts. We will now turn to an analysis of such attempts by Washington and Moscow to collaborate in settling the Arab-Israeli conflict.

Chapter 6

# Explaining Superpower Diplomacy: Attempts at U.S.-Soviet Collaboration in Resolving the Arab-Israeli Conflict

In this chapter I continue the discussion (begun in chap. 4) of high-level explicit great power diplomatic cooperation in regional conflict resolution. Yet while I focused on the highest level of such cooperation—a full-blown diplomatic concert—in chapter 4, in this chapter, I address a more limited and less ambitious level of great power diplomatic collaboration, that of concerted diplomacy in a certain issue or region. However, the same factors influencing the formation of great power concerts also affect the emergence of concerted diplomacy. Accordingly, the factors discussed in chapter 4 are applied in this chapter to an empirical case—the attempts at superpower diplomatic cooperation in the Middle East during the Cold War.

When we look at the record of superpower diplomacy in the Middle East, two puzzles confront us. First, needless to say, in view of the ideological-cultural divergence of the superpowers, a full-blown concert was a nonissue. Moreover, even regarding more limited concerted diplomacy, the intensity of the global U.S.-Soviet competition during the Cold War, which was sharper in the Middle East than in other third areas, should ostensibly have led us to expect a very low likelihood of explicit superpower cooperation in normal Middle Eastern diplomacy. Yet, surprisingly, the record of U.S.-Soviet interaction in noncrisis situations in this region shows that on various occasions both superpowers have tried to construct common diplomatic initiatives, sometimes even reminding us, although remotely, of the joint management of international conflicts by the Concert of Europe. At least, the superpowers have shown some willingness to behave responsibly and, at times, to take positions at some distance from their respective clients to advance the peacemaking process in the Middle East.

Yet—in contrast to the repeated success, as we saw in the last chapter, of superpower crisis management—the record of joint superpower attempts at regional *conflict resolution* in the Middle East was poor during the Cold War. In other words, while on the one hand the superpowers made more attempts at cooperation than should ostensibly have been expected, on the other, these attempts bore little fruit. Despite the large difference in capabilities between the superpowers and their clients, Moscow and Washington did not succeed in imposing a settlement in the Middle East or even in radically changing their allies' diplomatic positions, as we should supposedly have expected from a power-related analysis. Indeed, though the positions of the superpowers have at times been closer than at other times, their cooperative inclinations have rarely converged for any length of time; thus, they have never succeeded in sustaining collaboration long enough to decisively impel the region toward conflict resolution. Moreover, in contrast to the continuity and similarity of superpower crisis behavior, their attempts at conflict resolution, although recurrent, were occasional and characterized by discontinuity, and their approaches to cooperation were dissimilar. And to understand the reasons for this, we must focus on ideological, cognitive, and domestic factors that are not treated in a systemic, balance-of-power perspective. These factors include differences in U.S. and Soviet approaches toward the Arab-Israeli conflict, U.S. domestic and bureaucratic politics, and the beliefs of key American and Soviet policymakers.

Yet first it is necessary to explain why these attempts at cooperation were made at all. The first puzzle (attempts at concerted diplomacy taking place in the absence of similarity and moderation) is best addressed by the application of the factors discussed in chapter 4 with regard to the emergence and the form of concerts. Thus, four factors may explain the recurring attempts at superpower cooperation:

1. Common fears of escalation and inadvertent war
2. The inclination of a weaker or more vulnerable power to a cooperative approach
3. The absence in authoritarian states of domestic groups opposing cooperation
4. Certain dispositions and beliefs of individual decision makers toward the three images discussed in chapter 4, which are conducive to cooperation

These factors can lead to attempts at concerted diplomacy even in the absence of similarity and moderation. Yet these factors are insufficient to ensure the success of the attempts, to the extent that other factors may undermine cooperation.

Accordingly, the second puzzle—regarding the failure of the attempts at concerted diplomacy—is likewise explained by the factors addressed in chapter 4:

1. The tendency of the superior power to pursue a unilateral-exclusionary approach, not tempered in this case by similarity and moderation

2. The domestic opposition in a pluralist polity to any form of a condominium-like arrangement with an authoritarian power at the expense of small allies. This opposition will be led by domestic and transnational linkage groups sympathetic to the small ally. The disagreement between a pluralist and an authoritarian power over the form of their cooperation toward small states is likely to undermine any cooperation between them
3. Images and beliefs of other decision makers that are not conducive to cooperation, especially a negative image of the opponent
4. Most fundamentally, the domestic opposition in a pluralist democratic polity to any cooperation with an ideological rival

These factors detrimental to cooperation could only be reduced or superseded by growing similarity and moderation. Indeed, as the ideological gulf between the superpowers has started to narrow following the post-1985 changes in the Soviet Union, much more meaningful superpower concerted diplomacy could become possible in the late 1980s, even approaching, at least to some extent, the level of a concert.

Accordingly, this chapter is divided into sections that reflect these issues and that parallel the sections of chapter 4 while applying them to the Middle East. In the first section, I provide a brief survey of the main attempts at U.S.-Soviet diplomatic collaboration during noncrisis periods in the Middle East from the June War up to the mid-1980s. However, in the first section I also demonstrate that these attempts failed during this period because of the apparent dominance of competitive-unilateral inclinations on the part of both superpowers. The simultaneous concurrence of both competitive and collaborative incidents under essentially the same bipolar system demonstrates the indeterminacy of structural factors with respect to cooperation in conflict resolution. In the following sections, I explain both the recurrence and the failure of the attempts at cooperation by examining various factors in turn. In the second section, I suggest the influence of a common fear of escalation and inadvertent war on the willingness of both superpowers to attempt a collaborative strategy, at least to a certain extent. In the next two sections, I show that despite this common fear and despite being located similarly in the bipolar system, the superpowers in fact had different approaches toward collaboration in resolving the Arab-Israeli dispute and that this contrast reflected the uneven balance of nonmilitary capabilities between the two countries as well as domestic political differences between them. The combination of such differences constrained the feasibility and effectiveness of even limited concerted diplomacy.

In the fifth section, I address how the beliefs of different U.S. and Soviet leaders have affected the variations in their countries' inclination to cooperate or compete during different administrations. In the sixth section, I discuss the keen ideological differences between the superpowers, which have underlain all the other obstacles to cooperation and resulted especially in the U.S. rejection of Soviet participation in conflict resolution in the Middle East. Accordingly, in the final section, I discuss cognitive learning by policymakers, especially with regard to changes in the image of the opponent that are in turn, affected by changes in the domestic attributes of the great powers. This cognitive learning increases the policymakers' inclination to cooperate and supersedes the other factors detrimental to cooperation. In other words, the more similar and status quo oriented the great powers become, the greater the prospects for the pursuit of concerted diplomacy even if the structure of the international system does not basically change.

## Superpower Interaction in Normal Diplomacy in the Middle East: The Historical Record

The record of superpower diplomacy in the Middle East is a complex and mixed one and includes both cooperative and competitive elements. For the sake of clarity, in this section, I present these elements separately, and analyze them in subsequent sections.[1]

### Cooperative Elements—Joint Superpower Attempts at Resolving the Arab-Israeli Conflict

The first attempt at superpower cooperation for resolving the Arab-Israeli conflict resulted in the endorsement on November 22, 1967, of Resolution 242 by the UN Security Council. The resolution was based on a joint U.S.-Soviet formula that was first discussed during the Glassboro summit conference between President Johnson and Premier Kosygin, held a few weeks after the Six-Day War (Johnson 1971, 484) and later finalized in negotiations between Soviet Foreign Minister Gromyko and Secretary of State Rusk. The formula called for Israeli withdrawal from territories occupied in the June War in exchange for recognition of the right of every state in the region to live in peace within secure and recognized boundaries. Although a comprehensive settlement of the Arab-Israeli conflict has not been reached so far, this trade-off still constitutes the most widely accepted formula for settling the dispute.

A second attempt at superpower collaboration followed the U.S. presidential elections of 1968. The Soviets indicated their interest in joint diplomacy by putting forward in December, 1968, a plan for an overall peace settlement in the Middle East, calling for full implementation of Resolution 242. The incoming Nixon administration agreed that Secretary of State Rogers and Assistant Secretary of State Sisco should conduct substantive talks with Soviet Ambassador Dobrynin and ultimately with Foreign Minister Gromyko on this issue. Commencing in March, 1969, the two-power talks picked up considerable momentum in the following months with the great powers distancing themselves from their clients' stances, despite Soviet retrogressions in June, 1969 (Breslauer 1983a, 83-84). On October 28 the superpowers concluded a joint brief to guide Gunnar Jarring, the UN emissary, in the hoped-for negotiations over an Egyptian-Israeli agreement (Whetten 1974, 75-76). The joint document came to be known as the first Rogers Plan and was essentially based on the principle of trading territories for peace. However, this initiative was overshadowed by the escalating War of Attrition along the Suez Canal during the winter of 1969-70. Further progress was made in the two-power talks during the summer of 1970. But again, developments on the ground, notably U.S.-Israeli accusations of Egyptian-Soviet violations of the cease-fire, superseded the diplomatic collaboration, and the two-power talks were suspended (Whetten 1981, 63).

When a third attempt at cooperation was under way, about a year later, the leading role in the formulation of America's Middle East policy had already moved away from the State Department to the White House. The superpower dialogue on the Middle East was thus conducted from that point on by the top policymakers. Through an exchange of letters, Nixon and Brezhnev agreed to collaborate in the Middle East (Kissinger 1979, 1285-86, 1288-89); but the main substantive negotiations were handled by Kissinger and Gromyko during the May, 1972, summit. As a result, the superpowers concluded "general working principles" for a comprehensive peace agreement. The common principles indicated a major Soviet concession, as they made allowances for considerable retentions of captured territory by Israel (Kissinger 1979, 1293-94; Quandt 1977, 150-51).

Formal superpower cooperation seemed to culminate during the October War and in its immediate aftermath. In a meeting in Moscow held during the war, Kissinger and Brezhnev called for peace negotiations between the warring nations and stated that Moscow and Washington would play the role of cochairs of a multilateral peace conference (Quandt 1977, 192; Stein 1980, 507-8). In the aftermath of the war, in a scene reminiscent of the great diplomatic conferences of the nineteenth century, the great powers indeed cochaired the Middle East Peace Conference in Geneva in December, 1973.

Although in the next few years Kissinger engaged in unilateral step-by-step diplomacy, the Carter administration came into office in 1977 with a commitment to renew the superpower collaborative effort in the Middle East. It decided to move from Kissinger's strategy of partial agreements toward an attempt to achieve a comprehensive Arab-Israeli peace settlement. Closely related was the decision of the new foreign policy elite to change the exclusionary U.S. mediation to joint diplomacy with Moscow through the reconvening of the Geneva Conference cochaired by the superpowers.[2] The major manifestation of the renewed superpower diplomatic cooperation was a U.S.-Soviet joint communiqué of October 1, 1977, which called for "withdrawal of Israeli Armed Forces from territories occupied in the 1967 conflict; resolution of the Palestinian question, including ensuring the legitimate rights of the Palestinian people; termination of the state of war and establishment of normal peaceful relations . . . " (Quandt 1986a, 343–44).

Finally, the failure of U.S.-sponsored attempts to persuade other Arab states to join Egypt and Israel in the Camp David process has led since 1985 to a renewed interest in the idea of an international conference to resolve the Arab-Israeli dispute. The Soviets and their allies, the Syrians, have persisted in their support of multilateral diplomacy, which in their view meant an active and influential Soviet participation in the peace process, specifically through the device of an authoritative international conference. Although the Reagan administration did not show great enthusiasm for joint diplomacy with the Soviets, Washington's opposition to the notion of an international conference and to the inclusion of the Soviets has seemed to weaken in the course of time. With the help of American diplomats, King Hussein of Jordan and the then-Israeli Foreign Minister Peres reportedly concluded an agreement on April 11, 1987, on how an international conference would function.[3] Since this understanding did not gain the support of the Israeli Prime Minister Yitzhak Shamir and his Likud bloc, Secretary of State Shultz suggested in October, 1987, that Shamir and King Hussein come to Washington at the time of the superpower summit, which was scheduled for the end of the year, to receive a joint U.S.-Soviet blessing for negotiations. This time it was Jordan that turned down the American idea. Shortly after that, in December, 1987, the uprising or intifada of the Palestinians in the occupied territories erupted. The major American diplomatic response was the Shultz initiative of March 4, 1988, in which the secretary suggested that an international conference would precede bilateral negotiations between Israel and a Jordanian-Palestinian delegation (see Quandt 1988, 376–77).[4]

The recurrent efforts of the superpowers to coordinate their diplomacy in the Middle East appeared to indicate a certain degree of continued commitment to the idea of a joint managerial role of the superpowers in the international system in accordance with international society expectations.[5] This commitment lasted despite the keen competition between the superpowers as well as the numerous ideological, domestic, and bureaucratic obstacles, and occasional opposition of their clients, to great power cooperation. The commitment to superpower joint diplomacy was even institutionalized, to some extent, by the cochairship of the Geneva Peace Conference.

Thus Moscow and Washington were frequently aware of their responsibility, at a minimum, to work for war prevention in the Middle East, lest a local war would embroil them. Their joint diplomacy suggests, moreover, a certain willingness both to cooperate with the rival superpower, sometimes even at the expense of one's local allies, and to advance a peace settlement. And by accepting the superpowers' cochairship of the Geneva Peace Conference, the small states acknowledged their special role. Thus, the regional actors recognized, at least in the aftermath of the 1973 war, the necessity that both the U.S. and the Soviet Union be involved in the diplomatic process, at least in the formal sense.

## Competitive Elements—Unilateral-Exclusionary Superpower Behavior

Yet a closer look at superpower diplomatic conduct in the Middle East seems to suggest that it was characterized by unilateral inclinations of both sides. Many observers note that far from pursuing collaborative policies both great powers engaged in fact in competitive efforts in the region.

The major argument in the West and in Israel, though not necessarily in the Arab world, against the notion of a joint superpower role in Arab-Israeli diplomacy focused during the postwar era on the Soviets. It was claimed that the USSR was either unable or unwilling, or most probably both, to contribute to the peaceful settlement of regional conflicts and of the Arab-Israeli dispute in particular. The capability element is discussed below; but what of the element of Soviet intentions? The "no war, no peace" thesis on Moscow's Middle East policy, though accepting that the Soviets might not favor the breakout of a regional war because of its escalatory potential, claimed that they equally opposed an Arab-Israeli peace settlement because peace would undermine Moscow's influence in the Arab world.[6] In the absence of a conflict with Israel, it has been maintained, Arab states would not turn to Moscow anymore because they would not need the major Soviet comparative advantage: willingness to provide massive arms shipments to the Arabs.

Other observers, however, have seen U.S. behavior as irresponsible and as jeopardizing the Middle East peace process. It is alleged that an American bias in favor of Israel, expressed in generous military-economic-diplomatic assistance, reinforces Israeli intransigence and reduces its incentives to cooperate in promoting a settlement (see, e.g., Campbell 1972, 51; Neff 1988a and 1988b; Rubenberg 1986; Tillman 1982; Whetten 1974, especially the conclusions, and 1981).[7] Some of these observers also contend that U.S. policy has stymied Arab-Israeli peace because Washington has focused on excluding the Soviets from the Middle East rather than on a joint effort toward a settlement (see, e.g., Tillman 1982, especially chap. 6).[8]

Indeed, more frequently in normal periods than during times of crisis, both the United States and the Soviet Union have sought unilateral advantages in the Middle East. Accordingly, every attempt at collaboration was followed by unilateral policies, each power using its respective comparative advantages to build up its influence in the region. Moreover, the great powers did not persist in maintaining a distance between their own diplomatic positions and those of their clients; in the aftermath of the collaborative episodes, they were quick to return to supporting their protégés' stances. At any rate, neither superpower managed to persuade the other that it was willing or able to restrain its clients. The collective goods of an international society—war avoidance, crisis prevention, arms control, and conflict resolution—seemed to take a back seat to the particular interests of each superpower in its role as a protector of local protégés.

An examination of the historical record may indeed seem to suggest the dominance of competitive policies. On the whole, Washington has helped to maintain Israel's military advantage. It has also tended to exclude the Soviets from participation in the peace process and to reject Moscow's offers of collaboration in settling the dispute. It seems that Moscow, for its part, has focused on arming the Arabs, especially those who have opposed peacemaking efforts. The general consequences of these superpower policies have been an accelerated arms race in the Middle East, the outbreak of a number of regional wars, and the failure of attempts to achieve comprehensive peace. As a result, this conflict has continued to pose grave risks to the stability of the region and to the peacefulness of the world.

More specifically, in the wake of the superpower cooperation in reaching Security Council Resolution 242, the United States and the Soviet Union reverted, in 1968, to a focus on arming their respective allies without substantial efforts to ameliorate the conflict. In the following year, during the two-power talks, the Soviets backtracked twice just as an agreement on a settlement seemed to be close: in June, 1969, the Soviets withdrew previous concessions that included an acceptance of a lasting peace agreement and Arab recognition of Israel (see Breslauer 1983a, 83–84; Quandt 1977, 104; Whetten 1974, 73) and, most notably, six months later, when on December 23 the Soviets formally informed the United States of their objection to the first Rogers Plan although the plan was, in fact, identical with the joint U.S.-Soviet brief of October 28 of that year (Breslauer 1983a, 84; Whetten 1974, 79–80). The major, if not the only, reason for such Soviet about-faces appears to have been Arab opposition to progress in the peace process with Israel.[9]

On top of these diplomatic retrogressions, during 1970 Moscow deployed air-defense systems in Egypt. Thus, it does not seem surprising that Washington started to move away from the cooperative path in spring 1970 (Quandt 1977, 98–104) or that following the Soviet complicity in the Egyptian violations of the cease-fire in August, 1970, the United States formally disengaged from the two-power talks. Finally, the shipment of major Soviet military hardware to Egypt and Syria, beginning in February, 1973 (see chap. 5), enabled those countries to attack Israel on October 6, 1973, probably with some kind of Soviet approval of the use of the military option, if necessary, to take back the occupied territories (Heikal 1975, 181; Spechler 1986, and the sources she cites).[10]

Nevertheless, the Soviets were not the only great power that played power politics by preferring patron's commitments to larger managerial responsibilities. It is true that the United States' publicly stated diplomatic position, as expressed in the Rogers Plan, considerably diverged from its client's position (Quandt 1977, 91). Moreover, the United States delayed Israeli arms requests in spring 1970 (Kissinger 1979, 571; Quandt 1977, 98; Safran 1981, 438; Spiegel 1985a, 190). In the final analysis, however, the United States helped Israel to maintain its qualitative military edge, especially in air power, over the Arabs (Quandt 1977, 129–30) and did not lean too forcefully on Israel in the diplomatic field in the period before the 1973 war.

In the military domain, the arrival of Phantom aircraft in Israel in September, 1969, guaranteed Israeli air predominance (Aronson 1978, 116–17; Quandt 1977, 88; Riad 1981, 105; Spiegel 1985a, 163) and helped Israel inflict devastating losses on Egyptian forces in the fall of 1969. The probable effects of this tacit support for Israeli military activities on Soviet behavior were twofold. First, the Soviets decided at this time (fall 1969), in principle, to escalate their military involvement in the War of Attrition; second, on the diplomatic front, the apparent U.S.-Israeli collusion (Breslauer 1983a, 86–87) and the resultant Israeli military superiority (Whetten 1974, 82) were probably important factors in bringing about the Soviet decision to back off from their endorsement of the first Rogers Plan.

Although Secretary Rogers presented in this plan positions that departed from those of Israel,[11] the United States did not exert any pressure on Israel to accept what was supposedly the administration's policy. Thus, although Nixon authorized the Jordanian portion of the Rogers Plan, he reassured Golda Meir that the United States would go no further and would not press its proposal (Kissinger 1979, 376).[12] But the Israelis were not reassured, and provoked a domestic storm in the United States over the Rogers Plan. As a result, not only did Washington not press for the acceptance of its proposal, but it approved, earlier than planned, Israeli requests for economic and military aid.[13] Indeed, the first Rogers Plan and the State Department's Middle East policy in general, including collaboration with the Soviet Union, were not wholeheartedly supported by Nixon and in fact were opposed by his influential national security advisor of the time, Kissinger, although the State Department was ostensibly in charge of U.S. Middle East policy from 1969 to 1971.

Keeping Israel predominant and avoiding strong pressures on it (especially in the context of superpower collusion) were deliberate steps. As

Kissinger makes clear in his memoirs, these policies were two components of his strategy to establish a Pax Americana in the Middle East and to drastically reduce Soviet influence in the region. Kissinger aimed to accomplish these objectives by excluding the Soviets from real participation in the diplomatic process, which would, he hoped, be arbitrated exclusively by the United States. Thus, although he pursued a semblance of collaboration with the Soviets, the main thrust of his Middle Eastern policy was exclusionary, the major intended result of this policy being the expulsion of Soviet advisers from Egypt in July, 1972. (For a more detailed discussion of Kissinger's policy and its effects, see below.)

In the wake of the short interlude of superpower cooperation in bringing the 1973 war to an end and in cochairing the two-day Geneva Conference, U.S. unilateral policies and efforts intensified. In 1974 through 1975, Kissinger continued to conduct step-by-step diplomacy with the conscious goal of excluding the Soviet Union from having a voice in the international politics of the Middle East.[14]

Following the interval of the 1977 attempt to reconvene the Geneva Conference and the October 1 joint statement, the Carter administration likewise turned to what became, in fact, unilateral mediation. Even if that had not been its initial intention, this Democratic administration responded to the November, 1977, visit by Sadat to Jerusalem by embarking on an exclusionary brokerage of the Camp David accords (signed in September, 1978), which were later translated into a separate Israeli-Egyptian peace treaty (in March, 1979).[15]

When the Reagan administration came to power, the exclusionary policy was transformed from a mostly unplanned effect of external (global and regional) developments during Carter's term (such as Sadat's trip to Jerusalem and the 1979 Soviet invasion of Afghanistan)[16] to the hallmark of deliberate U.S. policy in the region. But whereas Kissinger's and Carter's unilateral courses, despite their many differences, had been geared to regional conflict resolution (although in Kissinger's case it was only a means toward attaining global goals), Secretary of State Haig's "strategic consensus" initiative was aimed at constructing an anti-Soviet coalition of Israelis and Arabs without making any real efforts to address the local dispute.[17] According to the rationale for that policy, the Soviet Union was the major security threat to the Middle East, whereas the Arab-Israeli conflict was secondary in importance. Thus the Reagan administration did not give high priority to the talks on autonomy for the Palestinians in the West Bank and Gaza, which had been agreed on at Camp David. In fact, these talks took a back seat to Haig's attempt to construct a multinational force (which would include U.S. troops) to oversee compliance with the Israel-Egypt peace accords following the completion of the Israeli withdrawal from the Sinai.

A short-lived exception to the Reagan administration's low interest in settling the Arab-Israeli conflict came in the wake of the Israeli invasion of Lebanon. The president's "fresh start" initiative of September 1, 1982, was announced after the seeming success of U.S. envoy Philip Habib in stabilizing the situation in Beirut in August, 1982, by achieving a cease-fire and the evacuation of the PLO fighters from the city. Reagan's peace plan drew on the Camp David accords but called, more specifically, for some form of association between the West Bank, Gaza, and Jordan. Yet no intensive follow-up was carried out, and soon, after the massacre of hundreds of Palestinians in refugee camps near Beirut around the middle of September, the attention reverted to Lebanon and was to remain focused there for two years. In the following months the United States attempted to broker unilaterally (that is, excluding the Soviets) an agreement between Israel and Lebanon that would lead to the withdrawal of all foreign forces (Israeli, Syrian, and Palestinian) from Lebanon and to the stabilization of this war-torn country (see Haig 1984; Zak 1986, 106–9). But strong Syrian opposition brought about the collapse of the accord a short time after it was signed (May 17, 1983). And instead of helping bring about a stabilization, the U.S. marines, who suffered heavy casualties in a terrorist attack, had to vacate the increasingly volatile Lebanese scene in early 1984.

After this American (and also Israeli) fiasco in Lebanon, the focus shifted again to an exclusionary mediation of the Arab-Israeli dispute. The main avenue was an effort during 1985 and 1986 to open negotiations, brokered by Washington, between Israel and a joint Jordanian-Palestinian delegation following the Hussein-Arafat agreement. Yet the overall attention top U.S. policymakers paid to this issue, at least up to the outbreak of the Palestinian uprising in the occupied territories in late 1987, continued to be very low compared to preceding administrations (cf. Saunders 1988, 571). Moreover, the Reagan administration was never enthusiastic about the idea of dealing with a joint Jordanian-PLO delegation (Quandt 1988, 369–72), and indeed consistently rejected during most of its tenure Soviet proposals for an international conference on Middle East peace with equal Soviet and U.S. participation.

Moscow, for its part, has refused from the outset to accept the legitimacy of a peace process that did not include a major role for itself. Thus, during the 1970s, the Soviets rejected Kissinger's step-by-step diplomacy,[18] Sadat's trip to Jerusalem, and the Camp David process.[19] During the 1980s, they opposed Reagan's "fresh start" plan (Golan 1990b, 75–79) and the U.S. attempts in 1985 and 1986 to initiate Israeli/Jordanian-Palestinian talks (Golan 1990b, 87; Primakov 1988, 404). Moscow claimed that these were unilateral American arbitrations designed to exclude it from the Middle East. The Soviet response was to reinforce its ties with those actors (Libya, Iraq, the PLO, and most important, Syria)[20] who opposed what they all saw as efforts to impose American hegemony in the Middle East through a separate Egyptian-Israeli peace and later a separate Israeli-Jordanian agreement. In the view of the Soviets and their clients, the Camp David process jeopardized Arab unity, and at the same time, it did not resolve the Palestinian problem and thus precluded the establishment of a comprehensive peace in the region.

The Soviets were also suspicious of the establishment of the multinational force and American warning stations in the Sinai as part of the Israeli-Egyptian peace treaty. Together with the formation of the Rapid Deployment Force and the U.S. naval buildup in the Indian Ocean (following the Soviet invasion of Afghanistan in late 1979) and the deployment of the multinational force in Lebanon (after the Israeli invasion), these measures were seen by Moscow as first steps toward large-scale U.S. military deployments in the Middle East (see Primakov 1988, 398, 402). The Soviets thus not only opposed the exclusionary American peace plans but played an important role in obstructing them. For example, there is some evidence of their role in opposing Reagan's "fresh start" initiative. According to King Hussein, who was supposed to be a key player in Reagan's plan, the Soviets exerted very heavy pressure on him to reject the initiative.[21] Indeed, on April 10, 1983, the king stated his inability to accept the American proposal without Palestinian support, while Jordanian officials charged pro-Soviet elements in the PLO with obstructing the attempt to coordinate the positions of Jordan and the PLO (Quandt 1988, 367). The Soviets also played a significant part in obstructing the envisaged Israeli/Jordanian-Palestinian talks in 1985 and 1986 (Golan 1990b, 159).

Thus at least in the eyes of Americans and Israelis and some Egyptians,[22] by helping the Arab opponents of Camp David (the so-called rejectionist front), the Soviets frustrated the peace process and constituted a major obstacle to the broadening of the Israeli-Egyptian peace through the hoped-for inclusion of other Arab states and the Palestinians in peacemaking.

At any rate, the end results of these unilateral policies of the superpowers were a diplomatic stalemate regarding a solution of the Palestinian problem, the outbreak of the Lebanon War in 1982,[23] the increasing strength of the extremists on both sides, mounting violence in the occupied territories especially since the outbreak of the intifada, and ever-growing chances of renewed warfare that might draw in external powers in one way or another.

Although more recent attempts at superpower cooperation appeared to be more promising than past efforts, they also failed until the late 1980s, and their failure also appeared to be accounted for by power-politics reasoning. Thus, the Soviets and their Arab supporters attributed the stalemate to the lack of U.S. enthusiasm for Soviet participation and Washington's unwillingness to exert moderating pressure on Israel. Americans and the Israeli government (especially the Likud bloc) maintained that the lack of diplomatic progress can be explained, at least partly, by Soviet insistence on their right to a veto power in an authoritative international conference, while not being ready to pay the full price for the entry ticket, i.e., more effective pressure on the intransigent Arabs and the PLO and the renewal of full diplomatic relations with Israel.[24]

Although in the course of time it became somewhat more receptive to the idea of Soviet involvement in Middle East diplomacy than at first, the Reagan administration never accepted the idea of an influential Soviet voice in the peace process. Consistent with this logic was the proposal for a joint Hussein-Shamir trip to the Washington summit in late 1987 to receive the blessing of the two superpowers' leaders. In other words, the United States was ready to accept a symbolic Soviet role, but it was expected that the United States would play the major mediating role and would in fact be the regional broker. Similarly, the role of the international conference in the March, 1988, Shultz plan seemed to the Soviets merely symbolic. "The Soviets wanted a real role in the negotiating process, not just an opportunity to legitimize a made-in-America initiative that would ultimately leave them on the sidelines" (Quandt 1988, 178).

The above short survey has advanced two interpretations of the superpower diplomatic conduct in the Middle East, the first focusing on collaborative elements and the second on competitive ones. However, what both have in common is that they attribute similar behavior to both superpowers. In the following section, I advance one explanation of the similarity in collaborative behavior.

## Common Fears of Escalation and Inadvertent War

The first and most fundamental factor that may serve to explain the willingness of both superpowers at least to make recurring attempts at collaboration is the common fear of inadvertent war as a result of the escalation of a regional crisis that may engulf them.

Indeed, in a nuclear-bipolar world, the superpowers were frequently worried that regional conflicts—especially in volatile locales such as the Middle East, where important superpower interests overlap—could escalate into global confrontations. To the extent that the superpowers were concerned that a certain local conflict had this high escalatory potential, they would try to ameliorate that conflict.[25]

Even the "no war, no peace" thesis concerning Soviet behavior in the Middle East recognized that the Soviets wanted to avoid uncontrolled escalation. However, proponents of this thesis claimed that the Soviets believed in their ability to control the Middle East conflict even if it was not settled diplomatically. It seems to me that this belief, whatever its merits for the pre-1967 era, has had little applicability since the Six-Day War. That war vividly dramatized to the Soviets how events could get out of hand in a tinderbox like the Middle East (see Breslauer 1983a, 67; MacFarlane 1987b,

192) so long as the Arab-Israeli conflict was not at least mitigated. The 1970 Jordanian crisis and the 1973 war could only reinforce this lesson. Indeed, as MacFarlane points out, "the Soviet fear of escalation from local crisis—particularly in regions where critical interests overlap (e.g., the Middle East)—never disappeared completely" (1985, 309; see also Golan 1990a, 98–99).

As noted in chapter 4, such common fears are a necessary factor in the establishment of both concerted diplomacy and full-blown diplomatic concerts. Yet it is insufficient and, in the absence of the other necessary factors of similarity and moderation, cannot ensure the success of attempts at collaboration. In addition, an explanation based on common fears cannot account for persistent differences between the attitudes of the two superpowers with regard to diplomatic cooperation for resolving the Middle East conflict (persistent in the sense of lasting beyond the term in office of a particular leader or party). Although the diplomatic record of both superpowers included both cooperative and competitive elements, on the whole, the Soviet Union has preferred the cooperative multilateral approach, while the main thrust of U.S. policy was unilateral-exclusionary and involved the rejection of Soviet offers of cooperation. In the next section, I provide the evidence for this assertion by demonstrating that the United States has indeed pursued a Pax Americana in the Middle East and that the "no peace, no war" thesis with regard to Soviet behavior in the region was mistaken. In the next section, I also provide an explanation of this difference in the strategies of the superpowers, based on the factor of relative capabilities.

## The Effects of the Balance of Nonmilitary Capabilities on the Choice of a Unilateral or Multilateral Approach to Peacemaking

In accordance with the argument in chapter 4 regarding the factors influencing great power approaches to cooperation, we need to look at both power-related and unit-level factors for explaining why it should necessarily have been the Soviet Union that has been inclined to prefer a multilateral approach to regional conflict resolution, whereas the United States has tended toward unilateral diplomacy.

The argument concerning power-related factors states that it is the superpower balance of nonmilitary capabilities that conditions their orientation toward joint conflict management. In other words, the distribution of economic and diplomatic resources affects the great powers' attitude toward cooperation with each other in conflict reduction in third areas. Whereas the stronger power attempts unilateral management, the weaker one is inclined toward multilateral cooperative measures to the extent that it seeks stabilization of volatile regions. In this section, I show that this proposition is strongly supported by the superpowers' diplomatic record in the Middle East.

## Pax Americana in the Middle East?

The objective American advantages in the Middle East, as compared to the limitations on the capacity of the Soviets to contribute to regional peacemaking, helped to make the unilateral-exclusionary approach the dominant inclination in U.S. Middle East policy. Thus, regional circumstances conducive to American-led brokerage have led even moderate policymakers who were inclined to collaborate with the USSR (such as Rogers-Sisco and Carter-Vance) to deviate from their initial preferences and to pursue unilateral diplomatic initiatives.[26]

The dominant strand in the American policy in the Middle East has been based on the assumption that superior U.S. capabilities for influencing events in the region would ensure the success of unilateral mediation. The United States has combined superior nonmilitary resources[27] with the willingness to sacrifice tangible short-term benefits for intangible long-term gains.[28] This U.S. leadership has been manifested in the willingness to invest scarce financial resources as well as top leaders' time and attention (thus, foregoing tangible resources) for the advancement of the peace process (the long-term objective).[29] Spending time and money, in turn, helps the United States "bribe" small states into peacemaking by offering them side payments in the form of financial assistance and technology transfers in addition to honest brokerage. Such payments facilitate the acceptance of Pax Americana in the Middle East and help secure peace, stability, mutual recognition, and territorial arrangements.

Although the USSR achieved impressive military capabilities (including some capabilities of power projection to third areas), the United States has been able to offer third world countries much more economically and technologically.[30] And at least since the 1980s, the Western ideas of the free market and democratic institutions have gained much more popularity in the Third World than the Soviet model of development or communist ideology. Furthermore, particularly in the Middle East, the United States has enjoyed a diplomatic leverage that the Soviets have lacked. Israel is the superior military power in the region; yet Soviet leverage over Israel has been limited because it has not maintained diplomatic relations with the Jewish state since the 1967 war, and already before the war relations were very strained. In contrast, the United States has, at least potentially, substantial leverage over Israel because of the great Israeli dependence on American military and economic aid and diplomatic support; a dependence further enhanced during the Cold War by Israel's lack of any real option of realignment.

Consequently, once Arab states realized that they could not recover the occupied territories by force because of Israeli military predominance, one could reasonably expect, as Kissinger (1979, 379, 559) did, that Arab leaders would turn to the United States as the chief arbiter. Only the United States, it seemed, could bring about a settlement that would satisfy the Arabs' territorial demands. Developmental and technological needs could only reinforce an inclination to the United States. For the United States, in turn, the manipulation of its foreign assistance and its pivotal diplomatic position could help it extract concessions from the local antagonists for attaining regional accommodation under Pax Americana. Israel, in particular, could be expected to prefer exclusive U.S. brokerage rather than the participation of the Soviet Union with its (at least until recently) widely perceived pro-Arab orientation.

Indeed, the source of Soviet diplomatic strength in the Middle East—its alliance with radical Arab states—would presumably have constrained Soviet diplomacy in the peace process by presenting a dilemma. If the Soviets had tried to exercise a moderating influence on their allies, such pressures might have antagonized them. As a result, some of them might even have turned to the United States, which appeared better able to deliver Israeli concessions in the event of an active peacemaking process and an Arab willingness to compromise. If, on the other hand, Moscow had maintained its support for the Arab maximal position, it might have kept the radicals' friendship in the short run but it would not have been able to help them achieve their objectives through war because of Israel's military superiority and the Soviet fear of the escalation of local hostilities to a global confrontation (see Porter 1984, 117–18). Thus, it was still bound to disappoint its allies in the long run. At the same time, if Moscow's Arab allies had continued to be intransigent, the Soviets would not have been able to contribute to the peace process.

The United States, for its part, would be ready to engage in such a difficult process because Pax Americana would stabilize this turbulent region and mitigate the main U.S. dilemma: the tension between the goals of supporting Israel versus maintaining good relations with the Arabs and ensuring an uninterrupted flow of oil from the Gulf. Furthermore, the likelihood of a superpower clash resulting from a local war would decline, and Pax Americana would also ensure U.S. predominance in the region by peaceful means.[31] Especially important in this respect is Kissinger's strategy in the Middle East throughout the Nixon and Ford years.[32]

### Kissinger's Strategy and its Effects

Although Kissinger embarked on a policy of détente and negotiations with the USSR, there still remained enough of a Cold War conception in him (and in Nixon) that his basic objective in the Middle East was to expand Washington's influence at the expense of Moscow's.[33] At a minimum, he hoped that Egypt would defect from the Soviet camp and enter the U.S. orbit; his maximal goal was to guarantee U.S. hegemony in the Middle East and to exclude the Soviets from any major role in the area. There were a number of policy implications to this strategy.

The first implication was to ensure Israel's military superiority, so that the Arabs would realize that Soviet arms could not bring about the recovery of the occupied territories.

The second was the frustration of the State Department's "even-handed" diplomatic initiatives to reach an overall settlement in collaboration with the Soviets (1969–70) or even its attempts to accomplish partial agreements unilaterally (1971).[34] The combined effect of strengthening Israel and obstructing the premature initiatives of Rogers and Sisco, Kissinger believed, would be to make the Arab position more flexible; only then could the American ally, Israel, be expected to reciprocate.[35] Most important, the credit for this newly won flexibility would be given to the United States, which would then emerge as the regional peacemaker.[36]

The third policy implication was to enlist Soviet participation in vague public statements. Such joint superpower declarations would demonstrate to the Arabs that the USSR cared more about the superpower détente than about its allies' concerns. At the same time, Washington was to engage Moscow in secret agreements so that the Soviets should have the feeling of equality in status with the United States and would then have incentives to slow down the arms supply to the Arabs. Such a scenario, Kissinger hoped, would both strain Soviet-Egyptian relations and frustrate the Arabs' military option.

Fourth, Kissinger embarked on a back-channel communication with Egypt and thus helped start the process of Cairo's realignment from the Eastern to the Western camp. But this exchange was not accompanied by a real effort to promote the peace process because of the just-mentioned logic of first creating a diplomatic stalemate.

Hence, the appearance of superpower collaboration was essentially a device to enhance U.S. influence with the Arabs. The major intended effect of Kissinger's strategy was the July, 1972, expulsion of the Soviet advisors from Egypt following the vague U.S.-Soviet declarations of May, 1972[37] (although Kissinger could not anticipate the precise form and timing of this effect). These statements created the impression of Soviet support for the status quo and thus alienated Sadat from the Soviets. The resulting expulsion was a serious blow to Soviet standing in the Middle East and the beginning of a rift between Moscow and Cairo.[38]

Indeed, an explanation based on U.S. comparative advantages in the Middle East can best account for the progress in the Arab-Israeli peace process achieved under American leadership in the aftermath of the 1973 war until the late 1970s.[39] Kissinger's unilateral, step-by-step shuttle diplomacy produced the disengagement accords of 1974 between Israel and Egypt (Sinai I, January, 1974) and between Israel and Syria (May, 1974). American exclusionary brokerage also generated the Sinai II interim accord between Israel and Egypt (September, 1975). U.S. mediation culminated, of course, with the achievement of the Camp David accords (September, 1978) and the Egyptian-Israeli peace treaty (March, 1979).[40]

The exclusion of the Soviets from any effective involvement in the peace process could be seen as beneficial not only from a narrow Cold War standpoint but also in the view of those local actors interested in reaching a settlement. Thus, in the aftermath of the 1973 war not only Egypt and Israel but also Jordan supported U.S.-sponsored negotiations. Most interestingly, "even President Assad of Syria indicated a willingness to let Kissinger try his hand, although his skepticism was considerably greater than Sadat's" (Quandt 1977, 211).[41] Sadat's support of diplomatic progress, moreover, appeared to be forthcoming only when the United States single-handedly presided over the peace negotiations like during 1974 through 1975 and 1978 through 1979.

Yet as we will see, the United States's pursuit of Pax Americana also depended on two sets of unit-level factors—domestic political support and the ideologically motivated rejection of an equal status for the Soviets—rather than only on the objective characteristics of a predominant power. Indeed, all these three factors undermined the standing of those policymakers who supported collaboration with the Soviets while strengthening the position of those who opposed the cooperative avenue.

## The Soviet Approach to Conflict Resolution in the Middle East: A Participant or a Spoiler?

The following analysis shows that far from obstructing any efforts at conflict resolution in the Middle East, as claims the "no peace, no war" thesis, the Soviets were in fact genuinely interested in peacemaking in the region and in collaborating with the United States for that purpose, albeit with certain conditions. The role of the spoiler, which they occasionally played, resulted from the unwillingness of the United States to recognize and accept these conditions and from the U.S. preference for an exclusionary approach.

As noted in chapter 4, there is evidence of Soviet eagerness during the postwar era to be recognized as an equal of the United States. Such

> preoccupation with the establishment of status equal to that of the U.S. in global security matters . . . gives the USSR a limited stake in cooperative arrangements which recognize this status and legitimize it. The Soviet aspiration to equality in the hierarchy of prestige in international politics may be achieved, in other words, not only by conscious challenge to the position of the previous hegemon, but through acts whereby the United States consciously concedes to the U.S.S.R. status commensurate with its

growing power to affect outcomes in the Third World. (MacFarlane 1987a, 13)[42]

Numerous Soviet statements since the early 1960s, cited by Jonsson (1984, 25–28), have highlighted their desire to fulfill the traditional great power role of taking part in the resolution of international conflicts, including even those that were far from its frontiers.[43] Since the Middle East is not remote from the Soviet Union—indeed, it is much closer to its borders than to the United States—it should not be surprising that the Soviets have especially insisted on their inclusion in the Middle East diplomatic process.[44] Thus, the Soviets have persistently proposed a wide range of joint political and military actions with Washington for regional conflict resolution. There have been five main attempts in the diplomatic field:

1. In the late 1940s and early 1950s, Moscow tried to participate in the peacemaking and peacekeeping activities of the UN machinery in the Middle East (see Roi 1974 and 1980).[45]
2. Throughout the 1950s, but especially in 1957 and 1958, Moscow asked to join a revised version of the Tripartite Statement of the three Western powers concerning arms control and the maintenance of peace in the Middle East (see Slater 1990–91, 564–65; Smolansky 1978; Zak 1986, chap. 2, especially 46–49).[46] This, however, was in the heyday of the Cold War, and the West sought to preclude any Soviet "penetration" of the Middle East and thus completely rejected any diplomatic role for the USSR, even if ostensibly for peacemaking purposes. However, the idea of Soviet participation (along with the United States) in superpower guarantees of the borders between Israel and its Arab neighbors has become, since the mid-1950s, a consistent theme of the Kremlin's Middle East peace proposals (cf. Golan 1990a, 99).[47]

The other three diplomatic attempts were already discussed earlier in this chapter.

3. Following the Six-Day War, the Kremlin demonstrated its interest in jointly working with the United States to reach a comprehensive Arab-Israeli settlement (albeit under certain conditions).
4. In the 1970s, in the aftermath of the Yom Kippur War, Moscow sought to play the role of cochair of the Geneva Conference together with Washington.
5. In the 1980s, the Soviets succeeded in mobilizing the Arab world and the majority of the UN members for supporting an international conference on Middle East peace with active Soviet participation. The

idea of an international conference was a major element in the Soviet Middle East peace plans advanced under Brezhnev in 1981, Chernenko in 1984, and Gorbachev in 1986.

Basically, the idea of a multilateral framework was designed to promote Moscow's aim to be recognized as an equal of Washington in the Middle East.[48] Thus, the Soviets sought to prevent separate deals between Israel and individual Arab states (most notably Jordan) that the United States would exclusively broker.[49]

In addition to diplomatic peacemaking, the Soviets expressed readiness to support their equal status by military presence for peacekeeping or even peace-enforcement purposes. Thus, in December, 1947, they proposed that U.S. and Soviet troops take part in an international force that would assist in implementing the UN partition resolution (this resolution, which the Arabs opposed, called for the establishment of a Jewish and an Arab state in the territory of Palestine, which was then under British control).[50] At the end of both the 1956 and 1973 wars, the Soviets suggested sending joint U.S.-Soviet forces to enforce the UN-sponsored cease-fires.[51] Finally, Brezhnev offered to contribute Soviet troops to the UN forces that would be deployed in demilitarized buffer zones separating Israel and its neighbors following a territorial settlement to be reached in an international conference (Brezhnev Plan, *Pravda*, February 24, 1981, cited in *The Soviet Union and the Middle East* 6, no. 2 [1981]: 5).

As Smolansky observes, "throughout all the convulsions of Moscow's Middle East policy since 1955, the one common theme that emerges is the Kremlin's quest for full superpower status and consequent recognition that its interests must be considered in whatever regional arrangements are reached" (1978, 105). Smolansky argues, moreover, that only some kind of peaceful arrangement would have enabled the Soviet Union to gain the great power status and international legitimacy it aspired to achieve through being recognized as the equal collaborator of the United States in settling regional disputes.[52]

Because of the intensity of the conflict in the Middle East, an Arab-Israeli peace was expected to be an armed peace (cf. Eran 1978, 47; see also MacFarlane 1987b, 194–95);[53] and one of the often-mentioned measures for preserving such a peace was great power guarantees (see Astor and Yorke 1978; Dowty 1975; Evron 1977, 29–36). Indeed, the Soviets consistently advocated this means of ameliorating the regional security dilemma. Superpower guarantees would ensure the Soviets the long-awaited, formally legitimized presence in the Middle East (cf. Golan 1979, 121) and recognized equality with the United States. As Eran suggests, "The achievement of such a status in the region by the Soviet Union would mean, at long last, the formalization and legitimization of Soviet Middle Eastern involvement by the international community" (1978, 46). Moscow also supported a superpower role in enforcing the peace because it "would make the Soviet Union less dependent on unstable regimes in the Arab world by providing it with an additional, more solid and secure means of participating in the politics of the region" (Eran 1978, 47).

A number of analysts have reached the conclusion that the Soviets have been interested in joint diplomacy with the United States to resolve the Middle East dispute and jointly guarantee the peace. This interest has been contingent, however, on U.S. willingness to reciprocate and has been valid only to the extent that the peaceful settlement would not reduce Soviet influence in the Arab world.[54] A rigorous examination of the "no war, no peace" hypothesis with respect to Soviet Middle East policy from 1967 to 1972 concludes that "the Soviet leadership sought a peace settlement based on superpower collaboration that would simultaneously reduce the probability of military confrontation with the United States in the Middle East, advance the cause of détente, and create a more stable base of influence for the USSR in Middle Eastern affairs. The Soviets sought to bring about an armed peace based upon Israeli withdrawal from occupied territories, Arab recognition of and normalization of formal relations with Israel, and a coequal superpower role in enforcing the peace" (Breslauer 1983a, 96).

A significant indicator of the Soviet commitment to conflict resolution is the restraints that the Soviets imposed on their arms supply to the Arabs. This commitment is seen especially in Moscow's refusal in 1971 and 1972 to ship sophisticated weapons to Egypt that would have enabled Sadat to launch a major offensive against Israel (especially MiG-23s and Scud surface-to-surface missiles) (Breslauer 1983a, 90–91; Garthoff 1985, 315–16; George, with others, 1983, 140; Glassman, 1975, 87–88; Golan 1977, 21–22; Heikal 1975, 112, 117; and 1978, 249–50; Karsh 1985, 39–40; Mangold 1978, chap. 7, 115–41; Porter 1984, 120–21; Quandt 1977, 151; Spechler 1986, 437–38; Tillman 1982, 251; Whetten 1974, 154; and 1981, 65–67). Such unwillingness by the Soviets severely frustrated Sadat, as he repeatedly makes clear in his memoirs (1977, 185–87, 198, 212, 219, 220–21, 225–31, 286–87). At the same time, Sadat was dismayed at the Soviet agreement with the United States at the May 1972 summit to call for "military relaxation" in the Middle East, which "practically" meant "an implicit acceptance of the status-quo" in the region (Kissinger 1979, 1247; see also Atherton 1985, 699; Garthoff 1985, 315–16; Quandt 1977, 151). This advocacy, Sadat recalls, "was a violent shock to us" because the status quo was seen in Cairo as beneficial to Israel (1977, 229; see also Ben-Zvi 1986, 76–77, and the references he cites in 132 n. 31–33). The result of this Soviet moderation and readiness to cooperate with the United States at the expense of their client was the expulsion two months later of their advisors from Egypt. Sadat continued to distrust Soviet intentions even after Moscow had resumed arms shipments in February, 1973.[55] This persistent distrust was a major factor in Egypt's gradual realignment with the

United States from 1972 to 1976. Indeed, the architect of this realignment on the American side, despite his exclusionary diplomacy and suspicion of Soviet motivations in the Middle East, admits that the Soviets paid a high regional price for the advancement of détente (Kissinger 1979, 1294, 1297).[56] The expulsion of the Soviet advisors from Egypt and Cairo's eventual reorientation toward the United States, suggest how costly cooperation with the United States could be for the Soviets, especially if it was carried out essentially under U.S. terms and without a genuine U.S. desire to reciprocate by exerting pressure on Israel and by pursuing joint diplomacy with Moscow (see Breslauer 1983a, 89–95; Garthoff 1985, chap. 9, especially 315–16; MacFarlane 1987b, 187–207).[57]

A dramatic illustration of Soviet eagerness to work together with the United States on Middle East conflict resolution took place at the June, 1973, San Clemente summit. According to Nixon (1978, 2:429–31), a secret service agent knocked on his door late at night with a message that the Russians wanted to talk. " 'I could not sleep, Mr. President,' Brezhnev said with a broad smile" (Nixon 1978, 2:430). The reason was the Middle East situation. The Soviet secretary general wanted a superpower agreement "on a set of 'principles' to govern a Middle East settlement." He warned that "without such an agreement . . . he could not guarantee that war would not resume." Nixon and Kissinger, however, dismissed this Soviet warning as "psychological warfare" (Kissinger 1982, 461) designed "to bulldoze us into solving his dilemmas without paying any price" (1982, 298). Nixon's anticommunist belief system probably played a major role in his interpretation of the midnight session as "a reminder of the unchanging and unrelenting Communist motivations beneath the diplomatic veneer of détente" (1978, 2:431; on the images and beliefs of American decisionmakers, see below). Nixon saw the Soviet initiative as an attempt to impose on Israel a settlement based on Arab terms, an attempt motivated by Moscow's concern about the progress that U.S. exclusionary diplomacy was making with Arab states. However, regardless of the substance of the Soviet proposals for a settlement, Kissinger makes clear in his memoirs that he and Nixon simply did not want to negotiate the Arab-Israeli conflict with the Kremlin (Garthoff 1985, 364).

By contrast, the Soviets were ready to demonstrate diplomatic flexibility in the event of a real chance for their inclusion in the diplomatic process. Thus, as the chances for reconvening the Geneva Conference grew when the Carter administration came to office in 1977, the Soviets were willing to make important concessions. Their draft of a "Joint Soviet-U.S. Statement on the Middle East" did not mention a Palestinian state or call for Israel to return to the 1967 borders or to abandon East Jerusalem (Quandt 1986a, 119; Vance 1983, 191–93). They agreed to take part in the conference without official PLO participation from the outset (rather, the issue was supposed to be solved at the conference itself; see Golan 1990b, 71; Vance 1983, 192–93) and to drop the word *national* from the phrase *the legitimate national rights* of the Palestinians. The Kremlin also agreed that the peace would have to constitute more than just the end of war in the Middle East: "The ultimate goal . . . was normal relationships between the Arab and Israeli governments and people" (Foreign Minister Gromyko to Carter, cited in Carter 1982, 293). Indeed, such Soviet concessions made it possible for the United States to issue in October, 1977, a joint communiqué with the Soviets regarding the settlement of the Arab-Israeli conflict.[58]

To sum up, the United States, at least at first glance, has had the potential to manage the Arab-Israeli conflict unilaterally. On the other hand, because of their inferior economic and diplomatic resources, the Soviets (to the extent that they were interested in the stabilization of the Middle East) needed to resort to collaboration with the United States.

This Soviet inclination to pursue a joint approach with Washington stemmed mainly from the Soviets' desire, as the newer (cf. MacFarlane 1987b, 190), weaker, and less secure great power in the postwar world, to be recognized as an equal superpower.[59] Indeed, the Soviets often preferred joint U.S.-Soviet diplomacy in the Middle East (with an equal role for each of the two superpowers) to the involvement of all five permanent members of the Security Council (cf. Zak 1986, 105). However, this inclination was reinforced by an additional incentive: even after attaining impressive military capabilities, the Soviets remained inferior to the United States in overall economic resources; thus, cooperation in conflict resolution could enhance U.S. readiness to provide Moscow with much-desired trade benefits and technology transfers. Joint regional diplomacy could also strengthen support in the United States for arms control,[60] in which the Soviets had an economic interest (to save costs by reducing defense spending and also to raise the likelihood of Western economic assistance).

However, the different approaches of the superpowers to peacemaking in the Middle East were not confined to the choice between a multilateral versus an exclusionary strategy (i.e., between cooperation and noncooperation) but also included a second dimension, that of disagreement over the form of the prospective cooperation toward small states (whether accommodative or coercive). While the first difference may be explained by relative capabilities, the second stems from state-level regime factors.

### Domestic Factors and the Preference for an Accommodative or a Coercive Form of Cooperation

According to the proposition in chapter 4, a centralist-hierarchical power is both willing and able to pursue a policy of coercive collaboration that may lead to the construction of a great power condominium. This proposition is confirmed not only by the general Soviet inclination to a condominiumlike arrangement in the postwar era but also by their position on the particular issue of peacemaking in the Middle East.[61] Some analysts argue that the Soviets have sought a virtual superpower condominium in the Middle East, either as a joint imposition of peace (Bell 1974, 535; Hoffmann 1984, 244; Jonsson 1984, chap. 5) or as a recognized division of the region into spheres of influence between the superpowers (Vital 1972, 84–85) or both (Ben-Zvi 1986, 6, 71; Zak 1986). At any rate, the Soviets seemed to prefer a superpower collusion behind closed doors in the Middle East (Breslauer 1983a; and 1983b, 334), without the presence of unruly allies.

With regard to the Soviet proposals for an international conference for settling the Middle East conflict, the Soviets were interested in reaching a superpower understanding on the outline of a regional settlement and then using the international conference to enforce a comprehensive arrangement on the local parties. For such enforcement, the Soviets demanded, somewhat similarly to the view of many of the Arabs (especially the Syrians), that the multilateral plenary supervise the work of the bilateral subcommittees and, on a number of issues, supersede them. Thus, Moscow "sought a multilateral, hierarchical framework in which it would first reach an agreement with the United States and then the two superpowers would persuade their respective Middle Eastern clients to accept it" (Touval 1987, 45). This orientation corresponds to the concept of an imposed peace—one of the forms of great power coercive collaboration in conflict management.[62] Breslauer (1983a, 74–75) suggests three major indicators of the Soviet commitment to conflict resolution in the Middle East that are associated with coercive collaboration: readiness to take some distance from maximal Arab positions; desire to collude with the United States behind closed doors; and insider testimony about Soviet pressures on the Arabs to accept a diplomatic settlement of the dispute.[63]

The Soviet emphasis on military measures for enforcing the peace is also associated with the idea of a condominium and with a policing role. As Eran puts it, "Moscow intends that any Arab-Israeli settlement be tied to the establishment of an international regime—one may call it Soviet-American condominium—which from time to time would require international policing; Moscow wishes to become co-gendarme of any Arab-Israeli settlement with the United States," (1978, 45–46).

Yet, the U.S. foreign policy elite has persistently and forcefully rejected such an idea of a condominium or an imposed solution in the Middle East, in a manner consistent with its traditional opposition to similar proposals of coercive collaboration and reflecting its pluralist political system (see chap. 4). This rejection had to do not only with an ideological unwillingness to take part in a condominium but especially with a domestic political inability to do so. The argument in chapter 4 concerning the form of great power collaboration stressed the domestic and allied opposition in a pluralist democracy to the pursuit of any semblance of coercive collaboration with another great power at the expense of small allies, especially those that have powerful domestic resources within the great power's polity, as has been the case with Israel's standing in the United States. Accordingly, the opposition of both Israel and pro-Israeli elements in the United States to any initiative that smacked of great power condominium at the expense of Israel was instrumental in obstructing such initiatives, as I demonstrate by the following two examples: the joint U.S.-Soviet statement of October, 1977, and the first Rogers Plan of December, 1969.

The 1977 communiqué contained important Soviet concessions (see above; see Quandt 1986a, 119-20; Spiegel 1985a, 338; Vance 1983, 192-93); nonetheless, as soon as it was made public, it became the target of sharp criticism by Israel's friends in the United States (Brzezinski 1983, 73, 108; Garthoff 1985, 580-81; Indyk 1984, 44; Quandt 1986a, 123; Spiegel 1985a, 338; Vance 1983, 192). To calm the strong domestic and Israeli opposition, President Carter, together with Israeli Foreign Minister Dayan, produced a working paper on October 4, 1977, that diluted the impact of the superpower communiqué (Brzezinski 1983, 107-10; Cohen 1978; Garthoff 1985, 581; Indyk 1984, 44; Quandt 1986a, 125-31; Saunders 1988, 568-69; Vance 1983, 192-94). As Quandt points out, both Arabs and Israelis felt that "Carter had backed down in the face of domestic and Israeli pressures. . . . Although Carter never wavered in thinking that he had held firm, the widespread perception, caused by the joint statement with Israel, was that the United States had abandoned the position it had just worked out with the Soviets" (1986a, 131).

The failure of superpower cooperation in 1977 was derived from the strength of domestic and allied opposition motivated by fears of Israel's supporters that cooperation with the Soviets would necessarily be harmful to Israel. The effectiveness of this opposition in the United States, in turn, influenced Sadat to try another road to peace, namely to travel to Jerusalem in November, 1977, rather than to wait endlessly for the convening of the Geneva Conference (Quandt 1986a, 131, 136, 139-42, 145; Sadat 1977, 304).[64]

An additional brief example further highlights the point, namely, the strong domestic opposition to Rogers I, the December, 1969, collaborative attempt with the Soviets to resolve the Arab-Israeli conflict. Secretary Rogers's speech on December 9 outlined his proposal, which had been worked out in collaboration with the Soviets during the two-power talks in 1969.[65] The plan called for an Israeli withdrawal from almost all the occupied territories in exchange for an agreement by the Arabs to some contractual arrangement guaranteeing a permanent peace with Israel. Rogers's speech triggered an outcry from Israel's supporters in Congress and in the Jewish community; this powerful protest, in turn, led to signals from Nixon to Jewish leaders that the United States would not impose a settlement on Israel. As a result of the domestic pressure, the president also backed off from the strong language used in the plan about the necessity for Israel's withdrawal from the occupied territories and pledged to continue delivering necessary military hardware to Israel (see Hersh 1983, 220; Kissinger 1979, 376–77; Spiegel 1985a, 186–89).

Because of the greater influence of domestic and transnational politics in a pluralist democracy in noncrisis periods, the effectiveness of U.S. pressures on Israel in normal diplomacy was thus considerably diminished. I show below that domestic factors, especially in a democratic polity, are relevant not only to the form of cooperation but also to the choice between a cooperative and an exclusionary strategy. However, before turning to other factors at the state and the individual levels of analysis that affected both the making of efforts at cooperation and their failure, it is helpful to consider the combined effects of the two factors just discussed, which, in the absence of similarity and moderation, conditioned the differences in the superpower approaches to regional peacemaking in the Middle East: relative capabilities and domestic regimes.

## The Combined Effects of Relative Capabilities and State Attributes on Great Power Inclination toward Concerted Diplomacy

The combination of these two causal factors discussed in this section and in the previous one—relative power and domestic regime—yields four possible orientations toward great power cooperation in regional conflict resolution. Each of the orientations, which are presented in figure 3, is composed of two major dimensions. The first concerns the strategy toward the other great powers—whether to cooperate with them in a multilateral approach or to go it alone. The second relates to the form of collaboration, which, in turn, is closely related to the great power's attitude to small states—whether to respect their autonomy (accommodative approach) or to infringe on it in some major ways (coercive strategy). On the whole, whereas the strategy toward cooperation with other great powers is influenced by relative capabilities, the attitude toward small states is conditioned by the domestic regime of the great power.

Approach 1 is typical of pluralist regimes that are more powerful and secure than their competitors at least in some regions or issue-areas. This approach consists of a disinclination to collaborate with other great powers (because of relative strength) but also a relatively tolerant attitude to small states (due to the democratic-pluralist regime of the great power), especially if they are also democratic. The best example is the postwar United States with its economic-technological advantages vis-à-vis the USSR. As I have shown, such nonmilitary advantages were especially remarkable in the Middle East

## Explaining Superpower Diplomacy

|  | Pluralist | Centralist-Authoritarian |
|---|---|---|
| Superior | 1<br><br>Unilateral-Accommodative<br><br>(United States in the Middle East) | 2<br><br>Unilateral-Coercive<br><br>(USSR in its exclusive sphere of influence) |
| Inferior (vulnerable) | 3<br><br>Multilateral-Accommodative<br><br>(the West Europeans in the Middle East) | 4<br><br>Multilateral-Coercive<br><br>(USSR in the Middle East) |

Domestic Regime ↙ ↘ ; Relative Capabilities ↗ ↘

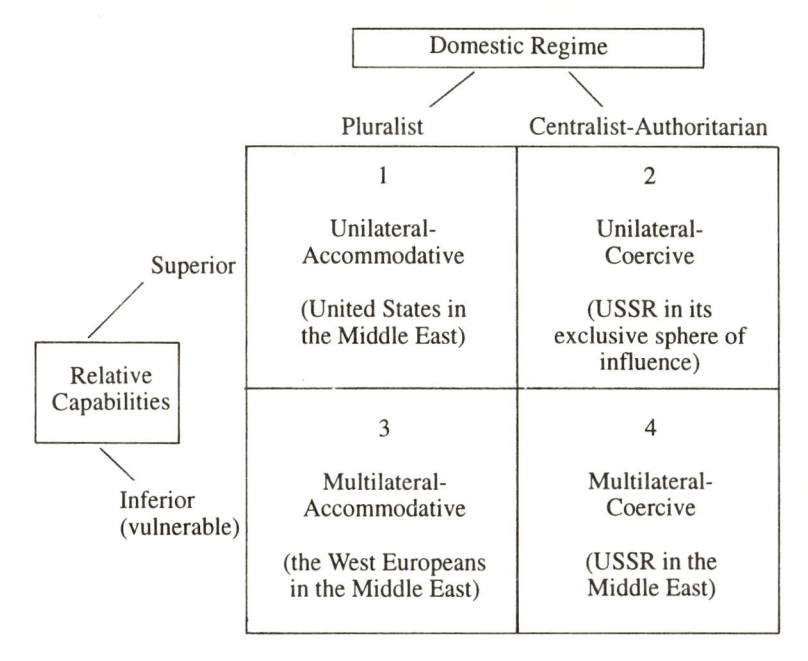

Fig. 3. Approaches toward great power cooperation in conflict resolution according to relative capabilities and state attributes

because the United States has enjoyed special diplomatic resources in that area that have enabled it to play the unilateral role of an honest broker and to exclude the Soviets from the international diplomacy of such an important region, while maintaining a tolerant and noncoercive attitude toward its ally Israel.

Orientation 2 characterizes the conduct of authoritarian great powers in situations or areas where they enjoy superior capabilities. Their conduct is intolerant both with regard to cooperation with great power rivals and to small state autonomy.[66] This orientation has no example in the postwar Middle East, but it is manifested in the Soviet attitude toward its exclusive sphere of influence in Eastern Europe. The opposite is inclination 3, which combines both cooperation with other powers and respect for the rights of small states. It is typical of democratic regimes that are inferior or vulnerable in comparison to other great powers. Such, for example, has been the approach of the Western Europeans during the postwar era with regard to an international conference to resolve the Arab-Israeli conflict. As relatively weak external powers in the Middle East, they were closer to the Soviet position of a multilateral forum (which should include the five permanent members of the Security Council) rather than to the U.S. preference for a unilateral strategy for resolving the Middle Eastern conflict under an exclusive U.S. leadership. Yet as democratic states, the Europeans were closer to the American position with regard to the noncoercive nature of the international engagement in the resolution of this regional conflict.

Centralist powers, especially when they are vulnerable and relatively weak as compared to other great powers, tend to prefer a condominium-like arrangement (inclination 4), that is, great-power collaboration that will jointly impose peace in third areas or divide them into spheres of influence between the powers. Such was the inclination of the Soviet Union in the Middle East during most of the postwar period.

In spite of the persistent attitudes of the superpowers to cooperation in conflict resolution, influenced by the long-term factors of relative capabilities and domestic regimes, one can also note in the superpowers' conduct in the Middle East both differences of views among decision makers within (U.S. or Soviet) administrations—such as the not infrequent disagreements about Middle East policy between the White House and the State Department[67]—and changes of policies from one administration to another—such as the change regarding Soviet participation in the Middle East peace process from the Ford to the Carter administration.[68] As we have seen, to explain such disagreements or changes, we need to look at the individual level of analysis, that is, decision makers' beliefs. Although, as we have noted, in crisis situations there is a greater likelihood of consensus within an elite, in noncrisis settings the cognitive attributes of policymakers, especially of those who have won the bureaucratic political infighting, tend to hold sway.[69]

In the next section, I address the cognitive differences among Soviet and especially American decision makers regarding the three images discussed in chapter 4. In addition to explaining the range of variations in a great power's normal foreign policy behavior, such differences can explain when and why attempts at concerted conflict resolution will be made and when and why they will not—depending on the specific content of the three images.

## Cognitive Differences among Decision Makers and Great Power Cooperation in Conflict Resolution

The content of decision makers' beliefs is a major factor that influences concerted diplomacy. In the postwar era, decision makers (especially in the United States) fell into three main orientations—each of which had its respective critical image as discussed in chapter 4. Yet because of the importance of the relations with the other superpower during the Cold War, the image of the opponent was an especially influential factor in affecting U.S. and Soviet foreign policies. Thus, an image of the adversary as an unalterable antagonist tended to fortify unilateralist-exclusionary policies; whereas perceiving the adversary as cooperative or as an adverse partner, with whom it is possible to do business, strengthened the multilateralist course. I illustrate this point briefly with regard to Soviet images of the United States and then address at somewhat greater length American orientations. Indeed, the greater availability of data on the U.S. side should enable us to consider also the influence of the two other images (the dynamics of world politics and the loci of primary problems) on the choice between a unilateral and an exclusionary course.

### Soviet Images of the United States and Willingness to Pursue Cooperation

Although, for the obvious reason that it was a closed society, far less is known about the subjective beliefs of Soviet decision makers during the postwar era than about their American counterparts, Spechler (1978, 64-68, and 1986) uses competing images of the United States held by the Soviet elite to analyze changes and inconsistencies in Soviet Middle East behavior from 1967 to 1973.[70] For those who saw the United States as an adverse partner, the United States, "while still an adversary, was a potential partner of the U.S.S.R. in solving key international problems (Spechler 1986, 448)."[71] Thus, in their view the superpowers "should strive for de-escalation of conflicts between their regional allies. A political agreement in the Middle East was particularly urgent" (Spechler 1986, 448). This view indicates that these decision makers also subscribed to the regionalist image, namely, regarding the conflict in the Middle East as a regional problem that might escalate and engulf the superpowers.

In contrast, for the holders of the unalterable antagonist image, the U.S. was

> necessarily hostile and threatening to the Soviet Union because of its economic and military power and aggressive intentions. The U.S. must be actively countered and restrained, both militarily and politically. The U.S.S.R. must acquire friends and military facilities and maintain local allies wherever these would help to combat, contain, or undermine American power. [Hence,] it would not be tragic—indeed, it might be fortunate—if events in the Middle East or elsewhere in the third world were to disrupt or prevent détente. . . . There was little reason to restrain the Arabs or demand that they seek a peaceful resolution of their conflict with Israel. (Spechler 1986, 449-50)

In his study of the views of six members of the upper reaches of the Soviet journalistic and academic elites on the Middle East, Breslauer (1990, chap. 7) found a strong linkage between the image of the adversary, optimism about long-term acquisitive goals (which parallels the distinction made here between believers in balancing versus bandwagoning), and the preferred intensity of competition with the United States versus collaboration with it. Those who viewed U.S. goals as global confrontation were optimistic about the Soviets' competitive prospects in the Third World; they also had low faith in diplomacy and preferred a high intensity of struggle. In contrast, commentators who saw U.S. goals in the Middle East as minimalist-defensive (securing the flow of oil) were more pessimistic about advancing Soviet goals in the region, and they preferred a low intensity of struggle and had high faith in diplomacy.

### American Images and Multilateral versus Exclusionary Diplomacy

Similarly, divergent images of the USSR in the U.S. foreign-policy elite led to different orientations with respect to conferring legitimacy on it as an equal superpower that should have a voice in managing world affairs. A general distinction can be drawn between administrations with a Cold War orientation (hard line) versus those that were more détente oriented (soft line). Thus, the Cold War administrations of Truman, Eisenhower, Kennedy, Ford, and Reagan rejected explicit superpower cooperation; whereas the more détente-oriented (in varying degrees) Johnson, Nixon, and Carter administrations were willing to pursue joint initiatives with Moscow for conflict mitigation in the Middle East. As the image of Moscow under Gorbachev changed and a new détente emerged in the final years of the Reagan administration, the willingness of that administration to try a multilateral road in the Middle East was also strengthened.

The most striking contrast is between the unilateral-exclusionary Middle East policies of the vehemently anticommunist (and believers in the global-bandwagoning outlook) John Foster Dulles and the early Ronald Reagan versus the collaborative-multilateral approach of the relatively soft-line Carter administration. The Eisenhower-Dulles administration rejected outright the numerous Soviet proposals in the 1950s for joint statements and actions concerning the Middle East. The administration, as the Eisenhower Doctrine indicated, did not recognize the legitimacy of Soviet interests in the Middle East; it wanted to make "the Mid East secure from Communist penetration" (Eisenhower to Dulles, cited in Spiegel 1985a, 84) by preventing any Soviet presence in the area, including the diplomatic manifestations of such a presence.[72] Even when the local parties, including, most surprisingly, Israel, were interested in Soviet participation, the Eisenhower administration vehemently opposed it. Thus, in 1960 Israeli Prime Minister Ben-Gurion proposed to Eishenhower that the United States try to reach an arms control agreement with the Soviets in the Middle East; after a couple of weeks, Secretary of State Herter called the Israeli ambassador and another senior Israeli diplomat to his office and asked them how the prime minister of Israel, a basically pro-Western country, could possibly have suggested to the Americans bringing the Soviets into the Middle East and granting them a status there.[73]

The Reagan administration, which on coming to power viewed the Soviet Union as an "evil empire," sought, at least initially, to form a grand anti-Soviet alliance of Israelis and Arabs that would displace Soviet influence in the Middle East;[74] that is, the Middle East was viewed primarily through the prism of U.S.-Soviet rivalry. Indeed, most foreign policy officials of the administration knew little about the Middle East (in contrast to the influential presence of some leading regional experts in the Carter administration and also, to a certain extent, in the Nixon and Ford administrations). Thus, some top aides argued that the most severe problem in the Middle East was the presence of twenty-plus Soviet divisions on Iran's northern border (Quandt 1988, 362).

In contrast to these two Republican administrations, when the Carter administration came to office, it prided itself on being "free of that inordinate fear of communism that had dominated American postwar foreign policy" (see the President's Notre Dame address, May 22, 1977, *Weekly Compilation of Presidential Documents,* 13, no. 22 [1977]).[75] A moderate image of the Soviets, together with a belief in balancing and a regional focus, led the new team to try a collaborative approach toward the Soviets in the Middle East, as the administration did throughout 1977, culminating in that year's October 1 joint statement.[76] Yet analogous to the differences between the Carter administration and some of its predecessors, the disagreements within the administration between National Security Adviser Brzezinski and Secretary of State Vance concerning the Soviet role in Middle East peace negotiations can also be accounted for by their divergent perceptions of Soviet intentions.

Brzezinski perceived that there was a "Soviet thrust toward global preeminence. . . . The Soviets subtly combined elements of cooperation and competition, not to preserve the status quo, but to transform it. . . . The Soviet Union might hope to displace America from its leading role in the international system . . . and to promote the 'world revolutionary process'" (1983, 148–49). By contrast, Vance had a more benign view of the Soviets. He "believed that [America] faced in the Soviet Union a powerful potential adversary with growing global interests and a compelling stake in avoiding military conflict with the U.S." (1983, 28). Vance suggested that "it was doubtful that there was a Soviet master plan for world domination, but rather an unceasing probing for advantage in furthering its national interests" (1983, 28). Thus, Vance was more forthcoming than Brzezinski regarding Soviet participation in the peace process.[77]

If we shift the focus to individual diplomats from different administrations, who held mitigated views of the Soviets (that is, neither hard-line ideologues nor pure soft-liners), we find a contrast between, on the one hand, Kissinger, who was less inclined to treat the Soviets as equals in resolving regional conflicts, and, on the other, Rogers and Vance, who were considerably more inclined to do so. Although Kissinger distrusted Soviet intentions more than Rogers and Vance did, the difference between them regarding cooperation with the Soviets cannot be explained only by differences in the image of the opponent. Rather, when we analyze the attitudes of decision makers with a mitigated image of the opponent, the two other images discussed in chapter 4 come into play. These images can also explain some of the differences in the Middle East strategies of Kissinger versus those of Eisenhower and Dulles and Reagan and Haig, although both these strategies were basically unilateral-exclusionary.

Those who subscribed to the bandwagoning-global outlook focused on the global rivalry in third areas as well and believed that local states would be inclined to align with the stronger party (or coalition). Thus, Kissinger's (1979, 379, 559, and 1982, 195, 196, 200, 202, 468, 1034) belief in diplomatic bandwagoning led him to expect that the United States could reach a hegemonic position in the Middle East because inherent U.S. advantages in the region would lead local states to accept Pax Americana and make it feasible for the United States to exclude the Soviets from the diplomacy of the region.[78]

For hard-line ideologues like Dulles and Haig, the exclusive focus was on the Soviet military threat; thus, they pursued a confrontational strategy expressed in the Middle East by the attempts at establishing anti-Soviet military alliances. But Kissinger was more attuned to regional nuances and, primarily, to the bandwagoning dynamics of international politics in various regions. Thus, Kissinger's fear of falling dominoes in south-east Asia influenced his behavior in Vietnam, whereas his optimism concerning U.S. diplomatic opportunities in the Middle East led him to invest his time and U.S. money (foreign aid) in an effort to resolve the Arab-Israeli conflict. In contrast, the Eisenhower and Reagan administrations put the resolution of this regional dispute on the back burner in relation to the priority given to the establishment of military alliances directed against the Soviet threat.

Somewhat similar to Kissinger, Rogers and Vance invested much effort in resolving the Arab-Israeli conflict. Yet in contrast to him, these two adherents to the balancing-regional approach were more inclined to cooperate with the Soviets in regional conflict resolution. This approach stressed the indigenous origins of regional conflicts and included a belief that states would tend to join the weaker coalition to protect their autonomy vis-à-vis the stronger one. This approach meant a lack of confidence that hegemonic policies could succeed in excluding a great power from a region that that power saw as vital to its national interests; indeed, that power would do all it could to resist its exclusion. Moreover, there were likely to be a number of regional actors, especially in areas with endemic conflicts, that would have their own interests (derived from local concerns) in allying with the excluded great power. Together, all these dissatisfied forces could obstruct the hegemon's attempt to pacify the region. Thus, State Department officials in the first Nixon administration and the Carter administration were more skeptical about U.S. ability to bring about a settlement unilaterally without some Soviet participation. If the Soviets had a voice in shaping the settlement, Secretaries Rogers and Vance believed, they could restrain their clients; but if the Soviets were excluded, they would help their intransigent clients to spoil the peace process. The Soviets would do so because Moscow had important interests in the area and would not accept being left out of the diplomatic process.[79]

The differences of opinion among U.S. decision makers about whether the United States could unilaterally bring about Pax Americana in a critical region indicate that the exclusionary pursuit of stabilizing policies is, at least partly, a subjective-cognitive matter influenced by leaders' perceptions, rather than only the objective effect of superior capabilities. The subjective component is reinforced, in turn, by the effects of the image of the opponent.

Secretary of State Rogers, for his part, believed that the Soviet Union was interested in a settlement (Safran 1981, 439) and that its participation was needed for progress in the peace process (Kissinger 1979, 378). Therefore, in the view of the Rogers' State Department, negotiations with Moscow could be useful (Kissinger 1979, 375–76; Spiegel 1985a, 175–76) and could even help the United States out of its Middle East predicament (Kissinger 1979, 368–69). In contrast, Kissinger describes his own view as "profoundly distrustful of Soviet motives, determined to prevent Soviet expansion, scornful of those critics who abjectly accepted Soviet advances or relied on history to undo them. To some extent my interest in détente was tactical, as a device to maximize Soviet dilemmas and reduce Soviet influence in the Middle East" (1979, 1254–55). Kissinger believed that "the Soviets would exploit the resulting turbulence for their hegemonic aims" (1982, 615).[80]

It is true that based on his scholarly writings on the Concert of Europe and his contribution to the policy of détente with Moscow, some observers have concluded that Kissinger intended to revive the idea of a great power concert (Bell 1977, 25ff.; Garrett 1976), perhaps also including China, and even Japan and Western Europe, (see Gaddis 1982, 280–83, and the sources he cites). The Arab-Israeli case shows, however, that Kissinger embarked on a strategy of competition with only limited collaboration, that is, he was inclined to cooperate with the Soviets only when there was no choice but to deal with them, like in the areas of arms control and European security. Thus, in the hour of crisis, Kissinger had to collaborate with the Soviets, as he did in the 1973 war.[81] But once he saw a possible gain to be made from successful unilateral steps by the

United States, he preferred to exclude the Soviets to the extent that it seemed possible to him. The point is that the cognitive-subjective elements predisposed him to believe that it was possible to do so in Middle East diplomacy. Thus, in the wake of the 1973 war, as we have seen, he pursued a unilateral course whose major goal was to exclude Moscow from the Middle East (Kissinger 1982, 747, 755, 794, 815, 843). It is true that Kissinger's rhetoric about Soviet participation in Middle East negotiations sounded more conciliatory than that of the pure hard-liners.[82] Kissinger was also more forthcoming than most previous administrations about the symbols of a Soviet role, such as the cochairship of the Geneva Conference.[83] Yet, as Ben-Zvi observes, "On the whole, Kissinger's Middle East policy was not less ambitious or maximalist than the posture advanced by the US during most of the Cold War era. And although he attempted to incorporate his policy into the framework of mitigated bipolarity, in practice he pursued an incremental undermining of Soviet strongholds in the area" (1986, 36).[84]

Apart from differences of opinion within the U.S. elite, another indicator that, in this context, shows the strength of cognitive factors in influencing U.S. Middle East policy is the resilience of preexisting images in the face of new external stimuli. The greater the closure of leaders' images to new information, the more attention we have to pay to individual-level elements. In United States administrations, like in other governments, a distinction must be made between open-minded leaders who are sensitive to contextual information versus close-minded leaders who are less so.[85] The importance of cognitive elements, however, is demonstrated when even relatively open-minded leaders become insensitive to external inputs. This phenomenon occurs quite often in noncrisis periods, when the intensity of international inputs is less than in times of crisis (see chap. 2).

It is true, for instance, that Kissinger was more open-minded than some of his predecessors regarding the Soviet Union. Still, because of his preexisting perception of Soviet intentions in the Middle East (and his belief that it was feasible to exclude the Soviets), he dismissed the considerable concessions they made in the May, 1972, summit concerning Arab-Israeli peace (1979, 1294, 1297).[86]

The slowness of the Carter administration in coming to support Sadat's 1977 Jerusalem initiative is another example of cognitive closure in normal diplomacy (Quandt 1986a, 137). Although one might have expected an enthusiastic U.S. endorsement of a trip by an Arab leader to Jerusalem, indicating a willingness to live in peace with Israel, such was not in fact the initial American reaction, which was at best lukewarm. Even after endorsing the initiative, the State Department contended that it was not in America's interest to support a bilateral Egyptian-Israeli peace and that every effort should be made to include other Arab parties and to reconvene the Geneva Conference (Indyk

1984, 49–50; Spiegel 1985a, 341–42). The reason for this response was the administration's intense commitment to the idea of a comprehensive peace with the participation of the Soviets and all the Arab parties.

Whereas the systemic factor (relations with the Soviets) was paramount in crisis settings, there has been a greater variation in the motivations of different policymakers in noncrisis situations. Thus, Carter's peacemaking was more motivated by human rights and an idealist perspective than Kissinger's, whose major interest was the strategic competition with the Soviets. The State Department, for its part, has tended to focus on regional concerns. In this sense, decision makers' personal values and beliefs have played a greater role in normal diplomacy than in crisis situations.[87]

## Ideological Differences and Domestic Factors

The opposition to diplomatic cooperation with an ideological rival may not be confined to individual policymakers from within the decision making elite, but may also stem from domestic groups who subscribe to a negative image of the opponent and consequently are opposed to cooperation with it. The effectiveness of this domestic opposition is conditioned by the domestic regime. In the diplomacy of a democratic great power, particularly when it involves collaboration with other great powers in normal diplomacy, domestic support is of key importance. Thus, one of the differences between crisis and noncrisis settings, at least throughout the postwar period, was the greater influence of domestic politics on U.S. foreign policy in noncrisis periods. In contrast, domestic influence could not play nearly so great a role in a country with a nondemocratic, centralist-hierarchical government. A pluralist great power is much more dependent than an authoritarian power on the support of public opinion and influential interest groups for carrying out its foreign policy, especially if it involves cooperation with an ideological rival.

The major factor that fueled the domestic opposition in the United States to cooperation with the Soviet Union was the ideological identity of the latter. Indeed, so long as the dominant perception of the rival is that of an expansionist, aggressive, revolutionary power, it is much easier to spoil the delicate enterprise of cooperation with it than to build a wide-based coalition in favor of this kind of controversial cooperation. This situation made any high-level cooperation with Moscow particularly vulnerable to domestic and bureaucratic political opposition[88] and placed severe domestic constraints on U.S. administrations. Thus, even when the U.S. leadership was ready to collaborate with the Soviets in a relatively benign form of prior superpower agreement on the outline of a regional Middle East settlement, American domestic politics obstructed the continuation of the joint superpower initiative. For example, the domestic opposition in the United States to the 1977 joint statement referred to above originated not only from pro-Israeli groups but also from anti-Soviet ones. These groups were not less offended by the mere fact of U.S. cooperation with the Soviets than by the substance of the statement, which was, in fact, moderate.[89] This opposition was motivated by a refusal to grant the Soviets an equal status in conflict resolution in the Middle East. Spiegel reports that

> At home, a political firestorm erupted as editorial and congressional critics charged that the administration—for no apparent reason—had invited the USSR back into the center of the Mideast diplomatic scene. Not one senator or congressman rose to defend the administration, which was widely seen as catering to the Russian and Arab positions. After American officials had worked successfully for years to reduce Russian influence over the Mideast peace process and in the area as a whole, critics could not understand why the administration had suddenly invited Moscow to return. In addition, the flat Israeli rejection appeared to foreclose further diplomatic progress. (1985a, 338)

Generally speaking, the ideological rivalry between communism and capitalism severely constrained U.S.-Soviet cooperation by reinforcing mutual images of enemies rather than of limited adversaries.[90] Strong commitments to their respective visions of the international order made it difficult for Washington and Moscow to agree about the legitimacy of the status quo (cf. Nye 1987, 393–94), to accept each other's spheres of influence, and to recognize each other's equal status.[91] This was particularly true regarding the Third World, where the Soviets were committed to support the "progressive forces" and national liberation movements and the United States was obligated to promote democracy and free enterprise, or at least to oppose the rise of pro-communist regimes. The lack of consensus on their balance of interests was especially notable in the Middle East. The combination of generally negative images of each other (shaped by ideology) and the specific content of their ideologies (i.e., the rejection of spheres of influence) undermined attempts at concerted diplomacy. Moreover, ideological or moral affiliation with at least some of their allies made their commitment to these allies stronger than if only traditional great power patronage were at issue. But, as noted, it was especially the United States that rejected the equal status of the Soviets and the legitimacy of their interests in the Middle East, both because U.S. advantages in the Middle East allowed it to afford such a rejection and because its domestic constraints precluded cooperation, especially in a coercive form. But what has underlain this rejection was the ideological rivalry and the derived dominant image of the Soviets as a revolutionary-aggressive power that does not deserve to be recognized as an equal by a democracy.

Conversely, it was easier for the USSR, as an authoritarian state and a closed society, to pursue a collaborative strategy in the Middle East, because no domestic groups could effectively oppose it—especially as this strategy was also in the interests of the USSR as the weaker power in the region. (Yet an opposition existed within the Soviet elite, on the part of ideologically hard-line fractions who opposed any cooperation with the United States).

Only growing similarity and moderation could make the United States willing to forego opportunities for exclusive brokerage and grant the USSR or Russia a role in the peace process in the region. Growing similarity could also create more positive mutual images among decision makers and domestic groups in both countries and reduce the disagreements between them over the form of cooperation.

Indeed, only when crucial domestic and cognitive changes took place in both superpowers in the mid-1980s could the collaborative element of U.S.-Soviet relations in the Middle East become more prominent, including with regard to some sorts of a multilateral framework for peace negotiations. These changes took place although the bipolar structure of the international system would not essentially change for a number of years and despite the continuity (or even the growth) of the basic power asymmetries in the Middle East.[92] These domestic and cognitive changes and their effects on the emergence of diplomatic collaboration in conflict resolution will occupy us next.

## Growing Similarity and Moderation and the Emergence of Concerted Diplomacy

The immediate explanation for the emergence of concerted superpower diplomacy in the Middle East from the mid-1980s until the early 1990s seems to lie in changes in the policy positions of the most important players, namely, the much greater flexibility and moderation of Soviet foreign policy under Gorbachev, including the openness toward Israel, and U.S. responsiveness to these changes.

Yet what has underlain these policy changes has been the fulfillment, to a considerable extent, of the basic prerequisites for cooperation: a convergence in outlook and aims as the great powers became more moderate (externally) and more similar (internally) that enhanced the prospects for the emergence of concerted diplomacy for the purposes of conflict resolution (see chap. 4). Thus, on the one hand, the translation of the Soviet new thinking into policy actions increased the Soviet capability to contribute constructively to peacemaking, while on the other hand, Gorbachev's domestic reforms (and not only the greater moderation in foreign policy) made Moscow a much more acceptable partner in American eyes for joint diplomacy in conflict resolution and brought about the growing willingness of the Reagan and the Bush administrations to involve the Soviets in Middle East peacemaking.

Let us now look more specifically at the policy changes among the involved actors.

## The New Political Thinking in Soviet Foreign Policy and Its Application to the Middle East

The new Soviet approach (see Breslauer 1990, especially 293–94; Breslauer and Tetlock 1991; Legvold 1988, 126–28; Weiss and Blight 1992, 158–61)[93] involved the following conceptual revisions in Soviet thinking on foreign affairs, which together amounted to a growing moderation.

The first revision is from a perception of a zero-sum superpower competition to a recognition of a high level of interdependence between the superpowers. Instead of a conception according to which a gain for one power meant a loss for the other and vice versa, a realization emerged that in many situations there might be joint losses and also joint gains for all the parties involved. (As noted in chapter 2, such subjective-cognitive interdependence is necessary for high-level cooperation and concerted diplomacy.)

The second revision is from a focus on the balance of superpower military forces to an emphasis on the balance of their interests. Instead of relying on military power as the major means of achieving absolute national security, the Soviet elite came to realize that there should be an attempt to reach mutual or common security between adversaries. This should be attempted through negotiated agreements between the superpowers based on the balance of their relative interests at stake in each conflict. These agreements should also include the area of arms control and thus help to reach the following objective.

The third conceptual change is a shift of military forces from an offensive to a defensive posture. Instead of aiming at superiority or even equality with the rival, a goal of reasonable sufficiency (in fact, minimal deterrence) emerged—that is, an ability to deter potential aggressors but also to reassure status quo states (and thus, in fact, to reduce the security dilemma). This change was also related to a greater priority of domestic and economic needs at the expense of defense spending and military intervention in foreign countries. The combination of the last two points meant that security was no longer defined in exclusively military terms.

The fourth cognitive shift is from unilateral means to multilateral approaches to problem solving. This revision meant a shift to cooperative measures and a greater use of international organizations such as the UN and the Conference on Security and Cooperation in Europe.

The fifth revision is from class interests to overall human interests. Instead of the classical Marxist-Leninist focus on the class struggle, priority was accorded to the concerns of humankind as a whole, such as the avoidance of nuclear war, the control of the arms race, the protection of the environment, and the resolution of regional conflicts.[94]

In the Middle East, we have seen that from 1967 till the Gorbachev era, the Soviets tried either to construct joint peace initiatives with the United States or to obstruct exclusionary U.S. moves by supporting Arab radicals. Gorbachev, however, as part of his new thinking in foreign policy and his new approach to regional conflicts in particular, initiated two important changes in this strategy (see Breslauer, ed., 1990; see also Rabinovich 1990).[95] On the one hand, since 1985 Moscow broadened its options by opening a dialogue with a greater variety of Middle East actors beyond the members of the "radical club." On the other hand, Gorbachev demonstrated a greater willingness than his predecessors to forcefully press traditional Soviet allies toward moderation.

These policy changes reflected a greater ideological flexibility and moderation. The new thinking suggested, in fact, the deideologization of foreign policy (as reflected especially in the fifth revision). It advocated improving Soviet relations with a wider range of states, including good ties with Third World countries with a capitalist orientation (cf. Golan 1990b, 157–58). In the Middle East, this new doctrine was expressed in overtures toward conservative Arab states and increasing contacts with Israel. Gorbachev indeed succeeded in upgrading relations with the Arab Gulf states, Egypt, and Jordan; that, in turn, solidified their support for the idea of an international conference. Even more innovative were the overtures made toward Israel, after two decades of estranged relations in the diplomatic and other fields. These moves included intensified diplomatic contacts and allowing unlimited Jewish emigration to Israel.

At the same time, Gorbachev publicly distanced himself from the positions of his closest ally in the Middle East—President Assad of Syria—by stating his opposition to the resolution of the Middle East conflict by military force (*Pravda,* April 25, 1987) and his support for the recognition of Israel (*New York Times,* April 11, 1988). Although the Soviets continued to supply Syria with sophisticated weapons, they failed to meet some of the Syrians' quantitative and qualitative requests and slowed their arms shipments (cf. *New York Times,* June 12, 1988; Breslauer 1990, 311; Golan 1990b, 160).

The Soviets were also instrumental in moderating the positions of the PLO in the winter of 1988. They pressured the Palestinian organizations to accept UN Resolutions 242 and 338, renounce terrorism, and recognize Israel's right to exist. Since the main short-term outcome of this new PLO moderation was the launching of a U.S.-PLO dialogue, the Soviets, in fact, helped to make it possible. This stands in marked contrast to the Soviets' anxieties earlier in the 1980s that talks between a joint Palestinian-Jordanian delegation and the United States would eventually lead to Pax Americana. Whereas at that time they activated their radical allies in the PLO to obstruct Jordanian-PLO negotiations with the United States, they now signaled to these allies to refrain from opposing the diplomatic road to the resolution of the conflict (interviews in Washington, D.C., April, 1990).

A related change took place in the Soviet position regarding the form of superpower cooperation, namely the procedures and authority of the international conference for the resolution of the Arab-Israeli conflict. The United States and Israel strongly opposed the traditional Soviet view in favor of a coercive role for such a conference, in which the superpowers would have real authority to promote (if not impose) a solution. Consequently, realizing the unworkability of its position, Moscow softened its stance and tended to minimize any element of imposed peace (see Ben-Zvi 1990, 102–3; see also Golan 1990b).

Such shifts in Moscow's position toward greater moderation, implied in the new thinking, could not be accounted for only by the desire to have better relations with the United States (a desire that was closely related to the enormous economic need of the Soviet Union for Western assistance in technology, investments, know-how, and credits and the related wish to reduce defense spending to release resources for the economy). Neither can they be explained by the accumulating domestic and economic pressures that have weakened the Soviet Union and have finally brought about its disintegration—for the new Soviet willingness to cooperate with the United States preceded by several years the process of Soviet disintegration and in fact began with the coming to power of Gorbachev and a new foreign policy elite. While the domestic and economic factors disposed the Soviets toward some sort of new thinking, the cognitive beliefs of Gorbachev and his team determined the timing and the specific content of the policies that Moscow pursued from 1985 until its disintegration. The new Soviet leadership seemed to accept the logic of the balancing dynamics of international politics more than its predecessors. As noted in chapter 4, an image of balancing is a prerequisite for moderation. In other words, the Soviets seemingly realized that it would be extremely difficult for any one of the superpowers to permanently exclude the other from such a turbulent and important region as the Middle East.[96] But by the same token, they also understood that to stay in the diplomatic picture, let alone advance Middle East stability and reduce the risk of inadvertent escalation, they had to show flexibility, moderation, and willingness to cooperate with the United States. Related cognitive changes also took place with regard to the other two images: a more benign view of the United States as a potential partner and an increased perception of the dangers of escalation of regional conflicts.

These moderating changes in foreign policy were accompanied by domestic reforms, which made the Soviet Union more similar to the United States in American eyes and contributed to the growing willingness of the United States to reciprocate by moderating their own position on Soviet participation in Middle Eastern diplomacy.

## Evolution of the Reagan and Bush Administrations' Attitude toward Cooperation with the Soviets in the Middle East

Because of Reagan's vehemently anti-Communist views, his administration was initially even less inclined than its predecessors to involve the Soviets in Middle East diplomacy (Ben-Zvi 1990; Quandt 1988; Saunders 1988, 572). But Soviet internal reforms and moderation in foreign affairs, including in the Middle East, and the overall improvement in U.S.-Soviet relations, especially in the last year of the administration, made even the hard-liners in the Reagan administration somewhat more flexible toward Moscow's role in the region.

One can discern three main stages in the evolution of the Reagan administration's position toward Soviet participation in Middle East peacemaking and the related idea of an international conference. This evolution confirms the strength of cognitive factors and their resilience to change, but it also indicates that dramatic changes in the external environment (international and regional) can eventually lead to modifications even in strongly held positions. Moreover, as cognitive theory would expect, changes in policy positions were relatively slow, gradual, and, at least initially, more sensitive to changes in the positions of friends and allies than of adversaries.

The first stage was dominated by the confrontational Cold War beliefs of the leading members of the administration. From its assumption of power in 1981 until 1985, this administration totally rejected recurring Soviet proposals for superpower cooperation in the Middle East in the framework of an international conference and was essentially opposed to any Soviet role in the peace process (as well as in a Lebanese settlement). This exclusionary position was fully consistent with the administration's highly ideological view of the Soviet Union as "the last great predatory empire on earth" (Dallin and Lapidus 1983, 210).

The second stage involved a change in the American position in the direction of accepting the need for some sort of international framework for resolving the Arab-Israeli conflict. But this change was more a response to modifications in the positions of local allies than a change of attitude toward the Soviet Union. Accordingly, the change was very limited and not wholeheartedly pursued by Washington. Confronted by King Hussein's insistence from 1984 onward on an international conference to legitimize any direct talks with Jerusalem, the Reagan administration reluctantly accepted the notion of a multilateral framework. The agreement of Israeli Prime Minister Peres, in 1985, to the notion of an international framework also played a critical role in making Washington more forthcoming about this idea, culminating in the support U.S. officials provided for the Peres-Hussein London Document of April, 1987. Yet in the U.S. interpretation, the envisioned role for the conference was a minimalist one, primarily as a starting point for launching the supposedly direct negotiations among the parties in which the United States would presumably play a key mediating role. Moreover, the administration's lukewarm attitude toward an international conference, which was due in part to a fundamental resistance to full-blown Soviet participation, was reflected in its failure to exert pressures on the right-wing Likud bloc in Israel to modify its opposition to the London Document and to an international conference with Soviet participation. Indeed, by mid-1987 it did not seem that there was a strong linkage between the gradual improvement in overall U.S.-Soviet relations and their minimal cooperation in the Middle East.

Two kinds of changes, one regional and the other global, brought about the third stage, in which there seemed to be a greater (although by no means unqualified) U.S. willingness to include Moscow in the peace process. The first was the uprising, or intifada, of the Palestinians in the territories occupied by Israel that erupted in late 1987.[97] The prolonged nature of the intifada lent itself to the emergence of diplomatic initiatives aimed not just at ending the immediate violence but also at resolving the Arab-Israeli conflict, or at least its critical Palestinian dimension.

The second change was the great improvement in superpower relations with the progress made in the negotiations on the agreement on intermediate-range nuclear forces in late 1987 and the signing of the treaty that December. Throughout 1988, not only did the bilateral relations continue to warm up (a summit took place in May–June, 1988, during which Reagan, the life-long communist-baiter, visited Moscow), but the accelerating domestic reforms in the Soviet Union markedly improved the image of the Soviets, and in particular that of Gorbachev personally, in American eyes.

Thus, Secretary of State Shultz's initiative of March 4, 1988, proposed that the direct negotiations between Israel and each of its neighbors would be preceded by an international conference to be convened on April 15, 1988.[98] But the authority of the conference was still envisioned as minimalist, and the change in the U.S. position was limited, at least partly, because there were still misgivings in the administration about full-blown and influential Soviet participation in the delicate Middle East diplomacy.

By the time the Reagan administration completed its term in office, the most important change was not any specific transformation in the parties' respective policy positions. Rather, it was the diplomatic legacy that the Reagan team left to its successor, that is, the removal of some important taboos in American public opinion concerning U.S. policy in the Middle East. One was the negotiations with the PLO; the other was the talks with the Soviets about Middle East problems and the related notion that some form of international framework was necessary for resolving conflicts in the region, notably the Arab-Israeli dispute. Especially significant was that the removal of these taboos was carried out by an administration with an unprecedented record of support for Israel and (initial) hostility toward the Soviets. This change could provide important domestic legitimacy for potential superpower cooperation in the next administration.

However, despite the persistence of political reforms in the Soviet Union and the continuation of Moscow's moderation in foreign affairs, the Bush administration, on coming to power, took a stance of extreme caution toward the other superpower. Even growing cooperation with the Kremlin in some regional conflicts did not at first alleviate the administration's reservations about a Middle East peace conference with Soviet participation. It seems that such reservations were, at least partly, influenced by Kissinger, who was the mentor of some influential members of the administration. The former secretary of state continued to articulate his doubts about an international conference[99] and this probably reinforced, at least at the outset, skeptical views about a Soviet role in the new administration.[100] Indeed, President Bush was reported to state in early 1989 that "the Soviet role in the Middle East should be limited" (*New York Times,* February 22, 1989, 2), and there were repeated complaints by U.S. officials about the absence of new Soviet thinking concerning the Arab-Israeli conflict.

Yet the accelerated pace of revolutionary changes in Soviet domestic affairs, in Eastern Europe, and in Soviet policies in the Third World under the leadership of Gorbachev in 1989 and 1990 made the Bush administration more receptive to Soviet participation and to ongoing diplomatic consultations with Moscow about the Middle East. The changing attitude saw its most public manifestation in the Malta Summit of late 1989, which reflected a new peak in the superpower rapprochement. In a considerable departure from his initial approach, President Bush stated at the summit that the Soviets could play a constructive role in the Middle East and that he did not think there was a great distance between the superpowers on the questions of Lebanon and the West Bank (*Haaretz,* December 6, 1989).

Indeed, during 1989 and 1990, some concrete elements of superpower cooperation emerged: for example, a joint action to prevent UN recognition of a declared Palestinian state; some degree of pressure on their respective allies (the United States on Israel; the Soviets on the PLO) to moderate their positions concerning the Israeli initiative to hold elections in the occupied territories; a joint declaration during the June, 1990, summit in Washington against the settlement of new immigrants (mostly from the Soviet Union) in the territories held by Israel; and talks on arms control and the nonproliferation of nonconventional weapons in the Middle East.

During summer and fall 1990, U.S.-Soviet cooperation peaked in confronting Saddam Hussein's aggression against Kuwait, making possible Security Council resolutions imposing economic sanctions and, in late November, authorizing the use of force against Iraq. Moreover, the superpowers agreed that following the resolution of the Gulf crisis, a major effort should be made to resolve the Arab-Israeli conflict and that they should cooperate in this enterprise.

Indeed, in the aftermath of the Gulf War, the United States, as the widely recognized leading world power, initiated precisely such an effort in close collaboration with Moscow, which has played a supportive, although essentially a secondary, role. By late 1993, the prospects for the post–Gulf War initiative to advance the Arab-Israeli peace process seemed much more promising than earlier attempts to resolve this conflict. Yet at the time of this writing, there is still a considerable degree of uncertainty with regard to the likelihood and the final shape of a comprehensive Arab-Israeli settlement. At any rate, it is clear that the current effort has departed from its numerous predecessors in at least two major respects that are related to the superpower role. First, there has been an unprecedented level of U.S.-Soviet (later U.S.-Russian) substantive agreement concerning the peace process, and there has also been a substantial degree of cooperation in trying to advance it. Second, all the regional parties have agreed that the superpowers should cosponsor and cochair the peace conference, although the former were, until recently, in dispute about the duration and nature of the conference and about the role and the representation of some of the other participants (the UN, the Europeans, and the Palestinians).

Thus, by attending the Madrid Conference in late October, 1991, both Arabs and Israelis responded to the joint call issued by Bush and Gorbachev in their Moscow summit of summer 1991 to convene a peace conference in that month. Moreover, the pressures exerted by the unified stance of the superpowers played a critical role in inducing the responsiveness of the local parties. Yet a short time after this successful peak in superpower cooperation in the Arab-Israeli peace process, the failed coup in Moscow drastically accelerated the disintegration process of the Soviet Union until it was replaced by a loose Commonwealth of Independent States in late 1991. At any rate, it is likely that Moscow (now as a capital of the Russian Republic) is, at least for the short-run, on a path of partial disengagement from world affairs, which would render it less relevant to Middle East diplomacy and leave the United States for the time being as the major power in the driving seat—a possibility the implications of which we examine briefly in the final section of this chapter and in the concluding chapter of the book.

### Conclusions

In this chapter we have seen the considerable explanatory power of nonsystemic factors (state attributes, domestic politics, cognitive attributes) for foreign policymaking in noncrisis settings. Fundamental changes in these factors brought about important changes in international and Middle East politics since the mid-1980s, including possibilities for joint diplomacy of the great powers in conflict resolution. These possibilities started to materialize in varying degrees in a number of regional conflicts, including the Middle East, several years before the structural changes that culminated in the disintegration of the Soviet Union and its disengagement from worldwide involvement. This disengagement, for its part, seems to open the way for a dominant American role in Middle East peacemaking, at least for the foreseeable future. Yet a great power concert might reemerge in the longer run, with a rise in the global engagement of an integrated Europe and of Japan. These powers could conceivably translate their economic might to the diplomatic domain and cooperate with the United States in managing international conflicts. At any rate, the strategy that the United States will choose to pursue in the Middle East, like in other international conflicts in the post–Cold War era, will heavily depend on domestic support and especially on the three beliefs discussed in this chapter.

We have seen that different U.S. administrations pursued three major strategies vis-à-vis the Soviets in the Middle East (sometimes there were also divisions of opinions within administrations on these strategies), in accordance with the three orientations and their associated images presented in chapter 4.

First, the confrontational orientation, which was dominant during the peak periods of the Cold War, was manifested in the Middle East by attempts at forming anti-Soviet military alliances by Eisenhower and Dulles (in the 1950s) and by Reagan and Haig (in the early 1980s). This strategy was informed by the image of the Soviet Union as an expansionist "evil empire."

Second, the competitive orientation, which was dominant during most of the détente period, was reflected in the Middle East by the strategy of unilateral diplomacy in the peace process (most notably, Kissinger's step-by-step diplomacy in 1974 through 1976). Belief in the bandwagoning dynamics of world politics—in this case, regarding U.S. ability for unilateral leadership—was the major image that guided this strategy (in addition to suspicion of Soviet intentions).

Third, the multilateral approach was expressed by attempts at joint superpower diplomacy such as the two-power talks (from 1969 to 1970), the Geneva Conference (December, 1973), and the joint statement of October, 1977. Such attempts at joint actions in the Third World were informed by the focus on regional problems as the major source of international conflicts and also by disbelief in the success of unilateral policies.

Although this strategy was supported by State Department officials in the first Nixon administration, and especially by leading members of the Carter administration at its initial stage, so long as the Cold War was ongoing, it did not have much of a chance. Indeed, the ideological rivalry with the Soviets meant that the impact of domestic politics in a pluralist democracy would make this strategy especially vulnerable to domestic and allied pressures. This could lead to the abandonment of the path of joint superpower diplomacy, as Carter reluctantly had to do by eventually moving to the Camp David course of U.S. unilateralism following Sadat's dramatic moves and the Soviet opposition to them. Similarly, the combination of domestic political constraints and bureaucratic politics undermined the standing of Rogers and the appeal of his approach in the struggle with Kissinger's strategy.

Whereas the three images determined which strategy was preferred by different administrations, state-level factors influenced to what extent leaders' beliefs were translated to state policy. Thus, the multilateralist strategy was severely undermined by the domestic constraints. At the same time, international factors determined the degree of eventual success of the two strategies that were more acceptable domestically. The confrontational approach failed to produce regionwide anti-Soviet alliances; the unilateral diplomatic strategy succeeded only partially—on the Egyptian-Israeli front—but failed on the other fronts, at least until the recent Gulf War. The absence of irrefutable accomplishments in the external arena increased even more the vulnerability of the multilateralist strategy to domestic and allied challenges.

Yet under the impact of Soviet moderating trends under Gorbachev, the superpowers have seemed to come to realize the balancing effects in international politics, in the sense that it is costly and useless to try to exclude from regional conflict resolution one of the powers who has important interests in the region, whereas the participation of all the interested great powers could reduce the incentives for any of them to spoil the peace process; instead, the powers could help to restrain their respective allies. The Soviets have recently done this in the Middle East with respect to Syria and the PLO.

A multilateral framework, furthermore, could enhance the international legitimacy of the settlement. Such legitimacy is especially critical to small states whose borders, or very existence, are controversial. In the Arab-Israeli context, this concern applies to Israel and to whatever Palestinian entity would emerge from the peace negotiations. It also applies to Jordan, whose legitimacy has been challenged by radical Palestinians as well as Israeli extremists. Indeed, it was, in particular, vulnerable Jordan that pushed for a multilateral framework for the negotiations. Such a framework would confer greater legitimacy to the outcome of the peace talks at home (within Arab states and among the Palestinians), and in inter-Arab relations, as well as internationally. An active Soviet role, in particular, appeared to encourage Syrian and Palestinian participation and to restrain obstruction by the radicals. The United States reciprocated, to some extent, by exerting some moderating influence on Israel's positions, especially after the Gulf War.

On the part of the superpowers, genuine collaboration has seemed to reflect the accumulated learning that unilateral policies jeopardize the improvement of their bilateral relations. The United States and the Soviet Union appeared to arrive at the insight that exclusionary strategies are dangerous and, in the final analysis, have questionable chances of success at affordable costs, at least in a bipolar world in which both superpowers are committed to their status as global powers.[101] And each side has seemed to come to a deeper appreciation of the uncontrollable character and escalatory potential of regional dynamics, which could result in a greater sense of urgency about the need to concert their efforts and a greater awareness of the futility of competitive policies. Indeed, in recent years there has been a growing understanding of the need to learn to cooperate also in noncrisis periods to ameliorate, if not resolve, those local conflicts that were costly, brought limited returns, poisoned superpower relations, and threatened escalation and thus posed a danger to world stability. Yet the growing cooperation became possible not only because of rising moderation in superpower foreign policy but also due to the domestic reforms in the USSR, which made it more similar to the United States; as a result, the United States became much more willing to involve a democratizing Soviet Union in the peace process, even if power asymmetries grew rather than narrowed.

However, since the disintegration of the USSR, U.S.-Russian cooperation, while still important for the Arab-Israeli peace process, does not at all mean an equal role for both powers. Already during the 1980s, U.S. advantages in the Third World have become very noticeable in the area of socioeconomic development and with respect to building democratic institutions, whose appeal has been increasing recently. More specifically to the Middle East, the United States has had, especially since the 1973 War, a potentially great leverage on the party that has controlled the major issue at stake in the Arab-Israeli conflict—the Israeli-held occupied territories. The Gulf War has demonstrated the dependence of Arab states, not only those in the Gulf, on the United States for their security against regional aggressors.

The sharp decline of the USSR, and eventually its breakdown at the end of 1991, have reinforced drastically the special U.S. standing as the dominant broker in the Middle East. In the aftermath of the disintegration of the Soviet Union and the disappearance of Gorbachev from power, Russia under Yeltsin has started to play a more minor role in world affairs, including in the Middle East, where it seemingly resigned itself to following the American leadership in the regional peace process, although maybe only for the short run. As a consequence, its chief client in the region, Syria, had no choice but to turn to Washington and to become more receptive to U.S. influence. Ironically, although the mass immigration of Jews from the collapsing Soviet Union to Israel could eventually make the Jewish state stronger, the immediate effect was to increase even more its dependence on U.S. assistance for coping with the big wave of immigrants and thus to increase Israel's susceptibility to U.S. pressures with regard to the promotion of the post–Gulf War peace process.

Since the Japanese and the Europeans are still mainly economic powers and not full-blown military-diplomatic powers, the United States would remain the only true superpower at least for the immediate future. Thus, with the decline of bipolarity in the early 1990s due to the fall of the Soviet empire, U.S. unilateral strategy in the peace process seems to be much more feasible than it has been until recently.

However, this scenario might be somewhat questionable in the longer run, because of the domestic political and economic as well as the regional and international constraints on successfully playing the role of a unilateralist hegemon for an extended period. Even if the hegemonic scenario is feasible, it might still make sense for the United States and the regional powers to try to engage other external powers as much as possible in the peace process. Although in a much smaller role than the United States, the Russians would presumably still have the capacity to contribute (through moderating pressures on allies and additional international legitimacy, but primarily through participation in arms control agreements) or to spoil. At any rate, in spite of its present relative retrenchment, Russia is likely to remain involved in the region, at least to some limited degree.[102] Moreover, the probable transition to a multipolar world with the strengthening of an integrated Europe and the rise of China and Japan might also necessitate their participation in Middle East peacemaking and peacekeeping through joint political-diplomatic and economic initiatives with the United States, to help Middle East peace and prosperity and thus also enhance world stability and energy security.[103]

Yet I have shown in this chapter that the choice of strategy by U.S. policymakers will heavily depend on their perceptions of other powers' intentions and capabilities as well as on their beliefs about the dynamics of the international system and the linkage between regional and global politics. More specifically, the image of the opponent will condition the willingness to engage other powers—depending largely on the perception of their similarity to the United States (i.e., a strong commitment to democracy and to the free market) and of their moderation (the absence of hegemonic-exclusionary inclinations and commitment to peaceful resolution of conflicts). Yet as noted in chapter 4, the other two images will become more crucial in the post–Cold War era, with the disappearance of the East-West ideological rivalry. The belief regarding the dynamics of world politics will affect American decision makers' confidence in the United States's ability to produce a Pax Americana alone and the perception to what extent and in what ways and domains there is a need for the participation of other powers. The perception of the loci of problems, for its part, will determine whether an isolationist or an internationalist approach is going to be selected in the policymaking process. To invest scarce resources in dealing with regional conflicts in the aftermath of the termination of the Soviet threat, key decision makers need to believe that these conflicts threaten vital U.S. interests as well as global stability.

However, for their preferences to become policy, leaders will have to work hard to convince the attentive public about the validity of these threats as well as the feasibility of pacifying policies in a region such as the Middle East. This will be a tough challenge, because in the post–Cold War era, public support for international engagements will be harder to achieve than in the bipolar era (see chap. 3). In the Conclusions, I focus on the post–Cold War feasibility and necessity of the highest form of international engagement discussed in this book—a great power concert. I also mention the challenges that a potential concert is likely to face.

# Conclusions: Intended and Unintended Consequences—Past and Future

In this chapter, I summarize the main findings of the book by briefly reviewing the major historical patterns of great power conflict and cooperation in the eras of the Concert of Europe and the Cold War, which are accounted for by the two schools presented in chapter 1—the structural balance of power and the international society—and the causal factors associated with each school. I focus, however, on the implications of the theoretical argument of this study for the post–Cold War era. Finally, I suggest some ideas for future research, which should build on the findings of this book concerning the *origins* of great power conflict and cooperation, especially in third regions, to address the *consequences* of international involvement for regional security.

## Explaining the Recurrence of Deliberate and Inadvertent Conflict and Cooperation

In this book, I have shown the recurrence of both intended and unintended conflict and cooperation in international politics in general. Yet in different historical periods, there are different combinations of these outcomes. Thus, the nineteenth century was characterized by deliberate high-level cooperation, but some inadvertent wars also took place. By contrast, the postwar era was characterized by successful unintended cooperation as well as the failure of attempts at intended cooperation. As I show in this chapter, the post–Cold War era might resemble more the nineteenth century, at least in the sense of much greater prospects for concerted diplomacy in conflict resolution, but there is also a greater danger of inadvertent wars as compared with the postwar era. The argument of this book is that a synthesis of the causal factors associated with the structural balance-of-power approach with those related to the international society school is essential to account for such variations. Yet such a synthesis can provide a useful explanation, rather than mere description, only if it is based on defining the relative strength of each of the schools for explaining different types of outcomes. This is indeed the major theoretical argument of this book, namely that unintended conflict or cooperation in times of crises is accounted for by structural factors, whereas success or failure of intended cooperation in conflict resolution is explained by unit-level elements.

Thus, such a model can advance two major predictions for the post–Cold War era:

1. Crisis management will be much more difficult than in the Cold War because of the structural change, namely, the disappearance of bipolarity.
2. Concerted diplomacy in conflict resolution will be more likely to succeed because of recent unit-level changes, which have made the great powers more similar and moderate.

In other words, the range of outcomes will be much greater than in the Cold War era: from protracted and large-scale wars in regions that did not know such conflicts during the Cold War due to the heavy involvement of one or two superpowers in that region (such as Eastern Europe and the Gulf), to negotiated settlements brokered (or facilitated) by the great powers in regions that have experienced conflicts intensified by superpower involvement and assistance to the local protagonists during the Cold War (notably in the Third World and the Middle East).

I first discuss the implications for crisis management, and then for concerted diplomacy in conflict resolution. The discussion of crisis management in the post–Cold War era, in turn, is also divided into two parts: the current postbipolar or unipolar era and the future multipolar system.

On the whole, each of the two schools best explains four major patterns of conflict and cooperation in the nineteeenth century, postwar, and post–Cold War eras. The structural balance-of-power school accounts for the following four patterns that are manifestations of unintended crisis outcomes:

1. the occurrence of inadvertent wars, notably under pre–World War I multipolarity
2. the crisis patterns, or tacit rules, of the Cold War
3. the growing problems for crisis management in the current postbipolar era
4. the potential for inadvertent escalation in a future multipolarity

The causal factors associated with the international society approach, for their part, best explain the following four phenomena, which are expressions of intended cooperation in conflict resolution.[1]

1. the emergence of the nineteenth century European Concert
2. the initiation, but also the failure, of limited attempts at concerted diplomacy in the postwar era, let alone the nonemergence of a full-blown concert in this era

3. the much more successful U.S.-Soviet attempts at concerted diplomacy since the mid-1980s until the disintegration of the USSR
4. the much brighter prospects for a concert in the post–Cold War era, at least in comparison with any other period in this century

Since the historical patterns (of both the Concert and the Cold War eras) were analyzed at length in the previous chapters, the focus of the concluding chapter is on the implications of the model for current and future patterns, notably the combination of growing difficulties for crisis management and rising prospects for conflict resolution.

**Outcomes Best Explained by the Structural Balance-of-Power School**

Failure in Crisis Management and Unintended Wars under Multipolarity

The Crimean War and World War I are good examples of the destabilizing effects of the multipolar structure on crisis management precisely because of the relative similarity and moderation of the great powers in that era. Their failure in crisis management is so remarkable also because it stood in marked contrast to their relative success in cooperative normal diplomacy. Indeed, the Concert members reached explicit agreements in noncrisis diplomacy on issues such as spheres of influence, equal status of the Concert members, the status quo, cooperation in conflict management, and the balance of stakes but were not as effective in developing the tacit understandings required for crisis management, although, by their effective noncrisis diplomacy, they succeeded in heading off many potential crises in the first place. But once crises had erupted, like in the Crimea and in the Balkans, the multipolar structure made it more difficult for the great powers to manage them and avoid a general war. Thus, whereas the Concert members had been more successful in establishing a crisis-*prevention* regime than were the superpowers during the Cold War, the United States and the Soviet Union never failed to *manage* crises, in contrast to the failure of the European powers on at least two fateful occasions: 1853–54 and 1914.[2]

The Emergence of Tacit Rules for Crisis Management under Bipolarity

When push came to shove, two of the most ideologically motivated powers in the modern states system became, under the constraints of bipolarity, status quo and moderate powers (although only for the duration of the crisis). As a result, the postwar system was relatively stable, although its major actors were less ideologically moderate and farther apart in their values than earlier great powers such as the members of the Concert.

In noncrisis times, however, the greater influence of causal factors below the system level considerably constrained superpower diplomatic cooperation in crisis prevention and in conflict resolution. Hence, while more able than earlier great powers to cooperate tacitly in crisis management, the postwar powers were, until recently, less capable of embarking on a long-term, concerted, and explicit collaboration as equal managers of the international system in normal periods, as the nineteenth-century Concert had been able to do. In noncrisis times during the Cold War, each of the superpowers tried to reach a hegemonic position and to exclude the other power from having a voice in the international politics of various parts of the Third World. Nevertheless, in crisis situations, both Washington and Moscow were more sensitive than previous great powers had been to the stakes of the rival power. Moreover, even during the Cold War, the United States and the Soviet Union tended to collaborate tacitly in controlling wars in the Third World and thus in maintaining de facto the major parameters of the postcolonial status quo in world politics.

Despite the absence of agreement in normal times on spheres of influence, equal status, the status quo, cooperation in conflict management, and the balance of stakes, in times of crisis the superpowers reached tacit-spontaneous understandings on these issues. Indeed, the patterns of U.S. and Soviet crisis interaction were not only persistent but also unintended, or at least unanticipated. The caution and tacit cooperation during periods of crisis could be anticipated neither from the internal attributes of the superpowers nor from their fundamental intentions toward each other and their competing visions of the desirable international and domestic orders. The success of U.S.-Soviet crisis management was all the more remarkable if we recall that in an earlier era, in contrast to this persistent success, even relatively more moderate and similar powers (including members of the usually cooperative Concert of Europe) found themselves embroiled in inadvertent wars. At the same time, there was a much stronger correlation between the internal attributes of the superpowers, with the constraints such factors imposed on deliberate cooperation and the highly competitive nature of U.S.-Soviet relations during noncrisis settings. More specifically, the images and beliefs of the leaders in both Washington and Moscow made a great deal of difference with respect to normal U.S.-Soviet relations.

Systems theory expects that great powers behave similarly when faced with similar situations. The explanatory power of this theory is especially strong if states respond similarly to external stimuli despite considerable differences in their domestic attributes. As we saw in chapters 3 and 5, a delicate balance of restraint and resolve characterized the crisis conduct of both superpowers. More specifically, in the context of regional crises, both Moscow and Washington tried to balance between a patron's commitments to its regional allies and a desire to avoid escalation to a major war. They succeeded in this balancing act by tacitly adhering to the balance of interests as the major determinant of crisis resolve, behavior, and outcomes. Indeed, while ready to defend the survival of their allies even by military intervention, the superpowers did not tend to become militarily engaged in offensive acts of their clients (that is, war operations conducted on the antagonist's soil). The interesting point is that the definition of *offense* in this context did not follow the superpowers' own particularistic ideological preferences but instead conformed to universal norms such as the sanctioning of every state's territorial integrity (irrespective of its political affiliation).[3] As Zacher (1979, 19–20, 73–79) observes, in conflicts between an aligned and a nonaligned state where the nonaligned state was the victim, both superpowers, including the patron of the aggressor, tended to support the victim. Indeed, the bipolar structure made it easier for the superpowers to restrain aggressive allies than was the case for past great powers under multipolarity, because of the extreme patron-client asymmetry in favor of the bipolar superpowers in times of crisis.

As the détente era of the 1970s (including the attempts at concerted diplomacy in the Middle East discussed in chap. 6) shows, domestic actors could constrain cooperation with the Soviet Union in normal diplomacy even if the U.S. foreign policy leadership was interested in such cooperation. In contrast, domestic factors could not undermine crisis collaboration with the Soviets even at the height of the Cold War (and at the time, the United States enjoyed clear-cut advantages in nuclear forces and in power projection outside of Europe). Crisis collaboration was not undermined even though it could imply, in contrast to the traditional U.S. view, a de facto recognition of spheres of influence (with regard to Soviet repressions in Eastern Europe in 1956 and 1968), joint coercion of U.S. allies (when they were seen as threatening the regional balance, as in the 1956, 1967, and 1973 Middle East crises), or at least sensitivity to Soviet concerns (in the Berlin and Cuban crises).

The joint restraint of victorious U.S. allies during regional wars demonstrated most vividly the marked difference between superpower normal diplomacy and crisis behavior. Although in normal times the United States rejected cooperation with the Soviets at the expense of allies, especially in a coercive mode, during crises Soviet threats helped Washington to restrain unruly allies. When faced with the danger of global escalation, domestic and allied politics had to take a back seat, as they indeed did with regard to the management of all major postwar crises (see chap. 3).[4]

The ideological dimension of U.S.-Soviet relations considerably intensified their competition during the Cold War. Yet by facilitating the emergence of tacit rules, bipolarity made crisis management possible, prevented inadvertent escalation, and helped to maintain the status quo and to contain and end local wars,[5] although not to resolve conflicts or prevent crises.

## The Growing Problems for Crisis Management in the Current Postbipolar-Unipolar Era

As I suggest in chapters 2 and 3, crisis management is conditioned by the international structure. Therefore, the critical variable for post–Cold War crises is the end of bipolarity and accordingly, the end of the tendency under bipolarity for international engagement and for a conduct of restrained resolve. As a result, in the postbipolar era one expects growing problems for crisis management, because of the disappearance of both superpowers as the "global policemen" from certain regions and the resultant decline of checks on aggressive local states.

On the other hand, there might also be a decline of balances (countervailing forces to the remaining superpower) in those regions in which only one of the superpowers ceased to be involved. Indeed, as a result of the disintegration of the USSR, a unipolar world has seemed to emerge, at least for the short run, because of U.S. dominance in overall power resources, especially in the military sphere, including a unique global power-projection capability. What are the implications of this structural change for patterns of crisis interaction? The main point is that in a unipolar or semi-unipolar system, there are both declining constraints and declining incentives for the hegemon with regard to regional crises. The Gulf Crisis and the war in Yugoslavia can illustrate the two main implications: the former demonstrates the effects of the decline of the external *constraints* on the freedom of action of the hegemon, whereas the latter shows the possible results of the declining *incentives* for international engagement in a postbipolar era. I now discuss in greater detail the main implications of the decline of bipolarity and the declining incentives and constraints on the hegemon for regional crisis management.

### Declining Checks on Aggressive (Former) Clients: Iraq and North Korea

The decline of bipolarity can provide some explanation for the behavior of Iraq in the Gulf Crisis. In a postbipolar world, those local actors that were aligned with the declining great power are less constrained by their weakened patron. Because of the end of the global rivalry, there might also be a greater likelihood of miscalculation on the part of aggressive local powers with respect to the hegemon's commitment to intervene against them. Indeed, Saddam Hussein probably shared these two perceptions: because of Soviet weakness, the USSR could not constrain him at all any more; the United States, for its part, might not have used force due to the disappearance of the global threat that served as the major motivation for its global engagement. Thus, the invasion of Kuwait could be accounted for by Saddam's (mis)perception of the emergence of a power vacuum in the Persian Gulf with the seeming disengagement of the superpowers from the Third World. Because of the Soviet withdrawal from Eastern Europe and from some parts of the Third World, Hussein perceived Moscow as a power in decline[6] and thus less of a restraint on his actions. Thus, he probably felt less constrained with respect to the invasion of Kuwait, since he could now more easily discount Moscow's tendency, manifest even during the Cold War, to oppose naked cross-border aggression by its clients. Moreover, Hussein was also not deterred by the United States because he thought the United States would see no Soviet military threat behind his invasion and thus he did not believe, until it was too late, that Washington would actually use its military power against him. Thus, the perception (in this case, misperception) of the declining incentives for U.S. involvement in the Third World significantly contributed to the outbreak of the Gulf Crisis.

Another example of aggressive behavior of a small state following the end of bipolarity might be the nuclear behavior of North Korea in the early 1990s, especially its withdrawal from the NPT regime during 1993. Some analysts have attributed this behavior, at least partly, to the loss of the restraining influence of the Soviet Union.[7]

*Disappearance of the Global Countervailing Force: From Management in Cold War Crises to Coercion in the Gulf Crisis*

The tacit rules that guided crisis management in the postwar era are not relevant in a postbipolar world. Rather, there is likely to be a transition from a focus on crisis management to a higher likelihood of war fighting and from a symbolic use of force to an actual resort to arms by the hegemon, notably in vital areas such as the Middle East. Because external constraints on the hegemon are substantially weakened in a unipolar world, it would be less willing to compromise and more quick to resort to massive use of force when its interests are threatened. This, indeed, happened in the Gulf following the Iraqi invasion of Kuwait.

Because of Soviet decline and disengagement, the United States was less constrained by its long-time adversary and thus could afford to deploy a massive force not far from Soviet frontiers, including by withdrawing some forces from the European theater, moves that were much less conceivable during the Cold War. In a world in which Soviet military intervention became much less likely, and in which, as a consequence, the danger of escalation to a global confrontation decreased drastically, the United States could afford not to compromise with Saddam Hussein and to contemplate and eventually carry out a massive use of force in a region considered vital to the Soviets. Thus, the decline of bipolarity made possible for the first time the outbreak of a war in the Middle East with the massive participation of a superpower, in fact, the only superpower in the international system, which became much less constrained by a countervailing force than had been the case during the bipolar era.[8]

*The Disappearance of One of the Poles: The Collapse of
Pax Sovietica and the Eruption of New Crises*
In the aftermath of the collapse of the USSR and its Pax Sovietica, the turbulent regions of the globe include not only the traditional Third World but also substantial parts of the former Second World, with its multiplicity of national-ethnic conflicts in Eastern Europe and the former Soviet Union. Soviet hegemony in Eastern Europe and bipolarity kept these conflicts in check during the postwar era (cf. Joffe 1992, 46; Larrabee 1992, 31–32), in contrast to the destabilizing effects of some of them on the eve of the two world wars. As Joffe suggests, "so long as bipolarity remained intact, the war in Yugoslavia would not—could not—have erupted" (1993, 30). The decay of Soviet power took the lid off ancient animosities, notably in the Balkans, and thus brought about protracted violence among Serbs, Croats, and Muslims in the former Yugoslavia but also in various trouble spots around the periphery of the former Soviet Union.

*Declining Incentives for the Remaining Superpower to
Intervene in Regional Conflicts: Yugoslavia*
Although Saddam's second assumption was a misperception, it is not illogical to expect that in a unipolar world, the incentives for external intervention by the hegemon will decline. In such a world, a well-defined great power rival that can pose a clear-cut global threat is absent. Thus, the hegemon might pursue a considerable degree of disengagement, especially from places that lack intrinsic value, namely, major economic resources and strategic value. The relatively low level of intervention by the United States in the Yugoslav crisis, at least until early 1994, has illustrated such a tendency in a postbipolar-unipolar world. Yugoslavia was an important prize in the context of superpower rivalry during the Cold War and a major concern to NATO regarding a possible Soviet invasion. Yet Tito's rule and the Pax Sovietica in Eastern Europe ensured stability in the potentially turbulent Balkans. But in the aftermath of Soviet collapse, when the multinational federation of Yugoslavia began to disintegrate violently, the United States was no longer concerned enough about Balkan stability to carry out, at least thus far, a potentially costly intervention in a quasi-internal-ethnic conflict.

Apart from the difference in the nature of the Gulf and Yugoslav conflicts (purely interstate in the former in contrast to the partly domestic nature of the latter), the difference in the U.S. behavior might be accounted for by the divergent interests that the United States has in the two regions and, accordingly, the different weight accorded to the decline in constraints versus the decline in incentives in these regions in a postbipolar world. The oil-rich Gulf is widely considered to be a vital U.S. interest; thus, the major factor that conditioned U.S. conduct in the aftermath of the Iraqi invasion of Kuwait (though not necessarily before) was the reduction in *constraints* and thereby the greater U.S. ability to use its massive military power in the gulf in the postbipolar era. In contrast, in the less-than-vital Balkans, the major element has been the decline in *incentives* for costly interventions by the sole superpower. Indeed, in Yugoslavia, the United States lacks intrinsic strategic or economic interests. Its major interest there was closely related to the bipolar competition. Thus, the end of the Cold War could lead us to expect a low likelihood of a major U.S. military intervention in Yugoslavia.

## The Implications of the Model Concerning Intended and Unintended Wars for the Future: Toward Nuclear Multipolarity

The model presented in chapter 3 leads us to be optimistic about the continued obsolescence of major intended wars in the foreseeable future because of the stabilizing presence of nuclear weapons. The unlikelihood of such wars is further strengthened by a development outside the scope of this model—namely, the recent unit-level changes, most notably the global democratization process. Because liberal democracies do not tend to fight each other (Doyle 1986), intended major wars among democratic great powers are virtually unthinkable.

One might ask whether the global tendencies toward greater democratization and liberalization may also solve the problem of inadvertent major war among the great powers. To the extent that the great powers in question are full-blown liberal democracies, constituting a "pluralistic security community" (Deutsch et al. 1957), crises among them are unlikely to arise; therefore, inadvertent escalation among them is highly unlikely. As I argue in chapter 2, the more moderate and similar the unit-level attributes of states, the more they can resolve their conflicts by peaceful means. Therefore, the problem of crisis management among them is almost irrelevant, as these states do not threaten to use force against each other and thus avoid military crises among themselves. Since liberal democracies are the only group of states to date to fit these criteria, an inadvertent war among the powers of the North Atlantic area is almost as unthinkable as an intended one, barring a regime change in Germany (which is unlikely in the foreseeable future).

Yet to the extent that at least some of the powers involved in a conflict are less than full-blown liberal democracies, the model gives us less reason to be optimistic about the occurrence of inadvertent wars than about intended ones, if the transition to multipolarity takes place, as indeed is to be expected.[9]

The most likely area for such inadvertent escalation is East Asia, where five actual or potential great powers (the United States, Japan, China, Russia, and India) are engaged in one way or another, as are a large number of other emergent powers.[10] The multiplicity of potential and actual conflicts in this area, in the absence of the clarity and simplicity of bipolarity, may well result in an inadvertent major war. Indeed, the model presented in this book alerts us to the possibility of such an escalation under multipolarity even among powers that are reluctant to go to war, or at least to a major war.

Moreover, even if the transition to multipolarity is irrelevant for the likelihood of inadvertent war among the liberal democratic powers of the North Atlantic region, it is highly relevant for their management of third-party (or regional) crises. Here the major adverse effect of the structural change is a growing likelihood of underreaction and disengagement by status quo powers and, as a result, a rising probability of failure in regional crisis management. The most likely areas for such failure are Eastern Europe and the former Soviet empire and also parts of the Third World. Problems in regional crisis management may take place according to three main scenarios or stages.

*Uninterrupted Continuation of Local Wars*
The most likely danger of the transition to multipolarity is failures in regional crisis management and in the termination of local wars. In the absence of highly focused threats and clear-cut leadership, multipolarity might encourage underreaction on the part of status quo powers. This could result in the absence of "global policemen," which would impose effective cease-fires on warring local parties in places like the Balkans or the former Soviet empire. So long as none of the local parties is able to decisively defeat its opponents, regional wars might drag on indefinitely, causing great destruction and casualties.

*The Encouragement of Local Aggression*
Furthermore, aggressive or revisionist local powers might take advantage of the disengagement strategy of the great powers and expand at the expense of their neighbors, committing ethnic cleansing and other atrocities without facing effective deterrence and retaliation. Such an indifference on the part of the great powers might encourage yet other local powers to violate international norms, abuse human rights, and commit aggression, thus causing further instability and destruction.

## *Inadvertent Escalation*

As noted in chapter 3, a disengagement strategy may in fact backfire and make inadvertent escalation more likely at a later stage. Growing confidence about the nonintervention of the great powers might lead aggressive local powers to such an outrageous behavior that some powers might feel compelled to intervene in the local conflict, at least partly due to a domestic outcry. Another reason for intervention might be a growing refugee problem and the possibly destabilizing effects of a mass flow of immigrants on the rise of extremist groups within the polities of some great powers. If the local aggressor could have expected in advance that crossing a certain red line might invite external intervention, it would not have done so. But the unclarity inherent in multipolarity and the tendency for buck-passing might mislead the regional challenger to expect no effective external intervention and thus to bring about inadvertent escalation by crossing the not-so-easily-identifiable threshold for external engagement in multipolarity. This inadvertent escalation may draw one or several powers into a regional conflict. Yet to the extent that the powers involved are liberal democracies, it will stop short of escalating to a major inadvertent war among them.

However, regional instability is a source of concern for the great powers even if it does not involve them directly in military actions against other powers. The reason is the proliferation of weapons of mass destruction, which could eventually pose a threat not only to Third World security but also to Western countries. Regional conflicts could endanger Western access to markets and resources, most notably Middle Eastern oil. As we have already witnessed in Europe, local conflicts could accelerate massive flows of refugees and thereby reinforce the power of antiforeigner extremists in the West, which could, in turn, potentially challenge political stability even in leading states such as Germany. Finally, there is always a residual worry that great powers may be drawn into regional conflicts, especially in important regions like the oil-rich Middle East and parts of Eastern Europe, because of its proximity to the Western part of the continent and the presence of nuclear arms in the former Soviet Union.

Thus, what is to be done? According to the model presented in this book, nuclear weapons are not a panacea for crisis management and for the prevention of inadvertent escalation. Thus, nuclear proliferation, advocated by some neorealists (Mearsheimer 1990; Waltz 1981), would not be of much help in this situation; indeed, it might increase the risk that nuclear weapons will be used inadvertently in multipolar crises, particularly between regional parties.

A more promising path might be an attempt to draw on the recent rapprochement among the great powers to institutionalize effective mechanisms for regional crisis prevention and conflict resolution under the leadership of a great power concert.

## From the Unintended Cooperation of the Structural Balance of Power to the Intended Cooperation of International Society?

Indeed, even if the probability of failure in crisis management was extremely low during the bipolar era, people could not feel comfortable relying exclusively on objective facts such as the bipolar structure (or, for that matter, MAD) for averting a disastrous World War III. In those regional conflicts that could potentially escalate to global crises, it is preferable to try to settle the underlying issues rather than to rely exclusively on spontaneous management of crises. Something can always go wrong in a crisis—and even could have, though it was highly unlikely, in a bipolar-nuclear confrontation (see Bracken 1983; Jervis 1989a; Lebow 1987). Crisis-prevention regimes, which explicitly regulate great power intervention in third areas, are also insufficient for the purposes of avoiding confrontations and preventing local (and even potentially global) wars. At any rate, so long as a regional dispute is not settled, there always exists the danger that the great powers will get entangled in a crisis; at the very least, the local conflict can be costly for them and impair their overall relations. At the same time, responsible great powers are uniquely qualified, if they concert their diplomacy, to advance the international and regional orders by helping to resolve, or at least facilitate the resolution of, local disputes and later to guarantee and sustain the peace.

Yet for understanding the conditions for the emergence of great power concerts, we must turn to the international society approach and to the causal factors associated with it. On the whole, four major historical, contemporary, and future patterns can be understood properly only with reference to factors highlighted by the international society school.

### Outcomes Explained by the International Society School

#### The Formation of the Concert of Europe

The unique combination of unit-level factors highlighted by the international society approach, namely shared domestic attributes and common fears by all the great powers from 1815 to 1854, explains why a concert could emerge in that era but neither earlier nor later. More specifically, great power similarity and moderation differentiates the post-Napoleonic period from later periods, while the presence of common fears of revolutions and inadvertent wars, based on cognitive and ideological elements, distinguishes the Concert from earlier periods. Thus, despite the differences among the Concert members in the degree of vulnerability and in the attitudes to the form of the Concert, these unit-level factors have made possible the endurance of joint great power diplomacy in the post-1815 era.

## The Initiation and Failure of Attempts at Concerted Diplomacy in the Postwar Era

Factors highlighted by the international society school can point out both some of the conditions for the initiation of attempts at concerted diplomacy and the likelihood of their success.

The initiation of such attempts is closely related to the three images discussed in chapter 4. Thus, on the cognitive level, the top leaders of the great powers have to believe in the collaborative inclinations of the adversary. They also have to hold the view that hegemonic policies cannot exclude, at affordable costs, the other great powers from having a voice in the international politics of a region that is vital to their national interests. In addition, decision makers should learn to recognize the indigenous roots of regional conflicts. To the extent that this learning takes place, the main danger in local disputes is seen not in the potential gains that the antagonist great power might make but in the escalation of the local conflict to a global confrontation and the hampering of great power relations. Thus, from being *objectively* interdependent (because of bipolarity), which is sufficient for crisis management, the superpowers must also become *subjectively* interdependent, which is necessary for the higher level of cooperation in conflict resolution. In other words, they must come to believe in the necessity and feasibility of superpower collaboration for purposes of conflict resolution.

President Carter's and Secretary Vance's subscription to these views facilitated the U.S.-Soviet joint statement on the Arab-Israeli conflict of October 1, 1977. In contrast, the two national security advisors, Brzezinski and even more so Kissinger, did not share these attitudes. They suspected that the Soviets had hegemonic designs in the Middle East and believed that it was feasible to reach a settlement of the dispute under exclusive U.S. sponsorship; this belief might explain their opposition to concerted superpower diplomacy in the Middle East.

Although there were some attempts to formally regulate the overall U.S.-Soviet relationship and their competition in the Third World[11] and to concert their diplomacy for purposes of conflict resolution (see chap. 6), these attempts did not go very far until the late 1980s. In other words, neither comprehensive nor specific crisis-prevention regimes were established, nor did the superpowers succeed in explicitly regulating their intervention or in pursuing joint peacemaking in third areas. The reasons are discussed in chapters 4 and 6; the differences in power resources in favor of the United States, the different attitudes regarding the form of collaboration, and the opposition in U.S.

domestic politics to concerted diplomacy with a nondemocratic power. Indeed, for concerted diplomacy to endure, there has to be a willingness in the pluralist great power's body politic to legitimize the adversary's role and presence in third areas. The ill fate of both the 1969 Rogers Plan and the 1977 joint statement can, at least partly, be accounted for by Israel's opposition and its ability to mobilize a powerful coalition against these plans within the American political system. This pro-Israeli coalition was joined by strong elements in the U.S. body politic who traditionally opposed granting equal status to the USSR in world politics.

These elements explain the differences in U.S. and Soviet attitudes toward concerted diplomacy and suggest the different factors that affect the ability of pluralist democracies and of authoritarian powers to pursue joint actions. Yet what underlies the consistent failure of the superpowers to collaborate in conflict resolution was the absence of the key elements of similarity and moderation during the Cold War. Indeed, changes in these elements have made concerted diplomacy much more likely in the Gorbachev era.

## The Growing Success of Concerted Diplomacy since the Mid-1980s

Only following the revolutionary domestic and cognitive changes in the Soviet Union under Gorbachev could there be considerable progress in superpower cooperation in conflict resolution in the Third World, notably with regard to Afghanistan, Angola–Southern Africa, Central America, Iran-Iraq, Cambodia,[12] and the Middle East (see chap. 6).

The emergence of U.S.-Soviet concerted diplomacy in the Third World in the mid to late-1980s—and until the Soviet disintegration in late 1991—started before the collapse of Soviet power but also well after the appearance of nuclear MAD two decades earlier. In other words, the joint superpower diplomacy cannot be explained by such systemic-structural forces[13] but rather by the major unit-level changes that occurred in the USSR in the mid to late-1980s. The main changes took place in the cognitive perceptions of the Soviet elite, especially toward the United States (which was viewed as a potential partner rather than enemy).[14] Added to this were Gorbachev's reforms that have made the Soviet regime appear somewhat more similar to the United States (internally) and moderate (externally), that is, more willing to collaborate and more in favor of peaceful resolution of conflicts.[15] Indeed, the greater moderation and flexibility Moscow showed in the Middle East and the Third World in general in the Gorbachev era reflected in part the Soviet new thinking on the Third World and the related perception of the growth of global interdependence in international politics in general (see chap. 6). There has been a growing recognition of the influence of local factors (as opposed to imperialist machinations) and, at the same time, a declining confidence in the bandwagoning dynamics of such factors in favor of the "progressive forces," that is, the Soviet Union and its allies; a rising concern about the potential for crisis escalation in some regions; and an increasing realization that competitive policies in the Third World jeopardize U.S.-Soviet détente, along with a growing skepticism about the Soviet Union's payoffs from such costly and futile policies in a time when it was having great economic problems. Indeed, in the Gorbachev period, Moscow placed the domestic economic problems at the top of the Soviet agenda and regarded good ties with the advanced industrialized West as much more important than any doubtful gains in the Third World. But the turn to accommodation was made possible, to a large extent, by a change in the image of the opponent Gorbachev held in comparison with his predecessors. Gorbachev was less pessimistic about U.S. intentions and therefore less concerned that Washington would take advantage of Soviet concessions (Lebow and Stein 1992).

The relative democratization in the Soviet Union under Gorbachev has made it, in the eyes of the American public and foreign policy elite, a much more acceptable partner for joint management of international problems and not only a tacit partner in times of crisis. The critical point is that the changes in the international behavior of the Soviet Union since the mid-1980s were not sufficient to generate a basic change in the U.S. attitude toward high-level cooperation with it. For a pluralist democracy to pursue such cooperation with the USSR, there also had to be a fundamental domestic change. Thus, "what gave some observers confidence early on that the changes in Soviet international behavior were both real and profound was that internal changes were also going on: at first *glasnost* (political openness) and growing press freedoms, and then the advent of real elections . . . taken together, these changes constituted a shift in the basis of legitimacy within the USSR" (Deibel 1993, 18).

As a result, domestic politics, bureaucratic politics, and the influence of small allies have become less of an obstacle for cooperation when the ideological component of the rivalry was drastically weakened. The Soviet democratization also reinforced the new thinking in Soviet foreign policy, including the peaceful resolution of regional conflicts in cooperation with the United States.

Indeed, these changes in Soviet foreign and domestic policies made the second Reagan and the Bush administrations much more willing than were earlier administrations to reciprocate and to involve Moscow in joint diplomacy for settling regional conflicts (see chap. 6).

The movement by the Reagan administration at the end of its second term toward greater collaboration with the Soviets in the Arab-Israeli conflict might be accounted for by the growing recognition in the administration that Gorbachev was different from his predecessors in some major ways. His willingness to cooperate with Washington on major international problems and his departure from the presumed previous Soviet commitment to world domination were perceived as constituting a break with past Soviet behavior. Washington's softening of its position on an international conference on the Middle East, particularly in the Shultz Plan of 1988, resulted in part from these changing perceptions.

Following an initial skeptical period, the Bush administration accelerated this trend toward more cooperation with the Soviets in the Middle East. The perception of the source of the threat to regional stability and to U.S. interests in the region has shifted from Moscow to regional sources such as Islamic fundamentalism, indigenous terrorism, the Palestinian problem and, most recently (also in the Clinton administration), Iraq and Iran and the proliferation of nonconventional weapons in such radical states. From being seen as entertaining hegemonic aspirations in the region, Moscow has now come to be viewed more as a useful potential partner (even if somewhat weakened because of domestic problems) in exercising moderating pressures on intransigent clients (or ex-clients such as Iraq).

## The Growing Prospects for Concerted Diplomacy in the Post–Cold War Era

The post–Cold War era might be the first period since the Concert of Europe in which there is a relatively high degree of great power similarity and moderation. This is due to the apparently increasing political-economic convergence of the major powers around the tenets of democracy (though that is still not the case with China) and capitalism. Thus, the chances for a concert look somewhat brighter than in earlier ages because democracies tend to be ready to legitimize explicitly the equal status of other democratic powers and to regard them as equal partners in managing international conflicts.

Similarity and moderation might help to overcome the following three obstacles to great power concerts, which are mentioned in chapters 4 and 6 and are related to differences between the great powers on three levels of analysis.

The first obstacle is at the systems level: relative power differences among the great powers. Similarity and moderation might weaken and overcome the inclination of the most powerful (or least vulnerable) state to go it alone; rather, these elements might encourage the dominant actor to play the role of a multilateralist leader, as might have been the case, to some extent, with the United States in the Western-dominated postwar international political economic regimes (such as in the trade and monetary areas). Thus, in contrast to the unilateral-exclusionary U.S. strategy vis-à-vis the USSR in third world regions during the Cold War, the recent domestic changes made Russia a much more acceptable partner in American eyes for joint conflict resolution.

The role of a multilateralist leader could thus be the future role of the United States in a potential concert that may include the other democratic powers (among them Russia—if it continues to be democratic, especially barring the coming to power of ultranationalist forces). Thus, from a hindrance to cooperation, a certain level of power gap could be transformed, under the subsystemic conditions of similarity and moderation, into a factor helpful in overcoming the collective goods problem (see Olson 1965) through the leading role played by the most powerful state.

The second obstacle is at the state level: regime differences among the concert members. In addition to preventing cooperation altogether in extreme cases like the Cold War, such differences can generate disagreements over the form of collaboration (coercive versus accommodative), as they did in the Concert of Europe. But the more democratic, and thus the more similar, the members become (as seems to be the case with a potential concert in the future), the weaker such disagreements are. Thus, a democratic concert is inclined toward accommodative multilateralism. Instead of managing external divergences with other concert members over the form of the concert, maintaining domestic support for the potentially costly participation in a concert is then the major challenge for the democratic members of the concert. Yet the public is more likely to support cooperation with other democratic great powers than with nondemocratic ones.

The third obstacle is at the individual level: a negative image of the opponent can constrain the likelihood and durability of a concert. Yet when all the members are similar and moderate, the image of the other concert members tends to become more benign.

Indeed, with regard to the effects of the end of the Cold War on the three orientations discussed in chapter 4, the multilateralists would seem to become relatively more powerful. More specifically, subscribers to the belief in balancing will tend even more forcefully toward multilateralism, that is, acting in concert with the other great powers, especially the seemingly potential superpowers (Germany or a united Europe and Japan), whose power and influence are likely to grow relative to the power and influence of the United States. In this view, it is unlikely that the United States could remain a single superpower for an extended period because of the balancing tendencies in world politics. Thus, the United States has to act through international institutions (such as the UN, the Security Council, the G-7, the International Monetary Fund, and the General Agreement on Tariffs and Trade), particularly regarding those issues that, in the view of the multilateralists, have important implications for U.S. as well as for global concerns. Those issues should include the pacification of conflict-ridden areas (like the Balkans and the former Soviet Union) because, according to the regionalist image, local conflicts in these areas could escalate and thereby threaten important U.S. and Western interests and values.

Yet the relative strengthening of the multilateralist approach does not mean that there are no opposing strategies, stemming from the application of the other two Cold War orientations (competition and confrontation) and their underlying images, to post–Cold War realities. Thus, believers in bandwagoning, who formerly advocated a competitive approach, are even more inclined than during the Cold War toward unilateralism in U.S. foreign policy, because of the supposed emergence of the United States as the sole global superpower. Accordingly, especially if they believe in a strong linkage between U.S. interests and regional politics (a version of the globalist image), they will support attempts at constructing Pax Americana in vital regions, such as the Middle East.

Yet it is the third strategy that provides the most powerful challenge to multilateralism: those who during the Cold War focused exclusively on the Soviet threat in globalist terms and consequently supported a confrontational strategy might now tend to become more isolationist because, in their view, with the disappearance of the Soviet Union, most regions (including the Balkans, for example) have lost their importance for U.S. interests. This loss of importance takes place because these regions do not really have intrinsic value; their significance during the postwar era was derived only from the superpower rivalry. Thus, according to this approach, with the end of the Cold War, the United States should disengage from most regional conflicts.

Indeed, a growing disinclination for any engagement (unilateral or multilateral) in regional conflicts may become a major obstacle to a concert in the post–Cold War era. This disinclination may occur because a concert of all the great powers of the day, by definiton, does not face a common global threat posed by another great power, so there might be a lack of incentives for costly interventions in remote places. Such a disinclination might be heavily influenced, especially in democracies, by a domestic opposition to external engagement in the absence of a clear-cut menace.

Thus, disengagement from third-area conflicts might be a possible scenario for the post–Cold War world because of the absence of a global threat facing the democratic powers. Yet, the negative elements conducive to joint actions (fear of transnational revolutionary threat or of inadvertent escalation) might play a role here in providing incentives for concerted actions by the major powers (at least diplomatic and economic, but possibly also military). Such actions might take place, for example, in the context of the transnational Fundamentalist Islamic threat to regional stability and to important status quo states in the oil-rich Middle East (Egypt, Algeria, Saudi Arabia, Turkey, Israel, and potentially also Central Asia), or due to the fear of unintended escalation in the Balkans and the former (but still nuclearized) USSR.

## Policy Implications: The Feasibility and the Necessity of a Concert

The implication of the present model is that in the 1990s, a great power concert seems to have become both more *feasible* than it has ever been since the nineteenth century and, at least in some senses, more *necessary* than has been the case in the postwar era. A concert has become more feasible because of the ideological convergence of the great powers, especially due to the domestic and cognitive changes in the Soviet Union that started under Gorbachev. Thus, already before the collapse of Soviet power, a U.S.-Soviet concert of sorts emerged following the major changes Gorbachev initiated with regard to the new thinking in foreign affairs and the internal liberalization in the Soviet Union. This concert can account for a major portion of the progress registered in conflict resolution in the Third World since the late 1980s.

In the aftermath of the disintegration of the Soviet Union, however, a U.S.-USSR concert has become irrelevant, yet the potential members of a new concert (the United States, the emerging great powers—most notably, Western Europe, or united Germany, Japan, and Russia, unless the ultranationalist elements take over) have more in common ideologically and with respect to a shared vision of the international and domestic orders than did the USSR, even under Gorbachev, and the United States. These powers also share a strong interest in maintaining stability or promoting peaceful change in turbulent areas by advancing peaceful conflict resolution. This could pave the way for a great power concert through some institutionalized adaption of the G-7 or, more likely, the UN Security Council (for example, by some gradual changes in the permanent membership to reflect new power realities, including some participation, perhaps on a rotating basis, of major regional powers such as Brazil, Nigeria, India, Indonesia, and Egypt). At any rate, for a concert to be effective, China must eventually be involved on an equal basis with the other great powers.

However, the logic of the model presented here suggests that the endurance of a concert heavily depends on the persistence of democratization and liberalization within the polities of the great powers. In other words, an antidemocratic backlash in Moscow or the rise of an antiliberal regime as a full-blown great power (China?) would considerably reduce the likelihood and effectiveness of a concert.

## The Decay of Bipolarity and the Necessity for an Institutionalized Concert

On the other hand, because of the new challenges to peace as a result of the decline of the stabilizing bipolar structure, a concert is also necessary and very desirable, especially for facilitating conflict resolution and helping to maintain the peace in various trouble spots of the former Second and Third Worlds. In other words, precisely because of the growing problems for successful regional crisis management (that is, terminating a crisis peacefully after it has already erupted) in a multipolar world as compared to the bipolar system, concerted diplomacy for conflict resolution is more necessary in the post–Cold War era to prevent crises from occurring in the first place.

Despite the keenness of the Cold War, the superpowers cooperated (even if only tacitly and spontaneously) in containing many conflicts in the Third World[16] and in their respective spheres of influence (see Keal 1983). The latter type of cooperation was notable with regard to the traditional powder keg of Eastern Europe and the Balkans, which the United States tacitly accepted during the Cold War as belonging to the Soviet sphere of influence. Thus, as a result of the decline of bipolarity, two sources of conflict have become more dangerous, replacing the East-West conflict that dominated the postwar era.

*East-East:* The reemergence of national-ethnic conflicts in Eastern Europe and the Balkans because of the disappearance of Pax Sovietica can be especially dangerous in the former Soviet empire because of the problem of control over nuclear weapons.

*South-South:* Obvious dangers are present in some parts of the Third World, as is evident from the combination of intense conflicts, the rise of fundamentalist forces, and the proliferation of ballistic missiles and nonconventional weapons of mass destruction, most notably in the Middle East. Indeed, one might argue that the end of the Cold War had some destabilizing effects on the Third World, as was manifested by Saddam Hussein's invasion of Kuwait. The disintegration of the Soviet Union might also have major destabilizing effects, because the Muslim republics could join the Middle Eastern game, thus increasing unpredictability and uncertainty in an already volatile region, and also because the breakup could aggravate the problem of nuclear proliferation due to the potential brain drain and technology transfers from the former USSR to the Third World. The disappearance of Soviet power could also lead to actual U.S. disengagement from the Third World and thus to a loss of what has been seen by many as a stabilizing influence in conflict-ridden regions.

Systemic factors cannot determine whether a concert is possible, but they affect the extent of the need for an explicit and institutionalized concert to settle conflicts effectively. In principle, as I discuss in this book, there are two major alternative modes of cooperation in conflict management: tacit-spontaneous and explicit-conscious. Although the tacit mode might have certain attractions, it is less effective in the complex system of multipolarity than in the relatively clear two-power system.[17] Spontaneous cooperation is based on tacit rules, which evolve most easily in a simple bipolar setting. In a multipolar setting, it is harder to coordinate expectations spontaneously, and tacit rules are less likely to evolve and to be a reliable source for durable cooperation. Thus, with the passing of the bipolar system, threats to regional peace could become more dangerous unless a concert is established to prevent them. In this sense, explicitly conscious attempts at conflict resolution are much more needed in the postbipolar world, especially with respect to the former Soviet bloc and the Third World, than during the period in which the superpowers tacitly cooperated in limiting conflicts in these regions.

It is true that the ideal solution to regional conflicts is, decidedly, indigenous reconciliation, yet in light of the local obstacles to indigenous conflict resolution in many conflict-prone regions and the rapprochement between the great powers in recent years, the most useful mechanism for settling, or at least ameliorating, disputes in the less developed world might be a great power concert. Such a concert would not be able to impose a settlement on reluctant regional disputants, but it could encourage them at least to reduce the intensity of their conflict through a mixture of incentives and pressures.

Hegemonic dominance of the United States (Pax Americana) can help to resolve conflicts as is evident from the recent progress in the Arab-Israeli peace process under overall American leadership. Yet the dominant power might tend to abuse and overuse its power in the absence of a countervailing force, as some critics have argued with regard to U.S. behavior in the 1990–91 Gulf Crisis (Tucker and Hendrickson 1992; Waltz 1991). Moreover, a hegemonic world is not feasible for the long run (Layne 1993; Rosecrance 1991, 376–77). For the purposes of worldwide conflict resolution, U.S. power and resources would not be enough, despite their critical importance. This is because of the growing American domestic and economic constraints and the limitations on U.S. patience, energy, and incentives to play the role of a unilateral hegemon for an extended period. Instead, the United States should play the leading role in a multilateral collaborative strategy with the Europeans, the Russians, the Japanese, and eventually the Chinese, in helping to bring about peace, prosperity, and arms control to conflict-ridden areas such as the Middle East. The participation of all these powers is needed for the following reasons: enhancing the international, regional, and domestic legitimacy of the settlement and of the external involvement in helping to bring it about; sharing the burden with the United States by taking part in the provision of economic sticks and carrots to the local parties; controlling arms supplies to the region; and minimizing the ability of the regional actors to play off the external powers.

Specific Policy-Relevant Proposals

Great power contribution to regional stability could be especially notable in the following five areas of cooperation.

*Peacekeeping and coguarantees for peace settlements:* Following the conclusion of a regional settlement, the major powers could contribute to its maintenance by sponsoring the deployment of multinational UN forces for peacekeeping purposes, providing security guarantees to the local parties, helping in the verification of the parties' compliance with the peace treaty, censoring the violators, and assisting in the introduction of confidence-building measures (such as prior notification of exercises and troop movements, troop reductions and disengagement along certain lines, and the demilitarization of certain territories). In this area, the recent European experience with such measures in the East-West context as well as the older UN record in peacekeeping could be relevant, with the big difference that now most or all the major powers are likely to be cooperative regarding the peacekeeping enterprise. More specifically, the powers could establish crisis-control centers in conflict-ridden regions such as the Middle East and early warning systems that would help to alleviate the security concerns of the regional actors.

*Deterring and containing regional aggressors:* The concert could issue threats to use force against aggressors under the authority of the Security Council, at least in major cases of naked cross-border military aggression. The concert would have to specify the rules that should guide its military intervention and also identify the conditions that could legitimize and necessitate humanitarian interventions even in the domestic affairs of states, especially in cases of ethnic or civil conflicts.

*Moving from arms races to arms control regimes:* The major powers should endorse major quantitative and qualitative limitations to their arms supplies to conflict-prone regions like the Middle East. Such limitations should help to create local balances of power at overall lower levels of armaments than the present balances. But the type of weapons to be deployed after the cuts should still provide effective deterrence against aspirants for regional hegemony. The regional arms control agreements should also reduce the security dilemmas of the local actors so that the fears of crisis instability, surprise attacks, preemptive strikes, and preventive wars would be reduced as much as possible. In accordance with these criteria, the regional arms control agenda should include major reductions in both conventional and nonconventional weapons of mass destruction. The powers, directly or through the UN Security Council, could help with on-site inspection of the local observation of these reductions. The powers should also cooperate in monitoring arms shipments to unstable regions and in preventing the proliferation of destabilizing technologies and weapon systems.

*Specific areas of cooperation for enhancing stability:* Collaboration in areas such as counterterrorism, socioeconomic development, and the resettlement of refugees should supplement the major diplomatic-security means for pacifying conflict-ridden regions. Especially in the economic field, Japan and

Western Europe should play the leading role alongside the United States in channeling investments, credits, technology, and know-how to turbulent regions such as the Middle East and in reaching free-trade agreements with the regional countries.

Yet it is critically important to bear in mind that all these measures should not overshadow or substitute the following major area of great power cooperation:

*Intensive and concerted efforts of the major powers for resolving political conflicts,* such as reaching a comprehensive settlement of the Arab-Israeli dispute: Indeed, economic aid and trade should be used as major incentives to encourage the local parties to move forward in the peace process, whereas economic sanctions could be applied against those local parties who refuse to compromise. The promise of security guarantees (especially via bilateral agreements with the United States) to the most vulnerable parties (the Gulf states, Jordan, the Palestinians, and even Israel in the event of a major withdrawal from the occupied territories) could also be used as an incentive for these parties to be flexible in their diplomatic positions so that a comprehensive settlement will be possible.

Especially in parts of the Third and the (former) Second Worlds, we might have to wait some time before democratization and liberalization take hold; thus, major reconciliations, let alone an "eternal peace," do not seem in the immediate offing. Until then, some combination of a concert (for conflict reduction, economic assistance, and arms control) and U.S. leadership (especially in times of major crises) could be useful for mitigating or containing regional conflicts.

Thus, a concert seems to be both feasible and desirable. Yet a cautionary note has to be added: in an anarchic world, especially a multipolar one, as the experience of the European Concert shows, there is always a danger of a breakdown of cooperation and the risk that institutions and rules will be too weak to be effective. Especially in multipolar crises, there is some danger of inadvertent escalation. Moreover, some regional disputes are quite intractable, and the concerted diplomacy of external powers may be far from sufficient to ensure peaceful outcomes. Joint diplomacy for conflict resolution, even if supported by explicit rules of conduct and the appropriate peacemaking and peacekeeping mechanisms and, more importantly, made possible by cognitive learning and democratization, cannot guarantee peaceful settlement of conflicts. However, it would still be preferable at least to attempt the road of concerted diplomacy, for the benefit of world peace and, especially, of those regions that have not enjoyed much calm in the last decades or in recent years.

It is worthy noting some important challenges that the concert is likely to face.

## Will a Concert Be Able to Achieve Effective Conflict Resolution?: Challenges to a Potential Concert

There are two main challenges to a concert on the regional level, while additional three are derived from the international arena. Further studies will have to examine whether a potential concert can successfully cope with these challenges.

*Resistance by the Local Parties*
Regional states, especially some of those in the East and South of the globe, might value their autonomy more than they value a settlement of the local conflict. Thus, they are likely to resist imposed solutions from the outside. But here the distinction made in chapter 4 between coercive and accommodative collaboration might be relevant; a strategy of accommodative collaboration, if pursued by the concert members, as is likely to be the case with a concert of democratic powers, is likely to minimize potential local opposition. As was shown by the attitude of most moderate Arabs and Israelis toward some sort of an international sponsorship of their peace talks, regional leaders do not necessarily oppose accommodative collaboration in which the great powers work together with the local actors to reach negotiated agreements, especially if the local actors perceive such collaboration as necessary for overcoming obstacles to reconciliation. Indeed, such collaboration has characterized the recent process of regional reconciliation in some of the trouble spots in the Third World and enjoyed considerable local support.

At any rate, while the great powers can be helpful in promoting regional conflict resolution, in practice, so long as the external powers and not the local parties play the critical role in the conflict resolution process, this process would frequently amount to no more than a mitigation or moderation of the dispute; thus, it would fall short of a full-blown indigenous reconciliation among the local parties. Further study should develop the distinctions among these various stages of conflict management and the relative role of local versus international forces in shaping each of them.

*The Substance of the Conflict*
A critical distinction has to be made here between an ethnic minority aspiring for self-determination within an existing state (such as the Kurdish and Shiite problems in Iraq and many of the conflicts in the former Soviet bloc) and an interstate conflict (the Gulf Crisis). An intermediate case is the Arab-Israeli conflict, which is essentially a dispute between existing states (thus, it differs from the internal problems of the Kurds and the Shiites in Iraq), but one which also includes the Palestinian demand for self-determination (thus, it is different from what was widely seen as a purely interstate conflict between Iraq and Kuwait).

Although a concert can be useful for managing both types of conflicts, internal conflicts might be especially hard to resolve. They can be difficult to resolve both because of the practical complications and ambiguities related to interventions in civil or ethnic conflicts and because in the case of such internal conflicts, two international principles clash: the right of every ethnic group to self-determination and the territorial integrity of states and the sanctity of their borders (cf. Hannum 1990; Ronen 1979). This is a difficult trade-off, but democratization, confederal solutions, free-trade agreements, and regional integration, alongside security arrangements, might play a role in reconciling these principles, especially if all these devices are strongly supported by the great power concert.

*Rising Inclination to Disengage in the Post–Cold War Era*
The combination of a multiplicity of complicated ethnic conflicts and the disappearance of the Soviet threat in the post–Cold War era reinforces the incentives of the powers—and the domestic and economic pressures they face—to disengage from local conflicts. Yet disengagement is less likely in a region like the Middle East where the powers have major economic interests related to oil. More generally, the recent surge of fundamentalism and nationalism in the South and the East might result in the spread of conflicts that, because of the proliferation of longer-range nonconventional weapons, might also pose threats to Western countries. In addition, a rising tide of refugees from conflict-ridden regions might pose an uneasy problem for the developed world and thus might also create an interest in the resolution of local conflicts.

*Leadership and the Collective Goods Problem*
The gradual transition to multipolarity will increase the problem of who will be in charge of the provision of collective goods (such as global and regional peace and security) in the absence of a clear-cut hegemon. For the foreseeable future, only the United States can lead a concert of powers, especially for the purpose of containing military aggression (such as Saddam Hussein's invasion of Kuwait), because of the unique combination of its power resources. Yet it should lead through a multilateral avenue rather than by unilateral steps. Thus, there should be a division of labor whereby the United States is in charge of the security aspects of the potential concert while the Japanese and the Europeans share the lead in the economic domain.

*Competition and Differences of Opinion between the Possible Concert Members*
A potential realist critique of the argument regarding the unit-level feasibility of a concert might suggest that as the Europeans (or specifically the Germans) and the Japanese become full-blown great powers,[18] in an anarchic system

they are likely to compete with the United States for security, influence, and control over resources, rather than establish a concert. Moreover, with regard to regional conflicts, there have already been disagreements between the United States and the Europeans, for example, vis-à-vis the Middle East and, more recently, the Balkans; such differences are likely to continue and even intensify as the Europeans and the Japanese become global powers engaged in different regions.

This subject calls for further research. One research possibility in this context is to examine the level and the extent of the factors highlighted in this study as favorable to a concert among today's great powers (similarity, moderation, and common fears). Another question is whether such common elements can overcome the differences among the powers to make concerted actions possible and whether and how the institutionalization of a concert will provide the members with a mechanism for consultations, ironing out their differences, and coordinating common strategies and joint actions in regional conflicts. In other words, can those unit-level factors that were underlined in the present study as conducive to the emergence of concerts, together with liberal mechanisms (notably, international institutions), overcome structural-realist tendencies against international cooperation among all the great powers of the day?

### Ideas for Future Research

Beyond these research questions, this book calls for another related area of research. The present book has focused on the sources of intended and unintended conflict and cooperation between the great powers. Future research should address the implications or consequences of these international factors for regional security. The objective of the future study will be to provide an analytical framework for addressing the effects of great power involvement, or lack of it, on regional conflicts. The thesis of the study will be that variations in the likelihood of successful conflict resolution in different regions are affected by the character of the great power involvement in these regions. My argument will be that although great power involvement or noninvolvement cannot either cause or terminate regional conflicts, which have indigenous origins, it can either intensify local conflicts or mitigate them and promote their resolution.

The project will propose causal linkages between the types of great power involvement in regional conflicts (the explanatory factors) and patterns of regional conflicts (the outcomes or dependent variables). Four patterns of regional conflicts will be differentiated.

1. Conflict resolution or mitigation—settlement, or at least mitigation, of the fundamental sources of the regional conflict

2. Conflict containment—limitation of the violent manifestations of the regional conflict, even if there is no resolution of the underlying sources of the conflict

3. Uninterrupted conflicts—no change in the level and intensity of the regional conflict and its amenability to successful resolution

4. Conflict intensification—escalation in the level and scope of the regional conflict

The study will also distinguish among four types of great power involvement: competition, cooperation, dominance, and disengagement. In competition and cooperation, several great powers are involved in the region. Dominance means that there is a single hegemon in the region, while in disengagement no great power is involved in the regional conflict. An important intervening variable that mediates between the explanatory factors and the outcomes refers to types of influence relations between the great powers and the small states in the region, or, more precisely, degrees of small state autonomy vis-à-vis the great powers.

The four major propositions will be based on the following causal chain: type of involvement—small states' autonomy—pattern of regional conflicts.

1. Competition—high positive autonomy (manipulation)—intensified local conflicts
2. Cooperation—low autonomy—regional settlements, or at least conflict mitigation
3. Disengagement—high negative autonomy (independence)—uninterrupted local conflicts
4. Dominance—no autonomy—highly effective conflict containment

Let me suggest very briefly the logic that informs the propositions.

1. Keen competition among the great powers permits the small states to play off the great powers by threatening to realign. This kind of ability to manipulate the great powers, in turn, makes it relatively easy for regional actors to obstruct great power attempts at conflict resolution. Moreover, the assistance granted by the patrons tends to shield the regional clients from the costs of the regional rivalry and thus makes it easier for the small states to intensify the local conflict.

2. Great power cooperation reduces the maneuvering room of the small states and enables the great powers to exert coordinated moderating pressures on their allies as well as broker settlements and mediate between the local parties. As a result, peacemaking efforts by the great powers will be much more effective than in a competitive setting, although cooperating great powers might not be able to prevent completely an occasional resort to violence by the regional actors.

3. Great power disengagement would mean a high independence of both the great powers and the regional parties from each other. The outcome would be a continuation of the regional conflict without interference from the outside and in accordance with the resources and motivation of the regional states.

4. Wherever there is one dominant power, the small powers will have very limited maneuvering room. A hegemon is very interested in stabilizing the area under its dominance. Thus, the greater the small parties' vulnerability and their dependence on the leader's power, the more the hegemon can effectively contain regional conflicts and prevent violence, although it will not necessarily attempt to resolve the fundamental sources of the conflict. The hegemon's efforts at containing regional violence are more effective than the coordinated efforts of several cooperating powers for two reasons. First, hegemony does not entail potential disagreements between the powers concerning burden sharing, especially in the highly sensitive and costly sphere of resort to military force. Second, the absence of small states' autonomy under hegemony would minimize the probability that they will dare to resort to military force, whereas the higher level of small state autonomy in the case of great power cooperation means that there will be a somewhat greater risk-taking propensity by the regional actors, yet the effectiveness of regional conflict containment by the hegemon might be achieved at the expense of the liberty of the small states, especially if the dominant power is nondemocratic.

## The Implications for International Security

The effects of great power involvement on patterns of regional conflicts will, in turn, have feedback implications for international security.

1. Competition will have destabilizing effects, as intensified local conflicts may escalate into crises that might engulf the great powers. Yet the likelihood of the escalation of regional crises into major wars involving the great powers will be affected by the international structure, namely, whether it is bipolar or multipolar. In bipolar systems regional crises are likely to be contained and successfully managed by the great powers, while in multipolarity there is a higher danger of failures in crisis management and of inadvertent escalation to the global level (see chap. 3).
2. Cooperation will have lasting stabilizing effects, because conflict resolution or mitigation, to the extent that it is successful, may minimize the outbreak of regional crises, or at least prevent their escalation into crises among the great powers themselves.
3. Disengagement, in principle, should not have major effects for international security, yet a protracted local conflict might spread from its

initial confined local arena and bring about destabilizing massive flows of refugees. Disengagement of status quo powers might also create temptations for potential aggressors. Thus, it could eventually force the great powers to intervene, resulting in the escalation of the conflict to the international level, especially in multipolar systems.
4. Hegemony should, on the whole, be stabilizing but the effects for international security will depend on tacit or explicit acceptance of the regional hegemony by the other great powers. Such an acceptance will reinforce the stabilizing effects of regional hegemony. Yet unless the hegemon goes beyond conflict containment and attempts to resolve or at least mitigate the conflict, it may flare up again as soon as hegemony wanes.

Thus, for international security, one may range the options from the best to the worst in the following order: cooperation, hegemony, disengagement, and competition.

The empirical part should examine the application of these propositions in several case studies, representing the four patterns of great power involvement in regional conflicts. Drawing on both the theoretical deductions and the historical case studies should make it possible to discuss the implications of great power involvement for regional conflicts in key regions in the post–Cold War era such as the Balkans, the Middle East, and East Asia.

# Notes

**Preface and Acknowledgments**

1. After the basic theoretical logic of this book was already conceived, I have learned that military psychologists investigated a battle in which I was intensely involved. One of their important findings was that situational factors are especially powerful in times of high threat and stress. This conclusion fits very nicely with the theoretical model presented in this book, and indeed, this study is cited in chapter 2.

**Introduction**

1. On deductive reasoning for the stability of bipolar systems, see Waltz 1964 and 1979, chap. 8, and Snyder and Diesing 1977, chap. 6. For empirical evidence that bipolar systems are more stable, see Levy 1985b, 54–58, 66; Brecher, James, and Wilkenfeld, 1990; and Midlarsky 1988. For a game theoretical perspective, see Oye 1985. For an application to the 1930s, see Posen 1984, and to the postwar period, see Gaddis 1987. For a similar rationale in different international contexts, see Gowa 1986 and 1989 and Mandelbaum 1988. For a recent refinement of the argument concerning the instability of multipolarity, see Christensen and Snyder 1990.

2. See, most notably, Mearsheimer 1990. For criticism of his view, see Keohane 1990, Hoffmann 1990, Van Evera 1990–91, Hopf 1991, and Kegley and Raymond 1992.

3. The most extreme representative is Fukuyama 1989. For a much more refined argument, see Mueller 1989. For a critique of their position, see Huntington 1989; see also Huntington 1993. On realist or Hobbesian pessimists versus liberal optimists regarding post–Cold War Europe, see Snyder 1990.

4. On democracies and war, see Doyle 1983 and 1986 and Maoz and Russett 1993. On the trading state, see Rosecrance 1986. For a brief recent review of the economic-liberal argument concerning the connection between a market economy and peace, see Levy 1989b, 89–90. On the effects of interdependence, see Keohane and Nye 1977 and 1987. For a critique of the liberal view of the connection between economics and security, see Buzan 1984.

5. On unintended consequences in international politics, see Waltz 1979; Jervis 1979, 212–45; and Gaddis 1987, 217–18. For more general discussions of unintended consequences, see Summer 1911, Deutsch 1973, 358, and Gleick 1988.

6. According to Weber, an ideal type is an arrangement of selected attributes detached from their contingent circumstances. See his *Methodology of the Social Sci-*

253

*ences* (1949, 89–110) and *Economy and Society* (1978, 20–22, 57–58). According to this definition, we could expect that some elements in each ideal type might be missing or appear in a different form in the real world and that only approximations of the ideal types might be found.

7. Although the following sources have different (and even opposite) views on the effects of crises on performance and decision making, all of them accept the distinction between crises and normal times as crucial for understanding state, elite, organizational, group, or individual behavior in different domains. See Williams 1976; James 1993; Oneal 1988; Wohlstetter and Wohlstetter 1971, 263; Verba 1961, 115; Ikenberry and Kupchan 1990b, 284; Gourevitch 1986, 240; Moltz 1993, 301; Wilensky 1967, 78; Lowi 1979, 128–29; Janis 1982; Lazarus, Averill, and Opton 1974. See also the useful overview of Holsti (1989), who cites some of these studies, and the references cited in chapter 2.

8. The original studies of the level of analysis problem in international relations are Waltz 1959, Singer 1961, and Kaplan 1957. For more recent contributions, see Wendt 1987; Hollis and Smith 1991; Buzan 1993; and Buzan, Jones, and Little 1993. Following Waltz 1959, three levels of analysis are commonly distinguished. The main distinction employed in the present model draws on Waltz's later work (1979) and thus is one between the system level and the unit level (although the unit level is also differentiated into state and individual levels in later chapters).

9. Such inside out theories expect a high correlation between internal attributes, states' foreign policies, and international outcomes. They include second-image theories (such as the Wilsonian, the liberal economic, and the Marxist schools; see Waltz 1959, chaps. 4 and 5; Doyle 1983 and 1986; and Hoffmann 1987; Bull's (1977) international society approach (see chap. 1); and related Grotian perspectives, which argue that common values and beliefs facilitate cooperation (most recently expressed in the regime literature, e.g., Puchala and Hopkins 1983; Ruggie 1983; Ruggie and Kratochwil 1986; Young 1983, 1986, and 1989; see also the overviews in Haggard and Simmons 1987, 509–13, and Cutler 1991). This line of argument is consistent "with a large body of research that shows that interpersonal attraction and help for others generally increases with similar beliefs and characteristics" (Patchen 1988, 70–71, and the references he cites). For criticism of inside-out theories, see Waltz 1959 and 1979.

10. The most influential structural-realist theory, which stresses the effects of the international system on state behavior, is Waltz's (1979). For criticism and Waltz's response, see Keohane 1986. See also Nye 1988a. For another variant of structural theory, see Gilpin's (1981) version of hegemonic theory. A more recent development related to structural theory is the emergence of the literature on cooperation under anarchy. See Axelrod 1984 and the special issue of *World Politics* (vol. 38, October 1985), edited by Oye. See also Jervis 1978 and 1988. Cooperation theory uses game theory, especially the Prisoner's Dilemma, to explain state behavior. For an attempt at an explanation of the foreign policies of a number of states "from the outside in," see Mandelbaum 1988. For a contribution in the area of international political economy, see Grieco 1990.

11. This is the implicit assumption—and the empirical conclusion—of theorists who examine the effects of the various levels of analysis. Jervis (1976, 16–17), for one, also states it explicitly. Even Waltz, who advances the most parsimonious theory that

explores the effects of a single (structural) level, explicitly recognizes the value and contribution of other (nonstructural) levels as well. See Waltz's (1986, 331, 339, 344) response to his critics. In fact, Waltz argues that he focuses on the effects of the structure precisely because these were overlooked by previous theories of international politics.

12. Some important works that have dealt with various aspects of this distinction include Schelling 1966, chap. 3; Jervis 1976, chap 3.; Smoke 1977; Frei 1983; George 1984a; Allison, Carnesale, and Nye 1985; Lebow 1987; and Gottfried and Blair 1988. For a major work on inadvertent wars, see George 1991.

13. Since the late 1970s, two new areas of research on international cooperation have emerged. Studies in international political economy have addressed the causes and the effects of international regimes (Krasner 1983; see also Rittberger 1993) and the related role of international institutions (Keohane 1984). Regarding cooperation among rivals in security affairs, traditionally the most sensitive area for states, the most important theorizing has been Waltz 1979 (especially chap. 9 on the management of international affairs by the great powers in bipolarity), a number of articles by Jervis (1978, 1983, 1985, and 1988, on the problem of "cooperation under the security dilemma"), and Bull's (1977) work (including on great power contribution to the international order, see especially chaps. 5 and 9). In addition, many studies have addressed crisis interaction between the superpowers; especially insightful are some of the works that followed Schelling's (1960) pioneering study and stressed tacit bargaining between rivals—most notably the works on crisis management by Young (1968) and Williams (1976), Snyder and Diesing's (1977), theoretically important book, and George's (1984a) and George, Hall, and Simons's (1971) more inductively oriented contribution. George and his colleagues also made a comprehensive empirical attempt to understand the obstacles and opportunities for U.S.-Soviet cooperation. George (1980c) developed the concept of a crisis prevention regime and later applied it, with collaborators (1983), to superpower détente in the Third World and to all aspects of U.S.-Soviet security regimes (George, Farley, and Dallin 1988). Another major approach is the application of game theory to international cooperation. Axelrod (1984) highlights the effectiveness of the tit-for-tat strategy for reaching cooperation among egoists without a central authority. Another important contribution was the special issue of *World Politics* (1985) devoted to cooperation under anarchy with an emphasis on game theory. Recent important works on superpower security cooperation in the postwar era include Gaddis 1987, Clark 1989, Allison and Williams 1990, Kanet and Kolodziej 1991, and Weber 1991. For a review of theories on cooperation, see Milner 1992.

14. For a somewhat related point, see George, Farley, and Dallin 1988, 5 n. 4, 11 n. 31, 14.

15. The postwar order approximates the former, while the nineteenth century Concert of Europe approximates the latter ideal type. Such a distinction might also be useful for understanding the recent rhetoric on a new international order for the post–Cold War era, which suggests at least a growing willingness to move from the former to the latter type of cooperation among the great powers.

16. For an excellent recent survey of the causes of war, see Levy 1989a. For useful comprehensive treatments from different perspectives, see Luard 1986b, Midlarsky 1989, and Rotberg and Rabb 1989.

17. Although Waltz (1979, 180–81) considers nuclear arms as a unit-level ele-

ment, they are qualitatively different from such internal factors as ideology and domestic politics. Rather, nuclear weapons are an indispensable part of the overall distribution of capabilities. Moreover, Mutual Assured Destruction (MAD) as an objective situational constraint (whether or not it is also the dominant strategic doctrine) accords well with the structural idea of objective factors that exercise restraining pressures on the actors regardless of their initial intentions, that is, their planned policies and strategic doctrines. On such a conception of nuclear deterrence, see Jervis 1989a. On nuclear weapons as a systemic factor, see Snyder and Diesing 1977, chap 6; Nye 1988a, 250; and Keohane and Nye 1987.

18. On the Long Peace, see Gaddis 1987, Lynn-Jones 1991, and Kegley 1991.

19. The Eastern question included both the contemporary Middle East and parts of the Balkans.

20. See the analysis in chapter 6 of the following cases: Security Council Resolution 242 of 1967; the two-power talks of 1969–70; the détente summits of 1972–73; the 1973 Geneva Conference; the October 1, 1977, Joint Statement on the Middle East; and the renewed attempts to convene an international conference on peace in the Middle East from the mid-1980s to the early 1990s.

21. In chapter 5, I discuss the most notable examples: the 1956 Suez crisis; the 1967 Six-Day War; the 1969–70 War of Attrition; the Jordanian crisis of September, 1970; the 1973 October War; and the 1982 Lebanese War.

22. The salience and dangers of regional conflicts are growing because of the combination of the rise of new regional conflicts (notably in the former Second World), the rising problems of nuclear proliferation and radical religious movements (notably in parts of the Third World), and the growing likelihood of great power disengagement from regional conflicts and thus the disappearance of one of the major ordering mechanisms for managing such conflicts.

23. See also Miller 1992b.

24. In constructing the book's theoretical model, I am following Waltz's conception of "a model of a theory" (1979, 7). Its chief objective is to explain rather than to describe, predict, or prescribe. Waltz argues that whereas a full description would be of lowest explanatory power, a greater comprehension is gained by moving away from reality, not by staying close to it. In contrast to Waltz, I am using causal factors at a number of levels of analysis and not only at a single level. I do so because a single-level explanation is insufficient to explain the considerable variance of the outcomes studied in this book. Yet by focusing on the differentiations among ideal types of outcomes and by offering a single set of explanatory factors for each of them, the parsimony of the explanation is maintained.

25. For a short discussion of these conditions, see Aggrawal 1985.

26. On this debate, see Nye 1988a, Keohane 1986 and 1989, Grieco 1988 and 1990, Stein 1990, and Baldwin 1993.

27. See the references in notes 1 and 2. See also Wagner 1993, Schweller 1993, Mansfield 1993, and Midlarsky and Hopf 1993.

## Chapter 1

1. Some of the more important works in the last two decades that see anarchy as a starting point for analyzing international politics are Axelrod 1984; Bull 1977; Buzan

1983; Buzan, Jones, and Little 1993; Jervis 1978; Keohane 1984; Nardin 1983; Posen 1984; Stein 1983; Waltz 1979; Wight 1978; the special issue of *World Politics,* edited by Oye, 1985; Mandelbaum 1981 and 1988; Clark 1989; Grieco 1990; and Weber 1991. See also Rosenau and Czempiel 1992. For a useful critique of the centrality of the assumption of anarchy for some of these theorists, especially Waltz, see Milner 1991.

2. For more elaborated differentiations among approaches to the international order, see Miller 1988, chap. 3, 1992c, and 1993.

3. Waltz is the major representative of the structural theory of the balance of power. On structural theory, see also chapter 2.

4. For a conception of order as a spontaneous arrangement, see Hayek 1973, 36 and 155 n. 3. In addition to the well-known example of a self-generating order in economic theory, the organism in biology and cybernetics in sciences (Hayek 1973, chap. 2) as well as language systems (Young 1983, 98) also constitute instances of automatic, self-generating orders.

5. For the distinction among the automatic, the semi-automatic, and the manually operated conceptions of the balance of power, see Claude 1962, 43–51. The manually operated conception is related to the international society school and to the operation of the Concert of Europe.

6. Classical realist writers include Carr (1964), Morgenthau (1978), and Aron (1967).

7. On the relations between the structural balance-of-power school, mutual deterrence as a conflict management mechanism, and the nuclear revolution, see Miller 1992c.

8. For a short review of these wars, see Levy 1985b, 345–46.

9. Indeed, as I show in chapter 3, in considering the causes of unintended wars, we have to specify how many great powers form the international structure.

10. In recent times, the international society approach has been represented mainly by British scholars such as Manning (1962), Butterfield and Wight (1966); see also Wight 1978 and Luard 1976. The best-known work, on which I rely most heavily in presenting this tradition, is by Bull (1977). See also Taylor 1982. For an overview of the Grotian tradition, see Cutler 1991. The most comprehensive treatment of the causes of war from the international society approach is by Luard (1986b and 1990, chap. 9).

11. Both approaches highlight the cooperation among states in place of the realist focus on conflict; but the regime approach introduces a more rigorous conception of the relations between basic explanatory factors (power and interests), rules (or institutions or regimes), and related behavior and outcomes. Most regime scholars agree that institutions and rules are intervening variables between the fundamental causal factors and outcomes (Keohane 1984, 64; Krasner 1983, 8; Stein 1983; Young 1986, 116). Yet after their formation, regimes "come to have their exogenous impact on outcomes and behavior" (Krasner 1983, 359). Furthermore, they change "the calculations of advantage that governments make" (Keohane 1984, 26) and "may alter the egoistic interests and power configurations that led to their creation in the first place" (Krasner 1983, 361). For a recent contribution to the regime literature, see Rittberger 1993.

12. For a detailed discussion of the promises and limitations of the contribution of the great powers to the international order, see Miller 1988, chap. 1.

13. On the capability of the great powers to project their power beyond their immediate borders, see Fox 1944, 21 and 1980 and Levy 1983b, 16. On the powers' global interests, see Keohane 1969, 295–97; Jervis 1979, 215; and 1976, 61; Levy 1983b, 16–17; and Claude 1986, 724. Although the worldwide interests of the great powers can also lead to expansionist policies, collective-goods theory (Olson 1965) leads us to expect that they will be ready to perform collective tasks for their own as well as others' sakes.

14. For the distinction between two modes and two substantive categories of great power collaboration, see below.

15. See Bull 1971, 145, although Bull does not make sufficiently clear the distinction between these competing conceptions. Indeed, he is much less interested in the sources of cooperation than in its consequences for the international order (see Holsti 1992, 32).

16. For a comprehensive study of the Security Council, see Hiscocks 1974.

17. Cooperation should be differentiated from harmony. Whereas a complete identity of interests is a prerequisite for harmony, cooperation occurs when there is a mixture of conflicting and complementary interests. Players are cooperative when they adjust their conduct to the actual or anticipated preferences of others. See Axelrod and Keohane 1985, 226. However, they need not always do it consciously and explicitly.

18. The security dilemma is discussed in the section on anarchy and conflict below.

19. See Gowa 1986, 176, who draws on Taylor's (1976) distinction between egoists and altruists. On this distinction, see also Stein 1983 and Keohane 1984, 27, 66, 74.

20. See, e.g., Keohane and Nye 1977; Krasner 1983; Jervis 1983; Lipson 1984; and Axelrod and Keohane 1985, who, however, try to stress the utility of a common analytical framework to account for cooperation in both arenas.

21. I am drawing here on Buzan 1983; Jervis 1983; Lipson 1984; and Axelrod and Keohane 1985. See also Mandelbaum 1988, 384–87.

22. The peacefulness of the post-1945 era, as I will elaborate in chapter 3, can be partly explained by the absolute nature of nuclear weapons.

23. In this situation, each actor's primary objective is to maximize the difference between its own payoffs and those of its rival. See Lipson 1984, 15, and Stein 1983. Whereas Lipson draws on Shubik's (1971) "games of status," Gowa (1986, 178), following Taylor (1976), uses the term "games of difference." Young calls this game "status-maximizing" (1986, 118). Grieco (1988 and 1990) argues that relative gains, rather than absolute ones, play a major role even in international political economy.

24. Snyder and Diesing (1977, 41–46) introduce four symmetric mixed-motive games.

25. On the interdependence of adversaries on the conflict-of-interest dimension and with respect to the interests that they have in common, see Snyder and Diesing 1977, 473. See also Lipson 1984, 13. For a useful analysis of the effects of U.S.-Soviet interdependence on their security cooperation, see George, Farley, and Dallin 1988, chap. 26. But whereas George deals only with subjective-cognitive interdependence (to be discussed in chap. 4 and the Conclusions), I also discuss the effects of objective or structural interdependence (chaps. 2, 3, and 5).

26. In a significant attempt at applying the logic of game theory to this field, Jervis (1978) identified conditions that are propitious for international cooperation under the security dilemma. Jervis termed such cooperation by the major powers either a "security regime" (1983) or a "concert" (1985).

27. Most notably, in the application of game theory to international politics (see Axelrod 1984; Jervis 1978; Oye 1985) and in the regime literature (see Krasner 1983; see also Keohane 1984; Young 1989).

28. Keohane refers to institutions in the broad sense of "sets of practices and expectations" (1984, 246). Most remarkable is the considerable consensus that was reached regarding the concept of regimes in a field of study as anarchical as international relations. In the most widely accepted formulation, Krasner defines regimes as "sets of implicit or explicit principles, norms, rules, and decision-making procedures around which actors' expectations converge in a given area of international relations" (1983, 2).

29. For critiques of the regime literature, see Strange 1983, Kratochwil 1984, Young 1986, and Rosenau 1986.

30. This is especially true for Keohane (1984, 76) and Stein (1983). See Young's (1983, 99, and 1986, 110–11) critique of their conceptions of order and regimes.

31. On this point, see also Nye 1987; George, Farley, and Dallin 1988; and Kanet and Kolodziej 1991.

32. On this point, see Jervis 1988; George, Farley, and Dallin (1988, 5 n. 4, 11 n. 31, 14; and Haggard and Simmons 1987, 504. In the structural–game-theoretical literature, the concepts *order, stability,* and *regime* have also not been clearly distinguished (Haggard and Simmons 1987, 496). Similarly, the all-too-general and all-too-often nonoperationalized notion of systems stability is not specified, for example, in Waltz's (1964 and 1979) work on bipolar stability, where it is not completely clear whether system stability means durability or peacefulness or both. See Ruggie 1986, 153–54 n. 10.

33. The examples are slightly modified variations on Schelling's (1960, chaps. 3–4).

34. On saliencies in international conflicts, see also Young 1968, especially chap. 1; Smoke 1977, 15–16, 32–34, 274–75; and Snyder and Diesing 1977, 500.

35. See Schelling's (1960, chaps. 1–3) theory of interdependent decisions.

36. An especially fascinating story of spontaneous cooperation during World War I is the Christmas Truce of 1914 along two-thirds of the trenches dug by the Germans and the British on the Flanders fields of Belgium and France. Many of the spontaneous incidents are described in letters reprinted in Brown and Seaton 1984; for a short review, see the *Boston Sunday Globe,* December 25, 1988.

37. Other examples of self-generating rules are Downs, Rocke, and Siverson's (1985) tacit bargaining in arms control, linguistic conventions (Hayek 1973, 37; Young 1983, 98), and Schelling's (1978, chap. 7; also cited among additional examples in Young 1986, 111) interactive conduct.

38. Nardin (1983) introduces a somewhat similar, though not identical, twofold distinction. Young (1983, 98–101, and 1986, 110–111) and Downs, Rocke, and Siverson (1985) advance different types of a threefold categorization of international arrangements; Kratochwil (1989, chap. 2) presents a fourfold typology of rules or norms;

and Cohen (1980) introduces a multifold classification of the "rules of the game," according to their explicitness. See also George, Farley, and Dallin 1988, especially chapters 26, 27, and 29. Although these useful typologies are closer to the real world and, in fact, do not depart from the logic of the fundamental distinction presented in this book, they blur its rigor and parsimony.

39. For a discussion of the logic of relating principles and norms to deliberate cooperation and power-related factors to spontaneous cooperation, see chapter 2.

40. On negotiations, see Raiffa 1982. Young (1983, 99–100) discusses negotiated orders and provides useful references.

41. "A partisan decisionmaker" is defined in Lindblom 1965, 3, 9.

42. In a sense, the tacit codes of conduct are heuristic intellectual constructs to the extent that they only approximate reality and are not an explicit set of norms that serves as a guideline for decision makers (Evron 1979, 22) but rather are detected by the outside analyst. Neither do these conventions spring from the realm of international law or morality, and they are usually not expressed in the course of diplomacy or public rhetoric (Gaddis 1986, 132–33; Keal 1983, 2–3).

43. The nature of a collaborative arrangement refers to the objectives promoted by the cooperation (Aggrawal 1985).

44. Young (1986 and 1989) distinguishes between international institutions and international organizations.

45. The distinction between collaboration out of "common interests" and coordination due to "common aversion" is presented in Stein 1983. He also provides references to scholars who distinguish between "positive" and "negative" kinds of cooperation (1983, 130 n. 27).

46. The scope refers to the range of issues that are regulated by the collaborative arrangement (Aggrawal 1985).

47. See, for example, the works of Brecher (1977); Young (1968); Snyder and Diesing (1977); and Craig and George (1983).

48. On the distinction between crisis management and crisis prevention, see George, with others, 1983, 365–69, and George, Farley, and Dallin 1988, especially chap. 23.

49. However, one of the most common definitions of an international crisis fails to address this element. See Hermann 1969, 414. See also Holsti 1989, 12. My definition, in turn, draws on Brecher 1977; Young 1968, 9–14; Snyder and Diesing 1977, 6–7; and Craig and George 1983, 205.

50. Thus the fundamental conflict concerning Germany was resolved only in 1990 in the aftermath of the fall of the Berlin Wall and with the processes of German unification and the end of the Cold War. For an analysis of the Berlin crisis, see Betts 1987, 83–109. For an account of the negotiations on Berlin and the Helsinki agreements, see George, Farley, and Dallin 1988, part 2.

51. These dominant elements are nonetheless manifested in a great variety of ways and degrees in different crises. The classical dilemmas of crisis management are to commit or preserve options and to manipulate or minimize risk. For an extended discussion, see Schelling 1960, 35–125; Williams 1976; and Snyder and Diesing 1977, 211–51.

52. Snyder and Diesing (1977, 248) advance a somewhat related argument. Their

impression is that the pattern of many more instances of backing down than of compromising is more characteristic of crisis interaction than of noncrisis bargaining.

53. On the definition of crisis management, see also George, Hall, and Simons 1971, 8–11, and Williams 1976, 27–32.

54. War between the great powers themselves, as Snyder and Diesing (1977, 7–8) note, should be excluded from the term *crisis*. Similarly, tacit rules for crisis management ought to be distinguished from the patterns of restraint for keeping a limited war from expanding. The former are designed to avoid a war between the great powers by controlling a local crisis or war. The function of the latter is to control the escalation of a limited war in which at least one of the superpowers is directly involved. See Jervis 1983, 188–89, on the patterns of restraint that kept the Korean and the Vietnam wars from expanding. The best discussions of escalation control are Schelling 1960 and Smoke 1977. That Jervis refers only to these patterns of restraint and not to the tacit understandings for the regulation of military intervention, which have been discussed by other analysts and are examined in this work, might partly explain why he so categorically rejects the possibility that there has been a security regime in the postwar era. On this point, although from different angles than presented here, see Nye 1987 and George, Farley, and Dallin 1988.

55. On this role conflict, see Snyder and Diesing 1977, 505–7; Stein 1980; George 1986; George, with others, 1983; Jonsson 1984; and Ben-Zvi 1988.

56. Inadvertent wars are defined in the next section, whereas the conditions for their occurrence are discussed in chapter 3.

57. By the state of war, Hobbes means not actual fighting but the "disposition thereto, during all the time there is no assurance to the contrary," that men "are in that condition which is called war; and such a war, as is of every man, against every man" (1962, 100).

58. Bull (1966, 42–43) contends that if one considers the states system not at a single moment but since its inception in 1648, one then finds that every state that has survived the period has at one point or another been disposed to war with every other one.

59. On the security dilemma, see Herz 1950; Jervis 1976, 1978, 1983, and 1985; and George, Farley, and Dallin 1988, 656–58.

60. See Blainey 1973, chap. 9 and Luard 1986b, chap. 5. It seems that their main criticism is directed not so much against the plausibility of inadvertent wars as they are defined in this book but against the concept of "accidental wars," which I differentiate from inadvertent wars.

61. See the extremely useful studies by Levy (1989a), Midlarsky (1989), Rotberg and Rabb (1989), and Holsti (1991).

62. For an extended discussion of the definition and identification of great power wars, see Levy 1983b, chap. 3.

63. As this book deals with cooperation and conflict among great powers, it will focus on major war. However, the main distinction developed in this book equally applies to local wars.

64. This definition is derived from Levy's (1987) useful analysis of preventive wars. It is worthwhile to emphasize that the main distinction in my model is not between aggressive and preventive motivations but between inadvertent and intended wars. For

this purpose, both preventive and aggressive wars are intended wars. On preventive war as a classical case of premeditation, see George 1991, 31. Both these types of objectives are acknowledged by theories of hegemonic war. A rising challenger may initiate a war against the hegemonic power in pursuit of aggressive objectives (Organski and Kugler 1980, 13–63). A declining hegemon, for its part, may resort to prevention (Gilpin 1981, 191, 201–2; Levy 1987, 97; see also Schweller 1992). For a recent overview of hegemonic theories, see Levy 1991a. In contrast, balance-of-power theory, as noted, would characterize many of the major intended wars as counterhegemonic (Levy 1991a, 148).

65. Alternative names of this phenomenon are spiral model, security dilemma wars, and uncontrolled escalation. On the critique of the deterrence model by advocates of the spiral model, see Jervis 1976, chap. 3. On inadvertent war, see Schelling 1966, chap. 3; Frei 1983; and George 1984a and 1991. Smoke (1977) deals with the question of controlling escalation.

66. For a useful overview of this cause, see Holsti 1989.

67. An inadvertent war should be distinguished from an accidental war. On this distinction, see George 1991, 8. An accidental war might break out as a result of technical-organizational problems. See especially the works of Bracken (1983), Steinbruner (1981), and Blair (1985), which focus on the implications of the vulnerability of strategic command, control, and communications in the nuclear age. Inadvertent wars, on the other hand, stem from broader political factors operating on the decision-making elite.

68. George (1984a, 225) applies the term "military logic" to the large-scale use of force as a "blunt, crude, instrument" for the actual negation of the rival's military capabilities; whereas according to "diplomatic logic," force is employed as a "flexible, refined psychological instrument of policy."

69. Appeasement can be seen, in fact, as a more active version of underreaction in the sense of making important concessions to revisionist powers in the misguided hope of satisfying their demands.

70. On the destabilizing effects of small allies, see Morgenthau 1978, 556; Gilpin 1981, 236; and Brown 1984. On the military bias in favor of offensive military doctrines, labeled the cult of the offensive, see Posen 1984, Van Evera 1984, and J. Snyder 1984. On the effects of domestic politics on the outbreak of wars, see Levy 1989a, 262–74, and 1989b.

71. The following discussion is based on Levy 1987. See also the distinction developed from the angle of political philosophy by Walzer (1977).

**Chapter 2**

1. These ideas are discussed in the Conclusions.

2. Haggard and Simmons specify that "game-theoretic approaches are strongest when they reveal the conditions which enable cooperation and stability; they say far less about whether regimes will actually arise, how they will be institutionalized, and, above all, the rules and norms which will comprise them" (1987, 506). They also have "difficulty explaining organizational form, scope, or change" (Haggard and Simmons

1987, 504). See Haggard and Simmons's (1987, 500–504) critique of the "hegemonic stability" explanation of regimes.

3. These subsystemic changes refer to the seemingly greater effect of domestic politics, ideology, and bureaucratic politics as well as crisis-induced stress (because of the presence of nuclear weapons) on policy outcomes in the post-1945 period. This point is addressed in chapter 3.

4. The literature on the European Concert is vast. For a political science perspective, the following works are particularly useful: Albrecht-Carrie 1968; Clark 1989; Craig and George 1983; Elrod 1976; Garrett 1976; Gulick 1955; Hinsley 1963; Hoffmann 1965; Holbraad 1970 and 1971; Holsti 1991, chaps. 6, 7; and 1992; Jervis 1983 and 1985; Kissinger 1964; Lauren 1983; Mandelbaum 1981; and 1988, chap. 1; Rosecrance 1963; Schroeder 1972 and 1986. The nature and form of great power concerts and the conditions for their emergence are discussed in chapter 4.

5. The Crimean War and World War I as inadvertent wars are analyzed in greater detail in chapter 3.

6. These assertions are examined in chapters 3 and 5.

7. Domestic constraints and this proposition on the whole, as is elaborated in chapters 4 and 6, refer mainly to the U.S. political system. The contrast between the superpowers' normal attitudes toward the status quo and their crisis conduct is presented in chapter 3.

8. These are the major themes of chapter 3.

9. For two analytical attempts to anticipate how such a scenario could have evolved, see Fukuyama 1985 and Gottfried and Blair 1988, 243–46. Obviously, since the end of the Cold War, such scenarios of U.S.-Soviet confrontation have become irrelevant.

10. For an elaboration of the distinctive effects of bipolarity and nuclear weapons on the postwar Long Peace, see chapter 3.

11. On the structural expectation that great powers will balance each other because of the dominance of security considerations in an anarchic system, see Wolfers 1962, 122–24; Waltz 1979, 123–28; Jervis 1979; and Walt 1987.

12. Waltz (1979, chap. 9) suggests that it should be easier to manage the international system when there are only two superpowers. For related points, see Snyder and Diesing 1977, 506–7; Oye 1985, 4; Gowa 1986, 172; and Mandelbaum 1988, 35 n. 26. In accordance with structural theory, the Third World was not very critical for the global distribution of capabilities in bipolarity, and the military and economic dependence of the superpowers on that part of the world was lower than the dependence of earlier powers on the periphery (Waltz 1979, chaps. 7 and 8, especially 190). Hence, the superpowers were expected either to disengage from most of these areas (for policy prescriptions in this light, see Posen and Van Evera 1983, Feinberg 1983, and Johnson 1985–86) or to cooperate in some way when their interests there converged (see Weber 1990), but probably not to pursue such an intense strategic-military-political competition as they did in the postwar era. However, structural theory also offers a contradictory expectation. For a discussion, see below.

13. I elaborate this argument in chapter 4.

14. Thus, as late as 1913, the great powers convened a conference in London to

address the Balkan conflict. As Mandelbaum commented, "the conference settled the most contentious issues in early 1913 without an expansion of the conflict. The London conference seemed to revive the Concert of Europe" (1988, 55). On the London conference, see also Lynn-Jones 1986, 129–30.

15. This discussion is further elaborated in chapter 3.

16. On concert and détente as forms of great power diplomatic cooperation, see chapter 4.

17. In presenting the ideal type conditions under which systemic or structural explanations are most useful, I am drawing mainly on the works of Waltz (1979) and Jervis (1976, 16–31, and 1979, 212–43), although they do not discuss some of these conditions explicitly in the same way as I do in this book. The system in Waltz's theorizing is composed of the structure (which Waltz contends was overlooked by previous systemic theorists) and interacting units (which he asserts belong to the theoretical realm of foreign policy). The international structure has three components: (1) The ordering principle is anarchy as against the hierarchy of the domestic order. (2) With respect to the functional character of the units, so long as the anarchic order endures, states (which are the central actors in international politics) remain functionally like units. (3) With respect to the distribution of capabilities, states are differentiated by their capabilities to perform similar tasks. A change in any one of these elements is a change of the international system. However, since the anarchic nature of the system has lasted for a very long time, the major source of change is changes in the distribution of capabilities, mainly between bipolarity and multipolarity. I also rely on the following sources: Morgenthau 1978; Allison's (1971, 10–38) Model I; Keohane and Nye's conception of realism (1977, 23–24); and Keohane's conception of structural realism (1983, 508, 529). I take issue with Morgenthau because of his focus on the concept of "interest defined as power." Following the logic of the structural balance-of-power perspective, I highlight minimal security interests rather than power maximization as a component of structural analysis. Allison's comprehensive rationality (and to a lesser extent, Keohane's more refined rationality assumption) are not viewed as essential expectations of structural theory in this book; instead, I accept a more modest conception of rationality.

18. On the term *situationally determined,* see Keohane 1984, 27–28.

19. For an example—Soviet emulation of American roles as a superpower—see Jonsson 1984, 22–23.

20. For overviews of the personality-situation debate in psychology, see Mischel 1973, cited in Larson 1985, 22; Ekehammar 1974; and Alker 1972. I am grateful to Reuven Gal for bringing the last two sources to my attention.

21. Although I took an active part in one of these battles, I was not interviewed by the military psychologists on my own involvement, so I do not have any personal relationship to Gal's studies.

22. As the Sprouts (1957) contend, the psychological milieu of policymakers could account for their decision making and the choices they make. At the same time, external factors (what the Sprouts call the operational milieu), such as the distribution of capabilities, are essential for understanding international political outcomes. Thus, cog-

nitive and domestic variables may explain foreign policy *choices*. But systemic factors affect the *outcomes* of states' interaction.

23. More precisely, the implications of such crisis cooperation are unintended. These implications could include an acceptance of the status quo and a recognition of the rival's interests, equal status, and spheres of influence, even if all these elements are undesired and unacceptable in normal times because of ideology or domestic politics or both. On the application of these elements to the postwar era, see chapter 3.

24. On the maxims of a state-as-actor (or a unitary actor) model, cf. Wolfers 1962, 3-24.

25. In chapter 1, however, I distinguish between the two ideal types of major war precisely on this point—whether they are preceded by a crisis (inadvertent war) or not (intended war). Obviously, a crisis manufactured by an aggressive state as a pretext for initiating war is not considered a genuine crisis in this sense.

26. More precisely, crisis decisions tend to be reached by ad hoc decisional units, composed of the chief executive and a selected group of advisers rather than the formal organizational machinery normally used to conduct foreign policy. See Frei 1983, 123; Paige 1968, 281, cited in Brecher 1980, 377; Williams 1976, 66-67, quoting Hermann 1969, 20.

27. Wilensky (1967), Holsti and George (1975, 297), Williams (1976, 66-67), Frei (1983, 122-23), and Snyder and Diesing (1977, 512) conclude that the degree of lower-level bureaucratic involvement does vary across cases—in general, in inverse ratio to the brevity and severity of the crisis.

28. See also the literature surveys in Holsti and George 1975, 285-93 and Stein 1976, cited in Frei 1983, 129-30. This conclusion is consistent with the insight of Simmel (1956) and Coser (1956) about the cohesive effects of an external threat.

29. At the same time, Adomeit recognizes that in comparison with the internal elite consensus in crisis settings, "there may be more room for disagreement over questions such as détente; the Strategic Arms Limitation Treaty (SALT); reduction of armed forces and armaments in Central Europe; East-West economic, scientific, and technological relations, and exchanges of information and ideas" (1981, 76). Thus, Adomeit also highlights the distinction between crisis behavior and normal diplomacy, similar to the distinction in the present book. But Adomeit's main explanation of the crisis consensus is nonstructural, namely, Soviet ideology. Although a common ideology might logically explain crisis consensus, it cannot account for the difference between the agreement during crises and the disagreements in noncrisis settings. In this sense, I believe that the distinction between the effects of different levels of analysis in crisis versus noncrisis situations provides a better explanation for the difference in behavior between the two types of situations.

30. On the concept *national interest* and the numerous problems in its definition and operationalization, see the useful discussions in Brodie 1973, chap. 8; George and Keohane 1980, 217-37, and the references they provide on 236-37; and Brown 1983, chap. 1. For a subtle distinction between values and interests, see Snyder and Diesing 1977, 183 n. 2. Structural theory does not expect, however, that states will necessarily be interested in power maximization. This is one of the key differences between classical realists, e.g., Morgenthau (1978, 215), and neorealists or structural theorists such as

Waltz. On this point, see Waltz 1959, 334; and 1979, 118, 126; Posen 1984, 68; and Keohane 1983.

31. This is not only the expectation of realists and many deterrence theorists but also of some students of organizational behavior (cf. Holsti 1989, 15–18).

32. For evidence supportive to the cited sources, see Paige 1972; Williams 1976, 68–69; and Adomeit 1982, 48–49.

33. A representation of comprehensive rationality is Allison's (1971, 10–38) Model I (this model is a simplification based on the "economic man" model and the writings of Morgenthau, Kissinger, and Aron in international relations). The comprehensive rationality model includes rigorous standards such as behavior as a unitary actor, a comprehensive search for information and sensitivity to pertinent new knowledge, the scrutiny of a well-defined set of alternatives according to their costs and benefits, and the selection of the alternative that maximizes expected utility, in accordance with the national interest. See also Schelling's conception of rationality as "value-maximizing" (1960, 15). For other references to comprehensive rationality, see also Verba 1961, 94–95, 106–8; Williams 1976, 61; Snyder and Diesing 1977, 340–41; and Stein 1978, 319. For a more recent definition of rationality, see Bueno de Mesquita 1981, 29–33, who sees leaders as strong rational calculators of expected utility. See also Huth and Russett 1984, 499. Some of these authors (Verba, Schelling, Bueno de Mesquita, and Huth and Russett) recognize the theoretical utility of the rationality assumption even if it does not describe real-world behavior.

34. The tradition of bounded rationality goes back to March and Simon's "satisficing" (1958). For a more recent discussion of rational choice and bounded rationality, see Keohane 1984. Somewhat similarly to bounded rationality, "sensitivity to costs" does not mean that leaders engage in intricate rational calculations. Rather, states act recklessly if the expected costs of aggressive actions are low or uncertain. States are more cautious if there is a high probability of resistance to expansionist moves, which might make it costly to threaten the status quo. The structure of the external situation can either enhance leaders' sensitivity to and awareness of costs or undermine them. This is the reason, as we will see in chapter 3, why bipolarity restrained superpower conduct in postwar crises. Studies that support the logic of the "sensitivity to costs" thesis include Mearsheimer's (1983) study of conventional deterrence and Posen's (1984) study of military doctrine.

35. See also Snyder and Diesing's (1977, 332–39) definition of rationality in the sense of information processing.

36. While explaining the sources of military doctrine, Posen suggests that "in times of relative international calm we should expect a high degree of organizational determinism. In times of threat we should see greater accommodation of doctrine to the international system—integration should be more pronounced, innovation more likely" (1984, 80, see also 40, 59).

37. This view is shared by organizational theorists such as Wilensky (1967, 78), who argues that decision makers are more likely to search past the first "satisficing" alternative, and Verba (1961), and to a lesser extent by March and Simon (1958, 116), who argue that the search for information under crisis conditions may be more extensive, if less productive. Lowi (1979, 128–29) argues that U.S. decision making during crises has been more rational than in noncrisis situations.

38. The classical study of misperceptions in international politics is Jervis 1976. See also Holsti 1976b, 18–54; Jervis 1970, 132.

39. Such as Schelling (1960), Mearsheimer (1983), and Quester (1989, 52–65).

40. For a very useful overview of crisis decision making from the theoretical perspective of four levels of analysis, see Holsti 1989. For the effects of individual-level causes, see especially Holsti 1972 and 1979; Hermann 1969 and 1972; Holsti and George 1975; and George 1980b, 47–49. Janis (1982) focuses on the effects of small groups. Allison (1971) emphasizes organizational routines and bureaucratic politics. Snyder and Diesing (1977) discuss information processing (chap. 4) and decision making (chap. 5) in crises. Lebow highlights the effects of "cognitive closure" (1981, 101–19) and of domestic politics (1981, 169–92) on crisis politics. The adverse effects of psychological factors on crisis management are also highlighted in Jervis, Lebow, and Stein 1985; Lebow (1987) sees U.S.-Soviet crisis management as a "dangerous illusion." For more recent studies, see Jervis 1989b and Lebow 1989. For a critique of some of these arguments, see Quester 1989. For a psychologist's (who specializes in nuclear crisis management) critique of the overemphasis on psychological factors in Lebow's and his associates' work, see Blight 1986–87. Another critique of Lebow (1981) and Janis (1982) from a psychological perspective is Larson 1985.

41. Compare the findings of Holsti (1972); Janis (1982); Lebow (1981); and Jervis, Lebow, and Stein (1985) with the evidence of, among others, Russett (1963 and 1967), Huth and Russett (1984 and 1988), Paige (1968, 81–93, 292), Brecher (1980), Stein and Tanter (1980), Shlaim (1983), and Dowty (1984) and a number of crisis simulations (see Morgan 1983, 181). Snyder and Diesing (1977, 405–8) have found in their comprehensive research that decision makers behave in crises according to bounded rationality or even some combination of utility maximization and bounded rationality. See also Patchen 1988, 103–8. Some major historical studies of the causes of war argue that even when the crisis escalates to war, it does not mean that decision makers behave irrationally: "The conflicts between states which have usually led to war have normally arisen, not from any irrational and emotive drives, but from almost a superabundance of analytic rationality" (Howard 1983, 14, see also 15). For similar points, see Blainey 1973, 127, chap. 9, and Luard 1986b, chap. 5.

42. Oye (1985, especially 18–20) surveys the game theory literature, including with respect to the effect of the number of players on cooperation. Olson (1965, especially chaps. 1 and 2) argues that the more concentrated the distribution of capabilities within a group, the more likely that public goods will be provided. See also Hardin 1982, chap. 3.

43. For a similar conclusion based on an overview of the literature, see Mandelbaum 1988. For a divergent opinion, see Snidal 1991.

44. See also the examples of situation-related cooperation, introduced in Schelling 1960 and Axelrod 1984.

45. Although, as Gottfried and Blair (1988, 270–73) note, there are many obstacles to the effectiveness of such intelligence efforts.

46. Since leaders tend to resist perceptual change, the less dramatic the external event, the less likely it is to generate such a change. On leaders' resistance to perceptual change, notably because of the effects of cognitive consistency, see Steinbruner 1974; Jervis 1976; Snyder and Diesing 1977, chap. 4; and Patchen 1988, 90. Patchen suggests

that the "general tendencies to resist change in perception will be greater to the extent that . . . new information contrary to existing perceptions is ambiguous and neither long-sustained nor dramatic" (1988, p. 90). On bureaucratic politics, see Allison 1971 and Halperin 1974. Although, on the whole, crisis situations are less ambiguous than normal diplomacy, certain crises (under multipolarity) are significantly more ambiguous than other (bipolar) ones (see chap. 3).

47. More precisely, state attributes have a large explanatory power when states with similar domestic attributes behave similarly, even if faced with significantly differing situations. Such conduct should differ from the behavior of states with different domestic characteristics, even if the international environment is the same (Jervis 1976, 22). A useful indicator, suggesting a need to focus on first-image factors, is the existence of disagreements within the elite over the government's policy (Jervis 1976, 23–24). More particularly, differences of opinion within a certain administration and discontinuity in policies between different administrations highlight the power of individual-level attributes.

48. See the discussion in chapter 1 of the distinction between a regime's principles and norms and its rules and procedures. See also the related discussion of the international society school.

49. Similarly, Haas, Williams, and Babai (1977, dealing with technological cooperation) highlight the linkage between cognitive congruence and cooperation. More specifically, Haas (1980) argues that as the number of areas on which there is consensual knowledge increases, so does the supply of regime principles and norms. The greater the number of goals decision makers seek to pursue, the more the demand for collaboration (see also Aggarwal 1985). Aggarwal suggests that cognitive theories such as Haas's are better at explaining the development of principles and norms (metaregime), whereas structural theories successfully account for the emergence of rules and procedures. The logic of the present argument is somewhat similar to Aggarwal's, although I am using different terms and the modes of collaboration and dependent variables in this book are also different, even if they parallel the regime terms. As noted above, spontaneous cooperation, manifested through tacit rules for regulating the use of force in crises, parallels the rules and procedures in the regime literature. The conscious collaboration manifested in concerted diplomacy (or a security regime) in the present book is close to the concept of metaregime and its principles and norms.

50. Krasner 1983, 361–67 specifies the ways in which regimes could change patterns of capabilities and interests.

51. On the BPA and its numerous weaknesses, see George, with others, 1983, chap. 5, especially 114–115 and 372–75; Gowa and Wessell 1982, 10–11; Jervis 1983, 187–94; and Garthoff 1985, 290–98.

52. Learning takes place internationally, according to Haas, when "new knowledge is used to redefine the content of the national interest. Awareness of newly understood causes of unwanted effects usually results in the adoption of different, and more effective, means to attain one's ends" (1980, 390). A useful distinction between levels of learning is Steinbruner 1974. For a recent comprehensive work on learning in U.S.-Soviet relations, see Breslauer and Tetlock 1991.

53. On interdependence among adversaries and tacit bargaining, see Schelling's (1960, chaps. 1–3) theory of interdependent decisions. On the positive effects of mutual

vulnerability on cooperation, see the experimental studies of Thibaut and his associates cited in Patchen 1988, 40–41.

**Chapter 3**

1. Of course, there have been many local and civil armed conflicts in the postwar period.

2. Following Waltz 1979, the polarity of a given system is defined in this book in accordance with the distribution of capabilities in that system or, more precisely, the number of great powers. For brief reviews of this debate, see Miller 1988, chap. 5, and Levy 1989a, 233–34.

3. In his earlier writings, Waltz (1964 and 1979, 180–81) attributed a much greater explanatory power to bipolarity but in his more recent publications (1981 and 1990) he seems to explain the postwar peace almost exclusively by nuclear weapons.

4. For an earlier argument on the irrelevance of nuclear deterrence, see Organski and Kugler 1980, chap. 4.

5. For a somewhat similar point, see also George, Farley, and Dallin 1988.

6. For useful analyses of the use of nuclear threats in superpower crises, see Betts 1987 and Trachtenberg 1991.

7. For analyses of this danger during the Cold War, see Allison, Carnesale, and Nye 1985; Bracken 1983; Gottfried and Blair 1988; and Lebow 1987.

8. On these demonstrative or show-of-force options, see Cohen 1980 and 1981; Frei 1983, 137–53; Jonsson 1984, chap. 5; and Osgood and Tucker 1967, 150–57. Conceptualizations of the diplomacy of force are advanced in Schelling 1960 and 1966; Jervis 1970; Young 1968; and Snyder and Diesing 1977, 452–57. Blechman and Kaplan (1978) provide a detailed description and analysis of the U.S. use of military force as a political instrument. The political use of the Soviet military is addressed by Dismukes and McConnell (1979, especially naval diplomacy) and Kaplan (1981). On signals, see Jervis 1970, 20–23.

9. Key advocates of multipolar stability include Kaplan (1957, 22–36) and Deutsch and Singer (1964). The major spokespeople in favor of bipolar stability are Waltz (1964 and 1979, chaps. 8 and 9), Snyder and Diesing (1977, chap. 6), Snyder (1984), Gaddis (1986), and Mearsheimer (1990). For a refinement of the argument regarding the instability of multipolar systems, see Christensen and Snyder 1990.

10. In contrast, some analysts who have investigated the nuclear revolution and appreciate its stabilizing effects think that the basic cause of postwar stability was indeed the bipolar structure. See especially Trachtenberg 1991, 232; see also Mearsheimer 1990.

11. This section and the next one draw especially on Waltz 1990; Levy 1989a, 291–95; Mandelbaum 1981; and Jervis 1989a.

12. In the same way, anarchy is a permissive factor allowing for wars in general. See Waltz 1959; see chap. 1.

13. MAD is a situation in which the opponents have the capability to inflict unacceptable punishment on each other even after absorbing a surprise nuclear first strike.

14. On crisis-induced stress and other psychological problems of crisis stability, see Jervis 1989a, chap. 5; Holsti 1989; and Fischhoff 1991.

15. For detailed studies of potential sequences of inadvertent escalation in the nuclear age, see Frei 1983; Allison, Carnesale, and Nye 1985; Lebow 1987; and Gottfried and Blair 1988.

16. However, although a common fear of war may not prevent an inadvertent escalation once the great powers find themselves in crisis, I show in chapter 4 that it may encourage deliberate cooperation in crisis prevention and conflict resolution designed to minimize the risk of their stumbling into a crisis in the first place.

17. However, control over allies is more directly influenced by the international structure.

18. See the citations in the Introduction. See also Layne 1993. The argumentation used in the debate on polarity and stability is deductive. Yet apart from the avoidance of a general war since World War II, substantial evidence from different historical periods has been advanced in support of the deductive logic of bipolar stability. See Brecher, James, and Wilkenfeld 1990; Levy 1985a, 54–58, 66; Thompson 1986. For formal deductive support of bipolar stability, see Saperstein 1991.

19. There are two sources of advantage in the balance of interests (see McConnell 1979, especially 245). The first is the value of the interest at stake, especially as it bears on national security. All other things being equal, the power that values the interest at stake more highly has the advantage in the balance of resolve. Even more important is the second dimension: the status quo. The superpower defending the status quo, an interest that is in its possession, tends to have greater motivation than does an opponent who is challenging the existing balance.

20. On the term *red lines,* see Evron 1979, especially 38–39; and 1987; and Bar 1990.

21. The argument that two-player games are more conducive to spontaneous cooperation and the evolution of tacit rules to coordinate and regulate behavior is supported by studies from the theory of the firm in microeconomics (see Scherer 1970, 7–8, who draws on the work of E. H. Chamberlin; see also Hardin 1982, 4–42; Olson 1965, chaps. 1 and 2); findings in social psychology (see, e.g., Thibaut 1968; Thibaut and Faucheux 1965; Thibaut and Gruder 1969; these studies are cited in Patchen 1988, 40); and some works in game theory (see Axelrod 1984; Gowa 1986; Oye 1985; Schelling 1960; but for a different argument, see Snidal 1991).

22. On the greater stability of bipolar alliances as compared to alliances in multipolarity, see Gowa 1989.

23. For a concise account of these adverse effects, see George 1980b, 47–49. Also very useful and updated are Holsti 1989, 8–84, and Jervis 1989a, chap. 5. The adverse effects of stress are also underlined by theories at the small-group level, especially Janis's (1982) "groupthink."

24. For an elaboration of this argument, see Miller 1992b.

25. See the lists of wars in Levy 1983b, chap. 3; 1985b; and 1987.

26. The discussion so far has been on the international system level, yet the same logic may be found to operate at the regional subsystem level, thus lending strength to the model. Indeed, in accordance with Mearsheimer (1990), polarity can be used for characterizing the distribution of capabilities not only in the system at large but also in a specific region. On the superpower role in the 1967 crisis, see chapter 5.

27. On the Crimean War, see Smoke 1991, 36; for references to other scholars who conceive of this war as a result of misunderstandings of interests and commitments, see Miller 1992b. On the Six-Day War as an inadvertent war, see Safran 1981; Quandt 1977, 168; Aronson 1978; Evron 1987; and Stein 1991, 126.

28. Jervis suggests that World War I "has provided much of the inspiration for the [spiral] model" (1976, 94–95; see also 1989b). Wildavsky contends that World War I is the "one historical case which the spiral model appears to fit" (1971, 165). Allison, Carnesale, and Nye (1985) argue that World War I illustrates the owlish (neither dovish—accommodation—nor hawkish—peace through strength) phenomenon of war through miscalculation. For similar arguments, see Snyder and Diesing 1977, 500–502; Kahler 1979–80; and Gaddis 1986, 122. A comprehensive study of the outbreak of World War I is the special issue of *International Security,* vol. 9, no. 1 (Summer 1984). For additional references, see Jervis 1976, 94 n. 70; Levy 1985b, 362 nn. 56–57; and 1991b; Lynn-Jones 1986; Sagan 1986; Orme 1987, 105–9; and Mearsheimer 1990.

29. Yet, global bipolarity prevented the escalation of the regional war to the global level, in contrast to the other two cases, which took place in a setting of global multipolarity. Moreover, bipolarity made possible a fairly early termination of this war without a major change in the regional status quo, as was also the case in the other Arab-Israeli wars. Indeed, these wars were terminated by superpower intervention according to certain tacit rules, to be discussed in chapter 5.

30. On the preemptive character of the Israeli strike in 1967, see Walzer 1977, 80–84.

31. For a useful overview of some of the historical questions involved here, see Sontag 1971, chap. 12, and the debate on A. J. P. Taylor's (1961) interpretation of Germany's aims in Robertson 1971.

32. On the unclarity of the balances before the two world wars, see Jervis 1989b.

33. For an analysis of this war from different theoretical perspectives, see Lebow and Strauss 1991.

34. Yariv (1985) analyzes to what extent the various Arab-Israeli wars were wars of no choice or wars by choice and concludes that the Lebanon War was a war by choice, in contrast to the no choice situation in 1967, which led to a preemptive strike. This distinction parallels the one between inadvertent and intended wars.

35. See Trachtenberg 1991, chap. 3, who analyzes the prevalence of the preventive war idea in the postwar American defense establishment and concludes that at no point was it seriously considered as practical policy.

36. For references, see chapter 1.

37. As Betts shows, "in terms of cautious estimates, Moscow had a finite deterrent even before the end of the Korean War" (1987, 147). See his useful analysis of "The Nuclear Balance before Parity: Myth of a Golden Age" (1987, 144–72).

38. This Soviet restraint stands in contrast to the fears of many commentators during the Cold War that the growing military capabilities of the Soviets might embolden them to take adventurous steps that would challenge the status quo. On these fears, see Pierre 1971, 183; Nitze, cited in Nacht 1985, 92 n. 14; Kissinger, cited in Legvold 1979, 755–57; and Brzezinski 1980, 321.

39. See, e.g., O. Holsti's (1967) work on Dulles's image of the Soviets.

40. For a sixfold typology of balances of superpower interests according to the strength of each superpower's stakes in a particular region and whether they are symmetrical, see George 1990, 108–20.

41. For a comprehensive study that highlights the cooperative elements of the Cold War in different regions, see Kanet and Kolodziej 1991. See also Allison and Williams 1990, chap. 13.

42. For a similar conclusion see the overviews by Frei (1983, 122, 133, 144), Holsti and George (1975, 296), and Oneal (1988, 602–11). On Soviet control over the military during crises, see Adomeit 1982, 344–45; see also Dallin 1988, 614.

43. For "overcontrol and overmanagement" by President Johnson over bombing targets during the Vietnam War, see Gelb with Betts 1979; Lebow 1981, 286; and George 1984a, 228.

44. For critiques of Allison (1971), see Krasner 1972; Art 1973; Williams 1976, 128–30; and Caldwell 1978, cited in Lebow 1981, 288 n. 54. Allison recognizes that there is much more presidential intervention in the implementation of policies during crises than in noncrisis periods (Allison 1971, 128). For more recent evidence about the crucial role of the president in the management of the Cuban crisis, see Blight, Nye, and Welch 1987.

45. For a related point, see Nye 1990, 92.

46. Mueller, for his part, suggests that "the structure of alliances therefore better reflects political and ideological bipolarity than sound nuclear strategy" (1991, 55).

47. This theory suggests that domestic instability is a major cause of interstate wars because insecure elites use aggressive foreign policy to strengthen their internal power. See the review in Levy 1989a, 271–74.

48. Notably, the most recent and comprehensive study of the Cuban Missile Crisis shows that domestic politics did not play any role in the president's decisions. See Welch and Blight 1987–88, 24–25; see also Patterson and Brophy 1986.

49. For a related point, see Russett 1990, 45.

50. On the U.S.-Soviet tacit mutual recognition of spheres of influence, see especially Keal 1983.

51. See also the overviews in Williams 1976; Morgan 1983, 181; Oneal 1988; and James 1993.

52. On World War I, see the Stanford findings as summarized by Holsti 1972 and Holsti, Brody, and North 1969; see also Jervis, Lebow, and Stein 1985 and Lebow 1981 and 1987. Jervis, Lebow, and Stein (1985) also discuss the 1973 Middle East war and the 1982 Falkland Islands War.

53. On the constraints bipolarity posed on the German room of maneuver to pursue basic territorial-political change, see Trachtenberg 1991, 232.

**Chapter 4**

1. Although the precise dates of the Concert are disputed, most scholars agree that it lasted from the Congress of Vienna until the Crimean War, namely 1815 to 1854. Some scholars regard the Concert as having lasted, to some extent, until 1914. See the citations for the different views in Chapter 2. At any rate, the Concert became much weaker and less effective after 1854. See Holsti 1992.

2. On the definition of institutions in Keohane 1984 and of regimes in Krasner 1983, see chapter 1. On a concert as a security regime, see Jervis 1983 and Lauren 1983. On the principles, norms, and rules of the European Concert, see Hinsley 1963, 224–25; Schroeder 1972, 405; and 1986; Garrett 1976, 391; Elrod 1976, 163–65; Jervis 1983; Lauren 1983, 33–34; and Clark 1989, 112–30.

3. On such a limited conception of a concert as a "temporary political agreement between two or more states," see Holbraad 1971, 11. The same factors that prevent the establishment of a concert may also constrain the more limited form of concerted diplomacy, as was the case with some recurring attempts at U.S.-Soviet concerted diplomacy during the Cold War, most notably in the Middle East (see chap. 6).

4. On détente and entente, see Craig and George 1983, chap. 17.

5. A concert as a mechanism of international order has to be differentiated from balancing on the one hand and from collective security on the other. For an elaboration of this distinction, see Miller 1992c. See also Kupchan and Kupchan 1991.

6. For example, see the insightful works of Jervis (1985), Weber (1990), and Kupchan and Kupchan (1991).

7. This is especially emphasized in the following writings on the Concert: Jervis 1983 and 1985; Hinsley 1963, 224–25; Elrod 1976, 168; and Kaplan 1979, 39, 73, 86.

8. See the accounts of the Concert by Holbraad (1971 and 1979), Bull (1977), Lauren (1983), Craig and George (1983, 31–32), Nardin (1983, 88), Schroeder (1972 and 1986), Mandelbaum (1988, chap. 1), and Clark (1989, chap. 6). These authors refer to both roles but stress the conceptualization of the Concert as joint management.

9. For a useful related conception, see Holbraad 1971, 11–12, and 1979, 151. On the high frequency of joint consultation and collective decision making in the post-Napoleonic Concert of Europe, see Hinsley 1963, 197, 224–25; Elrod 1976, 162–63; and Lauren 1983, 35–36. On the Concert's conscious management of the balance of power, see Hinsley 1963, 224; Kaplan 1979, 39, 73, 86, 136; Craig and George 1983, 30–31; and Lauren 1983, 33. On its pacific resolution or at least amelioration of conflicts, see Lauren 1983, 40–42, 48–50; Craig and George 1983, 31–32; Hinsley 1963, 225; and Clark 1989, 121. Schroeder (1986, 3) lists the Concert's diplomatic accomplishments in settling or ameliorating disputes.

10. On coercive diplomacy, see Lauren 1979, 193, and Craig and George 1983, 189. This concept corresponds to Schelling's "compellence" (1966, 70–71).

11. Young refers to imposed orders as "deliberately established by the dominant actors who succeed in getting others to conform to the requirements of these orders through some combination of coercion, cooption, and the manipulation of incentives" (1983, 100–101; see also Young 1986, 110).

12. Contrast, e.g., Hoffmann 1965, 105, 107; Holbraad 1979, 151–53; and Tucker 1977, 6–8, who underline the coercive elements, with Schroeder's (1972 and 1976) much more benign view of the Concert's attitude to weak states. He points out that lesser states in the nineteenth century probably had a greater voice on issues related to their vital interests than in other eras (1972, 405 and 1986, 25). For in-between positions, see Elrod 1976, 163; Lauren 1983, 46; and Nardin 1983, 88, who draws on the work of Klein (1974). For recent analysis, see Holsti 1991, chaps. 6 and 7.

13. On this point, see Hinsley 1963, 201–6; Rosecrance 1963, 61–62, who cites also Kissinger and Nicolson; Hoffmann 1965, 103; Albrecht-Carrie 1968, 10–11; Jervis

1978, 173; Craig and George 1983, 31–32; Mandelbaum 1988, chap. 1; and Holsti 1991, chap. 6.

14. The limits to this view are discussed below.

15. In contrast to the United States, the Soviet Union, like the Russian Empire before it, has historically been surrounded by unfriendly nations, especially, although by no means exclusively, in Eastern and Central Europe. Since the late 1950s, the hostile environment has included Communist China and, since the late 1970s, Islamic fundamentalism—the rising threat in Southwest Asia. In its final years, however, the source of its vulnerability turned inward: the sluggish performance of the Soviet economy and the threat of disintegration because of accelerating nationalist and ethnic tensions in the Soviet empire.

16. On Pax Britannica and Pax Americana, see Modelski 1978 and Gilpin 1981. However, for a useful critique that highlights the limits to hegemonic accounts of international politics, see Nye 1990. Pax Britannica was relevant at most to the British empire and to international political economy (notably, the issue-area of trade), but not to Europe. Indeed, it was the Concert (rather than hegemonic leadership by Britain) that played the major role in conflict management in the post-Napoleonic era (see Holsti 1992, 33–35). To the extent that the British attitude to the Concert was affected by relative capabilities, it resulted not so much from superior capabilities but rather from lesser vulnerability. Thus, the British attitude was manifested not so much in the desire for unilateral management but rather in relative noninvolvement in some regional conflicts. Pax Americana, for its part, was constrained by the bipolar structure of the postwar era. See Nye 1990, 87–95. Yet it is true that both Britain and the United States were relatively less inclined to take part in a multilateral cooperative framework of all the great powers. But a major common element in their lesser inclination was their objection to a certain form of such cooperation (that is, to a condominium), and this objection was largely due to unit-level factors.

17. According to balance-of-power theory, such a disappearance is likely to lead to the termination of the cooperation among previous allies.

18. On the concept "the image of the opponent," see George 1969. On such a positive image as a prerequisite for a concert, see Liska 1986b. See below for an extended discussion of this concept as a factor affecting the initiation of attempts at concerted diplomacy.

19. The positive effects of shared values on cooperation are especially highlighted by the international society approach (see Bull 1977); see chap. 1. See also Taylor 1982, 26–29, and the review and references in Patchen 1988, 70–71.

20. See especially Ruggie 1983, Puchala and Hopkins 1983, and Young 1983. A useful overview of different approaches to regimes is Haggard and Simmons 1987.

21. Ideological consensus as an explanation of the Concert's cooperation is advanced by the following authors: Albrecht-Carrie (1968, 6), Craig and George (1983, 33–34, 245), Holbraad (1971, 17, and 1979, 144–45), Lauren (1983, 57), Morgenthau (1978), Rosecrance (1963, 55–59, 77, 79–80), and Schroeder (1972, 404). For a more recent analysis, see also Kupchan and Kupchan 1991.

22. Morgenthau cites Guizot, a former prime minister of France, who wrote in the mid-nineteenth century, "The professional diplomats form within the European community, a society of their own which lives by its own principles, customs, lights, and

aspirations, and which amid differences and even conflicts between states, preserves a quiet and permanent unity of its own . . ." (1978, 250–51). For a similar point, see also Garrett 1976, 406, and Jervis 1983, 183–84.

23. For similar points, see Kissinger 1964, 1–6, 145–47, and Jervis 1983, 176–77. See also Kaplan's (1957) rules. For a useful critique of Kissinger's notion of "international legitimacy" in the context of both the Concert and the post-1945 system, see Hoffmann 1980, 37–40.

24. The classical analysis of legitimacy is Weber 1978, 212–16, which Habermas (1975) criticizes. I am drawing on the discussions of foreign policy legitimacy in George 1980a, 235 and of international legitimacy in Ikenberry and Kupchan 1990a.

25. This belief, which concerns the perception of the dynamics of international politics, is discussed in the next section.

26. On the tendency of monarchies to respect the traditional legitimacy of fellow kingdoms, see Walt 1987, 36–37. Kant predicted that republican states would avoid the use of force against each other but not against nonrepublican regimes (see Doyle 1983 and 1986). Moreover, democracies tend to respect the sovereignty of other popularly elected governments and to settle differences with them through negotiations, as a reflection of their domestic norm of nonviolently settling political disputes.

27. On the effects of this memory, see Rosecrance 1963, 59–60; Hinsley 1963, chap. 9; Garrett 1976; Holbraad 1979, 151–52; and Jervis 1985.

28. This is because the disintegration of the Ottoman Empire might have brought about a scramble over the spoils, since the Near East affected the interests of all the great powers. Such a scramble would have threatened the existing balance of power and the international order as agreed on in the Congress of Vienna in 1815 and consciously maintained by subsequent international conferences. Thus, to avoid this problem, so long as the Concert was effectively functioning, it maintained the integrity of the decaying Ottoman Empire through multilateral diplomacy and collective interventions. See, e.g., the above references and also Jervis 1983, 186 n. 25. For a useful analysis of the Eastern question, see Brown 1984. Brown also provides a useful bibliographical essay (1984, 280–329) and a detailed chronology of this question (1984, 331–55).

29. This kind of interdependence differs from the high interdependence of the superpowers in a bipolar world in their external security (see chap. 3).

30. Despite numerous differences, the growing concern of Western leaders in 1989–91 about the stability of Gorbachev's regime also fostered a somewhat similar sense of interdependence: it was feared that Gorbachev's fall from power would destabilize the Soviet Union and Eastern Europe and therefore have adverse consequences for international stability (mass emigration, the loss of control over nuclear weapons, spreading ethnic and civil wars, etc.). Hence, the West not only tried to avoid unilateral advantages but sought to be benign toward the Soviet government (i.e., to help it financially and to support the territorial integrity of the USSR) and especially toward Gorbachev personally. A similar process seems to be taking place toward Yeltsin in 1993–94 because of the fear that his fall might result in either chaos or a rise to power of the conservative-nationalist forces.

31. The difference between the unstable power politics of the eighteenth century and the cooperative concert of the post-1815 era is most dramatically underlined in the work of the historian Schroeder (1972 and 1986). He accounts for this difference by

what he calls "systemic" or "structural" changes from the eighteenth to the nineteenth centuries. However, rather than to structural changes, he refers, in fact, to changes in institutionalized arrangements (a great power concert, the separation between Europe and the colonial world, and small states as intermediary bodies in Europe). These institutional factors, in my view, constitute the intervening instead of independent variables. The formation of such cooperative arrangements, in turn, is explained by unit-level factors such as those highlighted here.

32. I am not referring primarily to individuals' processes of thinking and the structure of their decision making process, which Steinbruner (1974), Jervis (1976), Axelrod and his collaborators (1976), and Vertzberger (1990) have investigated. Rather, I highlight the content of state leaders' world views (or belief systems). See, on this point, Spiegel 1985b, 6, and Lipschitz 1989. As Holsti (1976a, 131) suggests, the content of a belief system refers to such concepts as image, operational code, world view, decisional premises, and the relevant theoretical literature on political philosophy and ideology. Drawing on Converse (1964) and Jervis (1976, chap. 4), Holsti and Rosenau define a belief system as "a complex, elaborate, and concrete set of attitudes and assessments that are tied together by their own logic in such a way as to be internally consistent" (1983, 375).

33. Drawing on Jervis (1976, 23–24), the presence of differences of opinion inside the foreign policy elite suggests the significance of individual-level factors (see chap. 2).

34. On the distinction between hard-liners and soft-liners, see Snyder and Diesing 1977, 297–310. See also Ben-Zvi's (1986, 9) critique of Snyder and Diesing's distinction.

35. American policymakers long tended to subscribe to the domino theory (Breslauer 1983b, 334; Feinberg 1983, 188–91; Garthoff 1985, 675; George, with others, 1983, 387; Johnson 1985–86, 39–40; Walt 1987, 20; Waltz 1979, 199–200). At the same time, the fundamental Soviet belief (as distinguished from operational behavior), at least until the Gorbachev era, was in a world revolution rather than in the emergence of an equilibrium of forces between competing powers. More specifically, optimistic Soviet assessments, especially in the 1970s, of the shifting "correlation of forces" in their favor led them to believe that many third world states would join the communist camp (see Menon 1986, 22–59) and, in more general terms, that the present historical era was marked, in the words of a prominent Soviet observer, by a "rejection of capitalism, [and] the victory of socialism as a world socio-economic formation" (cited in Menon 1986, 41). Somewhat similarly, the Reagan administration believed that its military buildup would create an environment more conducive to the spread of democracy, that is, to the realignment of Soviet clients. Both positions were informed by the view that third states join the strongest power.

36. On the differences between global and regional approaches of policymakers, see Marcum 1976, 418; Osgood 1981, 14; Jervis 1981, 55–59; George, with others, 1983, 388; and 1984c, 151; Feinberg 1983; Holsti and Rosenau 1983, 379 (one of the main elements in their differentiation between "Cold War Internationalists" and "Post–Cold War Internationalists" refers, in fact, to the global versus regional approaches); Garthoff 1985, 666–90; MacFarlane 1985; and Ben-Zvi 1986.

37. This was the position in the U.S. foreign policy elite that Osgood labels "Analysis B" (1981, 118), Holsti and Rosenau call "Cold War Internationalists" (1983,

379), Schneider characterizes as "Conservative Internationalism" (1984, 11–36), and Ben-Zvi terms the "Bipolar-Confrontational" conception (1986, 11–25).

38. Osgood labels this school "Analysis A" (1981), Holsti and Rosenau term it "Post-Cold War Internationalists" (1983, 379), Schneider defines it as "Liberal Internationalism" (1984, 11–36), and Ben-Zvi calls it "the Multipolar-Accommodative conception" (1986).

39. On pre-Gorbachev Soviet policy in the Third World, see MacFarlane 1985 and 1987a; Garthoff 1985, especially 679–89; Breslauer 1983b and 1987; Menon 1986; Shulman 1986; and Korbonski and Fukuyama 1987.

40. Such a capacity and willingness of a great power to collaborate with a rival power, while its ally is being attacked by the rival power (the mining of Haiphong harbor), will be discussed in the next section with regard to the preference of authoritarian regimes for a great power condominium.

41. Hence, the image of the opponent affects the actor's view of the essential nature of political life, namely, is the political universe essentially one of harmony or conflict? Whereas idealists underline the harmonious nature, realists highlight conflict. On the importance of the image of the opponent, see also Jervis 1976, chap. 2, and O. Holsti 1967.

42. On the difficulty in estimating rival intentions, see May 1984.

43. This is partly because of the development of the technology of reconnaissance satellites (see Gaddis 1986, 124 n. 71).

44. On the breakdown of the Cold War consensus in the U.S. foreign policy elite, see the studies of Schneider (1984, 11–35) and Holsti and Rosenau (1983, especially 377–82). The findings of Holsti and Rosenau indicate that U.S. involvement in Vietnam had a powerful impact on the leadership's beliefs. The war led to the replacement of the foreign policy consensus of the 1950s with three widely discrepant belief systems.

45. See, e.g., the competing interpretations of Soviet Foreign Minister Andrei Gromyko's statement that "Today, there is no question of significance which can be decided without the Soviet Union or in opposition to it" in Johnson 1983, 953 n. 3., citing Legvold and Pipes. See also Menon 1986, 238. For conflicting views of the détente in the 1970s, deriving from the image of Soviet intentions, see Gelman 1984 versus Garthoff 1985.

46. This has been especially true for the elites of the last two decades rather than for the populace. Thus, Schneider (1984, 14–17) distinguishes between liberal and conservative internationalism as the two major streams that have emerged in U.S. foreign policy elites since 1964. Hunt (1987) underlines the strong impact of ideology on the images, perceptions, and behavior of the makers of U.S. foreign policy. But see also Holsti and Rosenau 1983, 389–90, and Jervis 1981, 59.

47. On contending American beliefs about the Soviet Union during the Cold War, see, e.g., Pranger 1979, Osgood 1981, Zimmerman 1980, Dallin and Lapidus 1983, Holsti and Rosenau 1983, and Ben-Zvi 1986.

48. On learning and cooperation, see Haas 1980; Nye 1987; Legvold 1988, 120–24; Breslauer and Tetlock 1991; and chapter 2.

49. On this distinction, see Stoessinger 1979 and Stewart, Hermann, and Hermann 1989, 48–49.

50. These two factors (normative and structural) constitute the two main explana-

tions of the democratic peace thesis (see Maoz and Russett 1993; Starr 1992). See also Doyle 1983 and 1986, who draws on Kant. In this chapter, I examine these explanations in a different domain, namely, the inclination of a great power to take part in a condominium. This analysis may thus lend strength to the democratic peace theory while extending its utility.

51. Pluralism at home is usually associated with fragmented authority, multiple centers of power, and the legitimacy of diversity among the component parts of the whole. International pluralism is marked by the tolerance of diverse social systems and ideologies and a recognition that the locus of decision making ultimately rests with the nation rather than with centralized supranational leadership. An authoritarian great power, on the other hand, is more likely to favor centralized decision making, the conformity of small states, and a hierarchical organization of international affairs led by a great power condominium. This distinction draws on the well-documented argument in the alliance literature (see Holsti, Hopmann, and Sullivan 1973, 149–75) that pluralist societies tend to establish pluralist alliances, whereas centralist-hierarchical powers form monolithic blocs. These are ideal types, but they broadly reflect the differences between the Western and Eastern blocs from the late 1940s until the late 1980s.

52. Although this was not the only factor affecting the British attitude, Hinsley (1963, 205) also discusses the realpolitik dimension of British state interests as they were perceived by Castlereagh.

53. See especially the quotation in Craig and George 1983, 32.

54. See the citation of Castlereagh in Lauren 1983, 62. Rosecrance observes that "England abandoned its liberalism when the integrity of the Ottoman Power was at stake, and France was compelled to go along" (1963, 97).

55. For analyses that underline the domestic sources of the failure of détente, involving the opposition by both conservatives and liberals to Kissinger's policies, see George 1980a and Hoffmann 1980 and 1984.

56. See the above-cited normative explanation for the inclination of democracies to avoid war with other democracies (but not necessarily with nondemocratic regimes).

57. On the congruence between the hierarchical nature of the Soviet domestic system and its hierarchical relations with foreign communist parties, cf. Dittmer 1981, 496, 501.

58. The classical pluralist analyses of American politics in terms of interest groups are Bentley 1908 and Truman 1951. On the relations between interest groups and foreign policy, see Milbrath 1967.

59. For an analysis of domestic constraints on cooperation with the Soviets, see Nye 1984 and 1986. George (1983 and 1984c) focuses on the difficulties, including domestic ones, of cooperation with the Soviets in the Third World.

60. On linkage groups, see Bar-Siman-Tov 1983, 50–51, who draws on the work of Rosenau (1969) on linkage politics. Transnationalism is analyzed by Keohane and Nye (1972 and 1977). On transnational penetration as a cause of alliance formation, see Walt 1987, 46–49.

61. Other conditions for the effectiveness of these groups have included U.S. commitment to an internationalist strategy of containing Soviet expansion and the perception of the small ally as contributing to this strategy (see Keohane 1971). For an elaboration of the conditions for the effectiveness of transnational linkage groups, see Miller 1988, 355–56.

62. For instance, the Greek lobby, the Irish lobby, the Jewish lobby, and, more recently, the emergence of a lobby of African Americans supporting the struggle of black Africans against South Africa. On ethnic lobbies and U.S. foreign policy, see Said 1977, Mathias 1981, and Watanabe 1984. The U.S. ally that has been the most successful in using the transnational strategy is Israel. Its success is attributable to the intensive, persistent, well-organized, and almost unanimous backing of the American Jewish community for Israel's concerns. This community fulfills the conditions for an effective ethnic constituency. For comprehensive treatments of U.S.-Israeli relations, see Ben-Zvi 1993, Safran 1981, Spiegel 1985a, and Quandt 1977. For a critical portrait of the Israeli lobby, see Tivnan 1988.

63. Although the formation of a condominium has not been addressed in the literature in the terms used in this book, this section draws especially on the following sources: Destler, Gelb, and Lake 1984; George 1984c; George, with others, 1983; Keohane 1971; Mathias 1981; Quandt 1977; Spiegel 1985a; and Walt 1987.

64. I am striking here a middle ground between two extreme views of Soviet domestic politics since the death of Stalin and until the recent radical changes. See Simes 1986, 153, citing Hough and Pipes.

65. For analyses of the relations between domestic politics and Soviet foreign policy, see the articles in Hoffmann and Fleron 1980, 31–90, and by Dallin (1981, 335–408).

66. Cf. Jonsson 1984, 197–221, who reviews the literature on the superpowers and the nuclear nonproliferation treaty (NPT) regime. See also Nye 1988b.

67. For an account of how the USSR helped the cause of nonproliferation, see David 1992–93, 146 n. 51, citing Pilat. On Soviet support of the NPT and of International Atomic Energy Agency safeguards, see Duffy 1978, 95–99.

68. For an extended treatment of Stalin's policy toward the West, see Taubman 1982.

69. Bell (1974, 535) goes so far as to argue that the notion of condominium has deep roots in the Soviet world view from the Stalinist period on. In his memoirs, Kissinger writes about Brezhnev's efforts to draw the United States into a semialliance that would have served to isolate mainland China or to attain U.S. concurrence with potential Soviet actions against China (see Kissinger 1979, 1146, 1251–52; and 1982, 233, 274–86, 294–95, 1173). However, taking into account the huge disparity in capabilities between a U.S.-Soviet "semialliance" and China, such an arrangement would have amounted to a condominium rather than an alliance in the balance-of-power tradition. Of course, it is very difficult to gauge to what extent the USSR was sincerely interested in long-term durable collaboration.

70. See also Kissinger 1982, 287, with regard to the Soviets' preference of their relations with the United States to the concerns of their Vietnamese allies: the USSR was willing to collaborate with the United States while its ally was being attacked (the mining of Haiphong harbor).

**Chapter 5**

1. For a comment on this point, see Gaddis 1986, 135–36.

2. For a comprehensive study of many aspects of U.S.-Soviet competition in the Middle East, see Spiegel, Heller, and Goldberg 1988. See also Marantz and Steinberg 1985; Quandt 1986b; and Taylor 1991.

3. Strategic assets include overflight rights and air bases, port facilities, intelligence facilities, and the ability to station military forces permanently or to have access in times of need to military bases in strategic locations.

4. Rubinstein (1980, 326–27) presents a more "offensive" view of Soviet strategy. Fukuyama (1988) analyzes Soviet military power in the Middle East; he (1986b) also addresses U.S.-Soviet military competition in the Third World.

5. For discussions of superpower interests in the Middle East, see Quandt 1986b and the 1986 issue of *AEI*, which was devoted to this subject and was edited by Saunders.

6. On U.S. interests in the Middle East, see Quandt 1977, 9–15; Campbell 1979; Rosecrance 1980; Reich 1980; and Saunders 1986, 16–20.

7. For a statement by one of the leading Middle East specialists in the Soviet Union, see Primakov 1988, 387–89. On Soviet interests in the Middle East, see Golan 1979, Rubinstein 1980, Fukuyama 1981, Breslauer 1985, Ross 1985, and the special 1986 issue of *AEI* edited by Saunders. For a useful account of various aspects of Soviet Middle East policy, see the volume coedited by Dawisha and Dawisha (1982).

8. For an account of the positions taken on this issue by postwar administrations, see Zak 1986.

9. For a discussion of conflicting interpretations of Soviet Middle East policy, see Herrmann 1987. For a critique of the dominant U.S. interpretation during the Cold War (that is, the "expansionist" view) and useful references, see Slater 1990–91.

10. This is certainly true for the United States, including some efforts to court revolutionary Egypt (before its realignment) and Syria. But in different periods, the Soviets have also cultivated relations with such pro-Western states as Israel (supporting its War of Independence, even though they did so to undermine the British empire), the Shah's Iran, Turkey (since the 1960s), and conservative Arab states (especially in the last few years of the USSR's existence).

11. See Safran 1969 for the evolution of superpower involvement in the Middle East from 1945 to 1967. Quandt (1986b) provides a short account.

12. The Eisenhower Doctrine upgraded the U.S. commitment as compared to the Truman Doctrine, by pledging direct employment of U.S. military forces for defending states threatened by communist aggression.

13. Apart from the anti-imperialist agenda, the new revolutionary regimes were also attracted to the Soviet model of development (statism, central planning, and rapid industrialization). Moreover, they saw Zionism as an extension of Western imperialism supported by the United States. In contrast, the Soviet Union shifted from its initial support for Israel toward an endorsement of the Arab cause. Although the United States opposed the joint British-French-Israeli intervention in Suez (1956), subsequent U.S. support for the Arab monarchies and conservatives undermined U.S. standing with the "progressives."

14. The term that was used by many Westerners to describe Soviet involvement in the Third World—*penetration*—connoted the illegitimacy of Soviet engagement in that part of the world in the eyes of these observers, including many U.S. policymakers. The security dilemma made it very difficult, if not impossible or even sometimes irrelevant, to determine whether Soviet security interests in the Middle East were defensive or offensive. Defensive motives referred to the need to minimize potential threats to the

Soviet Union and to push them further and further away (Quandt 1986b, 20; Ross 1985, 166–67; Saunders 1986, 20–21). Offensive objectives alluded to the persistence of the old-time czarist desire for access to warm waters (cf. Golan 1979, 105) and alleged Soviet plans to expand their presence and control over states proximate to their borders (see the qualifications in Quandt 1986b, 21–22) and "from there to project their power internationally" (Ross 1985, 167–68).

15. For a useful study of the origins of alliances in the Middle East, see Walt 1987.

16. To a certain extent, Soviet ideological and state interests were complementary rather than competing. One of the most important characteristics of the revolutionary-socialist Arab regimes has been, from the outset anti-imperialism, that is, an anti-Western stance (at least until the pro-U.S. realignment of Egypt under Sadat, although by 1974 through 1976 the socioeconomic orientation of Egypt was hardly socialist anymore due to the disillusionment with the Soviet model of development). In other words, support of the "progressives" also served the Soviet state goal of weakening Western presence in the area. Yet whenever there was a clash between state interests and ideological interests, preference was given to the former. A major example is the subordination of party-to-party relations with communist parties in the Arab world to state-to-state interaction with "progressive" Arab governments, even when that was to the detriment of the local communists (Golan 1979, 109). At the same time, the radical regimes had a number of important ideological differences with communism: they were ultranationalist with strong ties to Islam and rejected the class struggle notion.

17. Yet it is important to bear in mind that direct arms supply from the United States to Israel began only during the Kennedy administration, that is, in the 1960s. Moreover, the current large allocations of U.S. economic and military assistance began only in the early 1970s, especially during and after the 1973 war. The most detailed accounts of the development of U.S.-Israeli relations are Safran 1981 and Spiegel 1985a.

18. For studies that show the limits to superpower influence in the Middle East, see, on the Soviet Union and Egypt, Roi 1979, chap. 7; on the Soviet Union and Syria, Roi 1979, chap. 8; on the Soviet Union and the Arab world, Dawisha 1982; and on the United States and Israel, Reich 1984 and Ben-Zvi 1993. Although Egypt provides the most dramatic example of a client state defying a patron by expelling Soviet advisers and abrogating the mutual friendship treaty, other Arab states have also not followed Soviet preferences (see Golan 1979, 113–14, and the sources she cites). Syria refused for a long time to sign a friendship treaty and behaved contrary to Soviet positions with respect to the Lebanese civil war and the Syrian Communist Party. Iraq turned down Soviet requests for extraterritorial rights for naval facilities or for support for its positions on the Horn of Africa and Afghanistan. The United States also had a difficult time in getting its allies in the Persian gulf to accept American military presence or even access to facilities (see McNaugher 1985, 15–16).

19. For a definition and discussion of crises, see chapter 1.

20. On these threats, see Bar-Joseph and Hannah 1988; Fukuyama 1981, 582–83; Glassman 1975, 15–16. Jonsson 1984, 154–57; Speier 1957. For a recent analysis of U.S. and Soviet threats to use nuclear weapons in the Suez crisis, see Betts 1987, 62–65. For a book-length account of the crisis, see Neff 1981.

21. See also the analyses of Soviet motivation in Roi 1974, 436–38, and Horelick 1972, 581–92, cited in Golan 1979.

22. For possible explanations of the Egyptian step, see Whetten 1981, 47; Mangold 1978, 117; and Jonsson 1984, 162.

23. This assertion was made not only by the Israeli foreign minister at the time of the crisis. Two other sources less friendly to Israel confirmed the absence of Israeli troop buildup along the Syrian border: UN observers (Glassman 1975, 40) and even the Egyptian chief of staff, General Mohammed Fawzi, who was dispatched to Syria on May 14 (Jabber and Kolkowicz 1981, 425; Jonsson 1984, 162).

24. Bar-Zohar served during the 1967 war as the spokesman of the Israeli Ministry of Defense and was closely affiliated with Defense Minister Dayan.

25. For a detailed study of the War of Attrition, see Bar-Siman-Tov 1980.

26. For a work representative of the charges that the Soviets behaved recklessly in the 1973 war and violated the rules of détente, see Kohler, Leon, and Mose 1974.

27. Some observers (Glassman 1975, 120–24; Kohler, Leon, and Mose 1974, 32–50; Laquer 1974, 71–75; Rubinstein 1977, 251–62; see also the references in Garthoff 1985, 366 n. 25) argue that there was a direct Soviet complicity in the Egyptian-Syrian war strategy and that the Soviets knew the date of the planned attack. They draw on Soviet-Arab exchanges on the eve of the war. However, Porter (1984, 124 n. 23) and Garthoff (1985, 366) persuasively refute their argument. On this point, see also Sadat 1977, 242, 246; and Heikal 1975, 21, 34–35; and 1978, 256, who say the Soviets found out about the attack only two days before it took place.

28. This was the first massive resupplying by the Soviets of any third world client involved in large-scale hostilities. For details on the Soviet airlift and sealift to Egypt, Syria, and Iraq during the 1973 war, see Kohler, Leon, and Mose 1974, 64–65; Glassman 1975, 130–31, 145–46; Quandt 1976, 18–27; and Porter 1984, 132–33.

29. Analysts disagree whether four divisions were placed on alert on October 24 in addition to the three alerted since October 11–12 (Blechman and Hart 1984, 277; Dowty 1984, 256; Jonsson 1984, 186, and the sources he cites) or whether all seven had already been placed on alert by October 11–12 (Garthoff 1985; 377, 378n; Golan 1977, 86; Jabber and Kolkowicz 1981, 447; Quandt 1977, 197).

30. Similarly, historian Pipes referred to Brezhnev's message as an "ominous ultimatum." He blamed the Soviets for violating "the spirit and letter of these accords [the BPA] almost at once" (1981, xiii).

31. Other related indicators included a reported Soviet request to Yugoslavia to overfly its territory and the establishment of a special airborne command post in the southern USSR (Betts 1987, 124; Blechman and Hart 1984, 278; Jonsson 1984, 186, citing Caldwell.

32. For an especially harsh criticism of Nixon's and Kissinger's handling of the crisis as a misperceived East-West contest, see Hersh 1983, 234–49.

33. On these accusations, see Nixon 1978, 500, 528, who provides a sarcastic account; Kissinger 1982, 596–98; and Dowty 1984, 261.

34. An excellent analysis of the date, meaning, and implications of nuclear parity is Betts 1987, especially chaps. 5 and 6. See also Schilling 1984, 183–214, for U.S. views of parity, and Lambeth 1984, 255–72, for Soviet views.

35. Menon (1986) provides a comprehensive analysis.

36. This view is partly based on the logic of hegemonic theories (especially the power-transition theory of Organski and Kugler (1980); for an overview of these theo-

ries, see Levy 1991a; see also Nye 1990, pt. 1; some of these theories and their major arguments are cited in chap. 1). But see also other related views on this subject, underlying the crucial effects of relative and changing military capabilities on great power crisis behavior, cited in other sources such as Levy 1989c, 100; McConnell 1979, 243; Gaddis 1982, 214; and Jervis 1984, 130–31 and in chap. 3.

37. On the effects of the balance of interests on the balance of resolve in a bipolar world, see chap. 3.

38. A tactical defeat is short of a total military collapse and is without the latter's destabilizing domestic effects on the loser's political system. An important criterion for identifying a danger to the survival of a client regime is a military threat to its capital city.

39. Regarding the effects of the balance of capabilities, I advance below the argument that in contrast to the expectations of hegemonic theories, Soviet military inferiority could lead to more reckless behavior and to more destabilizing outcomes than a situation of rough parity (as was the case in subsequent crises).

40. In an interview with Wells (1979, 166), Dean Rusk, then secretary of state, recalls that he and President Johnson were extremely concerned about Israeli actions, which in their view gave the Soviets a legitimate reason for intervention.

41. See the citation above from Whetten 1981, 54. Fukuyama (1981, 594) also mentions this seriousness.

42. Rusk thought at the time that "if, as a result of Soviet action, Israel had begun to fare badly, . . . Sixth Fleet aircraft could be landed at Israeli airfields to deter an attack on Israel itself; but he could not conceive of employing the Fleet in any capacity beyond that. His feeling . . . was one of despair if the cease-fire had not held and the Israelis not halted when they did" (Wells 1979, 166).

43. See the declarations of the Syrian president, Attassi, on the "liberation of Palestine," cited in Neff 1988b, 54, 56.

44. Even if the Soviet report was deceptive, it might not have been a completely calculated deception. As the specialist for Middle East affairs of the National Security Council, Harold Saunders, pointed out in a memorandum, "an Israeli attack seemed imminent whenever one of these Fatah attacks spilled Israeli blood. In this sense, the Soviet advice to the Syrians that the Israelis were planning an attack was not far off, although they seem to have exaggerated the magnitude. The Israelis probably were planning an attack—but not an invasion" (cited in Neff 1988b, 59). A leading Israeli intelligence official wrote twenty years after the war that the reason for the exaggerated Soviet reports on the Israeli buildup was an intelligence failure by the Soviets and not a calculated political step to increase the probability of war. Such a step would have been contrary to their interests in that the Soviets were well aware of the bad shape of the Egyptian army, which was involved at that time in a civil war in Yemen. Moscow also knew that the Syrians were not ready for a war (see Ben-Porat 1987).

45. On Arab charges of the Soviets letting them down in the 1967 war, see Heikal 1978, 181–91; Whetten 1981, 55 n. 33; and Fukuyama 1981, 584.

46. Heikal, Nasser's confidant, reports (*Al-Ahram,* August 25, 1967) that when Boumedienne, the Algerian leader, visited Moscow after the June war and complained about Soviet restraint in the war, the Soviet leader answered, "What is your opinion of nuclear war?" Heikal is cited in Quandt 1976, 24, and in Betts 1987, 128.

47. While the fear of undesired escalation provided an incentive for cautious conduct by the superpowers, it was increased under bipolarity by the realization that an intervention by one of the superpowers in an important region would be likely to bring about a counterintervention by the rival superpower.

48. The Israeli prime minister, Golda Meir, stated, for example, that "We shall not go into mourning if Nassar falls, but our Air Force operations are not intended to achieve this purpose. But if it also brings about a change of government in Egypt, we shan't waste any tears over it, but it's not a political aim of ours, and I don't know if Nasser's successor will be any better than he is, but I don't think he can be much worse. And that also holds good for Egypt. He's the one who's wrecked his people and its land. His influence in the Arab world is a threat to peace" (*Davar,* January 16, 1970, cited in Bar-Siman-Tov 1980, 123).

49. These Egyptian accounts provide a rare glimpse into Soviet decision making with respect to military intervention. As Nasser's confident, Heikal, reports, the initial Soviet response to Nasser's request for air defense crews was negative: "Brezhnev said that this would be a step with serious international implications. It would provide all the markings of a crisis between the Soviet Union and the United States. . . . This will involve a considerable risk (he said), and I don't know if we are justified in taking it" (1975, 86). Only after Nasser's threat to resign, Brezhnev told Nasser that "the Soviet Union has today taken a decision fraught with grave consequences. It is a decision unlike any we have ever taken before. It will need your help in carrying out, and it will call for restraint on your part" (1975, 88).

50. This is a central theme in Whetten 1974 and 1981. Soviet escalation could also be seen as a reaction to exclusionary U.S. diplomacy since April, 1970 (see Breslauer 1983a, 82–83; see chap. 6).

51. Whetten argues, moreover, that "Nasser succumbed to Soviet pressure" (1981, 61). In Bar-Siman-Tov's analysis, "the Soviet intervention achieved its goals since the way was opened for ending the war and for renewed attempts to secure a political solution of the conflict . . ." (1980, 173), and the "Soviet intervention was mainly what brought an end to the war . . ." (1980, 172).

52. On Soviet diplomatic behavior and arms shipments from 1971 to 1973, see also chap. 6.

53. For useful analyses that substantiate this argument, see, e.g., Porter 1984, 116–25; Garthoff 1985, 362–68; and Karsh 1985, 39–40. Sadat claims that when the military option was discussed with the Soviets several months before the war, "the USSR persisted in the view that a military battle must be ruled out and that the question must await a peaceful conference" (Cairo Radio, April 4, 1974, cited in Porter 1984, 118 n. 4). Sadat revealed that on four occasions before the war, Brezhnev warned him not to attack Israel (Garthoff 1985, 363 n. 12).

54. Although both the sealift (some 85,000 tons of material) and the airlift (approximately 10,000–12,500 tons of military hardware) were considerable, the main goal of the resupply venture was to replace Arab losses on the battlefield (Porter 1984, 132–33) and to prevent an Israeli (and American) military victory (Garthoff 1985, 370 n. 38, and the sources he cites). Sadat argues that much of the hardware delivered to Egypt during the war was already promised as early as April, 1971. He was content

neither with the speed and scope of the shipments nor with the performance of Soviet arms (Sadat 1977, 221, 247, 259, 267, 292).

55. The fullest account of Soviet naval activities during the October War is Roberts 1979, 192–210.

56. See also Heikal 1975, 208–9, 212–17, and the useful analyses in Golan 1977, 75–77; Stein 1982; and Porter 1984, 126–27. The Soviets suspended their pressures for a cease-fire, however, after realizing that the Arabs were doing well on the battlefield. Not only could this better-than-expected Arab performance enhance the prestige of Soviet arms, but it reduced the chances of superpower confrontation, since the most likely avenue for such a scenario was a decisive Arab defeat. Indeed, Moscow renewed its pressures on Egypt to accept a cease-fire as soon as the tide of battle turned in Israel's favor and Cairo seemed to face a major loss (Garthoff 1985, 369–70).

57. Kosygin presented to Sadat satellite photographs flown in from the Soviet Union that showed the seriousness of the threat Israel posed because of its growing presence on the west bank of the canal.

58. Porter (1984, 137 n. 54) cites a *London Times* report that the Soviet ambassador to Damascus ordered a temporary halt to the air bridge, apart from ammunition; he sent a Soviet cargo ship away without unloading and threatened to send home the technicians helping at the SAM sites.

59. As Golan remarks, "the Brezhnev letter, which was in fact the step which triggered the American alert, did not contain a direct threat to Israel . . . but even couched its threat in careful, somewhat hedging, terms" (1977, 123).

60. On Kissinger's calculations, see his memoirs (1982, 571); Quandt 1977, 191, 194; Garthoff 1985, 383–85; and the analysis of Kissinger's strategy in chapter 6. On the Soviets' reasoning, see Golan 1977, 123–24, 128; Jabber and Kolkowicz 1981, 457; Quandt 1977, 191–92; and Garthoff 1985, 382–83.

61. For a careful analysis that underlines the political, rather than the military, significance of the Soviet military moves toward the end of the war, see Golan 1977, 122–28.

62. As Porter points out, although "the Soviet Union made cautious and calculated responses to U.S. actions throughout the conflict" and "there is every evidence to indicate that the Kremlin wanted to contain the conflict and to avoid an overt confrontation with Washington . . . this does not mean that Brezhnev's threat was mere posturing or propaganda. . . . Brezhnev's communications to the White House arrived while confrontation was still a possibility, and the USSR had the necessary forces in readiness to carry it out. It was a credible threat, adroitly employed as an instrument of diplomatic pressure" (1984, 140–41).

63. On the domestic sources of Israel's influence on U.S. Middle East policy, see chapter 4.

64. Karsh (1985, 38–39) reports that this Soviet pattern of a complete avoidance of actual engagement in war operations outside its ally's territory has repeated itself in all the wars its clients initiated during the 1970s and early 1980s, including the Egyptian-Syrian offensive against Israel in 1973, despite that the hostilities took place in occupied Egyptian and Syrian territories. The other examples he cites are the invasions by Syria in Lebanon (1976), South Yemen in North Yemen (1979), and Iraq in Iran (1980).

65. Quandt's (1978) explanation of Soviet behavior fits neatly with the argument made in this chapter; see especially Quandt 1978, 279–81.

66. Some Middle East specialists argue that the internal rivalry between the Jadid and Asad factions played an important role in the Syrian withdrawal; specifically, that General Asad denied air cover to the invading Syrian tanks because the adventure was planned by his rival, Jadid. Yet in explaining the Syrian pullback, U.S. and Jordanian officials gave priority first to the performance of the Jordanian army, then to the threat of Israeli and U.S. intervention, and finally to Soviet pressure (Quandt 1978, 284).

67. This is especially stressed by Quandt (1977 and 1978) and Hersh (1983, especially 243–46). See also Garthoff 1985, 86. For an excellent analysis of U.S. policymakers' perceptions of the global and regional elements of the crisis, see the detailed study by Dowty 1984, 111–98.

68. Even such a dovish analyst as Garthoff agrees that "the Soviets would probably have provided forces if necessary, at least to defend Cairo and Damascus" (1985, 383).

69. Sagan reports that it was estimated that the Soviets could transfer 5,000 airborne troops a day into Egypt (1985, 125). For a detailed discussion of Soviet interventionary forces according to type and size of units and their estimated delivery time to the Middle East, see Karsh 1985, chap. 4, 56–69.

70. There are some differences between various accounts of the types of threats Kissinger used vis-à-vis Israel: sending U.S. forces to resupply the Third Army, allowing the Russians to do it, or cutting off U.S. assistance. See Ben-Zvi 1988, 352–53; Dowty 1984, 272–73; Garthoff 1985, 385; Glassman 1975, 164–65; Jonsson 1984, 188; Quandt 1977, 198 n. 7; Spiegel 1985a, 265, and the references he cites in nn. 217 and 218; Whetten 1981, 75. For variations in Israeli accounts, see Dayan 1977, 552–53; but see also different versions of Dayan, cited in Quandt 1977, 198 n. 7, and in Glassman 1975, 164–65, and Eban 1977, 537. There is a consensus, however, that Kissinger threatened Israel. He made it clear that the United States would not allow Israel to destroy the Third Army and that there must be nonmilitary supply for that encircled army. Otherwise, the United States would join the other members of the Security Council in imposing those conditions (Kissinger 1982, 602–9). The president was even tougher. He paraphrased *The Godfather,* "We gave 'em an offer . . . that they . . . could not refuse" (cited in Spiegel 1985a, 265).

71. Even with the alert there were allegations of U.S. appeasement at the end of the war (cf. Glassman 1975, 164–65; Sicherman 1976). Betts has argued that the administration "was actually doing what Moscow wanted—squeezing the Israelis" (1987, 126).

72. On the supposedly adverse effects of stress on crisis decision making, see chapter 3.

73. Another interesting finding that shows the great sensitivity to the external environment in times of crises is that "the higher the stress in a crisis situation, the greater the tendency to rely upon extraordinary and improvised channels of communication [and information]" (Dowty 1984, 307).

74. For recent research that suggests that the Soviet threats were the critical factor in influencing the Israeli decision to withdraw from the Sinai, see Lorch 1990; see also Eban 1977 and the references cited in Mangold 1978, 134 n. 4. On the considerable

influence of these threats on the Europeans, see Holbraad 1979, 26, and the references he cites, and Betts 1987, 63, 65.

75. For a useful analysis of the superpowers and the Lebanese War, see Jentleson 1988.

76. For a short account of the fighting and of the Soviet engagement, see Karsh 1985, 85–86.

77. Alford (1982, 134–46) provides a short analysis of the military dimension of the superpower rivalry in the Middle East.

78. Bar-Joseph and Hannah (1988, 440–41) analyzed the military limitations on Soviet ability to defend by brute (conventional) force the regime of a Middle East ally. The main problem, they suggested, was the distance from Soviet frontiers. As a consequence, the Soviets would have needed at least two months to assemble in the region an armored or mechanized army (three divisions), the minimum level of forces necessary to successfully engage the Israeli army, and even that might not have been sufficient to overcome the Israelis. Thus, the main function of a military intervention, especially for the short-term Arab-Israeli wars, would have been political—to demonstrate commitment and to deter Israel from further advance.

79. On this point, see also the useful analysis by Karsh 1985.

80. Lebow (1981, 64–66) provides a short bibliography of analysts who make this claim. See also Lebow 1981, 280–81, especially n. 32.

81. The latter part of the proposition, however, is debatable. Holbraad (1979, 25–28) reviews the scholarly dispute about the credibility of the Soviet threats and how seriously they were perceived by Western governments. Still, he concludes that "whatever importance the Soviet moves may have had in comparison with other factors influencing the decision-making of the British and French governments at the height of the crisis, few writers have denied that these threats had some influence on the course of events" (1979, 26). Similarly, Chester Cooper, who was a CIA representative in the U.S. Embassy in London in 1956, argues that "some accounts well after the event imply that officials in London discounted the Soviet threat. But that is not the way I remember the reactions at the time. 'Nuclear blackmail' rather than 'diplomatic bluff' were the words I heard during the twenty-four hours following the announcement of Bulganin's message . . ." (cited in Betts 1987, 65).

82. This section draws on the works of a number of observers of the superpower involvement in the Middle East who have addressed the regularities of U.S.-Soviet interaction during Middle Eastern wars. See Evron 1979, 17–45; George 1984c, 1985, and 1986; George, with others, 1983, chap. 15; George, Farley, and Dallin 1988, 583–85; Holbraad 1979, chap. 5; Jonsson 1984, chap. 5; McConnell 1979; Saunders 1988, 540–80; Stein 1980; Whetten 1981.

The basic elements of the tacit rules also apply to postwar superpower interaction in other third world wars such as India-Pakistan (1971), Angola (1975), and Ethiopia-Somalia (1977). See Dismukes and McConnell 1979; George 1984c; George, Farley, and Dallin 1988, 581–99; Matheson 1982. On superpower involvement in these regional conflicts, see also Blechman and Kaplan 1978; Garthoff 1985; George, with others, 1983; Kaplan 1981; Porter 1984.

83. For other Middle Eastern examples, see above.

84. In a comprehensive study, Neuman (1988) shows that in contrast to the con-

ventional wisdom, the dependence of third world states on superpower arms transfers was growing, at least until the late 1980s, rather than declining. Such dependence is especially critical during periods of crisis and for resupply during wars (Neuman 1988, 1054). See also Krause 1991.

85. Ben-Porat was a high-ranking officer in the Israeli military intelligence. His article is based on classified research he did for Israeli intelligence in cooperation with Dr. Levita. The published article has only one major reference that supports Ben-Porat's assertion about the Soviet success in averting the Arab attack. The reference is to an interview granted by President Sadat to an Egyptian newspaper, in which Sadat said that he had intended to attack Israel in May, 1973, but the Soviets had scheduled the second summit with Nixon in Washington for that month and out of "political considerations there is no need to expose now, I decided to postpone the timing" of the attack to September or October. Although he lacks references to declassified sources, Ben-Porat presents an interesting, and plausible, argument that clients are less likely to initiate wars when their patron strongly resists the use of force (as was the case with the Soviets and the Arabs in May, 1973) than when the patron does not apply restraining pressures even if it still prefers the client to avoid a resort to force (as was the case in October, 1973).

86. On the Soviet inclination to intervene militarily only in areas peripheral to U.S. interests and where the danger of superpower confrontation was remote, see Menon 1986, especially 13–14.

87. Israel claimed that the attack was accidental, and the Johnson administration accepted this claim; but some Americans, including presumably Central Intelligence Agency officers, dispute this and argue that the attack was deliberate. See Neff 1988b, 253–66, 273–74, 355–56.

88. Although the Israeli cabinet had appended a string of tough conditions to its consent to President Reagan's demand to accede to a cease-fire (Schiff and Ya'ari 1984, 169–70), Secretary of State Haig succeeded in arranging a cessation of hostilities between Israeli and Syrian forces independent of the PLO. He reportedly conveyed a warning to Israel from the USSR about the dire consequences of further attacks on the Syrians (Spiegel 1985a, 415).

89. See the references on postwar diplomacy of force, cited in chapter 3. It might be instructive that in the first post–Cold War crisis—the 1990 Gulf Crisis—there was a much more serious consideration on the part of the United States of an actual use of large-scale military power than during the bipolar crises of the Cold War, and eventually conventional force was used on a massive scale during the Gulf War in early 1991.

90. For a useful account of the efforts to establish a cease-fire in these two wars, see Stein 1980 and 1982.

91. On such conceptions of cooperation, see chapter 1. The term *partisan mutual adjustment* is Lindblom's (1965). See also George, Farley, and Dallin 1988, 649–53.

92. Quandt refers here to Nixon's weakened authority in the 1973 crisis because of Watergate.

93. Dowty's (1984, 313) research shows that even the widely assumed case of the influence of bureaucratic politics during the initial stage of the October War—the delay in the airlift to Israel—accords well with a unitary actor model. See also the essentially similar conclusion in Quandt 1977, 178–86, and Safran 1981, 481–83.

94. This conception could also apply to Soviet crisis decision making as evidenced from its behavior, although empirical research has yet to substantiate this claim.

95. Indeed, on a more general level, researchers in a number of disciplines have found that a mix of resolve and restraint, and more specifically, of initial firmness and a later switch to a more conciliatory approach, are effective in securing cooperation from an opponent. This is one of the major conclusions in a comprehensive study of international conflicts from the perspective of general social processes. This study also reviews a large body of literature in relevant fields. See Patchen 1988, 277–78, 291, 336. For a similar observation derived more specifically from international politics, see Snyder and Diesing 1977, 100; see also chap. 3.

96. On the distinction between types and levels of cooperation and learning and their relations with causal factors at different levels of analysis, see chaps. 1 and 2.

## Chapter 6

1. For a more elaborate description of these events than can be given in this book, see the following sources: Aronson 1978; Atherton 1985; Ben-Zvi 1986 and 1990; George, with others, 1983, Quandt 1977, 1986a, and 1988; Safran 1981; Saunders 1988; Spiegel 1985a and 1992; Spiegel, Heller, and Goldberg 1988; Whetten 1974 and 1981; Zak 1986. Sources that focus on Soviet Middle East behavior include Glassman 1975, Golan 1977 and 1990a; Rubinstein 1977; Freedman 1978 and 1988; Breslauer 1983a, 1985, and 1990; Roi 1974, 1979, and 1980; Zak 1988; and Slater 1990–91. Also useful are the memoirs of the relevant American, Egyptian, and Israeli policymakers. See Carter 1982 and 1985 (the latter focuses on the Middle East), Ford 1979; Nixon 1978; Johnson 1971; Brzezinski 1983; Kissinger 1979 and 1982; Vance 1983; Haig 1984; Sadat 1977; Riad 1981; Fahmy 1983; Heikal 1975 and 1978; Meir 1975; Rabin 1979; Eban 1977; and Dayan 1977.

2. See the writings of the following Carter administration officials: Vance (1983, 164, 166), Brzezinski (1983, 86–87), Atherton (1985, 704–5), Quandt (1986a, 39–40), and Saunders (1988, 568–69).

3. For a brief summary, see Quandt 1988, 373. For the full text of the agreement, see appendix G in Quandt 1988, 475–76. See also Ben-Zvi 1990.

4. The text is in Quandt 1988, appendix K, 488–89. See also Ben-Zvi 1990.

5. In the last section of this chapter, I refer to the more recent changes in U.S. and Soviet attitudes toward concerted diplomacy in the Middle East. See also Rabinovich 1990.

6. Breslauer (1983a, 99, n. 1) and Slater (1990–91, 560 n. 5) list the proponents of this viewpoint. See also Nixon 1978, 482–83, and, to a lesser extent, Atherton 1985.

7. This is, of course, a common position among Arab practitioners and scholars. More recently, some Israeli leftists also began to express such views, in particular with respect to the Reagan administration policy in the Middle East. There were rumors in the press that in private talks, even more mainstream Israeli officials tended to voice somewhat similar concerns.

8. In its extreme version, this position was shared by a minority of American (Ball 1976 and Senator Fullbright have been the most vocal) or Zionist (the late Nahum

Goldmann and, less forcefully, Arthur Hertzberg) public figures. This was also, of course, the standard Soviet position (cf. Primakov 1986 and 1988).

9. On Arab opposition in June, 1969, see Heikal 1978, 193–96, and Riad 1981, 112. Kissinger (1979, 378) relates the Soviet rejection of the Rogers Plan to Arab intransigence.

10. But see also more moderate interpretations of the pre-1973 Soviet behavior, cited in chap. 5 and below.

11. Especially with respect to the question of withdrawal from occupied territories (Quandt 1977, 91).

12. On Nixon's ambivalent position toward the Rogers Plan, see also Nixon 1978, 592–93; Hersh 1983, 220–21; and Spiegel 1985a 187–88.

13. As Kissinger suggests, "this set in motion a cycle in which every negotiating step of which Israel disapproved was coupled with a step-up of Israeli assistance programs without achieving a real meeting of minds with Israel" (1979, 377).

14. For a first-hand testimony of an insider, see the memoirs of the then-Egyptian foreign minister, Fahmy (1983). See also the relevant chapters in Kissinger's memoirs (1982, chaps. 17, 18, 21, 23) and the memoirs of a former Egyptian foreign minister and later secretary general of the Arab League, Riad (1981, 266–98). For useful analyses of Kissinger's shuttle diplomacy, see Quandt 1977, chap. 7; Safran 1981, 506–60; Spiegel 1985a, 267–314; Atherton 1985, 699–704; and Saunders 1988, 564–68. Quandt, Atherton, and Saunders were participants on the American side.

15. The most important study of this period is by an insider who was in charge of the Middle East in the National Security Council during the Carter administration. See Quandt 1986a. For an analysis of the Camp David negotiations, see Telhami 1990.

16. The exclusionary policy was unplanned at least in the eyes of some high-level officials of the Carter administration. The divisions of opinion within the Nixon and Carter administrations are discussed below.

17. For brief analyses of the strategic-consensus strategy, see Jentleson 1988, 322–24; Ben-Zvi 1986, 11–19; Saunders 1988, 571; and Quandt 1988, 361–63. On Haig's opinions, see his memoirs (1984). On Reagan's Middle East policy in the first term of the administration, see Novik 1985.

18. For the Soviet view, see Primakov 1988, 391–93. See also Ben-Zvi 1990, 96; Kissinger 1982, 940–43, 1022; Quandt 1977, 261. For a succinct summary, see Zak 1986, 85–92, who draws, among other sources, on the memoirs of American (Kissinger, Nixon, and Ford) and Egyptian (Fahmy) policymakers. For an analysis by a Soviet specialist, see Freedman 1978.

19. See Brezhnev's peace plan of February 23, 1981 (*Izvestia,* February 24, 1981), and Primakov 1988, 394–400. See also Ben-Zvi 1986, 58; and 1990, 96–97; Carter 1982, 223–24; Freedman 1978, 320–23; Garthoff 1985, 582; Zak 1986, 99–101.

20. The diplomatic climax was the signing of a Treaty of Friendship and Cooperation between Moscow and Damascus in October, 1980.

21. The king told an American journalist that during a visit to Moscow in December, 1982, Secretary-General Yuri Andropov had warned him, "I shall oppose the Reagan plan, and we will use all our resources to oppose it. With due respect, all the weight will be on your shoulders, and they aren't broad enough to bear it" (see Karen

Elliot House, "Hussein's Decision," *Wall Street Journal,* April 14, 1983, and April 15, 1983, cited also in Quandt 1988, 367 n. 13).

22. But not all the Egyptian officials: there were divisions of opinion even between Sadat and his foreign ministry with regard to the acceptance of a U.S. monopoly over the peace process (Fahmy 1983; see also Riad 1981, 299–340), let alone between Sadat and the Egyptian opposition, which rejected outright the closely related notions of a separate peace with Israel and an exclusive American brokerage.

23. One could argue that the separate peace treaty with Egypt made it much easier for Defense Minister Sharon to push for the Peace for Galilee operation than would have been the case in the absence of peace with the most powerful Arab state, which would have, in turn, increased the danger of a two-front war. Thus, an unintended effect (on the part of the Carter administration) of the U.S.-led separate peace on Israel's southern front was a dangerous escalation on its northern front.

24. The most recent changes in the positions of the local parties and the superpowers have been much more forthcoming regarding superpower collaboration; see below.

25. For a comprehensive analysis of superpower cooperation in regional conflict management during the Cold War, see Kanet and Kolodziej 1991.

26. With respect to the State Department in the first Nixon administration (the leading officials in charge of Middle Eastern affairs were Rogers and Sisco), the deviations leading to unilateral steps refer to Sisco's trip to Cairo in April, 1970, and later to the diplomatic initiatives in 1970 and 1971, dubbed Rogers II, III, and IV. On these plans, see Quandt 1977, chaps. 3 and 5; Safran 1981, 431–63; and Spiegel 1985a, chap. 6. The Carter-Vance deviation alludes to the Camp David process (1978 and 1979). The most comprehensive treatment of this process is Quandt 1986a. See also Saunders 1988, 568–70; Spiegel 1985a, chap. 8.

27. As I concluded in the chapter on crisis cooperation, the United States has not been the hegemon in the Middle East in the military-strategic sense, at least since the mid- to late-1960s and until the decline of the Soviet Union as a superpower in 1990 through 1991.

28. For such conceptions of *hegemony* and *leadership,* see Keohane and Nye 1977; Keohane 1984, 34–46; and Nye 1990.

29. The financial resources have been spent through foreign aid to those Middle Eastern states that cooperate in the U.S.-led peace process. Thus, following the step-by-step agreements, and later the Camp David accords between Egypt and Israel, these two states top, by far, the list of recipients of U.S. foreign assistance.

30. For an in-depth analysis of U.S. advantages in most power resources vis-à-vis the Soviet Union, see Nye 1990.

31. Another U.S. advantage is the relatively low American dependence on Middle East oil (as compared to Japan and Western Europe, for example). Such low dependence and vulnerability should make it easier for Washington to pursue flexible diplomacy and to play the honest broker in the Middle East.

32. The analysis here is based on the relevant Middle Eastern chapters in his memoirs (1979, chaps. 10, 14, 15, 28, 30, and 1982, chaps. 6, 11, 12, 13, 17, 18, 21, 23, 24; see especially 1979, 376, 379, 1247–48, 1279, 1285–90, 1292–96, 1300, and 1982, 196, 201–2) as well as the interpretations found in Quandt 1977, chaps. 3, 5; George,

with others, 1983, chap. 7; Garthoff 1985; Spiegel 1985a, chaps. 6, 7; Atherton 1985, 688–715; Ben-Zvi 1986; Saunders 1988; and Zak 1986. I also draw on interviews I held with U.S. officials who were involved in Middle East diplomacy.

33. For a cognitive explanation of Kissinger's position, see below.

34. As opposed to Kissinger's grand design, whose chief aim was to exclude the Soviets from the region even if that meant diplomatic stalemate (at least temporarily), the State Department focused on pragmatic ways to advance a regional reconciliation. Such practical tactics could include or exclude the Soviets, depending on regional circumstances. In contrast, Kissinger focused on the global rivalry and how the United States could best maximize its comparative advantages, such as those in the Middle East, in the context of this rivalry. Thus, the regional peace process was in Kissinger's strategy a means in the global competition, whereas it was a goal for its own sake in the State Department's policy. See also below on the explanation of these differences between the State Department and Kissinger.

35. Israel, as Kissinger realized very well, also commanded a good deal of domestic support in the United States; thus, premature pressure on Israel could backfire.

36. Another motive of Kissinger in frustrating the State Department's initiatives, however, was related to bureaucratic politics: to shift the control of U.S. Middle East policy to the National Security Council, which was under his leadership.

37. The effect of the U.S.-Soviet summits on the expulsion of the Soviet advisors and on the decision to go to war in 1973 is also discussed below.

38. Nevertheless, an unintended effect of the diplomatic stalemate was the outbreak of the 1973 war. The resort to force by the Arabs (especially Egypt) can be accounted for by their growing frustration at the lack of diplomatic momentum, notably expressed in the statements of the May, 1972, and June, 1973, superpower summits. Thus, Kissinger's efforts not only brought about the expulsion of the Soviet advisors from Egypt but also contributed to the eruption of an all-out regional war with all its dangers to world peace arising from the superpower confrontation at the end of the conflict (one of the consequences of the October War was also the oil embargo and the quadrupling of energy prices with its destabilizing effects on the world economy). Moreover, precisely because of the expulsion of their advisors, the Soviets became much more willing to accommodate Arab demands for arms delivery than they had been before; and these arms shipments, in turn, made it easier for Egypt and Syria to initiate the 1973 war.

39. Such progress may even confirm Kissinger's anticipations in the period preceding the 1973 war. But the outbreak of the war itself shows that the hegemon was either unwilling or unable to mobilize the necessary resources to stabilize the region or was more interested in playing power politics than in serious work to advance the cause of peace.

40. Useful analyses of these U.S. accomplishments in peacemaking are Quandt 1977 and 1986a, Aronson 1978, Safran 1981, Touval 1982, Spiegel 1985a, Atherton 1985, Ben-Zvi 1986, and Saunders 1988.

41. For Kissinger's account of Sadat's preference for American brokerage, see his memoirs (1982, chaps. 13, 18). Kissinger refers there to Assad's readiness to accept U.S. mediation (1982, chaps. 21, 23). On the regional actors' preference for U.S.

exclusionary diplomacy, see also Smolansky 1978, 100–101; Ben-Zvi 1986, 39–41; and Zak 1986, chap. 5.

42. On the Soviet conception of equality during the détente era, see also Blacker 1983, 119–37. The Soviet proclivity for declarative, political, and formal symbols that indicate a recognition of superpower parity is also discussed in Dallin 1988, 610.

43. The privileges of the permanent members of the UN Security Council are the postwar formal expression of such great power rights and responsibilities for international peace and security. On the Soviet desire for formal recognition of its superpower status and preference for formal international agreements, see also Golan 1979; Gowa and Wessell 1982, 2, 14; and Breslauer 1990.

44. This is the major theme of a book by a veteran Israeli journalist, Zak (1986; see also 1988). Zak argues that the common denominator of all Soviet steps in the Middle East since 1945 has been the struggle to reach a recognized partnership with the United States in the region. He documents the validity of this assertion in the different stages of Soviet involvement in the Arab-Israeli conflict.

45. These activities included, mainly, the so-called conciliation committee and the observation of the cease-fire agreements between Israel and its neighbors following the 1948 war. For a brief summary, see Zak 1986, 26–28. Because of U.S. domination of the UN and the subsequent denial of a role for the Soviets in its Middle East activities, Moscow supported in 1948 to 1950 the Israeli position advocating direct bilateral talks with the Arabs (Touval 1987, 45; Zak 1988, 369–70).

46. The authors of this statement (issued on May 25, 1950)—the United States, Britain, and France—called for the maintenance of the status quo and the military balance in the Middle East. See Hurevitz 1956, 2:308–11; Kirk 1954, 312–13.

47. An expression of such an idea (this time in the form of Soviet guarantees for Israel's security and independence) was made by Gorbachev in his meeting with congressional leaders during his June 1990 summit with President Bush (*Haaretz*, June 3, 1990).

48. This position seems to be one major manifestation of the general Soviet aim to be recognized as an equal superpower by playing a leading role in multilateral frameworks in different regions, notably in connection with the Conference on Security and Cooperation in Europe.

49. On the evolution of the Soviet position concerning the framework for Arab-Israeli negotiations, see Touval 1987, 45–46. For a detailed account of the Soviet view of an international conference, see Ben-Zvi 1990, 92–104.

50. Arkady Sovlov (a Soviet diplomat who served as a deputy secretary general of the UN) talked with Moshe Sharett (the man in charge of foreign affairs in the Jewish Agency) on the participation of two squadrons of Soviet bombers in an international force if such a force would be required for the enforcement of the resolution. This incident is mentioned in Ben-Gurion 1982, 86–87. Whereas the UN secretary general expressed his support for a superpower force (Ben-Gurion 1982, 239), the United States opposed such a force precisely because it required Soviet participation (Ben-Gurion 1982, 238).

51. On the Soviet proposal in the Suez crisis, see the memoirs of the then U.S. ambassador to Moscow, Bohlen (1973, 432). On Eisenhower's total rejection, see his memoirs (1965, 89–90) and Neff 1981, 403. The 1973 offer is mentioned in chapter 5.

52. For a discussion of the connection between the Soviet desire for a recognized equal status with the United States and its participation in the settlement of international problems, especially in the Middle East peace process during the détente era, see George, Farley, and Dallin 1988, 588–89, who draw on the work of Blacker (1983, 119–37).

53. On the nature of the Arab-Israeli conflict and ways to manage it, see articles in the volumes edited by Ben-Dor and Dewitt (1987) and Spiegel (1992).

54. See the sources cited in Breslauer 1983a, 99 n. 2, which refer especially to the 1967-72 period, and in Jonsson 1984, chap. 5. A similarly qualified conclusion is also reached by other scholars such as Golan (1977 and 1979); Garthoff (1985, especially 87); Herrmann (1987); Mangold (1978, 115–41); Tilman (1982, chap. 6, especially 251–53); George, with others (1983); George, Farley, and Dallin (1988); Karsh (1985, 39–40); MacFarlane (1985, 1987a, and 1987b); and Slater (1990–91); for corroboration, see especially the memoirs of Egyptian practitioners; President Sadat (1977, especially 228–29), and foreign ministers Riad (1981) and Fahmy (1983), and Nasser's confidant, Heikal (1975 and 1978) but also the work of a leading State Department Middle East specialist (Saunders 1988).

55. On these deliveries and possible motivations, see chapter 5 and below.

56. At the same time, Kissinger acknowledges not only that "we were not willing to pay for détente in the coin of our geopolitical position" (1982, 299) but also that "to some extent my interest in détente was tactical, as a device to maximize Soviet dilemmas and reduce Soviet influence . . . in the Middle East" (1979, 1255).

57. On pre-October, 1973, Soviet warnings to the United States about the danger of war in the Middle East if no settlement was achieved (through U.S.-Soviet cooperation), see George, with others, 1983, 145–48; George, Farley, and Dallin 1988, 589–90; Karsh 1985, 40; Garthoff 1985, 364–66; Ben-Porat 1985; and Zak 1986, 71, 74. I was also told about Brezhnev's warnings in an interview with an American official involved in U.S. Middle East diplomacy in that period.

58. The only major American concession also concerned the phrase *legitimate rights* of the Palestinians; Washington had previously used the term *national interests* (see Quandt 1986a, 120). Yet as we see below, despite all these Soviet concessions, the joint document triggered strong domestic opposition in the United States.

59. An additional explanation of the Soviet obsession with being recognized and treated as an equal might be related to the traditional Russian inferiority feelings toward the more technologically developed West.

60. Indeed, during the 1980s, there was a growing recognition in the Soviet elite that the competitive Soviet conduct of the mid- to late-1970s in parts of the Third World undermined the support for détente among the U.S. public (Breslauer 1990; George, Farley, and Dallin 1988, 597; MacFarlane 1985).

61. On the Soviet desire for an arrangement approaching a condominium with the United States in the postwar era, see chapter 4. According to Nixon (1978, 2:430) and Kissinger (1982, 583), the Middle East was one of the major areas in which the Soviets wanted to establish a superpower condominium based on an imposed peace.

62. The Soviets tried to legitimize the special role of the superpowers by arguing that "from the economic and military viewpoints, from the viewpoint of political influence, the U.S. and the Soviet Union are the two most powerful countries in the world. As

a consequence, they carry a special responsibility for world peace. Inherent in that responsibility is the obligation to apply our influence toward the resolution of regional conflicts, and in particular that of the Middle East" (Alexey Podtserob, counselor for Middle East Affairs at the Permanent Mission of the Soviet Union to the United Nations, reported in *Moscow Tass* [English], June 4, 1985, cited in Ben-Zvi 1990, 98).

63. For such a testimony, see, e.g., Heikal's (1978, 186–87) report that immediately after the Six-Day War, the Soviets started pressuring the Arabs to reach a settlement with Israel even if it required some form of diplomatic acceptance of the Jewish state. See also Whetten 1974, 46–47. Heikal (1978, 30) writes also about Soviet restraining pressures on Nasser in 1968 when he suggested a renewal of the military option against Israel. Sadat (see the citations in Golan 1977, 47–55; in Spechler 1986, 438n. 10; and in chap. 5) reports about Soviet pressures and their preference for a diplomatic solution in the months preceding the 1973 war. On the differences between the diplomatic positions of the Soviets and the Arabs, cf. Heikal 1978, 195.

64. At the same time, the intransigence of Arab radicals, and inter-Arab rivalries also affected the peace process. Thus, the absence of moderation on the part of the PLO, and even more so on the part of the Syrians, as well as the Syrian-Egyptian antagonism, also played an important role in Sadat's decision to abandon Geneva, at least for a while, in favor of Jerusalem (see Indyk 1984, 44–50; Quandt 1986a, 131–46, especially 146 n. 12). Some observers have claimed that Sadat was so worried about Soviet participation that his decision to go to Israel (or at least its timing) was actually triggered by the U.S.-Soviet joint statement a month earlier. Sadat, according to this view, decided to subvert the American diplomacy of cooperation with the Soviets by negotiating directly with Israel (cf. Ben-Zvi 1986, 56). Yet there is substantial evidence that counters this claim (see Brzezinski 1983, 110; Fahmy 1983, 234–36; Garthoff 1985, 581; Quandt 1986a, 123, 124–25, 131; Saunders 1988, 569; Tillman 1982, 237–38; Vance 1983, 192.

65. However, as noted above, the Soviets backed off from their support of the plan in December, 1969, although in this case this should be attributed to the Soviet refusal to press their allies—the Egyptians—when they were in a poor military situation (Breslauer 1983a, 86–87; MacFarlane 1987a; Whetten 1974, 82). The Soviet retrogression cannot be explained by domestic opposition, at least not opposition from outside the elite.

66. As noted, however, in the absence of a countervailing force, democratic powers have also abused their superior power in their spheres of influence, including coercive conduct by the United States in Central America. But relatively speaking, they tend to be somewhat less coercive than authoritarian powers, especially vis-à-vis other democracies.

67. That particular division of opinion was especially notable from 1969 to 1971 concerning the strategy of conflict resolution in the Middle East (see Atherton 1985, 694–95; Hersh 1983, 213–33; Kissinger 1979, chap. 10; Quandt 1977, chap. 3; Saunders 1988, 554–59; Spiegel 1985a, chap. 6).

68. See especially the memoirs of Carter's secretary of state, Vance (1983, chap. 9). For analyses, see Spiegel 1985a, chap. 8; Atherton 1985, 704–5; Quandt 1986a, chaps. 3–5; Ben-Zvi 1986, chap. 3; and Saunders 1988, 568–70.

69. Under the circumstances of normal diplomacy, bureaucratic political struggles (such as those between Kissinger and the State Department when it was under the

leadership of Secretary Rogers) could affect U.S. policymaking more than in crisis situations, particularly once the issue at stake had a low priority, as the Middle East did on the U.S. foreign policy agenda in the years preceding the 1973 war (because of higher priority issues such as the Vietnam War, détente with Moscow, and rapprochement with Peking (see Saunders 1988, 555) as well as due to Kissinger's strategy of creating a stalemate.

70. More generally about Soviet policy toward the United States, Griffiths argued that "there is an array of conflicting tendencies in the behavior of the Soviet system towards the U.S." . . . This can be explained by "stated Soviet perceptions of American foreign and military policymaking" (1984, 5). For a more recent discussion of the effects of the image of the opponent on U.S.-Soviet security cooperation, see George, Farley, and Dallin 1988, 658–61.

71. Spechler adds that "the holders of this image perceived the prevention of a military confrontation with the U.S. as the most acute problem facing the Soviet Union. . . . They did not want events in the Middle East (or in any other region) to cause or deepen mistrust and hostility between the U.S. and the U.S.S.R. The superpowers should come to an agreement specifying the activities permitted to each" (1986, 448).

72. The classic work on Dulles's enemy image of the Soviet Union is O. Holsti 1967. On the similarity between the views of Dulles and Reagan, see Ben-Zvi 1986, 15. On Eisenhower's and Dulles's world views and their application to the Middle East, see Spiegel 1985a, chap. 3. On the West's rejection of the Soviet calls for joint diplomacy or for mutual disengagement, led by the Eisenhower administration, see Roi 1974, 216, cited in Zak 1986, 46–48; Heikal 1978, 77; and Slater 1990–91, 564–65.

73. This episode is recounted by one of the Israeli participants in this meeting, Yaccov Herzog. See his book in Hebrew (1975, 83). The Kennedy administration, still in a basically Cold War mood, also rejected a related proposal by Ben-Gurion—this time for superpower coguarantees for the territorial integrity of all Middle Eastern countries (see Gazit 1983, 120–23).

74. At one point during his presidential campaign, Reagan was quoted as saying, "Let's not delude ourselves. The Soviet Union underlies all the unrest that is going on. If they weren't engaged in this game of dominoes, there wouldn't be any hot spots in the world" (from an interview with Karen Elliott House, "Reagan's World," *Wall Street Journal*, June 3, 1980, cited in Quandt 1988, 362). On Reagan's philosophy and its application to the Middle East, see Spiegel 1985a, chap. 10; Ben-Zvi 1990, 72–91; Lenczowski 1990, chap. 8. However, as I note below, changes in the local actors' attitudes toward the inclusion of the Soviets in the peace process and, more importantly, changes in Washington with respect to the perception of the Soviet leadership, following Gorbachev's domestic reforms and arms control offers, brought about a greater U.S. readiness to include the Soviets in Middle East diplomacy.

75. On the deemphasis of the Soviet threat by the Carter administration and the more benign interpretation of the Soviets and their proxies as compared to preceding administrations, see Spiegel 1985a, chap. 8, especially 318–23. Even the most hawkish and anti-Soviet member of the administration, National Security Adviser Brzezinski, "argued that we should move away from what I considered our excessive preoccupation with the U.S.-Soviet relationship. . . . Instead, I felt that the United States should address itself to a variety of Third World problems, either on its own or through trilateral

cooperation with Western Europe and Japan. The Soviet Union should be included in that cooperation whenever it was willing but should not be made the focal point of American interest to the detriment of the rest of the global agenda" (1983, 148–49).

76. Whereas the Eisenhower and Reagan administrations behaved more cautiously in crises than what their rhetoric and ideology would lead us to expect, the Carter administration behaved more resolutely during a crisis (such as the 1979 Soviet invasion of Afghanistan) than its initial rhetoric and beliefs may have indicated. On the hawkish effects of the Soviet invasion of Afghanistan on the administration, see Gaddis 1982, 348; Brzezinski 1983, 429; Garthoff 1985, 946; Betts 1987, 129–31. Hence, crises can push leaders to either more resolute or more cautious behavior than they initially intended, whereas there is a closer reflection of leaders' beliefs in normal diplomacy (especially, in the initial stage of an administration).

77. On his view of the Soviets, see Brzezinski 1980 and his memoirs (1983). In contrast, see the more benign image of the Soviets held by Vance's adviser on Soviet affairs, Shulman (e.g., 1980 and 1986). The differences between Brzezinski and Vance regarding collaboration with the Soviets in the Middle East are described in Quandt 1986a, 38–40, 61–62. See Smith 1986, 35–40 for a succinct account of their different world views in general. Whereas Vance's (1983, chap. 9) memoirs explain why he pursued collaboration with the Soviets in the Middle East, Brzezinski (1983, 107–10, 113) discusses the abandoning of the joint approach and argues that Washington should have been more cautious about bringing the Soviets into Middle East diplomacy. See, on this point, Garthoff 1985, 582–83.

78. On Kissinger's globalist approach, see George, with others, 1983, 388; Hoffmann 1980 and 1984; and Garthoff 1985, 674. For application to the Middle East, see Dowty 1984; Spiegel 1985a, chaps. 6, 7; and Ben-Zvi 1986, especially 19–20. On Kissinger's—and Brzezinski's—belief in U.S. hegemony, see Breslauer 1983b, 334. On Kissinger's belief in bandwagoning, see Walt 1987, 20, and the source he cites; George, with others, 1983, 387; and Hoffmann 1984, 242, 244. As a Nixon administration official indicated to me, there were moments in which Kissinger suspected that such a Pax Americana would not last more than ten years—but in the Middle East, ten years are a lot (interviews in Washington, D.C., April, 1986).

79. On the State Department's views during the first Nixon administration, see Quandt 1977, chap. 3; Kissinger 1979, chap. 10; Spiegel 1985a, chap. 6; Atherton 1985; and Saunders 1988. On the Carter administration's regionalist approach, see the references in chapter 4 and also George, with others, 1983, 388; and George 1984c, 151. As Secretary Vance put it when the administration came to office: "A flaw in our foreign policy . . . was that it was too narrowly rooted in the concept of an overarching U.S.-Soviet 'geopolitical' struggle. . . . But our national interests encompassed more than U.S.-Soviet relations. New crises unrelated to competition with the Soviet Union had and would occur around the globe with increasing frequency. . . . Many developments did not fit neatly into an East-West context . . . it had become essential for the United States to grapple with the North-South issues. . . . Global interdependence . . . had become a reality" (1983, 27). Vance also reports in his memoirs that "I advised President Carter in November of 1976 that as a practical matter the Soviet Union, with political interests in the region and as a patron of several Arab states, should be accorded a role in negotiations that would help to dissuade it from undermining our efforts"

(1983, 164). Similarly, during the presidential election campaign, Carter argued that "the Soviet Union is going to have to participate in a forceful way before Syria will be amenable to any productive negotiations with Israel" (cited in Ben-Zvi 1986, 51). The administration's views of the Soviet role in the Middle East are presented in Indyk 1984, 19–21; Atherton 1985, 704–5; Spiegel 1985a, chap. 8; Ben-Zvi 1986, chap. 3; Quandt 1986a, chaps. 3, 5, 6; Saunders 1988; and the memoirs of the administration's three major foreign policymakers: Carter (1982), Brzezinski (1983), and Vance (1983).

80. On Kissinger's "mitigated hard-line" view of Moscow, cf. Ben-Zvi 1986, 19–25. For a content analysis of Kissinger's image of the Soviets, see Starr 1984, chaps. 6, 7. Kissinger refers to his fairly hard-line approach to the Soviets in his memoirs (1979, 347, 351, 1256, and 1982, 239, 242, 245, 1034). Regarding the general approach of the administration, he reports that "Nixon's formal statements never failed to stress the competitiveness between the Soviet and American systems and the profound ideological gulf intensifying the rivalry" (1979, 1255–56), and about Nixon himself that "he was, in short, the classic Cold Warrior" (1982, 236).

81. The great sensitivity that Kissinger showed toward Soviet concerns throughout the crisis was highlighted to me in an interview (April, 1986) with a Nixon administration official who served on the National Security Council in that period.

82. On the more benign view of the Soviets by Kissinger as opposed to Dulles, see the detailed comparative content analysis by Starr (1984, chap. 6). Drawing on a common categorization of American images of the Soviet Union during the Cold War, one could label Dulles, Haig, and Reagan as pure hard-liners; Vance, and to a lesser extent Carter and Rogers, represent the mitigated soft-line view; Kissinger, Nixon, Brzezinski, and Shultz approximate the mitigated hard-line position. In terms of preferred strategies, these three categories parallel confrontation, multilateralism, and competition, respectively.

83. Kissinger's symbolic responsiveness to the Soviets was also raised in the interview mentioned in note 81. On the persistent U.S. objection to any Soviet participation in Middle East diplomacy from the Truman to the Kennedy administrations despite the keen Soviet interest in such a role, see Zak 1986, chaps. 1, 2.

84. For similar observations about the apparent contradiction between Kissinger's conciliatory rhetoric and sensitivity to symbols versus his actual exclusionary behavior vis-à-vis the Soviets (especially the rapid transition from Geneva to unilateral step-by-step diplomacy in 1974), see Quandt 1977, 213; Fahmy 1983; Breslauer 1983b, 327; George, with others, 1983, chap. 7, especially 149; Hoffmann 1984, 242–43; Zak 1986, 85–87; and Saunders 1988, 562, 564. As noted above, the conciliatory track of Kissinger's policy was designed to facilitate the achievement of his exclusionary objectives by giving the Soviets a sense of participation and thus presumably reducing their incentives to spoil Kissinger's strategy. Hence, his strategy was a continuation of the Cold War's goals through different, and more sophisticated, means.

85. On this point, see chapter 4. For a discussion, see Stewart, Hermann, and Hermann 1989, especially 44–45.

86. An additional case of closure to new information is Nixon's and Kissinger's response to Soviet warnings in the 1973 summit.

87. When there is a single major leader who exclusively dominates the foreign policymaking process, that leader's subjective beliefs alone can determine the course of

the state's normal diplomacy. But if two or more powerful individuals (and departments) are involved in the process, as is more often the case in noncrisis periods, the different orientations among them can lead to the internal bargaining known as bureaucratic politics. On this point, see Snyder and Diesing 1977, 355–61, and Stewart, Hermann, and Hermann 1989, 49–51. Changes in the political power of a coalition that holds a certain image relative to a competing coalition is likely to lead to changes in foreign policy. Thus, it could plausibly be argued, for example, that by 1971, Kissinger's views became U.S. Middle East policy because he had more resources in the bureaucratic political game than Rogers. Yet dramatic external inputs can also influence who wins the foreign policy debate. Such dramatic events as the expulsion of the Soviet advisors from Egypt or Sadat's trip to Jerusalem had major impacts on the internal debates within the Soviet and the U.S. foreign policy elites, respectively.

88. On Kissinger's obstruction of the State Department's initiatives in the Arab-Israeli peace process, including the attempts at collaboration with the Soviets, see Hersh 1983, 213, 217, 220, 226–28; Rabin 1979, 120–21; and Spiegel 1985a, 185.

89. Indeed, although Israel and its U.S. friends vehemently rejected the joint statement, even the right-wing Likud government in Israel did support during 1977 the reconvening of the Geneva Conference. Less than a year later, moreover, the same hardline Israeli government that had criticized the U.S.-Soviet statement essentially agreed to the same formulation of the solution to the Palestinian problem by accepting the Camp David accords, which suggest, like the 1977 statement, that "the solution from the negotiations must also recognize the legitimate rights of the Palestinian people and their just requirements." For the text of the Camp David Accords, see Quandt 1986a, appendix G, 376–87.

90. For a discussion of the adverse effects of ideology on U.S.-Soviet security cooperation, see George, Farley, and Dallin 1988, 658–61. See also Mandelbaum 1988, 29.

91. For a statement, see Betts 1987, 134–44. Whereas Betts argues that such disagreements have reduced the utility of the balance of interests as a determinant of crisis outcomes, I differentiate between the adverse effects of these ideological differences in normal or precrisis times and the spontaneous superpower cooperation in reaching tacit understandings on these issues during crisis periods because of the restraining and clarifying influence of systemic factors (bipolarity) in these periods.

92. The point about growing collaboration should not deny, as is discussed in the conclusions to this chapter, that the United States, reflecting its greater power resources in the Middle East, played a more active and important role than the Soviets in the peace process in 1988 through 1990, and especially in the aftermath of the Gulf War.

93. For a Soviet perspective on the new thinking in regional contexts, see Kremenyuk 1991 and Mirski 1990. For analyses of the changes in Soviet foreign and defense policies under Gorbachev, see the volume edited by Bialer and Mandelbaum (1988), their coauthored book (1989), and chapters in Breslauer 1990.

94. The reasoning behind the new thinking in regional contexts is discussed in the concluding chapter.

95. For a Soviet perspective, see Primakov 1988. I also draw in this section on interviews I held with Middle East observers and State Department officials in Washington, D.C. in April, 1990.

96. As Foreign Minister Shevardnadze bluntly put it, "without the Soviet Union, there can be no peace process" (*New York Times,* February 26, 1989).

97. The best book on the intifada is Schiff and Ya'ari 1990.

98. For more details on the plan and the negative reactions of the Soviets and the regional parties to it, see Quandt 1988; Ben-Zvi 1990; and Lenczowski 1990.

99. See, e.g., his joint article in *Foreign Affairs* with another former secretary of state, Vance (1988). The subject of the international conference was one of the few points on which the two still had explicit differences of opinion, and this obviously was a continuation of the debate from the 1970s. This is also a tribute to the continuing influence of cognitive beliefs even in the face of remarkable changes in the international and regional environments (Kissinger and Vance 1988, 915 n. 3).

100. Some of these members participated in coauthoring a 1988 report of the Washington Institute for Near East Policy. The report counseled a skeptical American approach toward an international conference as the forum for Arab-Israeli negotiations and an overall go-slow approach by the United States toward Middle East peacemaking (see the *Boston Globe,* January 27, 1989; see also Haas 1990, chap. 2). In contrast, a report of a study group sponsored by the liberal Brookings Institution urged a more activist U.S. involvement and was more sympathetic to the idea of an international conference; see Brookings 1988. This division of opinion is consistent with the difference between Kissinger and Vance, representing, in general, a conservative-liberal division of opinion on the role of the Soviets in regional conflicts. It again shows the consistency of domestic beliefs and opinions, at least up to a certain point, despite far-reaching external changes.

101. As Foreign Minister Shevardnadze pointed out, "if the U.S. can single-handedly resolve all the issues in the Middle East, we would applaud that. But no country in the world can do that. There must be a collective effort to defuse the Middle East crisis . . . the policy of pushing each other out of the region has to be abandoned in favor of constructive cooperation for the sake of peace and tranquility in the Middle East" (*New York Times,* February 24, 1989).

102. This involvement might be due to the strength of geographic (proximity), historic (traditional allies and a pre-Revolutionary tradition of involvement in the region), and demographic-transnational (Jewish emigration to Israel and the relations between the former muslim Soviet republics and the Islamic world) ties.

103. For more on the contribution of the great powers to regional peacemaking, including a possible concert of the United States, an integrated Europe, Japan, and Russia, see the concluding chapter.

**Conclusions**

1. As I suggest in chapter 3, the nuclear revolution has made intended great power wars obsolete; thus, our major concern regarding intended outcomes has been intended cooperation. This is also true for the future because the nuclear revolution cannot be disinvented. Thus, the major focus concerning future great power conflict is on inadvertent wars.

2. On the Concert as a crisis-prevention regime, see Lauren 1983. Indeed, in accordance with the distinction made by George, the essence of the cooperation be-

tween the Concert members was in *preventing* great-power crises rather than in *managing* them. When crises erupted during the peak period of the Concert, 1815 through 1854, the rivals were usually third parties and not more than a single great power was directly involved. To prevent escalation to a crisis among the great powers themselves, the Concert then acted multilaterally either through a joint intervention of the powers—like in the Ottoman crises of the 1830s and the 1840s (see Lauren 1983, 47–48)—or through joint diplomacy for conflict resolution—like in the crisis resulting in the establishment of Belgium in the early 1830s. On the Concert's accomplishments in settling disputes and averting dangers by diplomacy, see, especially, Schroeder 1986. In contrast, many local crises in the postwar era escalated to superpower crises and only then were successfully managed while the superpowers all along acted mainly through unilateral steps. On superpower failure in crisis prevention during the Cold War, see George, with others, 1983 and also George, Farley, and Dallin 1988, chap. 23.

3. The contradiction between ideology and practice was especially notable in the case of the more doctrinaire party, the Soviet Union (see Karsh 1985, 38).

4. On the United States, see Williams 1976, 89, and George 1984c, 153–54; on the Soviet Union, see Adomeit 1982.

5. Neuman's (1988, 1045–46) study of the superpowers and regional wars suggests that the dependence of Third World states on superpower arms supply, and especially resupply during crises, made it possible for the superpowers to limit the scope of regional wars.

6. See his Amman's speech of February 24, 1990, *International Affairs*, FBIS-NES-90-039.

7. More generally, the collapse of the Soviet Union has created a major problem for the NPT regime because of the much greater availability of nuclear knowledge and material due to the Soviet collapse, while the Soviets strictly played by the rules of NPT before the disintegration of central authority in Moscow (see chap. 4).

8. On the decisive effects of unipolarity on behavior and outcomes in the Gulf Crisis, see Krauthammer 1990/91 and Miller 1992c.

9. On the high likelihood of such a transition, see Layne 1993 and Waltz 1993.

10. For recent analyses of the arms race and the overall security situation in East Asia, see Klare 1993, Friedberg 1993–94, and Betts 1993–94.

11. The BPA (1972) and the Agreement on the Prevention of Nuclear War (1973) were failed attempts to address such issues (see chapter 2; see George, Farley, and Dallin 1988, 588–92, 713–14).

12. For treatments of superpower cooperation in each of these regional conflicts, see the detailed accounts in the following edited volumes dedicated to this subject: Katz 1991; Kanet and Kolodziej 1991; and Weiss and Blight 1992.

13. For an explanation of U.S.-Soviet cooperation based on the emergence of nuclear MAD as a structural change, see Weber 1990. At the same time, balance-of-power theory could suggest that the concert of the late 1980s was only a reflection of Soviet weakness, and thus was not a real concert between more or less equal powers.

14. On the importance of Gorbachev's more positive image of U.S. intentions as compared to his predecessors, see Lebow and Stein 1992 and Herrmann 1992, 462–64.

15. For a recent analysis that highlights the cooperative elements (rather than just unilateral disengagement and submission to U.S. pressures) in the new Soviet strategy

under Gorbachev toward conflict resolution in a number of regions, see Herrmann 1992. For a similar point with regard to the settlement in Southern Africa, see, for example, Hampson 1992, 141.

16. On the tacit rules of this cooperation, see chapters 3 and 5. See also Jervis 1991–92; and Keal 1983.

17. This is a specification and refinement of the overgeneralized and abstract argument that bipolar systems are more stable than multipolar ones (see Gaddis 1986; Mearsheimer 1990; Waltz 1979).

18. For a useful analysis of the emerging international structure, see Waltz 1993.

# Bibliography

Adomeit, Hannes. 1973. *Soviet Risk-Taking and Crisis Behavior: From Confrontation to Coexistence?* Adelphi Paper 101. London: International Institute for Strategic Studies.
———. 1981. "Consensus Versus Conflict: The Dimension of Foreign Policy." In Seweryn Bialer, ed. *The Domestic Context of Soviet Foreign Policy.* Boulder, Colo.: Westview.
———. 1982. *Soviet Risk-Taking and Crisis Behavior.* London: George Allen and Unwin.
Aggarwal, Vinod K. 1985. *Liberal Protectionism: The International Politics of Organized Textile Trade.* Berkeley: University of California Press.
Albrecht-Carrie, Rene, ed. 1968. *The Concert of Europe, 1815–1914.* New York: Harper and Row.
Alford, Jonathan. 1982. "Soviet-American Rivalry in the Middle East: The Military Dimension." In Adeed Dawisha and Karen Dawisha, eds., *The Soviet Union in the Middle East: Policies and Perspectives.* New York: Holmes & Meier.
Alker, Henry A. 1972. "Is Personality Situationally Specific or Intrapsychically Consistent?" *Journal of Personality* 40:1–16.
Allison, Graham T. 1971. *Essence of Decision.* Boston: Little, Brown.
Allison, Graham T., Albert Carnesale, and Joseph S. Nye, eds. 1985. *Hawks, Doves, and Owls: An Agenda for Avoiding Nuclear War.* New York: W. W. Norton.
Allison, R., and P. Williams, eds. 1990. *Superpower Competition and Crisis Prevention in the Third World.* Cambridge: Cambridge University Press.
Aron, Raymond. 1967. *Peace and War: A Theory of International Relations.* Translated by Richard Howard and Annette Fox. New York: Fredrick A. Praeger.
Aronson, Shlomo. 1978. *Conflict and Bargaining in the Middle East: An Israeli Perspective.* Baltimore: Johns Hopkins University Press.
Art, Robert. 1973. "Bureaucratic Politics and American Foreign Policy: A Critique." *Policy Science* 4:467–90.
Ashworth, Tony. 1980. *Trench Warfare, 1914–1918: The Live and Let Live System.* New York: Holmes & Meier.
Astor, David, and Valerie Yorke. 1978. *Peace in the Middle East: Superpowers and Security Guarantees.* London: Corgi.
Atherton, Alferd. 1985. "The Soviet Role in the Middle East: An American View." *The Middle East Journal* 39, no. 4 (Autumn): 688–715.
Axelrod, Robert. 1984. *The Evolution of Cooperation.* New York: Basic Books.

Axelrod, Robert, ed. 1976. *The Structure of Decision.* Princeton, N.J.: Princeton University Press.
Axelrod, Robert, and Robert O. Keohane. 1985. "Achieving Cooperation under Anarchy: Strategies and Institutions." *World Politics,* 38, no. 1 (October): 226–54.
Baldwin, David A., ed. 1993. *Neorealism and Neoliberalism: The Contemporary Debate.* New York: Columbia University Press.
Ball, George. 1976. "Kissinger's Paper Peace: How Not to Handle the Middle East." *The Atlantic Monthly,* February, 41–49.
Bar, Micha. 1990. *Red Lines in Israel's Deterrence Strategy.* Tel Aviv: Maarchot. Hebrew.
Bar-Joseph, Uri, and John Hannah. 1988. "Intervention Threats in Short Arab-Israeli Wars: An Analysis of Soviet Crisis Behavior." *The Journal of Strategic Studies* 11, no. 4 (December): 437–67.
Bar-Siman-Tov, Yaacov. 1980. *The Israeli-Egyptian War of Attrition, 1969–1970.* New York: Columbia University Press.
———. 1983. *Linkage Politics in the Middle East: Syria between Domestic and External Conflict.* Boulder, Colo.: Westview.
Bar Zohar, Michael. 1970. *Embassies in Crisis.* Englewood Cliffs, N.J.: Prentice-Hall.
———. 1978. *Ben-Gurion: A Political Biography.* Tel Aviv: Am Oved. Hebrew.
Becker, Abraham S. 1979. "Arms Transfer, Great Power Intervention, and Settlement of the Arab-Israeli Conflict". In M. Leitenberg and G. Sheffer, eds., *Great Power Intervention in the Middle East.* New York: Pergamon.
Bell, Coral. 1971. *The Conventions of Crisis: A Study in Diplomatic Management.* Oxford: Oxford University Press.
———. 1974. "The October Middle East War: A Case Study in Crisis Management during Detente." *International Affairs* 50 (October): 531–43.
———. 1977. *The Diplomacy of Detente: The Kissinger Era.* New York: St. Martin's.
Ben-Dor, Gabriel, and David Dewitt, eds. 1987. *Conflict Management in the Middle East.* Lexington, Mass.: Lexington Books.
Ben-Gurion, David. 1982. *War Diary.* Tel Aviv: Defense Ministry of Israel. Hebrew.
Ben-Porat, Joel. 1985. "The Yom-Kippur War—Error in May and Surprise in October." *Maarachot* 299 (July-August): 2–9. Hebrew.
———. 1987. "A Well-Functioning Intelligence." *Haaretz,* June 5, B4. Hebrew.
Bentley, Arthur. 1908. *The Process of Government: A Study of Social Pressures.* Chicago: University of Chicago Press.
Ben-Zvi, Abraham. 1986. *The American Approach to Superpower Collaboration in the Middle East, 1973–1986.* Tel-Aviv: Jaffee Center for Strategic Studies.
———. 1988. "The Management of Superpower Conflict in the Middle East." In Steven Spiegel, Mark A. Heller, and Jacob Goldberg, eds., *The Soviet-American Competition in the Middle East.* Lexington, Mass.: Lexington Books.
———. 1990. *Between Lausanne and Geneva: International Conferences and the Arab-Israeli Conflict.* Boulder, Colo.: Westview.
———. 1993. *The United States and Israel: The Limits of the Special Relationship.* New York: Columbia University Press.
Betts, Richard K. 1977. *Soldiers, Statesmen, and Cold War Crises.* Cambridge, Mass.: Harvard University Press.

———. 1987. *Nuclear Blackmail and Nuclear Balance.* Washington, D.C.: Brookings Institution.

———. 1993/94. "Wealth, Power and Instability: East Asia and the United States after the Cold War." *International Security* 18:34–77.

Bialer, Seweryn, and Michael Mandelbaum. 1989. *The Global Rivals.* New York: Vintage Books.

Bialer, Seweryn, and Michael Mandelbaum, eds. 1988. *Gorbachev's Russia and American Foreign Policy.* Boulder, Colo.: Westview.

Blacker, Coit D. 1983. "The Kremlin and Detente: Soviet Conceptions, Hopes, and Expectations." In Alexander George, ed., *Managing U.S.-Soviet Rivalry: Problems of Crisis Prevention.* Boulder, Colo: Westview.

Blainey, Geoffrey. 1973. *The Causes of War.* New York: Free Press.

Blair, Bruce. 1985. *Strategic Command and Control: Redefining the Nuclear Threat.* Washington, D.C.: Brookings Institution.

Blechman, Barry. 1988. "Efforts to Reduce the Risk of Accidental or Inadvertent War." In A. George, P. Farley, and A. Dallin, eds., *U.S.-Soviety Security Cooperation: Achievements, Failures, Lessons,* chap. 18. New York: Oxford University Press.

Blechman, Barry, and Douglas Hart. 1984. "The Political Utility of Nuclear Weapons: The 1973 Middle East Crisis." In Steven Miller, ed., *Strategy and Nuclear Deterrence: An International Security Reader,* 273–97. Princeton, N.J.: Princeton University Press.

Blechman, Barry, and Stephen Kaplan, eds. 1978. *Force without War, U.S. Armed Forces as a Political Instrument.* Washington, D.C.: Brookings Institution.

Blight, James G. 1986–87. "The New Psychology of War and Peace." *International Security* 11, no. 3 (Winter): 175–86.

———. 1992. *The Shattered Crystal Ball: Fear and Learning in the Cuban Missile Crisis.* Lanham, Md.: Littlefield Adams Quality Paperbacks.

Blight, James G., Joseph Nye, and David Welch. 1987. "The Cuban Missile Crisis Revisited." *Foreign Affairs* 66, no. 1 (Fall): 170–88.

Blight, James G., and David Welch. 1989. *On the Brink: Americans and Soviets Reexamine the Cuban Missile Crisis.* New York: Hill and Wang.

Bohlen, Charles. 1973. *Witness to History.* New York: W. W. Norton.

Bouchard, Joseph. 1991. *Command in Crisis: Four Case Studies.* New York: Columbia University Press.

Bracken, Paul. 1983. *The Command and Control of Nuclear Forces.* New Haven, Conn.: Yale University Press.

———. 1985. "Accidental Nuclear War." In G. Allison, Albert Carnesale, and Joseph S. Nye, eds., *Hawks, Doves, and Owls: An Agenda for Avoiding Nuclear War.* New York: Norton.

Brams, Steven. 1985. *Superpower Games: Applying Game Theory to Superpower Conflict.* New Haven, Conn.: Yale University Press.

Brecher, Michael. 1977. "Toward a Theory of International Crisis Behavior." *International Studies Quarterly* 21, no. 1 (March): 39–74.

———. 1978. "A Theoretical Approach to International Crisis Behavior." *The Jerusalem Journal of International Relations* 3 (2–3): 5–24.

———. 1980. *Decisions in Crisis: Israel, 1967 and 1973*. Berkeley: University of California Press.

———. 1986. "Polarity, Stability, Crisis: A New Look at an Unresolved Controversy." Presented at the annual meeting of the *American Political Science Association*, August 28–31.

Brecher, Michael, P. James, and J. Wilkenfeld. 1990. "Polarity and Stability: New Concepts, Indicators and Evidence." *International Interactions* 16 (1): 49–80.

Brecher, Michael, and J. Wilkenfeld. 1991. "International Crises and Global Instability: The Myth of the 'Long Peace.'" In C. Kegley, ed., *The Long Postwar Peace*. New York: Harper Collins.

Breslauer, George. 1983a. "Soviet Policy in the Middle East, 1967–1972: Unalterable Antagonism or Collaborative Competition?" In Alexander George, ed., *Managing U.S.-Soviet Rivalry: Problems of Crisis Prevention*. Boulder, Colo: Westview.

———. 1983b. "Why Detente Failed: An Interpretation." In A. George, ed., *Managing U.S.-Soviet Rivalry: Problems of Crisis Prevention*. Boulder, Colo.: Westview.

———. 1985. "The Dynamics of Soviet Policy Toward the Arab-Israeli Conflict: Lessons of the Brezhnev Era." In Dan Caldwell, ed., *Soviet International Behavior and U.S. Policy Options*. Lexington, Mass.: Lexington Books.

———. 1987. "Ideology and Learning in Soviet Third World Policy." *World Politics* 39 (April): 429–48.

Breslauer, G., ed. 1990. *Soviet Strategy in the Middle East*. Winchester, Mass.: Unwin Hyman.

Bresbauer, George, and P. Tetlock, eds. 1991. *Learning in US and Soviet Foreign Policies*. Boulder, Colo.: Westview.

Brodie, Bernard. 1973. *War & Politics*. New York: Macmillan.

Brodie, Bernard, ed. 1946. *The Absolute Weapon*. New York: Harcourt, Brace.

The Brookings Institution, Report of a Study Group. 1988. *Toward Arab-Israeli Peace*. Washington, D.C.: Brookings Institution.

Brown, Carl L. 1984. *International Politics and the Middle East: Old Rules, Dangerous Game*. Princeton, N.J.: Princeton University Press.

Brown, Malcolm, and Shirley Seaton. 1984. *Christmas Truce*. London: Leo Cooper.

Brown, Seyom. 1983. *The Faces of Power: Constancy and Change in United States Foreign Policy from Truman to Reagan*. New York: Columbia University Press.

Brzezinski, Zbigniew K. 1980. "U.S.-Soviet Relations." In Erik P. Hoffmann and Frederic Fleron, eds., *The Conduct of Soviet Foreign Policy*, 315–32. New York: Aldine.

———. 1983. *Power and Principle: Memoirs of the National Security Adviser, 1977–1981*. New York: Farrar, Strauss, Giroux.

Bueno de Mesquita, B. 1981. *The War Trap*. New Haven, Conn.: Yale University Press.

Bull, Hedley. 1966. "Society and Anarchy in International Relations." In Herbert Butterfield and Martin Wight, eds., *Diplomatic Investigations: Essays in the Theory of International Politics*. London: Allen and Unwin.

———. 1971. "World Order and the Super Powers." In Crasten Holbraad, ed., *Super Powers and World Order*. Canberra: Australian National University Press.

———. 1977. *The Anarchical Society: A Study of Order in World Politics*. New York: Columbia University Press.

———. 1980. "The Great Irresponsibles? The United States, the Soviet Union, and World Order." *International Journal* 35, no.3 (Summer): 437–47.
Bundy, McGeorge. 1988. *Danger and Survival: Choices about the Bomb in the First Fifty Years*. New York: Random House.
Butterfield, Herbert. 1966. "The Balance of Power." In Herbert Butterfield and Martin Wight, eds., *Diplomatic Investigations: Essays in the Theory of International Politics*. London: Allen and Unwin.
Butterfield, H., and M. Wight, eds. 1966. *Diplomatic Investigations: Essays in the Theory of International Politics*. London: Allen and Unwin.
Buzan, Barry. 1983. *People, States and Fear: The National Security Problem in International Relations*. Chapel Hill: University of North Carolina Press.
———. 1984. "Economic Structure and International Security." *International Organization* 38:597–624.
———. 1993. "The Level of Analysis Problem in International Relations Reconsidered." Paper presented at the International Studies Association Conference, Acapulco, Mexico, March.
Buzan, Barry, Charles Jones, and Richard Little. 1993. *The Logic of Anarchy: Neorealism to Structural Realism*. New York: Columbia University Press.
Calleo, David. 1987. *Beyond American Hegemony: The Future of the Western Alliance*. New York: Basic Books.
Campbell, John. C. 1972. "The Communist Powers and the Middle East: Moscow's Purposes." *Problems of Communism* 21, no. 5 (September–October): 40–54.
———. 1979. "The United States and the Arab-Israeli Conflict." In Robert Freedman, ed., *World Politics and the Arab-Israeli Conflict*. New York: Pergamon.
Carr, E. H. 1964. *The Twenty Years' Crisis, 1919–1939*. New York: Harper & Row.
Carter, Jimmy. 1982. *Keeping Faith: Memoirs of a President*. New York: Bantam Books.
———. 1985. *The Blood of Abraham*. Boston: Houghton Mifflin.
Christensen, Thomas, and Jack Snyder. 1990. "Chain Gangs and Passed Bucks: Predicting Alliance Patterns in Multipolarity." *International Organization* 44 (Spring): 137–68.
Clark, Ian. 1989. *The Hierarchy of States: Reform and Resistance in the International Order*. Cambridge: Cambridge University Press.
Claude, Inis. 1962. *Power and International Relations*. New York: Random House.
———. 1986. "The Common Defense and Great-Power Responsibilities." *Political Science Quarterly* 101 (5): 719–32.
Cohen, Raymond. 1978. "Israel and the Soviet-American Statement of October 1, 1977: The Limits of Patron-Client Influence." *Orbis* 22 (Fall): 613–33.
———. 1980. "Rules of the Game in International Politics." *International Studies Quarterly* 14, no. 14 (March): 121–50.
———. 1981. "Where Are the Aircraft Carriers? Nonverbal Communication in International Politics." *Review of International Studies* 7 (2): 79–90.
Converse, Philip. 1964. "The Nature of Belief Systems in Mass Publics." In David E. Apter, ed., *Ideology and Discontent*. New York: Free Press.
Corwin, Edwin S. 1940. *The President: Office and Powers*. New York: New York University Press.

Coser, L. 1956. *The Functions of Social Conflict.* New York: Free Press.
Craig, Gordon, and Alexander George. 1983. *Force and Statecraft.* New York: Oxford University Press.
Cutler, Claire. 1991. "The 'Grotian Tradition' in International Relations." *Review of International Studies* 17:41–65.
Dallek, Robert. 1979. *Franklin D. Roosevelt and American Foreign Policy, 1932–1945.* New York: Oxford University Press.
Dallin, Alexander. 1980. "Soviet Foreign Policy and Domestic Politics: A Framework for Analysis." In Erik P. Hoffmann and Fredric J. Fleron, eds., *The Conduct of Soviet Foreign Policy.* New York: Aldine.
———. 1981. "The Domestic Sources of Soviet Foreign Policy." In Seweryn Bialer, ed., *The Domestic Context of Soviet Foreign Policy.* Boulder, Colo.: Westview.
———. 1988. "Soviet Approaches to Superpower Security Relations." In A. George, P. Farley, and A. Dallin, eds., *U.S.-Soviet Security Cooperation: Achievements, Failures, Lessons.* New York: Oxford University Press.
Dallin, Alexander, and Gail W. Lapidus. 1983. "Reagan and the Russians: United States Policy toward the Soviet Union and Eastern Europe." In Kenneth A. Oye, Robert J. Lieber, and Donald Rothchild, eds., *Eagle Defiant: U.S. Foreign Policy in the 1980s.* Boston: Little, Brown.
David, Steven. 1992–93. "Why the Third World Still Matters." *International Security* 17, no. 3 (Winter): 127–59.
Dawisha, Adeed. 1982. "The Soviet Union in the Arab World: The Limits to Superpower Influence." In A. Dawisha and K. Dawisha, eds., *The Soviet Union in the Middle East: Policies and Perspectives.* New York: Holmes & Meier.
Dawisha, A., and K. Dawisha, eds. 1982. *The Soviet Union in the Middle East: Policies and Perspectives.* New York: Holmes & Meier.
Dawisha, Karen. 1982–83. "The U.S.S.R. in the Middle East: Superpower in Eclipse?" *Foreign Affairs* 61, no. 2 (Winter): 438–52.
Dayan, Moshe. 1977. *Story of My Life.* London: Sphere Books.
Deibel, T. 1993. "Internal Affairs and International Relations in the Post–Cold War World." *Washington Quarterly* 16, no. 3 (Summer): 13–33.
Destler, I. M. 1984. "Congress." In Joseph Nye, ed., *The Making of America's Soviet Policy.* New Haven, Conn.: Yale University Press.
Destler, I. M., Leslie H. Gelb, and Anthony Lake. 1984. *Our Own Worst Enemy: The Unmaking of American Foreign Policy.* New York: Simon and Schuster.
Deutsch, Karl, S. A. Brunell, R. A. Kann, M. Lee, Jr., M. Lichterman, R. E. Lindgren, F. L. Loewenheim, and R. W. V. Wagenen. 1957. *Political Community and the North Atlantic Area: International Organization in the Light of Historical Experience.* Princeton, N.J.: Princeton University Press.
Deutsch, Karl, and J. David Singer. 1964. "Multipolar Power Systems and International Stability." *World Politics* 16 (April): 390–406.
Deutsch, Morton. 1973. *The Resolution of Conflict: Constructive and Destructive Processes.* New Haven, Conn.: Yale University Press.
Dismukes, Bradford. 1979. "Large-Scale Intervention Ashore: Soviet Air Defense Forces in Egypt." In Bradford Dismukes and James M. McConnell, eds., *Soviet Naval Diplomacy.* New York: Pergamon.

Dismukes, Bradford, and James M. McConnell, eds. 1979. *Soviet Naval Diplomacy.* New York: Pergamon.
Dittmer, Lowell. 1981. "The Strategic Triangle: An Elementary Game-Theoretical Analysis." *World Politics* 33, no. 4 (July): 485–515.
Downs, George, David Rocke, and Randolph Siverson. 1985. "Arms Races and Cooperation." *World Politics* 38, no. l: 118–46.
Dowty, Alan. 1975. "The Role of Great Power Guarantees in International Peace Agreements." *Jerusalem Papers on Peace Problems.* Paper no. 3. The Leonard Davis Institute for International Relations, The Hebrew University of Jerusalem.
———. 1984. *Middle East Crisis: U.S. Decision-Making in 1958, 1970, and 1973.* Berkeley: University of California Press.
Doyle, Michael. 1983. "Kant, Liberal Legacies, and Foreign Affairs." *Philosophy and Public Affairs* 12 (Summer): 205–35.
———. 1986. "Liberalism and World Politics." *American Political Science Review* 80 (December): 1151–69.
Duffy, G. 1978. "Soviet Nuclear Exports." *International Security* 3, no. 1 (Summer): 83–111.
Easton, David. 1953. *The Political System: An Inquiry into the State of Political Science.* New York: Alfred A. Knopf.
Eban, Abba. 1977. *An Autobiography.* New York: Random House.
Eisenhower, Dwight. 1965. *The White House Years: Waging Peace 1956–1961.* Garden City, N.Y.: Doubleday & Co.
Ekehammar, B. 1974. "Interactionism in Personality from a Historical Perspective." *Psychological Bulletin* 81: 1026–48.
Elrod, Richard. 1976. "The Concert of Europe: A Fresh Look at an International System." *World Politics* 28 (January): 159–74.
Eran, Oded. 1978. "Soviet Policy between the 1967 and 1973 Wars." In Haim Shaked and Itamar Rabinovich, eds., *From June to October: The Middle East between 1967 and 1973.* New Brunswick, N. J.: Transaction Books.
Evron, Yair. 1973. *The Middle East: Nations, Superpowers, and Wars.* New York: Praeger.
———. 1977. "The Role of Arms Control in the Middle East." *Adelphi Papers,* no. 138. London: The International Institute for Strategic Studies.
———. 1979. "Great Power Military Intervention in the Middle East." In M. Leitenberg and G. Sheffer, eds., *Great Power Intervention in the Middle East.* New York: Pergamon.
———. 1987. *War and Intervention in Lebanon: The Israeli-Syrian Deterrence Dialogue.* London: Croom Helm.
Fahmy, Ismail. 1983. *Negotiating for Peace in the Middle East.* Baltimore: Johns Hopkins University Press.
Feinberg, Richard E. 1983. *The Intemperate Zone: The Third World Challenge to U.S. Foreign Policy.* New York: Norton.
Feldman, Shai. 1982. *Israeli Nuclear Deterrence.* New York: Columbia University Press.
Fischer, Fritz. 1967. *Germany's Aims in the First World War.* New York: Norton.
Fischhoff, Baruch. 1991. "Nuclear Decisions: Cognitive Limits to the Thinkable." In P.

Tetlock, J. Husbands, R. Jervis, P. Stern, and C. Tilly, eds., *Behavior, Society and Nuclear War,* 2:110–92. New York: Oxford University Press.
Ford, Gerald. 1979. *A Time to Heal.* New York: Harper & Row.
Fox, William T. R. 1944. *The Super-Powers.* New York: Harcourt Brace.
———. 1980. "The Super-Powers Then and Now." *International Journal* 35 (3): 417–36.
Freedman, Robert. 1978. *Soviet Policy toward the Middle East since 1970.* Rev. ed. New York: Praeger Special Studies.
———. 1988. "Moscow and the Arab States since 1967." In Y. Lukacs and A. Battah, eds., *The Arab-Israeli Conflict: Two Decades of Change.* Boulder. Colo.: Westview Press.
Frei, Daniel. 1983. *Risks of Unintentional Nuclear War.* Totowa, N. J.: Rowman & Allanheld.
Friedberg, Aaron L. 1993–94. "Ripe for Rivalry: Prospects for Peace in a Multipolar Asia." *International Security* 18:5–33.
Fukuyama, Francis. 1981. "Nuclear Shadowboxing: Soviet Intervention Threats in the Middle East." *Orbis* 25, no.3 (Fall): 579–605.
———. 1985. "Escalation in the Middle East and Persian Gulf." In Graham T. Allison, Albert Carnesale, and Joseph S. Nye, eds., *Hawks, Doves, and Owls: An Agenda for Avoiding Nuclear War.* New York: W. W. Norton.
———. 1986a. "Gorbachev and the Third World." *Foreign Affairs* 64, no. 4 (Spring): 715–31.
———. 1986b. "Military Aspects of U.S.-Soviet Competition in the Third World." In Marshall D. Shulman, ed., *East-West Tensions in the Third World.* New York: W. W. Norton.
———. 1986c. "U.S.-Soviet Interactions in the Third World." In Arnold L. Horelick, ed., *U.S.-Soviet Relations: The Next Phase.* Ithaca, N.Y.: Cornell University Press.
———. 1988. "Soviet Military Power in the Middle East; or, Whatever Became of Power Projection?" In Steven Spiegel, Mark A. Heller, and Jacob Goldberg, eds. *The Soviet-American Competition in the Middle East.* Lexington, Mass.: Lexington Books.
———. 1989. "The End of History?" *The National Interest* 16 (Summer): 3–18.
Gaddis, John L. 1972. *The United States and the Origins of the Cold War, 1941–1947.* New York: Columbia University Press.
———. 1982. *Strategies of Containment.* New York: Oxford University Press.
———. 1986. "The Long Peace: Elements of Stability in the Postwar International System." *International Security* 10, no. 4 (Spring): 99–142.
———. 1987. *The Long Peace: Inquiries into the History of the Cold War.* New York: Oxford University Press.
Gal, Reuven. 1983. "Courage under Stress." In Shlomo Breznitz, ed., *Stress in Israel.* New York: Van Nostrand Reinhold.
———. 1985. "Combat Stress as an Opportunity: The Case of Heroism." Paper presented at the Northeast Regional Conference of the Inter-University Seminar on Armed Forces and Society. Albany, New York, April 11–13.
Gal, Reuven, and M. IsraelashWili. 1978. "Personality Traits versus Situational Factors as Determinants of Individual Coping with Stress: A Theoretical Model." Paper

presented at the International Conference on Psychological Stress and Adjustment in Time of War and Peace, Jerusalem.

Garfinkle, Adam. 1985. "U.S. Decision Making in the Jordan Crisis: Correcting the Record." *Political Science Quarterly* 100, no. 1 (Spring): 117–38.

Garrett, Stephen A. 1976. "Nixonian Foreign Policy: A New Balance of Power—or a Revised Concert?" *Polity* 8 (Spring): 389–421.

Garthoff, Raymond. 1985. *Detente and Confrontation: American-Soviet Relations from Nixon to Reagan*. Washington, D.C.: Brookings Institution.

Gazit, Mordechai. 1983. *President Kennedy's Policy towards the Arab States and Israel: Analysis and Documents*. Tel Aviv: Shiloah Center.

Gelb, Leslie H. 1971. "Vietnam: The System Worked." *Foreign Policy* 3:140–67.

Gelb, Leslie H., with Richard Betts. 1979. *The Irony of Vietnam: The System Worked*. Washington, D.C.: Brookings Institution.

Gelman, Harry. 1984. *The Brezhnev Politburo and the Decline of Detente*. Ithaca: Cornell University Press.

George, Alexander. 1969. "The 'Operational Code': A Neglected Approach to the Study of Political Leaders and Decision-Making." *International Studies Quarterly* 13, no. 2 (June): 190–222. Reprinted in E. Hoffmann and F. Fleron, eds., *The Conduct of Soviet Foreign Policy*. New York: Aldine, 1980.

———. 1980a. "Domestic Constraints on Regime Change in U.S. Foreign Policy: The Need for Policy Legitimacy." In O. R. Holsti, R. M. Siverson, and A. George, eds., *Change in the International System*. Boulder, Colo.: Westview.

———. 1980b. *Presidential Decisionmaking in Foreign Policy: The Effective Use of Information and Advice*. Boulder, Colo: Westview.

———. 1980c. "Towards a Soviet-American Crisis Prevention Regime: History and Prospects." *CISA Working Paper* No. 28. Los Angeles.

———. 1982. "Case Studies and Theory Development." Paper presented to the Second Annual Symposium on Information Processing in Organizations, Carnegie-Mellon University, October 15–16.

———. 1984a. "Crisis Management: The Interaction of Political and Military Considerations." *Survival* 26 (September/October): 223–34.

———. 1984b. "Ideology and International Relations: A Conceptual Analysis." Draft of a paper prepared for a conference on Ideology and Its Influence on International Politics, The Hebrew University of Jerusalem, December.

———. 1984c. "Political Crises." In Joseph Nye, ed., *The Making of America's Soviet Policy*. New Haven, Conn.: Yale University Press.

———. 1985. "U.S. Global Rivalry: Norms of Competition." Paper presented to the Thirteenth International Political Science Association World Congress, Paris, July 10–15.

———. 1986. "Mechanisms for Moderating Superpower Competition." In *AEI (American Enterprise Institute) Foreign Policy and Defense Review* 6 (1): 5–13.

———. 1990. "Superpower Interests in Third Areas." In R. Allison, and P. Williams, eds., *Superpower Competition and Crisis Prevention in the Third World*. Cambridge: Cambridge University Press.

———. 1991. *Avoiding War: Problems of Crisis Management*. Boulder. Colo.: Westview.

George, Alexander, with others. 1983. *Managing U.S.-Soviet Rivalry: Problems of Crisis Prevention*. Boulder, Colo.: Westview.

George, Alexander, Philip Farley, and Alexander Dallin, eds. 1988. *U.S.-Soviet Security Cooperation: Achievements, Failures, Lessons*. New York: Oxford University Press.

George, Alexander, David Hall, and William Simons. 1971. *The Limits of Coercive Diplomacy*. Boston: Little, Brown.

George, Alexander, and Robert O. Keohane. 1980. "The Concept of National Interests: Uses and Limitations." In A. George, *Presidential Decisionmaking in Foreign Policy*. Boulder, Colo.: Westview.

Gilpin, Robert. 1981. *War and Change in World Politics*. Cambridge: Cambridge University Press.

Glassman, Jon D. 1975. *Arms for the Arabs*. Baltimore: Johns Hopkins University Press.

Gleick, James. 1988. *Chaos: Making a New Science*. New York: Penguin.

Golan, Galia. 1977. *Yom Kippur and After: The Soviet Union and the Arab-Israeli Crisis*. Cambridge: Cambridge University Press.

———. 1979. "The Middle East." In K. London, *The Impact of Soviet Foreign Policy*, 105–26. Boulder, Colo.: Westview.

———. 1982. "The Soviet Union and the Israeli War in Lebanon." Research paper no. 46. The Soviet and East European Research Center. The Hebrew University of Jerusalem.

———. 1990a. *Soviet Policies in the Middle East*. Cambridge: Cambridge University Press.

———. 1990b. "The Soviet Union and the Palestinian Issue." and "Gorbachev's Middle East Strategy." In G. Breslauer, ed., *Soviet Strategy in the Middle East*. Winchester, Mass.: Unwin Hyman.

Gottfried, Kurt, and Bruce G. Blair, eds., 1988. *Crisis Stability and Nuclear War*. New York: Oxford University Press.

Gourevitch, Peter. 1986. *Politics in Hard Times: Comparative Responses to International Economic Crises*. Ithaca, N.Y.: Cornell University Press.

Gowa, Joanne. 1986. "Anarchy, Egoism, and Third Images: The Evolution of Cooperation and International Relations." *International Organization* 40, no. 1 (Winter): 167–86.

———. 1989. "Bipolarity, Multipolarity and Free Trade." *American Political Science Review* 83 (4): 1245–56.

Gowa, Joanne, and Nils H. Wessell. 1982. *Ground Rules: Soviet and American Involvement in Regional Conflicts*. Philadelphia Policy Papers. Foreign Policy Research Institute, Philadelphia.

Grieco, Joseph M. 1988. "Anarchy and the Limits of Cooperation: A Realist Critique of the Newest Liberal Institutionalism." *International Organization* 42, no. 3 (Summer): 485–507.

———. 1990. *Cooperation among Nations*. Ithaca, N.Y.: Cornell University Press.

Griffiths, Franklyn. 1984. "The Sources of American Conduct: Soviet Perspectives and Their Policy Implications." *International Security* 9, no. 2 (Fall): 3–50.

Gulick, Edward. 1955. *Europe's Classical Balance of Power*. New York: W. W. Norton.

Haas, Ernst B. 1980. "Why Collaborate? Issue-Linkages and International Regimes." *World Politics* 32, no. 1 (April): 357–405.

———. 1983. "Regime Decay: Conflict Management and International Organization 1945–1981." *International Organization* 37, no. 2 (Spring): 189–256.

Haas, Ernest B., Mary Williams, and Don Babai. 1977. *Scientists and World Order: The Uses of Technical Knowledge in International Organizations.* Berkeley: University of California Press.

Haas, Richard. 1990. *Conflicts Unending: The United States and Regional Conflicts.* New Haven, Conn.: Yale University Press.

Habermas, Jurgen. 1975. *Legitimation Crisis.* Boston: Beacon.

Haggard, Stephan, and Beth A. Simmons. 1987. "Theories of International Regimes." *International Organization* 41, no. 3 (Summer): 491–517.

Haig, Alexander. 1984. *Caveat: Realism, Reagan, and Foreign Policy.* New York: Macmillan.

Halperin, Morton. 1974. *Bureaucratic Politics and Foreign Policy.* Washington, D.C.: Brookings Institution.

Hampson, F. O. 1992. "Winding Down Strife in Southern Africa." In T. Weiss and J. Blight, eds., *The Suffering Grass: Superpowers and Regional Conflict in Southern Africa and the Caribbean.* Boulder, Colo.: Rienner.

Hampson, F. O., and Brian Mandell. 1990. "Managing Regional Conflict: Security Cooperation and Third Party Mediators." *International Journal* 45, no. 2 (Spring): 191–201.

Hannum, H. 1990. *Autonomy, Sovereignty, and Self-Determination: The Accommodation of Conflicting Rights.* Philadelphia: University of Pennsylvania Press.

Hardin, Russell. 1982. *Collective Action.* Baltimore: Johns Hopkins University Press.

Hart, D. M. 1984. "Soviet Approaches to Crisis Management: The Military Dimension." *Survival* 26, no. 5 (September–October): 214–22.

Hayek, Friedrich A. 1973. *Law, Legislation, and Liberty.* Vol. 1: *Rules and Order.* Chicago: University of Chicago Press.

Heikal, Mohamed. 1975. *The Road to Ramadan.* New York: Quadrangle.

———. 1978. *The Sphinx and the Commissar.* New York: Harper & Row.

Hermann, Charles F. 1969. "International Crisis as a Situational Variable." In J. N. Rosenau, ed., *International Politics and Foreign Policy,* rev. ed. New York: Free Press.

———. 1972. "Threat, Time, and Surprise: A Simulation of International Crises." In C. F. Hermann, ed., *International Crises: Insights from Behavioral Research.* New York: Free Press.

Hermann, Richard. 1987. "Soviet Policy and the Arab-Israeli Conflict: Actions, Patterns, and Interpretations." *Political Science Quarterly* 102, no. 3 (Fall): 417–40.

———. 1992. "Soviet Behavior in Regional Conflicts: Old Questions, New Strategies, and Important Lessons." *World Politics* 44 (April): 432–66.

Hersh, Seymour M. 1983. *The Price of Power: Kissinger in the Nixon White House.* New York: Summit Books.

Herz, John H. 1950. "Idealist Internationalism and the Security Dilemma." *World Politics* 2, no. 2 (January): 157–80.

Herzog, Chaim. 1975. *The War of Atonement*. London: Weidenfeld and Nicolson.
Herzog, Yaccov. 1975. *Am Levadad Ishcon*. Tel Aviv: Maariv. Hebrew.
Hinsley, F. H. 1963. *Power and the Pursuit of Peace: Theory and Practice in the History of Relations between States*. Cambridge: Cambridge University Press.
Hiscocks, Richard. 1974. *The Security Council*. New York: Free Press.
Hoagland, S. W., and S. G. Walker. 1979. "Operational Codes and Crisis Outcomes." In L. S. Falkowski, ed., *Psychological Models in International Politics*. Boulder, Colo.: Westview.
Hobbes, Thomas. 1962. *Leviathan*. New York: Macmillam.
Hoffmann, Erik P., and Fredric J. Fleron, eds. 1980. *The Conduct of Soviet Foreign Policy*. New York: Aldine.
Hoffmann, Stanley. 1965. *The State of War: Essays on the Theory and Practice of International Politics*. New York: Praeger.
———. 1972. "Will the Balance Balance at Home?" *Foreign Policy* no. 7 (Summer): 60–86.
———. 1980. *Primacy or World Order*. New York: McGraw-Hill.
———. 1984. "Detente." In Joseph Nye, ed., *The Making of America's Soviet Policy*. New Haven, Conn.: Yale University Press.
———. 1987. "Liberalism and International Affairs." In Stanley Hoffmann, *Janus and Minerva*. Boulder, Colo.: Westview.
———. 1990. "Correspondence." *International Security* 15, no. 2 (Fall): 191–92.
Holbraad, Carsten. 1970. *The Concert of Europe: A Study in German and British International Theory, 1815–1914*. London: Longmans, Green.
———. 1979. *Superpowers and International Conflict*. London: Macmillan.
Holbraad, Carsten, ed. 1971. *Super Powers and World Order*. Canberra: Australian National University Press.
Hollis, Martin, and Steve Smith. 1991. *Explaining and Understanding International Relations*. Oxford, England: Clarendon.
Holsti, K. J. 1967. *International Politics: A Framework for Analysis*. Englewood Cliffs, N.J.: Prentice-Hall.
———. 1991. *Peace and War: Armed Conflicts and International Order 1648–1989*. Cambridge: Cambridge University Press.
———. 1992. "Governance without Government: Polyarchy in Nineteenth-Century European International Politics." In J. N. Rosenau and E. O. Czempiel, eds., *Governance without Government: Order and Change in World Politics*. Cambridge: Cambridge University Press.
Holsti, Ole R. 1967. "Cognitive Dynamics and Images of the Enemy: Dulles and Russia." In D. J. Finlay, O. R. Holsti, and R. R. Fagen, eds., *Enemies in Politics*. Chicago: Rand McNally.
———. 1970. "Individual Differences in 'Definition of the Situation.'" *Journal of Conflict Resolution* 14, no. 3 (September): 303–10.
———. 1972. *Crisis, Escalation, War*. Montreal: McGill-Queens University Press.
———. 1976a. "Foreign Policy Decision Makers Viewed Psychologically: 'Cognitive Process' Approaches." In James N. Rosenau, ed., *In Search of Global Patterns*. New York: Free Press.

———. 1976b. "Foreign Policy Formation Viewed Cognitively." In R. Axelrod, ed., *The Structure of Decision.* Princeton, N.J.: Princeton University Press.

———. 1979. "Theories of Crisis Decision Making." In Paul G. Lauren, ed., *Diplomacy: New Approaches in History, Theory, and Policy.* New York: Free Press.

———. 1989. "Crisis Decision Making." In P. Tetlock, J. Husbands, R. Jervis, P. Stern, and C. Tilly, eds., *Behavior, Society and Nuclear War.* New York: Oxford University Press.

Holsti, Ole R., Richard A. Brody, and Robert C. North. 1969. "Measuring Affect and Action in International Reaction Models: Empirical Materials from the 1962 Cuban Crisis." In J. N. Rosenau, ed., *International Politics and Foreign Policy,* rev. ed. New York: Free Press.

Holsti, Ole R., and A. George. 1975. "The Effects of Stress on the Performance of Foreign Policy-Makers." *Political Science Annual* 6:255–319.

Holsti, Ole R., Terrence P. Hopmann, and John D. Sullivan. 1973. *Unity and Disintegration in International Alliances.* New York: Wiley-Interscience.

Holsti, Ole R., and James Rosenau. 1983. "U.S. Leadership in a Shrinking World: The Breakdown of Consensus and the Emergence of Conflicting Belief Systems." *World Politics* 35 (3): 368–92.

Hopf, Ted. 1991. "Polarity, the Offense-Defense Balance, and War." *American Political Science Review* 85, no. 2 (June): 475–94.

Horelick, A. 1972. "Soviet Policy in the Middle East." In P. Y. Hammond, ed., *Political Dynamics in the Middle East.* New York: Elsevier.

Horelick, A., ed. 1986. *U.S.-Soviet Relations: The Next Phase.* Ithaca, N.Y.: Cornell University Press.

Howard, Michael. 1983. *The Causes of Wars.* Cambridge, Mass.: Harvard University Press.

Howe, J. R. 1971. *Multicrises: Sea Power and Global Politics in the Missile Age.* Cambridge, Mass: MIT Press.

Hunt, Michael H. 1987. *Ideology and U.S. Foreign Policy.* New Haven, Conn.: Yale University Press.

Huntington, Samuel. 1989. "No Exit: The Errors of Endism." *The National Interest* no. 17 (Fall): 3–11.

———. 1993. "The Clash of Civilizations." *Foreign Affairs* 72, no. 3 (Summer): 22–49.

Hurevitz, J. C., ed. 1956. *Diplomacy in the Near and Middle-East, A Documentary Record 1914–1956.* 2 vols. Princeton, N.J.: D. van Nostrand.

Huth, Paul, and Bruce Russett. 1984. "What Makes Deterrence Work? Cases from 1900 to 1980." *World Politics* 36, no. 4 (July): 496–526.

———. 1988. "Deterrence Failure and Crisis Escalation." *International Studies Quarterly* 32 (March): 29–46.

Ikenberry, John G., and Charles A. Kupchan. 1990a. "The Legitimation of Hegemonic Power." In D. Rapkin, ed., *World Leadership and Hegemony.* Boulder, Colo.: Lynne Rienner.

———. 1990b. "Socialization and Hegemonic Power." *International Organization* 44 (Summer): 283–315.

Indyk, Martin. 1984. *"To the Ends of the Earth": Sadat's Jerusalem Initiative.* Cambridge, Mass.: Harvard University, Center for Middle Eastern Studies.
Jabber, P., and R. Kolkowicz. 1981. "The Arab-Israeli Wars of 1967 and 1973." In S. S. Kaplan, ed., *Diplomacy of Power.* Washington, D.C.: Brookings Institution.
James, Alan. 1973. "Law and Order in International Society." In A. James, ed., *The Bases of International Order.* London: Oxford University Press.
James, Patrick. 1993. "Neorealism as a Research Enterprise: Toward Elaborated Structural Realism." *International Political Science Review* 14 (2): 123–48.
Janis, Irving. 1982. *Groupthink.* 2d ed. Boston: Houghton Mifflin.
Jentleson, Bruce W. 1988. "The Lebanon War and the Soviet-American Competition: Scope and Limits of Superpower Influence." In Steven Spiegel, Mark A. Heller, and Jacob Goldberg, eds., *The Soviet-American Competition in the Middle East.* Lexington, Mass.: Lexington Books.
Jervis, Robert. 1970. *The Logic of Images in International Relations.* Princeton, N.J.: Princeton University Press.
———. 1976. *Perception and Misperception in International Politics.* Princeton, N.J.: Princeton University Press.
———. 1978. "Cooperation under the Security Dilemma." *World Politics* 30, no. 2 (January): 167–214.
———. 1979. "Systems Theories and Diplomatic History." In Paul G. Lauren, ed., *Diplomacy: New Approaches in History, Theory, and Policy.* New York: Free Press.
———. 1981. "Beliefs about Soviet Behavior." In R. Osgood, ed., *Containment, Soviet Behavior, and Grand Strategy,* Policy Papers in International Affairs, no. 16, 55–59. Berkeley: Institute of International Studies, University of California.
———. 1983. "Security Regimes." In Stephen Krasner, ed., *International Regimes.* Ithaca, N.Y.: Cornell University Press.
———. 1984. *The Illogic of American Nuclear Strategy.* Ithaca, N.Y.: Cornell University Press.
———. 1985. "From Balance of Power to Concert: A Study of International Security Cooperation." *World Politics* 38, no. 1 (October): 58–79.
———. 1988. "Realism, Game Theory and Cooperation." *World Politics* 40 (April): 317–49.
———. 1989a. *The Meaning of the Nuclear Revolution.* Ithaca, N.Y.: Cornell University Press.
———. 1989b. "War and Misperception." In R. Rotberg and T. Rabb, eds., *The Origin and Prevention of Major Wars.* Cambridge: Cambridge University Press.
———. 1991. "The Political Effects of Nuclear Weapons: A Comment." In Sean M. Lynn-Jones, ed., *The Cold War and After: Prospects for Peace,* 70–80. Cambridge, Mass.: The MIT Press.
———. 1991/92. "The Future of World Politics: Will It Resemble the Past?" *International Security* 16 (Winter): 39–73.
Jervis, Robert, R. N. Lebow, and J. G. Stein. 1985. *Psychology and Deterrence.* Baltimore: Johns Hopkins University Press.

Jervis, Robert, and J. Snyder. 1991. *Dominoes and Bandwagons.* New York: Oxford University Press.
Joffe, Josef. 1992. "Collective Security and the Future of Europe." *Survival* 34 (Spring): 36–50.
———. 1993. "The New Europe: Yesterday's Ghosts." *Foreign Affairs* 72 (1): 29–43.
Johnson, L. B. 1971. *The Vantage Point: Perspectives on the Presidency 1963–1969.* New York: Holt, Rinehart and Winston.
Johnson, Robert H. 1983. "Periods of Peril: The Window of Vulnerability and Other Myths." *Foreign Affairs* 61, no. 4 (Spring): 950–70.
———. 1985–86. "Exaggerating America's Stakes in Third World Conflicts." *International Security* 10, no. 3 (Winter): 32–68.
Joll, James. 1984. *The Origins of the First World War.* London: Longman.
Jonsson, Christer. 1984. *Superpower: Comparing American and Soviet Foreign Policy.* New York: St. Martin's.
Kahler, Miles. 1979–80. "Rumors of War: The 1914 Analogy." *Foreign Affairs* 58, no. 2 (Winter): 374–96.
Kahn, Herman. 1962. *Thinking about the Unthinkable.* New York: Horizon Press.
Kalb, Bernard, and Marvin Kalb. 1975. *Kissinger.* New York: Dell.
Kanet, R., and E. Kolodziej, eds. 1991. *The Cold War as Cooperation.* Baltimore: Johns Hopkins University Press.
Kant, Immanuel. 1949. "Eternal Peace." In Carl J. Frederich, ed., *The Philosophy of Kant.* New York: Modern Library.
Kaplan, Morton A. 1957. *System and Process in International Politics.* New York: John Wiley & Sons.
———. 1979. *Towards Professionalism in International Theory.* New York: Free Press.
Kaplan, S .S., ed. 1981. *Diplomacy of Power.* Washington, D.C.: Brookings Institution.
Karsh, Efraim. 1985. *The Cautious Bear: Soviet Military Engagement in Middle East Wars in the Post-1967 Era.* Tel Aviv: Jaffee Center for Strategic Studies.
Katz, Mark N., ed. 1991. *Soviet-American Conflict Resolution in the Third World.* Washington, D.C.: United States Institute of Peace Press.
Keal, Paul. 1983. *Unspoken Rules and Superpower Dominance.* London: Macmillan.
Keeng, S. M., and W. K. H. Panofsky. 1985. "MAD versus Nuts." In M. Bundy, ed., *The Nuclear Controversy.* New York: New American Library.
Kegley, Charles, ed. 1991. *The Long Postwar Peace.* New York: Harper Collins.
Kegley, Charles, and Gregory Raymond. 1992. "Must We Fear a Post–Cold War Multipolar System?" *Journal of Conflict Resolution* 36, no. 3 (September): 573–85.
Kennedy, Paul M. 1987. *The Rise and Fall of the Great Powers: Economic Change and Military Conflict from 1500 to 2000.* New York: Random House.
Keohane, Robert O. 1969. "Lilliputians' Dilemmas: Small States in International Politics." *International Organization* 23, no. 2 (Spring): 291–310.
———. 1971. "The Big Influence of Small Allies." *Foreign Policy* no. 2 (Spring): 161–82.
———. 1980. "The Theory of Hegemonic Stability and Changes in International Economic Regimes, 1967–1977." In Ole Holsti, R. M. Siverson, and A. George, eds., *Change in the International System,* 131–62. Boulder, Colo.: Westview.

———. 1983. "Theory of World Politics: Structural Realism and Beyond." In Ada Finifter, ed., *Political Science: The State of the Discipline*, 503–40. Washington, D.C.: American Political Science Association. Reprinted in Robert O. Keohane, ed., *Neorealism and its Critics*, 158–203. New York: Columbia University Press, 1986.

———. 1984 *After Hegemony: Cooperation and Discord in the World Political Economy*. Princeton, N.J.: Princeton University Press.

———. 1989. *International Institutions and State Power: Essays in International Relations Theory*. Boulder, Colo.: Westview.

———. 1990. "Correspondence." *Internatonal Security* 15 (Fall): 192–94.

Keohane, Robert O., ed. 1986. *Neorealism and Its Critics*. New York: Columbia University Press.

Keohane, Robert O., and Joseph Nye. 1977. *Power and Interdependence: World Politics in Transition*. Boston: Little Brown.

———. 1987. "Power and Interdependence Revisited." *International Organization* 41 (Autumn): 725–53.

Keohane, Robert O., and Joseph Nye, eds. 1972. *Transnational Relations and World Politics*. Cambridge, Mass.: Harvard University Press.

Khrushchev, Nikita S. 1974. *Khrushchev Remembers: The Last Testament*. Translated and edited by Strobe Talbott. Boston: Little Brown.

Kirk, George. 1954. *The Middle-East 1945–1950, Survey of International Affairs*. London: Oxford University Press.

Kissinger, Henry. 1964. *A World Restored*. New York: Universal Library.

———. 1979. *White House Years*. Boston: Little, Brown.

———. 1982. *Years of Upheaval*. Boston: Little, Brown.

Kissinger, Henry, and Cyrus Vance. 1988. "Bipartisan Objectives for Foreign Policy." *Foreign Affairs* 66, no. 5 (Summer): 193–222.

Klare, M. 1993. "The Next Great Arms Race." *Foreign Affairs* 72 (Summer): 136–52.

Klein, Robert A. 1974. *Sovereign Equality among States: The History of an Idea*. Toronto: University of Toronto Press.

Kohler, Foy, Goure Leon, and Harvey Mose. 1974. *The Soviet Union and the October 1973 Middle East War: The Implications for Detente*. Monographs in International Affairs. Miami: Center for Advanced International Studies, University of Miami.

Korbonski, A., and F. Fukuyama, eds. 1987. *The Soviet Union in the Third World after 30 Years*. Ithaca, N.Y.: Cornell University Press.

Krasner, Stephen D. 1972. "Are Bureaucracies Important? (Or Allison Wonderland)." *Foreign Policy* no. 7 (Summer): 159–79.

———. 1978. *Defending the National Interest*. Princeton, N.J.: Princeton University Press.

Krasner, Stephen D., ed. 1983. *International Regimes*. Ithaca, N.Y.: Cornell University Press.

Kratochwil, Friedrich V. 1984. "The Force of Prescriptions." *International Organization* 38, no. 4 (Autumn): 685–708.

———. 1989. *Rules, Norms and Decisions*. Cambridge: Cambridge University Press.

Krause, Keith. 1991. "Military Statecraft: Power and Influence in Soviet and American Arms Transfer Relationships." *International Studies Quarterly* 35, no. 3 (September): 313–36.
Krauthammer, Charles. 1990/91. "The Unipolar Moment." *Foreign Affairs: America and the World* 70:23–33.
Kremenyuk, Victor. 1991. "The Cold War as Cooperation: A Soviet Perspective." In R. Kanet and E. Kolodziej, eds., *The Cold War as Cooperation*. Baltimore: Johns Hopkins University Press.
Kubalkova, V. and A. A. Cruickshank. 1989. *Thinking New about Soviet "New Thinking."* Berkeley, Calif.: Institute of International Studies.
Kupchan, Charles, and Clifford Kupchan. 1991. "Concerts, Collective Security, and the Future of Europe." *International Security* 16 (Summer): 114–61.
Lambeth, Benjamin S. 1984. "The Political Potential of Equivalence." In S. Miller, ed., *Strategy and Nuclear Deterrence*. Princeton, N.J.: Princeton University Press.
Laqueur, Walter Z. 1974. *Confrontation: The Middle East War and World Politics*. London: Wildwood House.
Larrabee, Stephen. 1992. "Instability and Change in the Balkans." *Survival* 34 (Summer): 31–49.
Larson, Deborah. 1985. *Origins of Containment: A Psychological Explanation*. Princeton, N.J.: Princeton University Press.
Larson, Thomas B. 1978. *Soviet-American Rivalry*. New York: W. W. Norton.
Lauren, Paul G. 1979. "Theories of Bargaining with Threats of Force: Deterrence and Coercive Diplomacy." In Paul G. Lauren, ed., *Diplomacy: New Approaches in History, Theory, and Policy*. New York: Free Press.
———. 1983. "Crisis Prevention in Nineteenth-Century Diplomacy." In A. George, ed., *Managing U.S.-Soviet Rivalry: Problems of Crisis Prevention*. Boulder, Colo.: Westview.
Layne, Christopher. 1993. "The Unipolar Illusion: Why New Great Powers Will Rise." *International Security* 17, no. 4 (Spring): 5–51.
Lazarus, R., J. Averill, and E. Opton. 1974. "The Assessment of Coping." In G. V. Coelho, D. A. Hamburg, and J. Adams, eds., *Coping and Adaption*, 249–399. New York: Basic Books.
Lebow, Richard Ned. 1981. *Between Peace and War: The Nature of International Crisis*. Baltimore: Johns Hopkins University Press.
———. 1987. *Nuclear Crisis Management*. Ithaca, N.Y.: Cornell University Press.
———. 1989. "Deterrence: A Political and Psychological Critique." In P. Stern, R. Axelrod, R. Jervis, and R. Radner, eds., *Perspectives on Deterrence*. New York: Oxford University Press.
———. 1991. "Thucydides, Power Transition Theory, and the Causes of War." In Richard Ned Lebow and B. Strauss, eds., *Hegemonic Rivalry: From Thucydides to the Nuclear Age*. Boulder, Colo.: Westview.
Lebow, Richard Ned, and Janice Stein. 1992. "Preventing War in the Middle East: When Do Deterrence and Reassurance Work?." In S. Speigel, ed., *Conflict Management in the Middle East,* Boulder, Colo.: Westview.

Lebow, Richard Ned, and B. Strauss, eds. 1991. *Hegemonic Rivalry: From Thucydides to the Nuclear Age.* Boulder, Colo.: Westview.

Legvold, Robert. 1977. "The Nature of Soviet Power." *Foreign Affairs* 57, no. 4 (October): 755–78.

———. 1979. "The Super Rivals: Conflict in the Third World." *Foreign Affairs* 57 (Spring): 755–78.

———. 1988. "War, Weapons, and Soviet Foreign Policy." In S. Bialer, and Michael Mandelbaum, eds., *Gorbachev's Russia and American Foreign Policy.* Boulder, Colo.: Westview.

Lenczowski, George. 1990. *American Presidents and the Middle East.* Durham, N.C.: Duke University Press.

Levy, Jack. 1983a. "Misperception and the Causes of War." *World Politics* 35 (1): 76–99.

———. 1983b. *War in the Modern Great Power System, 1495–1975.* Lexington, Ky: University Press of Kentucky.

———. 1985a. "The Polarity of the System and International Stability: An Empirical Analysis." In Alan Ned Sabrosky, ed., *Polarity and War.* Boulder, Colo.: Westview.

———. 1985b. "Theories of General War." *World Politics* 37, no. 3 (April): 344–74.

———. 1987. "Declining Power and the Preventive Motivation for War." *World Politics* 40 (October): 82–107.

———. 1989a. "The Causes of War: A Review of Theories and Evidence." In P. Tetlock, J. Husbands, R. Jervis, P. Stern, and C. Tilly, eds., *Behavior, Society and Nuclear War.* New York: Oxford University Press.

———. 1989b. "Domestic Politics and War." In R. Rotberg and T. Rabb, eds., *The Origin and Prevention of Major Wars.* Cambridge: Cambridge University Press.

———. 1989c. "Quantitative Studies of Deterrence Success and Failure." In P. Stern, R. Axelrod, R. Jervis, and R. Radner, eds., *Perspectives on Deterrence.* New York: Oxford University Press.

———. 1991a. "Long Cycles, Hegemonic Transitions, and the Long Peace." In C. Kegley, ed., *The Long Postwar Peace.* New York: Harper Collins.

———. 1991b. "The Role of Crisis Management in the Outbreak of World War I." In Alexander George, ed., *Avoiding War: Problems of Crisis Management.* Boulder, Colo.: Westview.

Lindblom, Charles E. 1965. *The Intelligence of Democracy.* New York: Free Press.

Lipschutz, Ronnie D. 1989. *When Nations Clash: Raw Materials, Ideology and Foreign Policy.* Cambridge, Mass.: Ballinger.

Lipson, Charles. 1984. "International Cooperation in Economic and Security Affairs." *World Politics* 37, no. 1 (October): 1–23.

Liska, George. 1986a. "Concert through Decompression." *Foreign Policy* no. 63 (Summer): 108–29.

———. 1986b. "From Containment to Concert." *Foreign Policy* no. 62 (Spring): 3–23.

Lorch, Nathenel. 1990. *Bizvat Hmatsamot.* Tel Aviv: Maarchot. Hebrew.

Lowi, Theodore. 1979. *The End of Liberalism.* 2d. ed. New York: W. W. Norton.

Luard, Evan. 1976. *Types of International Society.* New York: Free Press.

———. 1986a. "Superpowers and Regional Conflicts." *Foreign Affairs* 64, no. 5 (Summer): 1006–25.

———. 1986b. *War in International Society*. New Haven: Yale University Press.
———. 1990. *International Society*. New York: New Amsterdam.
Lynn-Jones, Sean M. 1986. "Detente and Deterrence: Anglo-German Relations, 1911–1914." *International Security* 11, no. 2 (Fall): 121–50.
Lynn-Jones, Sean M., ed. 1991. *The Cold War and After: Prospects for Peace*. Cambridge, Mass.: The MIT Press.
MacFarlane, Neil S. 1985. "The Soviet Conception of Regional Security." *World Politics* 37, no. 3 (April): 295–316.
———. 1987a. "Soviet Perspectives on Third World Security." University of California, Berkeley, and Stanford University, Program on Soviet International Behavior. Draft manuscript, February 23.
———. 1987b. "The Soviet Union and Conflict Management in the Middle East." In Gabriel Ben-Dor and David Dewitt, eds., *Conflict Management in the Middle East*. Lexington, Mass.: Lexington Books.
Mandelbaum, Michael. 1981. *The Nuclear Revolution: International Politics before and after Hiroshima*. New York: Cambridge University Press.
———. 1988. *The Fate of Nations*. New York: Cambridge University Press.
Mangold, Peter. 1978. *Superpower Intervention in the Middle East*. New York: St. Martin's.
Manning, C. A. W. 1962. *The Nature of International Society*. London: Bell.
Mansfield, Edward. 1993. "Concentration, Polarity, and the Distribution of Power." *International Studies Quarterly* 37, no. 1 (March): 105–28.
Maoz, Zeev, and Bruce Russett. 1993. "Structural and Normative Causes of Peace between Democracies." *American Political Science Review* 87, no. 3 (September): 624–38.
Marantz, Paul, and Belma S. Steinberg, eds. 1985. *Superpower Involvement in the Middle East: Dynamics of Foreign Policy*. Boulder, Colo.: Westview.
March, James G., and Herbert A. Simon. 1958. *Organizations*. New York: Wiley.
Marcum, John. 1976. "Lessons of Angola." *Foreign Affairs* 54 (April): 407–25.
Matheson, Neil. 1982. *The "Rules of the Game" of Superpower Military Intervention in the Third World 1975–1980*. Lanham, Md: University Press of America.
Mathias, Charles. 1981. "Ethnic Groups and Foreign Policy." *Foreign Affairs* 59, no. 5 (Summer): 975–98.
May, Ernest R., ed. 1984. *Knowing One's Enemies: Intelligence Assessment before the Two World Wars*. Princeton, N.J.: Princeton University Press.
McConnell, James. 1979. "The 'Rules of the Game': A Theory on the Practice of Superpower Naval Diplomacy." In B. Dismukes and J. McConnell, eds., *Soviet Naval Diplomacy*. New York: Pergamon.
McNaugher, Thomas L. 1985. *Arms and Oil: U.S. Military Strategy and the Persian Gulf*. Washington, D.C.: Brookings Institution.
Mearsheimer, John. 1983. *Conventional Deterrence*. Ithaca, N.Y.: Cornell University Press.
———. 1990. "Back to the Future: Instability in Europe after the Cold War." *International Security* 15, no. 1 (Summer): 5–56.
Meir, Golda. 1975. *My Life*. New York: Deli.

Menon, Rajan. 1986. *Soviet Power and the Third World.* New Haven, Conn.: Yale University Press.
Midlarsky, M. I. 1988. *The Onset of World War.* Boston: Unwin Hyman.
———. 1991. "International Structure and the Learning of Cooperation." In C. Kegley, ed., *The Long Postwar Peace.* New York: Harper Collins.
Midlarsky, M. I., ed. 1989. *Handbook of War Studies.* Boston: Unwin Hyman.
Midlarsky, M. I., and Ted Hopf. 1993. "Controversy: Polarity and International Stability." *American Political Science Review* 87, no. 1 (March): 173–80.
Milbrath, Lester. 1967. "Interest Groups and Foreign Policy." In J. Rosenau, ed., *Domestic Sources of Foreign Policy.* New York: Free Press.
Miller, Benjamin. 1988. "Can Opponents Cooperate: Explaining Great Power Cooperation in Managing Third Area Conflicts." Ph.D. diss., University of California, Berkeley.
———. 1992a. "Explaining Great Power Cooperation in Conflict Management." *World Politics* 45, no. 1 (October): 1–46.
———. 1992b. "International Systems and Regional Security: From Competition to Cooperation, Dominance or Disengagement?" Paper presented at the annual meeting of the American Political Science Association, Chicago, September.
———. 1992c. "A 'New World Order': From Balancing to Hegemony, Concert or to Collective Security?" *International Interactions* 18:1–33.
———. 1993. "From Balance of Power to International Society or to Hegemonic Stability: Competing Theoretical Models and Great Power Crisis Interaction." The Hebrew University of Jerusalem. Manuscript.
Milner, Helen. 1991. "The Assumption of Anarchy in International Relations Theory: A Critique." *Review of International Studies* 17:67–85.
———. 1992. "International Theories of Cooperation among Nations." *World Politics* 44 (April): 466–96.
Mirski, G. 1990. "The New Political Thinking and Soviet Approach to Regional Conflicts." Paper presented at the International Studies Association meeting, Washington, D.C., April.
Mischel, Walter. 1973. "Toward a Cognitive Social Learning Reconceptualization of Personality." *Psychological Review* 80:252–83.
Modelski, George. 1978. "The Long Cycle of Global Politics and the Nation-State." *Comparative Studies in Society and History* 20 (April): 214–35.
Moltz, James C. 1993. "Divergent Learning and the Failed Politics of Soviet Economic Reform." *World Politics* 45 (January): 301–25.
Morgan, Patrick M. 1983. *Deterrence: A Conceptual Analysis.* 2d ed. Beverly Hills, Calif.: Sage Publications.
Morgenthau, Hans J. 1978. *Politics among Nations.* 5th ed. New York: Knopf.
Mueller, J. E. 1989. *Retreat from Doomsday: The Obsolescence of Major War.* New York: Basic Books.
———. 1991. "The Essential Irrelevance of Nuclear Weapons: Stability in the Postwar World." In Sean M. Lynn-Jones, ed., *The Cold War and After: Prospects for Peace,* 45–69. Cambridge, Mass.: MIT Press.
Nacht, Michael. 1985. *The Age of Vulnerability: Threats to the Nuclear Stalemate.* Washington, D.C.: Brookings Institution.

Nardin, Terry. 1983. *Law, Morality, and the Relations of States*. Princeton, N.J.: Princeton University Press.

Neff, Donald. 1981. *Warriors at Suez: Eisenhower Takes America into the Middle East*. New York: Simon & Schuster.

———. 1988a. *Warriors against Israel: How Israel Won the Battle to Become America's Ally 1973*. Brattleboro, Vt: Amana Books.

———. 1988b. *Warriors for Jerusalem: The Six Days That Changed the Middle East*. Brattleboro, VT: Amana Books.

Neuman, Stephanie. 1986. *Military Assistance in Recent Wars: The Dominance of the Superpowers*. New York: Praeger.

———. 1988. "Arms, Aid and the Superpowers." *Foreign Affairs* 66, no. 5 (Summer): 1044–66.

Nicolson, Harold. 1946. *The Congress of Vienna*. New York: Harcourt Brace.

Nitze, Paul H. 1976. "Assuring Strategic Stability in an Era of Detente." *Foreign Affairs* 54 (January): 207–32.

Nixon, Richard. 1978. *The Memoirs of Richard Nixon*. 2 vols. New York: Warner Books.

Novik, Nimrod. 1985. *Encounter with Reality: Reagan and the Middle East during the First Term*. Tel Aviv: Jaffee Center for Strategic Studies.

Noyes, James H. 1982. *The Clouded Lens: Persian Gulf Security and U.S. Policy*. Stanford, Calif.: Hoover Institution Press.

Nye, Joseph. 1984. "The Domestic Roots of American Policy," and "Can America Manage Its Soviet Policy?" In J. Nye, ed., *The Making of America's Soviet Policy*. New Haven, Conn.: Yale University Press.

———. 1986. "The Domestic Environment of U.S. Policy Making." In Arnold Horelick, ed., *U.S.-Soviet Relations: The Next Phase*. Ithaca, N.Y.: Cornell University Press.

———. 1987. "Nuclear Learning and U.S.-Soviet Security Regimes." *International Organization* 41 (Summer): 371–402.

———. 1988a. "Neorealism and Neoliberalism." *World Politics* 40, no. 2 (January): 235–51.

———. 1988b. "U.S.-Soviet Cooperation in a Nonproliferation Regime." In Alexander George, Phillip Farley, and Alexander Dallin, eds., *U.S.-Soviet Security Cooperation*. New York: Oxford University Press.

———. 1990. *Bound to Lead*. New York: Basic Books.

Olson, Mancur. 1965. *The Logic of Collective Action*. Cambridge. Mass.: Harvard University Press.

Oneal, J. R. 1982. *Foreign Policy Making in Times of Crisis*. Columbus: Ohio State University Press.

———. 1988. "The Rationality of Decision Making during International Crises." *Polity* 20: 598–622.

Organski, A. F. K. 1968. *World Politics*. 2d ed. New York: Knopf.

———. 1990. *The $36 Billion Bargain: Strategy and Politics in U.S. Assistance to Israel*. New York: Columbia University Press.

Organski, A. F. K., and Jacek Kugler. 1980. *The War Ledger*. Chicago: University of Chicago Press.

Orme, John. 1987. "Deterrence Failures: A Second Look." *International Security* 11, no. 4 (Spring): 96–124.

Osgood, Robert, ed. 1981. *Containment, Soviet Behavior, and Grand Strategy.* Policy Papers in International Affairs, no. 16. Berkeley: Institute of International Studies, University of California.

Osgood, Robert, and Robert W. Tucker. 1967. *Force, Order, and Justice.* Baltimore: Johns Hopkins Press.

Oye, Kenneth, ed. 1985. "Explaining Cooperation under Anarchy: Hypotheses and Strategies." *World Politics* 38, no. 1 (October): 1–24.

Paige, Glenn D. 1968. *The Korean Decision.* New York: Free Press.

———. 1972. "Comparative Case Analysis of Crisis Decisions: Korea and Cuba." In C. Hermann, ed., *International Crisis: Insights from Behavioral Research.* New York: Free Press.

Patchen, Martin. 1988. *Resolving Disputes between Nations: Coercion or Conciliation?* Durham, N.C.: Duke University Press.

Patterson, T. G., and W. J. Brophy. 1986. "October Missile and November Elections: The Cuban Missile Crisis and American Politics, 1962." *Journal of American History* 73:87–119.

Pierre, Andrew J. 1971. "America Down, Russia Up: The Changing Political Role of Military Power." *Foreign Policy* no. 4 (Fall): 163–87.

Pipes, Richard. 1980. "Detente: Moscow's View." In Erik P. Hoffmann and Frederic Fleron, eds., *The Conduct of Soviet Foreign Policy.* New York: Aldine.

———. 1981. *U.S.-Soviet Relations in the Era of Detente.* Boulder, Colo.: Westview.

Polsby, Nelson W. 1983. *Consequences of Party Reform.* Oxford: Oxford University Press.

Porter, Bruce D. 1984. *The USSR in Third World Conflicts.* Cambridge, Mass.: Cambridge University Press.

Posen, Barry R. 1982. "Inadvertent Nuclear War? Escalation and NATO's Northern Flank." *International Security* 7:28–54. Reprinted in S. Miller, ed., *Strategy and Nuclear Deterrence: An International Security Reader.* Princeton, N.J.: Princeton University Press.

———. 1984. *The Sources of Military Doctrine: France, Britain, and Germany between the World Wars.* Ithaca, N.Y.: Cornell University Press.

Posen, Barry R., and Stephen Van Evera. 1983. "Defense Policy and the Reagan Administration: Departure from Containment." *International Security* 8, no. 1 (Summer): 3–45.

Pranger, Robert. 1979. "Six U.S. Perspectives on Soviet Foreign Policy Intentions." *AEI Foreign Policy and Defense Review* 1, no. 5 (October): 2–25.

Primakov, Yevgeny. 1986. "The Soviet Union's Interests: Myths and Reality." *AEI Foreign Policy and Defense Review* 6, no. 1: 26–34.

———. 1988. "Soviet Policy toward the Arab-Israeli Conflict." In W. Quandt, ed., *The Middle East: Ten Years after Camp David.* Washington, D.C.: Brookings Institution.

Puchala, Donald J., and Raymond F. Hopkins. 1983. "International Regimes: Lessons from Inductive Analysis." In Stephen D. Krasner, ed., *International Regimes,* 61–92. Ithaca, N.Y.: Cornell University Press.

Quandt, William. 1976. *Soviet Policy in the October 1973 War.* Santa Monica, Calif.: RAND.
———. 1977. *Decade of Decisions: American Policy toward the Arab-Israeli Conflict, 1967–1976.* Berkeley: University of California Press.
———. 1978. "Lebanon 1958, and Jordan 1970." In B. Blechman and S. Kaplan, eds., *Force without War, U.S. Armed Forces as a Political Instrument.* Washington, D.C.: Brookings Institution.
———. 1986a. *Camp David: Peacemaking and Politics.* Washington, D.C.: Brookings Institution.
———. 1986b. "U.S.-Soviet Rivalry in the Middle East." In Marshall D. Shulman, ed., *East-West Tensions in the Third World.* New York: W. W. Norton.
———. 1988. "U.S. Policy toward the Arab-Israeli Conflict." In William Quandt, ed., *The Middle East: Ten Years after Camp David.* Washington, D.C.: Brookings Institution.
Quester, George. 1989. "Some Thoughts on 'Deterrence Failures.'" In P. Stern, R. Axelrod, R. Jervis, and R. Radner, eds., *Perspectives on Deterrence.* New York: Oxford University Press.
Rabin, Yitzhak. 1979. *The Rabin Memoirs.* Jerusalem: Steimatzky's Agency.
Rabinovich, Itamar. 1987. "Controlled Conflict in the Middle East: The Syrian-Israeli Rivalry in Lebanon." In Gabriel Ben-Dor and David B. Dewitt, eds., *Conflict Management in the Middle East.* Lexington, Mass.: Lexington Books.
———. 1990. "The Middle East." In Nicholas Rizopoulos, ed., *Sea-Changes: American Foreign Policy in a World Transformed.* New York: Council on Foreign Relations Press.
Raiffa, Howard. 1982. *The Art and Science of Negotiation.* Cambridge, Mass.: Harvard University Press.
Reich, Bernard. 1980. "United States Interests in the Middle East." In Haim Shaked and Itamar Rabinovich, eds., *The Middle East and the United States: Perceptions and Policies.* New Brunswick, N.J.: Transaction Books.
———. 1984. *The United States and Israel: Influence in the Special Relationship.* New York: Praeger.
Riad, Mahmoud. 1981. *The Struggle for Peace in the Middle East.* London: Quartet Books.
Richardson, Lewis F. 1960. *Arms and Insecurity.* Chicago: Quadrangle.
Rittberger, Volker, ed. 1993. *Regime Theory and International Relations.* Oxford: Clarendon Press.
Roberts, S. S. 1979. "Superpower Naval Confrontations: The October 1973 Arab-Israeli War." In B. Dismukes and J. McConnell, eds., *Soviet Naval Diplomacy.* New York: Pergamon.
Robertson, E. M., ed. 1971. *The Origins of the Second World War: Historical Interpretations.* London: Macmillan.
Roi, Ya'acov. 1974. *From Encroachement to Involvement, A Documentary Study of Soviet Policy in the Middle East 1945–1973.* Jerusalem: Israel Universities Press.
———. 1980. *Soviet Decision-Making in Practice, The U.S.S.R., and Israel 1947–1954.* New Brunswick, N.J.: Transaction Books.

Roi, Ya'acov, ed. 1979. *The Limits to Power: Soviet Policy in the Middle East*. London: Croom Helm.
Ronen, Dov. 1979. *The Quest for Self-Determination*. New Haven, Conn.: Yale University Press.
Rosecrance, Richard N. 1963. *Action and Reaction in World Politics: International Systems in Perspective*. Boston: Little, Brown.
———. 1980. "Objectives of U.S. Middle East Policy." In Haim Shaked and Itamar Rabinovich, eds., *The Middle East and the United States: Perceptions and Policies*. New Brunswick, N.J.: Transaction Books.
———. 1981. "International Theory Revisited." *International Organization* 35, no. 4 (Autumn): 691–713.
———. 1986. *The Rise of the Trading State: Commerce and Conquest in the Modern World*. New York: Basic Books.
———. 1991. "Regionalism and the Post–Cold War Era." *International Journal* 46 (Summer): 373–93.
Rosenau, James N. 1986. "Before Cooperation: Hegemons, Regimes, and Habit-Driven Actors in World Politics." *International Organization* 40, no. 4 (Autumn): 849–94.
Rosenau, James N., ed. 1967. *Domestic Sources of Foreign Policy*. New York: Free Press.
———. 1969. *Linkage Politics*. New York: Free Press.
Rosenau, James N., and E. O. Czempiel, eds. 1992. *Governance without Government: Order and Change in World Politics*. Cambridge: Cambridge University Press.
Ross, Dennis. 1985. "The Soviet Union and the Persian Gulf." In Dan Caldwell, ed., *Soviet International Behavior and U.S. Policy Options*. Lexington, Mass.: Lexington Books.
———. 1990. "The Soviet Union and the Lebanon War, 1982–1984." In G. Breslauer, ed., *Soviet Strategy in the Middle East*. Winchester, Mass.: Unwin Hyman.
Rotberg, R, and T. Rabb, eds. 1989. *The Origin and Prevention of Major Wars*. Cambridge: Cambridge University Press.
Rubenberg, Cheryl. 1986. *Israel and the American National Interest*. Urbana: University of Illinois Press.
Rubinstein, Alvin Z. 1977. *Red Star on the Nile*. Princeton, N.J.: Princeton University Press.
———. 1980. "The Evolution of Soviet Strategy in the Middle East." *Orbis,* Summer, 323–38.
———. 1981. "Air Support in the Arab East." In S. S. Kaplan, *Diplomacy of Power.* Washington, D.C.: Brookings Institution.
Ruggie, John G. 1983. "International Regimes, Transactions, and Change: Embedded Liberalism in the Postwar Economic Order." In S. Krasner, ed., *International Regimes*. Ithaca: Cornell University Press.
———. 1986. "Continuity and Transformation in the World Polity: Toward a Neorealist Synthesis." In Robert Keohane, ed., *Neorealism and Its Critics*. New York: Columbia University Press.
Ruggie, John G., and Friedrich Kratochwil. 1986, "International Organization: The State of the Art or an Art of the State." *International Organization* 40 (Autumn): 753–76.

Russett, Bruce. 1963. "The Calculus of Deterrence." *Journal of Conflict Resolution* 7 (June): 97–109.
———. 1967. "Pearl Harbor: Deterrence Theory and Decision Theory." *Journal of Peace Research* 4: 89–105.
———. 1983. *The Prisoners of Insecurity*. San Francisco: W. H. Freeman.
———. 1990. *Controlling the Sword: The Democratic Governance of National Security*. Cambridge, Mass.: Harvard University Press.
Sadat, Anwar. 1977. *In Search of Identity*. New York: Harper & Row.
Safran, Nadav. 1969. *From War to War*. New York: Pegasus.
———. 1981. *Israel—The Embattled Ally*. Cambridge, Mass.: Belknap.
Sagan, Scott. 1979. "Lessons of the Yom Kippur Alert." *Foreign Policy* 36 (Fall): 160–77.
———. 1985. "Nuclear Alerts and Crisis Management." *International Security* 9, no. 4 (Spring): 99–139.
———. 1986. "1914 Revisited: Allies, Offense, and Instability." *International Security* 11, no. 2 (Fall): 151–75.
Said, Abdul A., ed. 1977. *Ethnicity and U.S. Foreign Policy*. New York: Praeger.
Saperstein, Alvin. 1991. "The 'Long Peace'—Result of a Bipolar Competitive World?" *Journal of Conflict Resolution* 35, no. 1 (March): 68–79.
Saunders, Harold H. 1986. "Superpower Stakes in the Middle East." In *AEI Foreign Policy and Defense Review* 6 (1): 14–26.
———. 1988. "Regulating Soviet-U.S. Competition and Cooperation in the Arab-Israeli Arena, 1967–86." In Alexander George, Philip Farley, and Alexander Dallin, eds., *U.S.-Soviet Security Cooperation*, 540–80. New York: Oxford University Press.
Saunders, Harold H., ed. 1986. "The Superpowers in the Middle East." AEI *Foreign Policy and Defense Review*, 6(1): n.p.
Schelling, Thomas C. 1960. *The Strategy of Conflict*. Cambridge, Mass.: Harvard University Press.
———. 1966. *Arms and Influence*. New Haven, Conn.: Yale University Press.
———. 1978. *Micromotives and Macrobehavior*. New York: W. W. Norton.
Scherer, F. M. 1970. *Industrial Pricing: Theory and Evidence*. Chicago: Rand-McNally.
Schiff, Ze'ev and Ehud Ya'ari. 1984. *Israel's Lebanon War*. New York: Simon and Schuster.
———. 1990. *The Intifada*. Tel Aviv: Shocken Books. Hebrew.
Schilling, Warner R. 1984. "U.S. Strategic Nuclear Concepts in the 1970s: The Search for Sufficiently Equivalent Countervailing Parity." In Steven Miller, ed., *Strategy and Nuclear Deterrence: An International Security Reader*. Princeton, N.J.: Princeton University Press.
Schneider, William. 1984. "Public Opinion." In J. Nye, ed., *The Making of America's Soviet Policy*. New Haven, Conn.: Yale University Press.
Schroeder, Paul W. 1972. *Austria, Great Britain, and the Crimean War: The Destruction of the European Concert*. Ithaca, N.Y.: Cornell University Press.
———. 1986. "The 19th-Century International System: Changes in the Structure." *World Politics* 34, no.1 (October): 1–26.
Schweller, Randall. 1992. "Domestic Structure and Preventive War: Are Democracies More Pacific?" *World Politics* 44 (January): 235–69.

———. 1993. "Tripolarity and the Second World War." *International Studies Quarterly* 37, no. 1 (March): 73–104.
Seabury, Paul. 1978. "Realism and Idealism." In Alexander De Conde, ed., *Encyclopedia of American Foreign Policy*, 3:856–66. New York: Charles Scribner's Sons.
Sella, Amnon. 1982. "The Soviet Attitudes towards the War in the Lebanon–Mid-1982." Research paper no. 47. Jerusalem: The Soviet and East European Research Center, The Hebrew University of Jerusalem.
Sestanovich, Stephen. 1987. "The Third World in Soviet Foreign Policy." In A. Korbonski and F. Fukuyama, eds., *The Soviet Union in the Third World after 30 Years*. Ithaca, N.Y.: Cornell University Press.
Shamir, Shimon. 1980. "Egypt's Reorientation towards the U.S.—Factors and Conditions of Decision Making." In Haim Shaked and Itamar Rabinovich, eds., *The Middle East and the United States: Perceptions and Policies*. New Brunswick, N.J.: Transaction Books.
Shlaim, A. 1983. *The United States and the Berlin Blockade 1948–1949*. Berkeley: University of California Press.
Shoemaker, Christopher, and John Spanier. 1984. *Patron-Client State Relationships: Multilateral Crises in the Nuclear Age*. New York: Praeger.
Shubik, Martin. 1971. "Games of Status." *Behavioral Science* 16 (March): 117–29.
Shulman, Marshall D. 1980. "Toward a Western Philosophy of Coexistence." In Erik P. Hoffmann and Fredric J. Fleron, eds., *The Conduct of Soviet Foreign Policy*, 333–53. New York: Aldine.
———. 1986. "An Alternative Policy for Managing U.S.-Soviet Relations." In Arnold Horelick, ed., *U.S.-Soviet Relations: The Next Phase*, 259–75. Ithaca, N.Y.: Cornell University Press.
Shulman, Marshall D., ed. 1986. *East-West Tensions in the Third World*. New York: W. W. Norton.
Shulsky, Abram. 1979. "The Jordanian Crisis of September 1970." In Bradford Dismukes and James M. McConnell, eds., *Soviet Naval Diplomacy*. New York: Pergamon.
Sicherman, Harvey. 1976. *The Yom Kippur War: End of Illusion?* Vol. 1, no. 4 of *The Foreign Policy Papers*. Beverly Hills and London: Sage.
Simes, Dimitri K. 1986. "The Domestic Environment of Soviet Policy Making." In Arnold Horelick, ed., *U.S.-Soviet Relations: The Next Phase*. Ithaca, N.Y.: Cornell University Press.
Simmel, G. 1956. *Conflict*. Translated by K. H. Wolff. Glencoe, Ill.: Free Press.
Singer, David J. 1961. "The Level of Analysis Problem." *World Politics* 14, no. 1 (October): 77–92.
Slater, Jerome. 1990–91. "The Superpowers and an Arab-Israeli Political Settlement: The Cold War Years." *Political Science Quarterly* 105 (4): 557–78.
Smith, Adam. 1776. *An Inquiry into the Nature and Causes of the Wealth of Nations*. Edited by Edwin Cannan. New Rochelle, N.Y.: Arlington House.
Smith, Gaddis. 1986. *Morality, Reason and Power: American Diplomacy in the Carter Years*. New York: Hill and Wang.
Smith, Gerard. 1980. *Doubletalk: The Story of the First Arms Limitation Talks*. Garden City, N.Y.: Doubleday.

Smith, Roger K. 1987. "Explaining the Non-Proliferation Regime: Anomalies for Contemporary International Relations Theory." *International Organization* 41, no. 2 (Spring): 253–81.
Smoke, Richard. 1977. *War: Controlling Escalation.* Cambridge, Mass.: Harvard University Press.
———. 1991. "The Crimean War." In Alexander George, ed., *Avoiding War: Problems of Crisis Management.* Boulder, Colo.: Westview.
Smolansky, O. M. 1978. "The United States and the Soviet Union in the Middle East." In G. Kirk and N. Wessell, eds., *The Soviet Threat: Myths and Realities,* 99–109. New York: Academy of Political Science.
Snidal, Duncan. 1991. "International Cooperation among Relative Gains Maximizers." *International Studies Quarterly* 35 (December): 387–402.
Snyder, Glenn. 1965. "The Balance of Power and the Balance of Terror." In P. Seabury, ed., *The Balance of Power,* 185–201. San Francisco: Chandler.
———. 1984. "The Security Dilemma in Alliance Politics." *World Politics* 36, no. 4 (July): 461–95.
Snyder, Glenn, and Paul Diesing. 1977. *Conflict among Nations.* Princeton, N.J.: Princeton University Press.
Snyder, Jack. 1984. "Civil-Military Relations and the Cult of the Offensive, 1914 and 1984." *International Security* 9, no. 1 (Summer): 108–46. Reprinted in S. Miller, ed., *Military Strategy and the Origins of the First World War.* Princeton, N.J.: Princeton University Press.
———. 1990. "Averting Anarchy in the New Europe." *International Security* 14, no. 4 (Spring): 5–41.
Snyder, Mark, and William Ickes. 1985. "Personality and Social Behavior." In Gardner Lindzey and Elliot Aronson, eds., *Handbook of Social Psychology,* 3d ed., vol. 2, chap. 28. New York: Random House.
Sontag, Raymond. 1971. *A Broken World: 1919–1939.* New York: Harper.
Spechler, Dina Rome. 1978. *Domestic Influences on Soviet Foreign Policy.* Washington, D.C.: University Press of America.
———. 1986. "The U.S.S.R. and Third-World Conflicts: Domestic Debate and Soviet Policy in the Middle East, 1967–1973." *World Politics* 38, no.3 (April): 435–61.
Speier, Hans. 1957. "Soviet Atomic Blackmail and the North Atlantic Alliance." *World Politics* 9 (April): 307–28.
Spiegel, Steven L. 1985a. *The Other Arab-Israeli Conflict: Making America's Middle East Policy, from Truman to Reagan.* Chicago: University of Chicago Press.
———. 1985b. "Unnoticed Policy Makers: The President and His Crowd." Paper presented at the annual meeting of the American Political Science Association, New Orleans, August 29–September 1.
Spiegel, Steven L., ed., 1992. *Conflict Management in the Middle East.* Boulder, Colo.: Westview.
Spiegel, Steven L., Mark A. Heller, and Jacob Goldberg, eds. 1988. *The Soviet-American Competition in the Middle East.* Lexington, Mass.: Lexington Books.
Sprout, Harold, and Margaret Sprout. 1957. "Environmental Factors in the Study of International Politics." *Journal of Conflict Resolution* 1, no. 4 (December): 309–28.

Starr, Harvey. 1984. *Henry Kissinger: Perceptions of International Politics.* Lexington: University Press of Kentucky.
———. 1992. "Why Don't Democracies Fight One Another?: Evaluating the Theory-Findings Feedback Loop." *Jerusalem Journal of International Relations* 14:41–59.
Stein, Arthur. 1976. "Conflict and Cohesion: A Review of the Literature." *Journal of Conflict Resolution* 20 (1): 143–72.
———. 1983. "Coordination and Collaboration: Regimes in an Anarchic World." In Stephen Krasner, ed., *International Regimes.* Ithaca, N.Y.: Cornell University Press.
———. 1990. *Why Nations Cooperate.* Ithaca, N.Y.: Cornell University Press.
Stein, Janice G. 1978. "Can Decision-Makers Be Rational and Should They Be? Evaluating the Quality of Decisions." *Jerusalem Journal of International Relations* 3 (2–3): 316–39.
———. 1980. "Proxy Wars—How Superpowers End Them: The Diplomacy of War Termination in the Middle East." *International Journal* 35, no. 3 (Summer): 478–519.
———. 1982. "The Termination of the October War." In Nissan Oren, ed., *Termination of Wars,* 226–45. Jerusalem: Magnes.
———. 1991. "The Arab-Israeli War of 1967: Inadvertent War through Miscalculated Escalation." In A. George, *Avoiding War: Problems of Crisis Management.* Boulder, Colo.: Westview.
Stein, Janice G., and R. Tanter. 1980. *Rational Decision-Making: Israel's Security Choices, 1967.* Columbus: Ohio State University Press.
Steinbruner, John D. 1974. *The Cybernetic Theory of Decision.* Princeton, N.J.: Princeton University Press.
———. 1981. "Nuclear Decapitation." *Foreign Policy* 45:16–28.
Stewart, P., M. Hermann, and C. Hermann. 1989. "Modelling the 1973 Soviet Decision to Support Egypt." *American Political Science Review* 83, no. 1 (March): 35–60.
Stoessinger, John G. 1979. *Crusaders and Pragmatists: Movers and Makers of American Foreign Policy.* New York: W. W. Norton.
Strange, Susan. 1983. "Cave! Hic Dragones: A Critique of Regime Analysis." In S. Krasner, ed., *International Regimes.* Ithaca, N.Y.: Cornell University Press.
Summer, William G. 1911. "War." In *War and Other Essays.* New Haven, Conn.: Yale University Press. Reprinted in L. Bramson and G. Goethals, eds., *War.* New York: Basic Books, 1968.
Tanter, Raymond. 1975. "Crisis Management: A Critical Review of Academic Literature." *Jerusalem Journal of International Relations* 1, no. 1 (Fall): 71–102.
———. 1978. "International Crisis Behavior: An Appraisal of the Literature." *Jerusalem Journal of International Relations* 3, nos. 2–3 (Winter-Spring): 340–74.
Taubman, William. 1982. *Stalin's American Policy.* New York: W. W. Norton.
Taylor, A. J. P. 1961. *The Origins of the Second World War.* New York: Atheneum.
———. 1992. *The Struggle for Mastery in Europe, 1848–1914.* London: Oxford University Press.
Taylor, Alan. 1991. *The Superpowers and the Middle East.* Syracuse: Syracuse University Press.
Taylor, Michael. 1976. *Anarchy and Cooperation.* London: Wiley.

———. 1982. *Community, Anarchy and Liberty.* Cambridge: Cambridge University Press.

Telhami, Shibley. 1990. *Power and Leadership in International Bargaining.* New York: Columbia University Press.

Thompson, William R. 1986. "Polarity, the Long Cycle, and Global Power Warfare." *Journal of Conflict Resolution* 30, no. 4 (December): 587–615.

Thucydides. 1954. *The Peloponnesian War.* Translated by Tex Warner. New York: Penguin Books.

Tillman, Seth. 1982. *The United States in the Middle East.* Bloomington: Indiana University Press.

Tivnan, Edward. 1988. *The Lobby: Jewish Political Power and American Foreign Policy.* New York: Simon & Schuster.

Touval, Saadia. 1982. *The Peace Brokers: Mediators in the Arab-Israeli Conflict, 1948–1979.* Princeton, N.J.: Princeton University Press.

———. 1987. "Frameworks for Arab-Israeli Negotiations—What Difference Do They Make?" *Negotiation Journal,* January, 37–52.

Trachtenberg, Marc. 1991. *History and Strategy.* Princeton, N.J.: Princeton University Press.

Truman, David. 1951. *The Governmental Process.* New York: Alfred A. Knopf.

Tucker, Robert W. 1968. *Nation or Empire? The Debate over American Foreign Policy.* Baltimore: Johns Hopkins University Press.

———. 1977. *The Inequality of Nations.* New York: Basic Books.

Tucker, Robert W., and David C. Hendrickson. 1992. *The Imperial Temptation: The New World Order and America's Purpose.* New York: Council on Foreign Relations Press.

Ulam, Adam B. 1983. *Dangerous Relations: The Soviet Union in World Politics, 1970–1982.* Oxford: Oxford University Press.

Vance, Cyrus. 1983. *Hard Choices: Critical Years in America's Foreign Policy.* New York: Simon and Schuster.

Van Evera, Stephen. 1984. "The Cult of the Offensive and the Origins of the First World War." *International Security* 9, no. 1 (Summer): 58–107.

———. 1990–91. "Primed for Peace: Europe after the Cold War." *International Security* 15, no. 3 (Winter): 7–57.

Vasquez, John. 1991. "The Deterrence Myth: Nuclear Weapons and the Prevention of Nuclear War." In C. Kegley, ed., *The Long Postwar Peace.* New York: Harper Collins.

Verba, Sidney. 1961. "Assumptions of Rationality and Non-Rationality in Models of the International System." *World Politics* 14, no. 1 (October): 93–117.

Vertzberger, Yaacov. 1990. *The World in Their Minds.* Stanford, Calif.: Stanford University Press.

Viotti, Paul. 1992. "Review of J. Bouchard, 'Command in Crisis.'" *Political Science* 86, no. 3 (September): 836–37.

Vital, David. 1972. *The Survival of Small States: Studies in Small Power/Great Power Conflict.* London: Oxford University Press.

Wagner, Harrison R. 1993. "What Was Bipolarity?" *International Organization* 47, no. 1 (Winter): 77–106.

Walt, Stephen. 1987. *The Origins of Alliances.* Ithaca, N.Y.: Cornell University Press.
Waltz, Kenneth. 1959. *Man, the State and War.* New York: Columbia University Press.
———. 1964. "The Stability of a Bipolar World." *Daedalus* 93, 881–909.
———. 1974. "America's European Policy Viewed in Global Perspective." In Wolfram F. Hanrieder, ed., *The United States and Western Europe.* Cambridge, Mass.: Winthrop
———. 1979. *Theory of International Politics.* Reading, Mass.: Addison-Wesley.
———. 1981. "The Spread of Nuclear Weapons: More May Be Better." Adelphi Paper 171. London: International Institute for Strategic Studies.
———. 1986. "Reflections on Theory of International Politics: A Response to My Critics." In R. Keohane, ed., *Neorealism and its Critics.* New York, N.Y.: Columbia University Press.
———. 1990. "Nuclear Myths and Political Realities." *American Political Science Review* 84, no. 3 (September): 731–46.
———. 1991. "America as a Model for the World? A Foreign Policy Perspective." *Political Science* 24:667–70.
———. 1993. "The Emerging Structure of International Politics." *International Security* 18, no. 2 (Fall): 44–79.
Walzer, Michael. 1977. *Just and Unjust Wars.* New York: Basic Books.
Washington Institute for Near East Policy. 1988. *Building for Peace: An American Strategy for the Middle East.* Washington, D.C.: The Institution.
Watanabe, Paul Y. 1984. *Ethnic Groups, Congress, and American Foreign Policy.* Westport, Conn.: Greenwood.
Weber, Max. 1949. *The Methodology of the Social Sciences.* Translated by Edward Shils and Henry Finch. Glencoe, Ill.: Free Press.
———. 1978. *Economy and Society: An Outline of Interpretive Sociology.* 2 vols. Edited by Guenther Roth and Claus Wittich. Berkeley: University of California Press.
Weber, Steve. 1990. "Realism, Detente, and Nuclear Weapons." *International Organization* 44:55–82.
———. 1991. *Cooperation and Discord in U.S.-Soviet Arms Control.* Princeton, N.J.: Princeton University Press.
Weiss, Thomas, and James Blight, eds. 1992. *The Suffering Grass: Superpowers and Regional Conflict in Southern Africa and the Caribbean.* Boulder, Colo.: Rienner.
Welch, D. A., and J. G. Blight. 1987–88. "An Introduction to the Ex Comm Transcripts." *International Security* 12, (3): 5–29.
Wells, A. R. 1979. "Superpower Naval Confrontations: The June Arab-Israeli War." In B. Dismukes and J. McConnell, eds., *Soviet Naval Diplomacy.* New York: Pergamon.
Wendt, Alexander E. 1987. "The Agent-Structure Problem in International Relations Theory." *International Organization* 41 (3): 335–70.
Whetten, Lawrence L. 1974. *The Canal War: Four-Power Conflict in the Middle East.* Cambridge, Mass.: The MIT Press.
———. 1981. "The Arab-Israeli Dispute: Great Power Behaviour." In G. Treverton, ed., *Crisis Management and the Superpowers in the Middle East.* Aldershot, Hampshire: Gower.

Wight, Martin. 1966. "The Balance of Power." In Herbert Butterfield and Martin Wight, eds., *Diplomatic Investigations: Essays in the Theory of International Politics,* 149–75. London: Allen and Unwin.

———. 1978. *Power Politics.* Edited by Hedley Bull and Carsten Holbraad. Leicester, England: Leicester University Press with the Royal Institute of International Affairs.

Wildavsky, Aaron. 1971. "Practical Consequences of the Theoretical Study of Defense Policy." In Aaron Wildavsky, *The Revolt against the Masses: And Other Essays on Politics and Public Policy.* New York: Basic Books.

Wilensky, H. O. 1967. *Organizational Intelligence.* New York: Basic Books.

Williams, Phil. 1976. *Crisis Management: Confrontation and Diplomacy in the Nuclear Age.* London: Martin Robertson.

Wohlstetter, Albert, and Roberta Wohlstetter. 1971. "Controlling the Risks in Cuba." In R. Art and K. Waltz, eds., *The Use of Force.* Boston: Little, Brown.

Wolfe, Alan. 1979. *The Rise and Fall of the "Soviet Threat": Domestic Sources of the Cold War Consensus.* Washington, D.C.: Institute for Policy Studies.

Wolfers, Arnold. 1962. *Discord and Collaboration.* Baltimore: Johns Hopkins University Press.

Wright, Quincy. 1965. *A Study of War.* 2d ed. Chicago: University of Chicago Press.

Yariv, Aaron. 1985. *War by Choice.* Tel Aviv: Hakibbutz Hameuchad. Hebrew.

Young, Oran. 1968. *The Politics of Force: Bargaining during International Crises.* Princeton, N.J.: Princeton University Press.

———. 1983. "Regime Dynamics: The Rise and Fall of International Regimes." In Stephen Krasner, ed., *International Regimes.* Ithaca, N.Y.: Cornell University Press.

———. 1986. "International Regimes: Toward a New Theory of Institutions." *World Politics* 34, no. 1 (October): 104–22.

———. 1989. *International Cooperation: Building Regimes for Natural Resources and the Environment.* Ithaca, N.Y.: Cornell University Press.

Zacher, Mark. 1979. *International Conflicts and Collective Security, 1946–77.* New York: Praeger.

Zak, Moshe. 1986. *Israel and the Superpower Game in the Middle East.* Tel Aviv: Hakibbutz Hameuchad. Hebrew.

———. 1988. *Israel and the Soviet Union—A Forty Years Dialogue.* Tel Aviv: Ma'ariv. Hebrew.

Zimmerman, William. 1969. *Soviet Perspectives on International Relations.* Princeton, N.J.: Princeton University Press.

———. 1980. "Rethinking Soviet Foreign Policy: Changing American Perspectives." *International Journal* 35, no. 3 (Summer): 548–62.

Zoppo, Ciro E. 1966. "Nuclear Technology, Multipolarity and International Stability." *World Politics* 18, no. 4 (July): 579–606.

# Index

Accidental wars, 261n.60, 262n.67
Adomeit, Hannes, 46, 265n.29
Aggarwal, Vinod K., 268n.49
Agreement on the Prevention of Nuclear War (1973), 134
Allies
   control of, 68–71, 74–75, 87, 167–68, 227–29, 270n.17, 281n.18
   Soviet Union and, 87, 129–30, 140–50, 167–68, 227, 279nn. 69, 70, 280n.13, 281nn. 16, 18
   United States and, 129–30, 140, 167–68, 227, 281n.18
Allison, Graham T., 84, 264n.17, 266n.33, 271n.28, 272n.44
Anarchy, 9–32
   conflict under, 9, 26–31
   cooperation under, 3–4, 9, 15–26, 31–32, 245, 255n.13
   crisis management under, 14–15, 22–26
   defined, 10
   international order under, 10–15
   overview of, 9, 31–32
   state of nature vs. states system, 10, 26
   *See also* Conflict; Conflict resolution; Cooperation; Crisis management
Andropov, Yuri, 290–91n.21
Arab-Israeli conflict, 173–221
   cognitive factors in, 200–207, 212–16
   bandwagoning outlook in United States, 202, 204
   Bush administration and, 209, 215–16, 237–38, 300nn. 99, 100
   Carter administration and, 202, 203, 204–5, 206–7, 217–18, 296–97nn. 75, 76, 297–98n.79
   competitive strategy in United States, 217, 218–19, 298n.82
   confrontational strategy in United States, 204, 217, 218, 298n.82
   Eisenhower administration and, 202–3, 204, 217, 296n.73
   Gorbachev regime and, 212, 236–37
   Kennedy administration and, 296n.73
   Kissinger and, 204, 205–6, 207, 217, 297n.78
   multilateralist strategy in United States, 217–18, 298n.82
   Nixon administration and, 202, 205, 217–18, 298n.80
   in post–Cold War United States, 220–21
   Reagan administration and, 202, 203, 204, 213–15, 217, 237–38, 296n.74
   Soviet images of United States, 201–2
   United States and in post–Cold War, 220–21
   United States images of Soviet Union, 202–7
   common fear of unintended conflict and, 185–86
   competitive orientation in, 179–85
   arms sales, 130, 180–81, 193, 211, 281n.17

335

Arab-Israeli conflict (*continued*)
   Camp David accords and, 182, 183, 218, 291nn. 22, 23, 29
   Carter administration and, 182, 184, 291nn. 22, 23
   and future peace process, 218–19
   Kissinger and, 181–82, 217, 218, 292nn. 34, 35, 36, 38, 39, 294n.56, 298–99nn. 84, 87
   Reagan administration and, 182–83, 185
   recent cooperative efforts and, 184–85, 218
   Rogers Plan and, 180, 181
   Soviet "no war, no peace" hypothesis, 179, 185–86, 190, 193
   Soviet Union and, 183–85, 218–19, 290–91n.21
   United States and, 179, 182, 187–88, 204, 205, 217, 218–19, 289n.7, 290n.13, 298n.82
  concerted diplomacy and, 173–76, 198–200, *199*, 209–16, 219
  cooperative-multilateral orientation in, 176–79
   Bush administration and, 209, 215–16, 237–38, 300nn. 99, 100
   Carter administration and, 177–78
   and Gulf War (1991), 215–16
   international peace conference proposals, 178
   Kissinger and, 177
   moderation in Soviet foreign policy and, 209–12, 218–19, 236–37
   Reagan administration and, 209, 213–15, 237–38
   Rogers Plan, 121, 176–77
   Soviet Union and, 190–95, 293nn. 44, 45, 47, 48, 50, 294–95nn. 59, 60, 61, 62
   UN Resolution 242 (1967), 176
  domestic constraints and, 195–98, 207–9, 227
   and forms of cooperation, 195–98
   and images of opponent, 207–9
   in post–Cold War era, 221
   and Rogers Plan, 197–98, 236
   Soviet Union and, 208–9, 227
   United States and, 121, 197–98, 207–9, 227
   and U.S.-Soviet statement of October, 1977, 121, 197, 236, 299n.89
  overview of, 37, 173–76, 216–21
  in post–Cold War era, 218–21, 300n.103
  Soviet Union and
   balancing and, 212, 218
   commitment to multilateral conflict resolution, 190–95, 293nn. 44, 45, 47, 50, 294–95nn. 59, 60, 61, 62
   competitive orientation and, 183–85, 218–19, 290–91n.21
   cooperation with United States, 193–95
   and disintegration of, 216, 217, 219, 220
   and domestic constraints, 208–9, 227
   and formation of condominiums, 195–96, 211–12
   and images of United States, 201–2
   and "loss" of Egypt, 167, 193–94, 281n.18, 298–99n.87
   military, economic, and diplomatic capabilities, 188
   moderation of Soviet foreign policy, 209–12, 218–19, 236–37
   "no war, no peace" hypothesis, 179, 185–86, 190, 193
   in post–Cold War era, 218–20, 300n.102
   and Rogers Plan, 295n.65
   and Syria, 219, 281n.18
   and U.S.-Soviet statement of October, 1977, 194–95
  tacit rules in, 83, 160–66
  United States and
   balancing, 218

bias toward Israel, 179, 289n.7, 290n.13
competitive orientation and, 182, 187–88, 204, 205, 217, 218–19, 298n.82
competitive strategy, 217, 218–19, 298n.82
confrontational strategy, 217, 218, 298n.82
and decision makers' beliefs in post–Cold War, 220–21
domestic constraints and, 121, 197–98, 207–9
after Gulf War, 216, 219, 220
and images of Soviet Union, 202–7
and "loss" of Iran, 168
military, economic, and diplomatic capabilities, 186–88, 291nn. 29, 31
multilateralist strategy, 217–18, 298n.82
Pax Americana and, 182, 187–88, 204, 205, 220
in post–Cold War era, 219–21
and resistance to condominiums, 196–97, 211–12
and U.S.-Soviet statement of October, 1977, 121, 178, 194–95, 197, 207–8, 235, 236, 299n.89
*See also* Kissinger; Middle East crises
Arms control agreements, 15–16, 121, 134, 244
Arms sales, 130, 134, 147, 161, 180–81, 193, 211, 281n.17, 301n.5
Ashworth, Tony, 18
Assad, Hafiz al, 164, 190, 211
Asymmetrical intervention outside spheres of influence, 83
Axelrod, Robert, 19, 43, 255n.13

Balance of forces. *See* Military
Balance of interests. *See* Interests
Balancing, 106–7, 112, 212, 218
Balkans, 74, 75, 230–31
Bandwagoning, 106–7, 112, 202, 204, 237, 240, 276n.35

Bargaining, in crises, 52–53
Bar-Joseph, Uri, 287n.78
Bar-Siman-Tov, Yaacov, 284n.51
Begin, Menachem, 79
Beliefs. *See* Cognitive factors
Bell, Coral, 279n.69
Ben-Gurion, David, 202–3, 296n.73
Ben-Porat, Joel, 162, 288n.85
Ben-Zvi, Abraham, 206
Berlin crises, 23–24, 83, 87, 157, 260n.50
Betts, Richard K., 271n.37, 299n.91
Bipolarity, 59–60, 67–69, 78–87
and balance of forces vs. balance of interests, 156–59, 283n.39, 287n.78
and causes of Long Peace, 58–60, 65–66, 269n.10
in Cold War, 80–88, 227–28
and concerts, 94
and control of allies, 68–69, 87, 227
and control of military, 69, 81, 83–84, 169–70
conventional bipolarity, *62*, 62, 78–79
crisis-induced stress and, 86–87
and crisis management, 4, 39–42, *40*, 50–52, 61, *67*, 80–82
decision makers and, 67, 68, 69, 70
domestic constraints and, 69, 81–86, 168–69, 227
intended conflict and, 4–6, 60–62, *62*, 66–68, *67*, 78–79
"maturation" of bipolar world, 157
Middle East crises and, 63, 78–79, 84, 87, 125, 126, 166–71, 227, 281n.18
military technology and, 60–62, *62*
misperceptions and, 86–87
vs. multipolarity, 1, 4–5, 50–52, 60–62, *62*, 66–68, *67*, 70, 72
nuclear bipolarity, 5, 8, 57–66, *62*, 80–83, 271nn. 37, 38
overreaction or underreaction and, 67
Peloponnesian War and, 63, 78
in post–Cold War era, 241–43
in post–World War II era, 49–50

Bipolarity (*continued*)
  "red lines" and, 68, 79, 87
  resolve and, 67–68, 226–27
  simplicity and clarity of, 68, 159
  stability and, 1, 8, 259n.32
  structural theory and, 50
  tacit rules and, 68, 78–79, 80–83, 225–28
  unintended conflict and, 4–6, 60–62, *62*, 66–68, *67*, 78–79, 80–82
  United States foreign policy and, 81–82, 84–86
  unit-level theory and, 50–52
  *See also* Arab-Israeli conflict; Cold War; Middle East crises; Multipolarity
"Blank check" alliances, 74, 75, 161
Bouchard, Joseph, 84
Boumedienne, Houari, 283n.46
"Bounded rationality," 48, 266n.34
BPA (U.S.-Soviet Basic Principles Agreement) (1972), 54, 134
Breslauer, George, 155, 193, 196, 201–2
Bretton Woods, 54
Brezhnev, Leonid, 135–36, 137–38, 148–49, 163, 164, 192, 194, 279n.69, 282n.30, 284n.49, 285nn. 59, 62
Brzezinski, Zbigniew, 203, 235, 296–97nn. 75, 77
Bulganin, Nikolai, 131, 141, 155
Bull, Hedley, 10, 13, 92, 99, 261n.58
Bureaucratic politics. *See* Domestic constraints
Bush, George. *See* Arab-Israeli conflict

Camp David accords, 182, 183, 218, 291nn. 22, 23, 29, 299n.89
Carnesale, Albert, 271n.28
Carter, Jimmy, 197, 203, 235
  *See also* Arab-Israeli conflict
Castlereagh, Viscount Robert Stewart, 116
Causal relations. *See* Structural balance-of-power theory; Unit-level theory

Caution. *See* Resolve
China, 122, 220, 232, 241, 243
Clients. *See* Allies
Coercive cooperation. *See* Condominiums
Cognitive factors
  in concerts, 104–15, *113, 123,* 235, 276nn. 32, 33, 277n.40
  in crises, 44–45, 52–53, 264–65n.22
  ideological convergence or polarization, 39–42, *40,* 53–55, 268nn. 49, 52
  *See also* Arab-Israeli conflict; Decision makers; Images
Cohen, Raymond, 19–20, 21–22
Cold War
  bipolarity in, 80–88, 227–28
  causes of Long Peace, 58–60, 65–66, 269n.10
  military technology and, 60–62, *62,* 65–66
  overview of, 57–58
  primacy of security interests in, 47
  tacit rules in, 82–83, 227–28
  *See also* Arab-Israeli conflict; Berlin crises; Bipolarity; Cuban Missile Crisis; Middle East crises; Multipolarity; Nuclear weapons; Post–Cold War era; Post–World War II era
Collaboration. *See* Cooperation
Common fears, 102–4, 105, 185–86, 270n.16
Competitive orientation, 112–15, *113, 123,* 128, 174, 186, 240, 247–51
  *See also* Arab-Israeli conflict; Confrontational orientation; Multilateralist orientation
Complex learning, regimes and, 54–55
Comprehensive rationality model, 264n.17, 266n.33
Concerted diplomacy
  in Arab-Israeli conflict, 173–76, 198–200, 209–16, 219
  Concert of Europe and, 39–40, 263–64n.14

in post–Cold War era, 224, 236–40
in post–World War II era, 235–36
relative capabilities, domestic regime and, 198–200, *199*
since mid-1980s, 236–38, 301n.13
See also Arab-Israeli conflict; Concerts; Conflict resolution
Concert of Europe
as a concert or a condominium, 93
Britain and, 95, 96, 101–2, 116–17
common fears and, 102–4
and concerted diplomacy, 39–40, 263–64n.14
convergence of beliefs and, 55
and crisis management, 34–36, 38, 39–42, 225, 300–301n.2
duration of, 272n.1
image of opponents in, 110–11
international relations theory and, 13, 34–36, 42
international society approach and, 13, 42, 234–35, 255n.15
moderation of intentions and, 100, 101–2
Ottoman Empire and, 109, 275n.28, 278n.54
vs. post–World War II cooperation, 17, 36, 99, 100, 104, 255n.15
regionalist approach to third-area conflicts in, 108–9
relative capabilities and degree of vulnerability in, 95
similarity of great powers and, 99, 100, 101–2
structural theory and, 35, 38
and types of cooperation, 26
unit-level theory and, 34–35, 38, 98
Concerts, 89–124, 241–48
active/affirmative vs. passive/negative concerts, 92
cognitive factors in, 104–15, *113, 123*, 235, 276nn. 32, 33, 277n.40
vs. condominiums, 92–93
cooperative-multilateral orientation toward, 112–15, *113, 123*
crisis management and, 24, 25

defined, 90–93, 273nn. 3, 5
vs. détente or entente, 90
differences in forms of, 115–23, 195–98
formation of, 93–105, 238, 270n.16, 274n.15, 274–75n.22
Kissinger and, 205–6
overview of, 89–90, *123*, 123–24
passive/negative vs. active/affirmative concerts, 92
in post–Cold War era, 6–7, 8, 238–48
structural theory and, 93–94
unilateral-exclusionary orientation toward, 112–15, *113, 123*
See also Condominiums; Conflict resolution; Cooperation, intended; Crisis management
Condominiums
in Arab-Israeli conflict, 195–98, 211–12
arms control as, 121
authoritarian states and, 115–16, 118, 277–78nn. 50, 51
vs. concerts, 92–93
defined, 93
liberal democracies and, 115–18
Soviet Union and, 121–23, 195–96, 211–12, 279n.69
strong states, weak states, and, 118–19
United States and, 96, 117–18, 119–21, 196–98, 211–12
See also Concerts
Conflict
under anarchy, 9, 26–31
crises as a surrogate for war, 167
future research and, 248–51
intended conflict
anarchy and, 31
bipolarity and, 4–5, 60–62, *62*, 66–68, *67*, 78–79
defined, 27–28
global democratization and, 231–32
Lebanon War (1982) and, 79, 271n.34
military technology and, 4–5, 8, 60–62, *62*

Conflict (*continued*)
    multipolarity and, 60–62, *62*
    in normal times vs. crises, 2
    nuclear bipolarity and obsolescence of, 5, 8, 60, 61, *62*, 63, 64–66, 80, 271nn. 37, 38
    settings and explanations for, *3*
    types of, 2
    vs. unintended conflict, 9, 27–31
    unit-level theory and, 3, 5
  international society approach and, 13–14
  major wars, 27, 60–62, *62*, 265n.25
  neorealism vs. neoliberlism and, 7–8
  overview of, 4–5
  polarity, military technology, and probability of, 60–62, *62*
  preventive vs. preemptive wars, 29, 30–31, 261–62n.64, 271n.35
  regional conflicts
    active/affirmative concerts and, 92
    crisis management and, 25, 36–37
    disengagement and, 230–31, 247, 256n.22
    future research and, 248–51
    global vs. regional images of, 107–10, 112, 277n.40
    Middle East crises as third-area conflicts, 126–27
    orientations toward regional conflict resolution, 112–15, *113, 123*
    in post–Cold War era, 1–2, 224, 228–33, 244, 246–47, 256n.22
    tacit rules and, 83
    U.S.-Soviet relations and, 36–37
    World War III and, 81
  security dilemma and, 26–27
  unintended conflict
    anarchy and, 31
    bipolarity and, 4–5, 60–62, *62*, 66–68, *67*, 78–79, 80–82
    Crimean War as, 73–77, 225
    crisis management and origins of, 28, 29–30
    defined, 28
    in East Asia, 232
    examples of multipolarity and, 73–78
    and formation of concerts, 102–4, 105
    inadvertent wars vs. accidental wars, 261n.60, 262n.67
    vs. intended conflict, 9, 27–31
    loss of control and, 29–31
    military technology and, 4–5, 8, 60–62, *62*
    miscalculation and, 28–30
    multipolarity and, 4–5, 60–62, *62*, 66–72, *67*
    in normal times vs. crises, 2
    nuclear bipolarity and avoidance of, 61–62, *62*, 80–82
    origins of, 38–41
    over- or underreaction, resolve and, 29–30
    security dilemma and, 28, 42–43
    settings and explanations for, *3*
    Six Day War (1967) as, 73–77, 271n.29
    structural theory and, 2–3, 12, 42–43, 54, 55, 166
    types of, 2
    World War I as, 31, 73–74, 225, 271n.28
  *See also* Crimean War; Middle East crises; World War I; World War II; World War III
Conflict management. *See* Crisis management
Conflict resolution, 22–26
  cooperation and, 3–4, 25–26, 33
  vs. crisis management, 22–26
  future research and, 248–51
  multilateralist, confrontational, and competitive orientations toward, 112–15, *113, 123*
  in post–Cold War era, 1–2, 245
  tacit rules and, 22
  and use of force, 22, 25
  *See also* Arab-Israeli conflict; Concerted diplomacy; Concerts; Co-

operation, intended; Crisis management
Confrontational orientation, 112–15, *113,* 204, 217, 218, 240, 298n.82
See also Competitive orientation; Multilateralist orientation
Cooperation
under anarchy, 3–4, 9, 15–26, 31–32, 245, 255n.13, 258n.23
conflict resolution and, 3–4, 25–26
in crisis management, 3–4, 25–26, 33–55, *40,* 300–301n.2
economic vs. security cooperation, 15–16, 258n.23
future research and, 249–51
game theory and, 18, 50–52, 255n.13, 270n.21
vs. harmony, 258n.17
intended cooperation
anarchy and, 31–32
and crisis management vs. conflict resolution, 25–26
in normal times vs. crises, 2
regimes and, 19–20
settings and explanations for, *3*
types of, *2*
vs. unintended cooperation, 9, 18–22
unit-level theory and, 3, 6, 54, 55
international institutions and, 17–18
international society approach and, 13–14
mixed-motive games and, 16
neorealism vs. neoliberalism and, 7–8
in normal times vs. crises, 22
overview of, 3–4
"partisan mutual adjustment" and, 20, 166
in post–Cold War era, 244–45
Prisoner's Dilemma and, 17, 18, 51–52
regimes and, 17–21
security cooperation vs. economic cooperation, 15–17, 258n.23
security dilemma and, 15–16
structural theory and, 37–39, 41–50, 228–31, 263n.12, 264n.17
tacit rules and, 19–22
in trench warfare, 18, 259n.36
unintended cooperation
anarchy and, 31
and crisis management vs. conflict resolution, 25–26
game theory and, 18
vs. intended cooperation, 9, 18–22
in normal times vs. crises, 2
Prisoner's Dilemma and, 18
regimes and, 19–20
settings and explanations for, *3*
structural theory and, 2–3, 12, 42–43, 54, 55, 166
tacit rules and, 19–22
types of, *2*
unit-level theory and, 50–55
See also Arab-Israeli conflict; Concerts; Conflict; Conflict resolution; Crisis management; Middle East crises
Cooperative-multilateralist orientation. See Multilateralist orientation
Copper, Chester, 287n.81
Craig, Gordon, 82
Crimean War, 35, 73–77, 225
Crises
bargaining in, 52–53
cognitive factors in, 44–45, 52–53, 264–65n.22
in Cold War, 225–26
consensus within elites in, 200
cooperation in, 22
crisis management in, 22–24, 41, 225–26
defined, 23–24
domestic constraints and, 207
focus of values in, 53
intended and unintended outcomes in, 2
vs. normal times, 23–24
in post–World War II era, 226
and primacy of security interests, 47–48

Crises (*continued*)
  rationality in, 48–50
  and resolve, 167
  and situational influences on unintended outcomes, 43–44
  and the state as a unitary actor, 46
  structural theory and, 48–49
  as a surrogate for war, 167
  and use of force, 23–24
  *See also* Crisis management; Middle East crises; Normal times
Crisis-induced stress
  bipolarity and, 86–87
  in Middle East crises, 153, 169–70, 286n.73
  multipolarity and, 70, 75–76
  nuclear weapons and, 65, 263n.3
  in World War I, 76, 86
Crisis management, 14–15, 22–26, 33–55
  under anarchy, 14–15, 260n.51
  bipolarity and, 4, 39–42, *40*, 50–52, 61, *67*, 80–82
  Concert of Europe and, 34–36, 38, 39–42, 225, 300–301n.2
  concerts and, 24, 25
  vs. conflict resolution, 22–26
  cooperation in, 3–4, 25–26, 33–55, *40*, 50–52, 300–301n.2
    bipolarity, multipolarity and, 4, 39–42, 50–52
    Concert of Europe and, 34–36, 38, 39–42, 300–301n.2
    game theory and, 50–52
    ideological convergence or polarization and, 39–42
    international relations theory and, 33–39
    new model of, 39–42, *40*
    overview of, 3–4, 25–26, 33–34
    post–World War II era and, 36–42
    *See also* Structural balance-of-power theory; Unit-level theory
  vs. crisis prevention, 23
  game theory and, 34, 50–52, 262–63n.2
  and ideological polarization or convergence, 39–42, *40*
  international society approach and, 41–42
  multipolarity and, 39–42, *40*, 50–52, 61, *67*
  in normal times vs. crises, 22–24, 41, 225–26
  and origins of unintended conflict, 28, 29–30
  over- or underreaction and, 29–30
  in post–Cold War era, 1–2, 224, 228–31
  resolve and, 29–30, 226–27
  security regimes and, 24, 41
  structural theory and, 37–39, 41–50, 228–31, 263n.12, 264n.17
  tacit rules and, 22, 24–25
  *See also* Concerts; Conflict resolution; Cooperation, unintended; Middle East crises
Crisis prevention, 23, 64–65, 234
Cuban Missile Crisis (1962), 24, 84, 87, 157, 272nn. 44, 48

Dayan, Moshe, 168, 197
Decision makers
  bipolarity and, 67, 68, 69, 70
  multipolarity and, 70
  nuclear MAD and, 64–66
  "operational code" of political actors, 110
  and resistance to change, 267–68n.46
  *See also* Cognitive factors; Crisis-induced stress; Images
Deibel, T., 237
Democracies
  and concerts, 100–102
  and condominiums, 115–16, 118, 277–78nn. 50, 51
  and intended wars, 231
  and self-determination of states, 116–18
  and spheres of influence, 295n.66
Democratic peace thesis, 277–78n.50

Democratization, 231, 237
Détente, 90
Deutsch, Morton, 98
Diesing, Paul, 16, 24, 46, 48, 51–52, 160, 260–61n.52, 261n.54, 267n.41
Diplomacy
  diplomatic logic vs. military logic, 29, 158, 165, 262n.68
  diplomatic use of military in Middle East crises, 157–58, 165, 287n.81
  *See also* Concerted diplomacy; Conflict resolution
Disengagement
  future research and, 249–51
  multipolarity and, 71–72, 77–78
  in post–Cold War era, 229–31, 232–33, 240, 242, 247, 250–51, 256n.22
  *See also* Engagement
"Disputed interest symmetry," 128
Dobrynin, Anatoly, 177
Domestic constraints
  bipolarity and, 69, 81–86, 168–69, 227
  multipolarity and, 72, 76–77
  in United States
    Arab-Israeli conflict and, 121, 197–98
    foreign policy and, 119–21, 227, 279n.62, 295–96n.69
    Middle East crises and, 168–69
    Rogers Plan and, 197–98, 236
    U.S.-Soviet relations and, 81–82, 84–85
    U.S.-Soviet statement of October, 1977 and, 121, 197, 236, 299n.89
    and Yom Kippur War (1973), 138, 151, 153
    *See also* Arab-Israeli conflict; Military
Dowty, Alan, 153, 169–70, 286n.73, 288n.93
Dulles, John Foster, 129, 154–55, 202–3, 204, 217

East Asia; unintended conflict in, 232
Eastern Europe, 230
Economic cooperation, 15–17, 258n.23
Eden, Anthony, 131–32
Egypt. *See* Arab-Israeli conflict; Middle East crises
Eisenhower, Dwight D., 80, 129, 132, 154–55, 159, 202, 280n.12
Eisenhower administration. *See* Arab-Israeli conflict
Elrod, Richard, 91
Embedded liberalism, 54
Engagement
  disinclination for, 230–31, 240, 242, 247, 256n.22
  and restrained resolve in Middle East crises, 170–71
  *See also* Disengagement
Entente, 90
Eran, Oded, 192–93, 196
Europe in post–Cold War era, 97, 220, 239, 241, 243, 244–45, 247–48
Evron, Yair, 79, 260n.42

Feldman, Shai, 48
Fischer, Fritz, 31, 73–74
Focus of values, 53
Force, use of. *See* Military
Fukuyama, Francis, 143, 149, 156
Fundamentalism, Islamic, 7, 240, 274n.15
Future research, 248–51

Gaddis, John L., 60
Gal, Reuven, 45
Game theory
  and cooperation, 18, 50–52, 255n.13, 270n.21
  and crisis management, 34, 262–63n.2
  and focus of values in crises, 53
  mixed-motive games, 13, 16
  Prisoner's Dilemma, 17, 18, 51–52, 53
  and security dilemma, 259n.26
  status games, 16, 258n.23

Game theory (*continued*)
  zero-sum games, 16, 161, 258n.23
Geiss, Imanuel, 73
George, Alexander, 23, 29, 30, 82–83, 110, 117, 128, 165, 255n.13, 262n.68
Global democratization, 231–32
"Global policeman," 232
Global vs. regional images of third-area conflicts, 107–10, 112, 277n.40
Gorbachev, Mikhail, 202, 209–12, 215, 216, 236–38, 241, 275n.30
Gowa, Joanne, 52, 159
Great powers, 11, 14–15, 248–51
  *See also* Arab-Israeli conflict; Concerts; Middle East crises; Post–Cold War era; Regimes; Soviet Union; State; United States
Griffiths, Franklyn, 296n.70
Gromyko, Andrei, 176, 177, 195, 277n.45
Gulf War (1991), 215–16, 218, 219, 228–31, 243, 288n.89

Haas, Ernst B., 268nn. 49, 52
Habib, Philip, 183
Haggard, Stephan, 262–63n.2
Haig, Alexander, 182, 204, 217, 288n.88
*Handbook of Social Psychology* (Snyder and Ickes), 44–45
Hannah, John, 287n.78
Harmony, vs. cooperation, 258n.17
Hayek, Friedrich A., 19
Heikal, Mohamed, 168, 283n.46, 284n.49, 295n.63
Herter, Christian, 203, 296n.73
Herzog, Yaccov, 296n.73
Hinsley, F. H., 107
Hitler, Adolf, 77
Hobbes, Thomas, 10, 26, 261n.57
Holbraad, Carsten, 141, 145, 166, 273n.3, 287n.81
Holsti, Ole R., 46, 276n.32, 277n.44
Howard, Michael, 267n.41

Hunt, Michael H., 277n.46
Hussein, King Ibn Talal, 134, 149, 150–51, 178, 183, 184, 213, 290–91n.21
  *See also* Arab-Israeli conflict; Jordan; Middle East crises
Hussein, Saddam, 215–16, 228–29, 230, 242

Ickes, William, 44–45
Ideological convergence, 39–42, *40,* 53–55, 268nn. 49, 52
  *See also* Cognitive factors
Images
  of dynamics of international politics, 106–7, 112
  of opponents
    concerts and, 110–12
    and domestic constraints, 207–9
    Soviet images of United States, 201–2
    United States images of Soviet Union, 111–12, 202–7
  of third-area conflicts, 107–10, 112, 277n.40
  *See also* Cognitive factors; Decision makers
Implicit rules. *See* Tacit rules
Inadvertent wars
  vs. accidental wars, 261n.60, 262n.67
  *See also* Conflict, unintended
India, 232
Inside-out theory. *See* Unit-level theory
Institutions, cooperation and, 17–18
Intended conflict. *See* Conflict, intended
Intended cooperation. *See* Cooperation, intended
Interest groups. *See* Domestic constraints
Interests
  balance of interests, 68, 83, 140, 156–59, 270n.19, 283n.39, 287n.78
  in Middle East crises, 127–28, 140, 159, 280–81n.14
  primacy of security interests, 47–48
International Crisis Behavior Project, 59

International order under anarchy, 10–15
International relations theory
  and Concert of Europe, 13, 34–36, 42
  and cooperation under anarchy, 17–18, 255n.13
  and cooperation in crisis management, 33–39
  and crisis management vs. conflict resolution, 23
  "model of a theory," 256n.24
  neorealism vs. neoliberalism, 7–8
  post–Cold War era and, 1–2, 7–8
  *See also* International society approach; Structural balance-of-power theory; Unit-level theory
International society approach
  and Concert of Europe, 13, 42, 234–35, 255n.15
  and cooperation vs. conflict, 13–14
  and crisis management, 41–42
  and international order under anarchy, 12–15
  outcomes best explained by, 224–25, 234–40
  regimes and, 12, 257n.11
  and role of great powers, 14–15
  vs. structural balance-of-power theory, 5, 12–13, 234, 254–55n.11
  *See also* International relations theory; Mixed-motive games; Structural balance-of-power theory; Unit-level theory
Iran, 168
Iraq, 281n.18
  *See also* Gulf War
Islamic fundamentalism, 7, 240, 274n.15
Israel. *See* Arab-Israeli conflict; Middle East crises

Jackson, Sen. Henry, 135
Japan in post–Cold War era, 97, 220, 232, 239, 241, 243, 244–45, 247–48
Jarring, Gunnar, 177

Jervis, Robert, 15, 17, 27, 28, 58–59, 91, 103, 104, 110–11, 255n.13, 259n.26, 261n.54, 271n.28
Joffe, Josef, 230
Johnson, Lyndon B., 80, 133, 152, 163, 176, 283n.40, 288n.87
Jonsson, Christer, 157–58, 191
Jordan, 74, 77, 218
  *See also* Hussein
Jordanian civil war (1970), 134, 136–37, 149–52, 165, 169, 286n.66

Kant, Immanuel, 101, 275n.26
Karsh, Efraim, 285n.64
Kennedy administration, 296n.73
Keohane, Robert O., 20, 120, 259n.28, 264n.17
Khruschev, Nikita, 142
Kissinger, Henry
  and Brezhnev, 194, 279n.69
  and Bush administration, 215, 300nn. 99, 100
  and competitive orientation, 181–82, 217, 218, 292nn. 34, 35, 36, 38, 39, 294n.56, 298–99nn. 84, 87
  and cooperative-multilateral orientation, 177
  on crisis management, 47
  globalist approach of, 108, 204, 297n.78
  and great power concerts, 205–6
  and images of Soviet Union, 204, 205–6, 207, 217, 235, 294n.61
  and Jordanian civil war (1970), 134, 136–37, 149, 151, 169
  and Nixon, 117–18, 298n.80
  and Rogers Plan, 181
  on Soviet "loss" of Egypt, 194
  on U.S.-Israeli relations, 290n.13
  on U.S.-Soviet relations, 279nn. 69, 70
  and War of Attrition (1969–1970), 134
  and Yom Kippur War (1973), 135, 149, 152–53, 164, 169, 286n.70, 292n.38

Kissinger, Henry (*continued*)
  See also Arab-Israeli conflict; Middle East crises; Nixon
Kosygin, Alexi, 133, 143, 146–48, 162–63, 176, 285n.57
Krasner, Stephen D., 19, 54, 118–19, 121, 257n.11, 259n.28
Kuwait, 215–16, 229, 231, 242

Leaders. *See* Decision makers
Learning, simple vs. complex, 54–55
Lebanon War (1982), 63, 78–79, 155–56, 164–65, 271n.34, 288n.88
Lebow, Richard Ned, 65, 78
Legislatures. *See* Domestic constraints
Legitimacy, and formation of concerts, 99–100
Levy, Jack, 30, 31, 73
Liberal democracies. *See* Democracies
Liberalism, 7–8, 54
Lindblom, Charles E., 20, 166
Liska, George, 110
Local wars. *See* Conflict, regional conflicts
Long Peace. *See* Cold War
Loss of control, 29–31, 157–58, 228–29, 281n.18
  See also Conflict, unintended; Miscalculation; Misperception
Lowi, Theodore, 266n.37
Luard, Evan, 13

MacFarlane, Neil S., 186, 190–91
MAD. *See* Nuclear MAD
Major wars, 27, 60–62, 62, 265n.25
  See also Conflict; Crimean War; World War I; World War II
March, James G., 266n.37
Mass media. *See* Domestic constraints
"Maturation" of bipolar world, 157
McConnell, James, 161, 165
McNamara, Robert, 163
Mearsheimer, John, 60, 65
Media. *See* Domestic constraints
Meir, Golda, 181, 284n.48
Metternich, Klemens von, 95

Middle East crises, 125–71
  balance of forces
    vs. balance of interests, 156–59, 283n.39, 287n.78
    effects of changing, 138–39, 153–56
  bipolarity and, 63, 78–79, 84, 87, 125, 126, 166–71, 227, 281n.18
  competitive orientation in, 128
  concerts and, 6–7
  crisis management and, 125–26
  great power conduct in, 125, 126, 130–53
    apparent recklessness of Soviet Union, 130–36
    apparent recklessness of United States, 131, 136–38
    arms sales, 130, 134, 147, 161, 193, 211, 281n.17
    and balance of interests, 140, 159
    and changing military balance, 138–40, 153–56
    diplomatic use of military capabilities, 157–58, 165, 287n.81
    effects of changing balance of forces, 138–39, 153–56
    overview of, 125, 126, 130–31, 139–40
    restrained resolve by Soviet Union, 140–50, 160–66, 170, 226–27, 284n.47
    restrained resolve by United States, 150–53, 160–61, 162–66, 170, 226–27, 284n.47
    tacit rules and, 83, 125–26, 160–67, 170–71
  great power interests, 126–30
  nuclear weapons and, 126, 167
  overview of, 37, 125–26
  "red lines" in, 160, 170
  security dilemma in, 129, 154, 280–81n.14
  Soviet Union and, 127–50, 153–56
    and allies, 87, 129–30, 140–50, 167–68, 227, 280n.13, 281nn. 16, 18

apparent recklessness of, 130–36
and changes in military balance,
 138–39, 155–59
and crisis-induced stress, 169,
 286n.73
and Israel, 280nn. 10, 13
and Jordanian civil war (1970),
 134, 136–37, 149–50, 165
and Lebanon War (1982), 155–56,
 164–65, 288n.88
military capabilities, 153–56,
 287n.78
restrained resolve in, 140–50, 160–
 66, 170, 226–27, 284n.47
security dilemma and, 129
and Six Day War (1967), 74, 132–
 33, 136, 142–45, 155, 162–63,
 164, 165, 176, 283nn. 44, 46,
 284nn. 49, 51, 295n.63
strategic interests, 127–28, 280–
 81n.14
and Suez crisis (1956), 131–32,
 140–42, 154–55, 157–58, 165
and War of Attrition (1969–1970),
 133–34, 136, 145–47, 160–61,
 162, 165
and Yom Kippur War (1973), 134–
 36, 137–38, 147–49, 162–63,
 164, 165, 282nn. 27, 28, 30, 31,
 284–85nn. 53, 54, 55, 56, 57, 58,
 59, 62, 64, 286nn. 68, 69, 288n.85
tacit rules in, 83, 125–26, 160–67,
 170–71
as third-area conflicts, 126–27
United States and, 127–31, 136–39,
 150–56
and allies, 87, 129–30, 140, 167–
 68, 227, 281n.18
apparent recklessness of, 131, 136–
 38
and changes in military balance,
 138–39, 153–55, 156–59
containment policies, 129
and control of military, 169
crisis-induced stress and, 169–70,
 286n.73
domestic constraints and, 168–69
and Jordanian civil war (1970),
 134, 136–37, 149, 150–52, 169
and Lebanon War (1982), 288n.88
security dilemma and, 154, 280–
 81n.14
and Six Day War (1967), 74, 143,
 155, 162–63, 164, 176, 288n.87
strategic interests, 127–28
and Suez crisis (1956), 132, 141,
 154–55
and War of Attrition (1969–1970),
 134, 145–46, 160–61, 165
and Yom Kippur War (1973), 135,
 137–38, 148, 149, 151, 152–53,
 158, 162–63, 164, 169, 286nn.
 70, 71, 292n.38
*See also* Arab-Israeli conflict
Military
 balance of forces, 138–40, 153–59,
  283n.39, 287n.78
 control of, 69, 72, 76–77, 81, 83–84,
  169–70
 diplomatic use of, 157–58, 165,
  287n.81
 military logic vs. diplomatic logic, 29,
  158, 165, 262n.68
 military technology, 4–5, 8, 57–66,
  62
 use of force, 22, 25, 243, 288n.89
 *See also* Domestic constraints; Nuclear weapons
Minimalist conception of rationality, 48
Miscalculation
 examples, 157–58
 "miscalculated fait accompli," 29
 nuclear weapons and, 65, 81
 structural theory and, 49
 unintended conflict and, 28–30
 *See also* Crisis-induced stress; Loss of control; Rationality
Misperception
 bipolarity and, 86–87
 by Saddam Hussein, 229, 230
 multipolarity and, 70, 75–76
 nuclear weapons and, 65, 81

Mixed-motive games, 13, 16
  See also Game theory
"Model of a theory," 256n.24
Moderation of intentions
  concerted diplomacy and, 209–16, 219, 238
  concerts and, 99–102, 105, 238
  in post–Cold War era, 238
  in Soviet foreign policy, 209–12, 218–19, 236–37
Monarchies, and concerts, 100–101
Morgan, Patrick M., 47, 48, 63
Morgenthau, Hans J., 264n.17, 274–75n.22
Mueller, J. E., 59, 272n.46
Multilateralist orientation, 112–15, *113, 123*, 239–40
  See also Arab-Israeli conflict; Competitive orientation; Confrontational orientation
Multipolarity, 59–60, 69–78
  vs. bipolarity, 1, 4–5, 50–52, 60–62, 62, 66–68, *67*, 70, 72
  and causes of Long Peace, 59–60
  complexity and discontinuity of, 69–70, 74
  and concerts, 94
  and control of allies, 70–71, 74–75
  and control of military, 72, 76–77
  conventional multipolarity, *62*, 62, 73–74
  Crimean War and, 73–77, 225
  crisis-induced stress and, 70, 75–76
  and crisis management, 39–42, *40*, 50–52, 61, *67*
  decision makers and, 70
  and disengagement, 71–72, 77–78
  and domestic constraints, 72, 76–77
  intended conflict and, 60–62, *62*
  misperception and, 70, 75–76
  nuclear multipolarity, 8, *62*, 62, 233
  in post–Cold War era, 231–33
  in post–World War II era, 49–50
  "red lines" and, 71
  Six Day War (1967) and, 73–77, 271n.29
  stability and, 1, 8
  structural theory and, 50
  unintended conflict and, 4–6, 60–62, 62, 66–78, *67*, 232
  unit-level theory and, 50–52
  World War II and, 77–78
  See also Bipolarity; Cold War; Concert of Europe
Mutual Assured Destruction. See Nuclear MAD

Nasser, Gamal Abdel, 74–75, 76–77, 132–33, 145, 146, 284nn. 48, 49, 51, 295n.63
Neoliberalism, 7–8
Neorealism
  vs. classical realism, 265–66n.30
  and explanation of concerts, 94
  vs. neoliberalism, 7–8
  and nuclear proliferation, 233
Neuman, Stephanie, 301n.5
Nixon, Richard M.
  and Brezhnev, 194
  and Jordanian civil war (1970), 134, 136–37, 149, 151
  Nixon-Kissinger détente, 117–18
  and Rogers Plan, 181, 198
  on Soviet Union in Middle East, 294n.61
  and War of Attrition (1969–1970), 134, 146
  and Yom Kippur War (1973), 135, 138, 163, 286n.70
  See also Arab-Israeli conflict; Kissinger
Nixon administration, 176–77, 202, 205, 217–18, 298n.80
Normal times
  cognitive factors in, 52–53
  consensus within elites in, 200
  cooperation in, 22
  vs. crises, 23–24
  crisis management in, 22–24, 41, 225–26
  domestic constraints and, 207
  focus of values in, 53

intended and unintended outcomes in, 2
nonsystemic factors in, 216–17
in post–World War II era, 226
See also Concerted diplomacy; Conflict resolution; Crises
North Korea, 229
"No war, no peace" hypothesis, 179, 185–86, 190, 193
Nuclear MAD, 63, 64–66, 80, 167, 236, 255–56n.17, 269n.13, 271nn. 37, 38
Nuclear weapons, 57–88
  as a systemic factor, 255–56n.17
  and avoidance of unintended conflict, 61–62, 80–82
  as cause of Long Peace, 57–60, 65–66, 269n.10
  and crisis-induced stress, 65, 263n.3
  crisis management and, 47–48
  crisis prevention and, 64–65
  decision makers and, 64
  disintegration of Soviet Union and, 301n.7
  Middle East crises and, 126, 167
  misperception, miscalculation and, 65
  multipolarity and, 8, 60–62, *62*, 233
  neorealism and nuclear proliferation, 233
  nuclear bipolarity, 5, 8, 57–66, *62*, 80–83, 271nn. 37, 38
  nuclear multipolarity, 8, *62*, 62, 233
  and obsolescence of intended conflict, 5, 8, 60, 61, 63, 64–66, 80, 271nn. 37, 38, 300n.1
  and preventive wars, 80
  and probability of intended and unintended conflict, 60–62, *62*
  stability-instability paradox and, 59
  and tacit rules for crisis management, 80–83
  and United States foreign policy, 84–85
  See also Military
Nye, Joseph, 54–55, 111–12, 271n.28

October War (Yom Kippur War) (1973). See Middle East crises
Olson, Mancur, 267n.42
"Operational code" of political actors, 110
Opponents, images of. See Images
Osgood, Robert, 99
Ottoman Empire, 109, 275n.28, 278n.54
Outcomes. See Conflict; Cooperation
Outside-in theory. See Structural balance-of-power theory
Overreaction, 29–30, 67, 136–38
  See also Resolve; Underreaction
Oye, Kenneth, 52

Palestinians, 134, 136–37, 149, 155–56, 183, 184, 194–95, 211, 214, 218, 299n.89
"Parallel but unconcerted and coordinated steps," 166
"Partisan mutual adjustment," 20, 166
Passive/negative concerts, 92
Patchen, Martin, 254n.9
Pax Americana, 96, 182, 187–88, 204, 205, 220, 240, 243, 274n.16
Pax Britannica, 95, 96, 274n.16
Pax Sovietica, 230
Peacekeeping, in post–Cold War era, 244
Peloponnesian War, 63, 78
Peres, Shimon, 178, 213–14
PLO. See Palestinians
"Pluralistic security community," 231
Pluralist states. See Democracies
Podtserob, Alexey, 294–95n.62
Polarity. See Bipolarity; Multipolarity; Structural balance-of-power theory
Policy-relevant proposals for post–Cold War era, 243–45
Porter, Bruce D., 285nn. 58, 62
Posen, Barry R., 266n.36
Post–Cold War era
  bandwagoning in, 240
  concerted diplomacy in, 224, 236–40
  concerts in, 6–7, 8, 238–48

Post–Cold War era (*continued*)
conflict resolution in, 1–2
confrontational orientation in, 240
crisis management in, 1–2, 224, 228–31, 281n.18
disengagement in, 229–31, 232–33, 240, 242, 247, 250–51, 256n.22
international relations theory and, 1–2, 7–8
multilateralist orientation in, 239–40
multipolarity in, 231–33
overview of, 223–25
"red lines" in, 233
refugees in, 233
regional conflicts in, 1–2, 224, 228–33, 244, 246–47, 256n.22
Russia in, 218–20, 241, 243, 300n.102
unilateral-exclusionary orientation in, 240
United States in, 97, 219–21, 230–31, 236–40, 242, 243, 301n.13
*See also* Structural balance-of-power theory
post–World War II era
cognitive factors in, 105
concerted diplomacy in, 235–36
vs. Concert of Europe, 17, 36, 99, 100, 104, 255n.15
convergence of beliefs and, 55
crisis management in, 36–42
global vs. regional images of third-area conflicts in, 108, 109, 277n.40
multipolarity and bipolarity in, 49–50
nonemergence of concert in, 96–97, 99, 100, 104
structural theory and, 37–39
unit-level theory and, 38–39
*See also* Arab-Israeli conflict; Cold War; Middle East crises
Preemptive wars, 29, 30–31, 261–62n.64, 271n.35
*See also* Conflict, intended; Miscalculation

Premeditated wars. *See* Conflict, intended
Preventive wars, 29, 30–31, 80, 261–62n.64, 271n.35
*See also* Conflict, intended
Primacy of security interests, 47–48
Prisoner's Dilemma, 17, 18, 51–52, 53
*See also* Game theory
Public opinion. *See* Domestic constraints

Quandt, William, 163, 168–69, 190, 197
Quemoy-Matsu crisis (1958), 83–84, 87
Quwatli, President, 142

Rabin, Yitzak, 144
Rationality, 48–50, 267n.41
Reagan, Ronald, 184, 213, 214, 288n.88, 290–91n.21, 296n.74
Reagan administration, 182–83, 185, 202, 203, 204, 209, 213–15, 217, 237–38, 296n.74
Realism. *See* Neorealism
"red lines"
bipolarity and, 68, 79, 87
in Middle East crises, 160, 170
multipolarity and, 71
in post–Cold War era, 233
Refugees, in post–Cold War era, 233
Regimes
attributes of and concerted diplomacy, 198–200, *199*
and convergence of beliefs, 54
cooperation and, 17–21
security regimes, 24, 41, 110–11, 259n.26
similarity of regimes
concerted diplomacy and, 209–16, 219, 238
concerts and, 98–99, 100–101, 105, 238, 274–75n.22
in post–Cold War era, 238
and similarity of conduct, 44–45, 231, 268n.47
simple vs. complex learning and, 54–55
tacit rules, explicit agreements and, 54

theory of, 12, 257n.11, 259nn. 28, 32
U.S.-Soviet Basic Principles Agreement (BPA) (1972) and, 54
Regional conflicts. *See* Conflict
Relative capabilities, 94–97, 198–200, *199,* 295–96n.69
Research, future, 248–51
Resolve
  balance of interests and, 68, 83, 270n.19
  bipolarity and, 67–68
  crises and, 167
  crisis management and, 29–30, 289n.95
  in Middle East crises, 140–53, 160–66, 170–71, 226–27, 284n.47
  over- or underreaction and, 29–30
  in United States foreign policy, 85–86, 226–27, 297n.76
  *See also* Overreaction; Underreaction
Revolutions, 102–5
Rogers, William P., 204–5, 298–99n.87
Rogers Plan, 121, 146, 176–77, 180, 181, 197–98, 236, 295n.65
Roosevelt, Franklin D., 117
Rosecrance, Richard N., 99, 278n.54
Rosenau, James N., 277n.44
Ross, Dennis, 136
Rostow, Eugene, 163
"Rough parity," 159
Ruggie, John G., 54
Rules. *See* Tacit rules
Rusk, Dean, 133, 162–63, 176, 283nn. 40, 42
Russia, 74, 75, 76, 77, 95, 218–20, 232, 241, 243, 300n.102
  *See also* Soviet Union

Sadat, Anwar, 147, 148, 190, 193, 197, 206–7, 218, 284–85nn. 53, 54, 57, 288n.85, 295n.64, 298–99n.87
Saudi Arabia, 74
Saunders, Harold, 283n.44
"Scapegoat theory," 85, 272n.47

Schelling, Thomas C., 16, 18, 19, 24, 30–31, 43, 64
Schilling, Warner R., 46
Schneider, William, 118, 277n.46
Schroeder, Paul W., 273n.12, 275–76n.31
Second-strike capability. *See* Nuclear MAD
Security dilemma
  conflict and, 26–27
  cooperation and, 15–16
  defined, 26–27
  game theory and, 259n.26
  in Middle East crises, 129, 154, 280–81n.14
  unintended conflict and, 28, 42–43
Security interests, 47–48
Security regimes, 24, 41, 110–11, 259n.26
Self-determination, condominiums and, 116–18
"Sensible decisionmaking," 48, 63
"Sensitivity to costs," 48
Serbia, 74, 75, 230–31
Shamir, Yitzak, 178
Sharett, Moshe, 293n.50
Sharon, General Ariel, 291n.23
Shepilov, Dmitri, 141
Shevardnadze, Eduard, 300n.101
Shulsky, Abram, 137
Shultz, George, 178, 185, 214, 238
Similarity of regimes. *See* Regimes
Simmons, Beth A., 262–63n.2
Simon, Herbert A., 266n.37
Simple learning, 54–55
Sisco, Joseph, 176–77
Situational determinism, 44–45
Situational influences on unintended outcomes, 42–44
Six Day War (1967). *See* Middle East crises
Small states, 44, 92–93, 116–18
Smolansky, O. M., 192
Snyder, Glenn, 16, 24, 46, 48, 51–52, 59, 160, 260–61n.52, 261n.54, 267n.41

Snyder, Mark, 44–45
Soviet Union
  as a strong state and a weak society, 119, 121
  bandwagoning and, 237, 276n.35
  and condominiums, 121–23, 195–96, 211–12, 279n.69
  and control of allies, 87, 129–30, 140–50, 167–68, 227, 280n.13, 281nn. 16, 18
  disintegration of, 216, 217, 219, 220, 230, 241, 242, 274n.17, 301n.7
  and Eastern Europe, 230
  *glasnost,* 237
  and Gulf War (1991), 229–30
  and nonemergence of post–World War II concert, 96–97, 99, 100, 104
  and obsolescence of intended conflict, 80, 271nn. 37, 38
  Pax Sovietica, 230
  and regional approach to third-area conflicts, 109–10
  relations with allies vs. U.S.-Soviet relations, 279nn. 69, 70
  vulnerability of, 274n.15
  and World War II, 78
  and Yugoslavia, 230
  *See also* Arab-Israeli conflict; Berlin crises; Brezhnev; Bulganin; Cold War; Cuban Missile Crisis; Gorbachev; Kosygin; Middle East crises; post–World War II era; Russia; Stalin; U.S.-Soviet relations; World War II
Sovlov, Arkady, 293n.50
Spechler, Dina Rome, 201, 296n.71
Spheres of influence, 83, 85, 96, 122, 128, 280n.10, 295n.66
Spiegel, Steven L., 208
Sprout, Harold and Margaret, 264–65n.22
Stability, bipolarity and, 1, 8, 259n.32
Stability-instability paradox, 59
Stalin, Joseph, 117, 122
State
  as a unitary actor, 45–46, 48
  responsiveness of to external stimuli, 48–50
  states system vs. state of nature, 10, 26, 261n.57
  *See also* Great powers
Status games, 16, 258n.23
Status quo, defined, 140
Stein, Arthur, 20, 21, 260n.45
Stein, Janice G., 169
Stress. *See* Crisis-induced stress
Strong states, vs. weak states, 118–19
Structural balance-of-power theory, 5, 11–15, 224–34
  and concerts, 93–94
  and cooperation in crisis management, 37–39, 41–50, 228–31, 263n.12, 264n.17
  and crises, 48–49
  and international order under anarchy, 11–12, 14–15
  vs. international society approach, 5, 12–13, 234, 254–55n.11
  Middle East crises and, 165–66
  and miscalculation, 49
  outcomes best explained by, 224, 225–31, 270n.17
  and post–Cold War multipolarity, 231–33
  and role of great powers, 14–15
  unintended outcomes and, 2–3, 12, 42–43, 54, 55, 166
  *See also* Bipolarity; International relations theory; International society approach; Multipolarity; Nuclear weapons; Unit-level theory
Subjective factors. *See* Cognitive factors; images
Suez crisis (1956), 87, 131–32, 140–42, 154–55, 157–58, 165
  *See also* Middle East crises
Superpowers. *See* Concerts; Great powers
Symmetry
  asymmetrical intervention outside spheres of influence, 83

"disputed interest symmetry," 128
Systems theory. *See* Structural balance-of-power theory

Tacit rules
  in Arab-Israeli conflict, 83, 160–66
  bipolarity and, 68, 78–79, 80–83, 225–28
  conflict resolution and, 22
  cooperation and, 19–22, 260n.42
  crisis management and, 22, 24–25, 225–28
  in Middle East crises, 83, 125–26, 160–67, 170–71
  regimes and, 54
Taylor, A. J. P., 31
Third-area conflicts. *See* Conflict, regional conflicts
Thucydides, 78
Tito, Marshal Josip, 230
Trench warfare, 18, 259n.36
Truman, Harry, 80, 129, 159, 280n.12
Turkey, 74, 75, 77, 109, 275n.28, 278n.54

Ulam, Adam, 122
Underreaction, 29–30, 67, 232, 262n.69
  *See also* Overreaction; Resolve
Understandings. *See* Tacit rules
Unilateral-exclusionary orientation. *See* Competitive orientation; confrontational orientation; multilateralist orientation
Unintended conflict. *See* Conflict, unintended
Unintended cooperation. *See* Cooperation, unintended
Unipolar era. *See* Post–Cold War era
United Nations, 148, 164, 176, 244, 293n.43
United States
  bandwagoning and, 202, 204, 276n.35
  bipolarity and, 81–82, 84–86, 227
  and condominiums, 96, 117–18, 119–21, 196–98
  and control of allies, 87, 129–30, 140, 167–68, 227, 281n.18
  disengagement and, 230–31, 240, 242
  foreign policy and domestic constraints, 119–21, 227, 279n.62, 295–96n.69
  and global vs. regional approaches to third-area conflicts, 108, 109
  Gulf War (1991), 215–16, 218, 219, 228–31, 243, 288n.89
  and nonemergence of post–World War II concert, 96–97, 99, 100, 104
  Pax Americana, 96, 182, 187–88, 204, 205, 220, 240, 243, 274n.16
  in post–Cold War era, 97, 219–21, 230–31, 236–40, 242, 243, 301n.13
  and resolve
    in Middle East crises, 150–53, 160–61, 162–66, 170, 226–27
    in United States foreign policy, 85–86, 226–27, 297n.76
  and Vietnam War, 163
  and World War II, 77–78
  and Yugoslavia, 230–31
  *See also* Arab-Israeli conflict; Berlin crises; Carter; Cold War; Cuban Missile Crisis; Eisenhower; Johnson; Kennedy; Kissinger; Middle East crises; Nixon; Roosevelt; Truman; World War II
U.S.-Soviet relations
  balance of forces vs. balance of interests and, 156–59, 283n.39, 287n.78
  cognitive factors in, 105
  and crisis management in post–World War II era, 36–39
  differences in preferred forms of cooperation, 122–23
  and global vs. regional approaches to third-area conflicts, 108, 109–10, 277n.40
  and multilateralist, confrontational, and competitive orientations toward conflict resolution, 114–15
  in post–Cold war era, 236–40

U.S.-Soviet relations (*continued*)
  Soviet images of United States in Arab-Israeli conflict, 201–2
  Soviet relations with allies vs., 279nn. 69, 70
  structural theory and, 37–39
  tacit rules in, 82–83, 227–28
  United States domestic influences on, 119–21, 227
  United States images of Soviet Union as an opponent, 111–12
  United States images of Soviet Union in Arab-Israeli conflict, 202–7
  U.S.-Soviet Basic Principles Agreement (BPA) (1972), 54, 134
  U.S.-Soviet statement of October, 1977, 121, 178, 195, 197, 207–8, 235, 236, 299n.89
  unit-level theory and, 38–39
  *See also* Arab-Israeli conflict; Cold War; Middle East crises; Post–World War II era; Soviet Union; United States
Unit-level theory
  and concerts, 94, 97–98
  and cooperation in crisis management, 34–35, 38–39, 50–55, 268nn. 49, 52
  intended outcomes and, 3, 5, 6, 54, 55
  Middle East crises and, 125
  overview of, 254n.9
  *See also* International relations theory; International society approach
Use of force. *See* Military

Vance, Cyrus R., 203, 204–5, 235, 297n.77, 297–98n.79, 300nn. 99, 100
Vasquez, John, 59
Verba, Sidney, 47, 266n.37
Vietnam War, 163
Viotti, Paul, 84
Vulnerability, 94–97, 274n.15

Waltz, Kenneth, 1, 10, 11, 15, 26, 47, 48, 50–51, 52, 54–55, 60, 63, 64, 65, 66, 93–94, 157, 255n.13, 255–56n.17, 256n.24, 259n.32, 263n.12, 265–66n.30, 269n.3
Wanted wars. *See* Conflict, intended
War of Attrition (1969–1970), 133–34, 136, 145–47, 160–62, 165, 177
Wars. *See* Conflict; Crimean War; Middle East crises; Preemptive wars; Preventive wars; World War I; World War II; World War III
Watergate, 138, 151, 153
Weak states, vs. strong states, 118–19
Wells, A. R., 158
Wessel, Nils H., 159
Western Europe in post–Cold War era. *See* Europe
Whetten, Lawrence L., 284nn. 50, 51
Wildavsky, Aaron, 271n.28
Wilensky, H. O., 266n.37
Wili, M. Israelash, 45
Williams, Phil, 48–49, 165
Wolfers, Arnold, 43, 44
World War I, 18, 31, 35–36, 39–40, 73–77, 86, 104, 225, 259n.36, 271n.28
World War II, 31, 40, 77–78
World War III, 81, 167

Yariv, Aaron, 271n.34
Yeltsin, Boris, 219, 275n.30
Yom Kippur War (1973). *See* Middle East crises
Young, Oran, 273n.11
Yugoslavia, 230–31

Zacher, Mark, 154, 227
Zak, Moshe, 293n.44
Zero-sum games, 16, 161, 258n.23
Zhukov, Georg Konstantinovich, Marshal, 142